Kō

Walk the road

Melodies of a New Monasticism

together

Melodies of a New Monasticism

Bonhoeffer's Vision, Iona's Witness

Craig Gardiner

With a foreword by
Rowan Williams

scm press

This edition published in 2018 by SCM Press
Editorial office
3rd Floor, Invicta House,
108–114 Golden Lane,
London EC1Y 0TG, UK
www.scmpress.co.uk

SCM Press is an imprint of Hymns Ancient & Modern Ltd
(a registered charity)

Hymns Ancient & Modern® is a registered trademark of
Hymns Ancient & Modern Ltd
13A Hellesdon Park Road, Norwich,
Norfolk NR6 5DR, UK

First published in the United States in 2018 by Cascade Books

British Library Cataloguing in Publication data

A catalogue record for this book is available
from the British Library

978 0 334 05720 8

Printed and bound in Great Britain by
CPI Group (UK) Ltd, Croydon

This work is dedicated to the people,
the place,
the purpose,
and the promise of Camas,
in whose stones
melodies (both old and new)
resound.

Out of silence, a voice speaks.

It's saying . . .
the economy of God is different
listen to the ground bass
listen to the bottom line
I listen, and I hear it, endlessly repeated . . .
don't be afraid. Beyond the judgements of the world,
you are precious. You need no value addition.
I am for you.

I begin to hear differently. The faint refrain becomes a
silver clarion horn:
never less than justice
never less than justice
And there are grace-notes, dancing, generous:
Yes, you too
Yes, you too

This is the music of the kingdom.
And I don't mind that many will go in before me.
Now, when I am afraid, I will listen for the ground bass,
the bottom line.
And my soul will sing.[1]

1. Galloway, "The Workers in the Vineyard," in *Talking to the Bones,* 27–28. Used with the kind permission of the author.

Contents

Permissions

Acknowledgment is gratefully extended for permission to reproduce extracts from the following:

John L. Bell, *States of Bliss and Yearning: The Marks and Means of Authentic Christian Spirituality* (Glasgow: Wild Goose, 1998).

John L. Bell and Graham Maule, "Heaven Shall Not Wait," in *Heaven Shall Not Wait: Songs of Creation, The Incarnation, and The Life of Jesus,* (Glasgow: Wild Goose, 1994). © 1987 The Iona Community.

Ian Cowie, *Prayers and Ideas for Healing Services* (Glasgow: Wild Goose, 1995).

David S. Cunningham, *These Three Are One: The Practice of Trinitarian Theology* (Oxford: Blackwell, 1998). © David S. Cunningham 1998.

Ronald Ferguson, *Chasing the Wild Goose: The Story of the Iona Community* (Glasgow: Wild Goose, 1988).

Ron Ferguson, *Daily Readings with George MacLeod* (Glasgow: Wild Goose, 2001).

Ron Ferguson, *George MacLeod: Founder of the Iona Community* (Glasgow: Wild Goose, 2001).

Stanley Hauerwas and William Willimon, *Resident Aliens: Life in the Christian Colony* (Nashville: Abingdon, 1989).

Iona Abbey Worship Book (Glasgow: Wild Goose, 2001).

Martyn Joseph, Liner Notes from *Till the End: For the MST* (Christian Aid/Pipe Records, 2002).

Fred Kaan, "The Church is Like a Table." © 1989 Hope Publishing Company, Carol Stream, IL 60188. All rights reserved. Used by permission.

George F. MacLeod, "Man is Made to Rise," and "A Temple Not Made with Hands," in *The Whole Earth Shall Cry Glory: Iona Prayers by Rev. George F. MacLeod* (Glasgow: Wild Goose, 1985).

Peter Millar, *An Iona Prayer Book* (Norwich: Canterbury, 1998).

Michael O'Siadhail, "That in the End," in *Our Double Time* (Newcastle upon Tyne: Bloodaxe, 1998).

Adrienne Rich, "Natural Resources," in *The Dream of a Common Language: Poems 1974–1977* (New York: Norton, 1978).

Frances Young, T*he Art of Performance: Towards a Theology of Holy Scripture* (London: Darton, Longman and Todd, 1990).

Bible quotations, unless otherwise noted, are from the New Revised Standard Version of the Bible, © 1989 by the Division of Christian Education of the National Council of the Churches of Christ in the USA.

Foreword

This is a work of outstanding originality, a hugely fresh and far-reaching essay on Christian community drawing on both ancient and modern Christian sources. It takes two iconic twentieth-century figures who have transformed the theology and practice of life in community—George MacLeod of Iona and Dietrich Bonhoeffer—and relates them both to the major themes of Christian theological thinking and to the history and vision of classical monasticism.

But it does a good deal more besides. It takes a single metaphor, that of *polyphony*, as the essential character of Christian community, and develops it with elegance and boldness. Gardiner is not content with a general appeal to polyphony as a model of unity-in-difference, but explores the crucial question of what actively unifies a diverse process, and comes up with a full exposition in terms of seeing Christ as the *cantus firmus* underlying and tying together the diversity. On this basis, he develops two parallel threefold structures for thinking about the Christian community as it expresses its identity in relation to God and the world—worship, ecumenism, and healing alongside peace, justice, and ecological responsibility. In each of these, the church is completely itself, singing its primary *cantus firmus*, but weaving interconnecting patterns around it in a differentiated unity.

It is a work that passes fluently and helpfully between the two poles of biographical and historical exposition on the one hand and direct doctrinal exploration on the other. As regards the former, Gardiner elaborates a comparison between Dietrich Bonhoeffer and George MacLeod that illuminates both men and draws out a theme in twentieth-century Christianity that has not been sufficiently dealt with. He shows how both grow from the soil of a "dynasty," academic or ecclesiastical, from different kinds of aristocracy, and then how both are challenged by exposure to the majority experience of their generation—war, mass privation, the secularity of the environment—and outgrow their inherited Protestant conventions without abandoning the central passions of the Reformation. Finally, he demonstrates how both find in the re-creation of a sort of monasticism an effective response to the modern crisis of religious credibility. All of this is argued with enthusiasm and vividness, and the reflection on what the monastic witness really means and might mean is appropriately challenging.

Both the writing and the practice of these two iconic figures then leads into a constructive exposition of the nature of the church and its contemporary vocation, using the same focal musical metaphor. In a way, what emerges is a very fully worked theological grounding for the view of the church that might be taken as basic for the Iona Community—and similar contemporary attempts to reimagine the church outside both narrowly local and narrowly hierarchical structures. The whole discussion is really a meditation on the fundamental integrity of the church, which is what every serious study of spirituality should be.

The contemporary pertinence of this work should be clear. Bonhoeffer, as we have been reminded a good deal in recent years, is someone whose disturbing legacy has yet to be really digested by the church. MacLeod stands at the origins of one of the most effective and credible Christian communities in the English speaking world. Neither of them can easily be pigeonholed in the terms of current conservative-liberal polarities. And the theology that emerges from this, as Gardiner states it, is itself something that transcends these glib oppositions. If it is true that we urgently need theological work that gets us out of the traps of ecclesiastical politics—and if it is also true that we need a few modern "Church Fathers" to look to as sources and touchstones of a rediscovered classical balance—this book offers something of quite exceptional importance and timeliness to the church overall. It defines a theological spirituality that is disciplined, imaginative, and engaged, that balances contemplation and action, and that shapes not just the life of an enclosed elite but the whole vision of the Christian community in its specific modern setting, a community promising and manifesting transformation.

So this is not an abstract essay. Both in style and in subject matter, it is as engaged as its two heroes are. It succeeds in being thoroughly well-resourced academically while never losing accessibility. It was, for me personally, a privilege to be involved in supervising some of the research that led to this book, and I am confident that Craig Gardiner is someone who will make a serious mark as a theologian of an unusual kind. He occupies the sort of territory currently inhabited by a Stanley Hauerwas or a Walter Brueggemann—someone with ample scholarly credentials but able to speak directly into the most pressing concerns of the contemporary church and its ambient society. It is an exhilarating study, whose richness will serve the sharing of the gospel and the vision of the Kingdom in all kinds of ways. I am delighted to see it in print.

Rowan Williams
Magdalene College, Cambridge

Acknowledgements

This book began as doctoral research but don't let that put you off! Writing is famously a solitary task and attempting to write on community is therefore not without its ironies. But there are some communities and individuals to whom appreciation and thanks should be extended. Firstly, thanks are owed to the Baptist Union of Great Britain, without whose generous financial support none of this might have been possible.

My appreciation must also be extended to the staff, past and present, of South Wales Baptist College, and everyone at the Department of Theology in Cardiff University, especially John Weaver, Simon Woodman, Peter Stevenson, and Ed Kaneen. A university grant made it possible to visit the Bonhoeffer Archive at Union Theological Seminary, New York, where Claire McCurdy helped my research, and Larry Rasmussen and Ralf Wüstenberg offered useful advice. Over lunches in Oxford, the late F. Burton Nelson also provided further insight on Bonhoeffer and I am grateful for other conversations with Ian Bradley and Mary Grey.

My indebtedness to many members of the Iona Community must be acknowledged: the late Uist MacDonald provided insight to the "early years," and Duncan Finlayson Sr. gave access to his collection of *Coracle* and personal papers. Similar courtesies were extended by Ian Fraser who also kindly commented on final drafts of the work. Good advice came from Graeme Brown, Ron Ferguson, and Norman Shanks. Kathy Galloway has not only shaped the writing, but the writer, too. Thanks, too, to Peter MacDonald, to Robert and Alison Swinfen, Iona Cymru, and all at the Bristol Iona Family Group. Wardens and staff on Iona, together with those at Camas, have regularly ensured enriching visits and appreciation is due to Carol Dougal, the late Dafydd Owen, Peter Millar, Philip Newell, Jan Sutch Pickard, and Brian and Sheila Woodcock. Thanks, too, to successive Abbey musicians and the Wild Goose Worship Group, particularly Alison Adam,

Mairi Munro, Graham Maule, and Gail Ullrich. Special appreciation is due to John Bell, who introduced me to the Iona Community (and so indirectly to my wife), for his hymns, humor, and wisdom, and whose every conversation leaves me with the gentle but persistent thought that life can be deeper.

My gratitude, too, to Brendan O'Malley and Tony Nolan for their spiritual direction and to Sister Veronica and the community at Ty-Mawr for the quiet space they have regularly provided. Particular appreciation must be expressed to all those at Calvary Baptist Church, Cardiff, whose generous patience gave their pastor the time to write and whose fellowship has been a crucible and inspiration for the thinking.

This has been my first real experience of the world of publishing, and so thanks must go to Anthony R. Cross for initially typesetting the material, together with Chelsea Lobey, Robin Parry, and all the folks at Wipf and Stock for guiding me through it all so skillfully. Additional thanks to Ben Dare for reading many proofs.

Of course, heartfelt thanks must be extended to the two incomparable individuals who supervised the research. First, to Rowan Williams for shaping my early thinking and for remaining committed to the project even after leaving Wales for Canterbury. Second, to Karen Smith, for adopting the project halfway through, for her indefatigable balance of criticism and encouragement, and for her personal and academic dedication which goes far beyond any call of duty.

Deep thanks must go to my parents, Singleton and Ann, for singing the song before I knew how to listen, for the sacrifices made to help the music-making of my youth, and for their steadfast love and encouragement through the diverse directions of more recent years. Thanks, too, to Ian and Jennifer Currie for their support and for sharing their daughter.

Words have never been enough to express how much I owe to Meredith, but it has been my deepest joy to listen to the melodies of her heart and the rhythms of her soul. It is my greatest privilege to join my faltering harmonies to the music that we share and to enjoy the considerable counterpoint brought to us in our children Niamh and Euan.

In the beginning was the song, the song was God and the song was given for all. And there is the reason to sing: *Laudate Dominum: Cantate Domino canticum novum.*

CHAPTER I

Introduction

The Melodies of George MacLeod
and Dietrich Bonhoeffer

Have I spoken something, have I uttered something worthy of God?
No . . . if I did say something, it is not what I wanted to say.
—AUGUSTINE[1]

For we are not trying to build community. We can never do that.
God sets us in community and it is man's sin that he is always
breaking it.
—RALPH MORTON[2]

From harmony, from heavenly harmony,
This universal frame began;
From harmony to harmony

1. Augustine, *On Christian Teaching*, 17.
2. Morton, *Household of Faith*, 122.

Through all the compass of the notes it ran,
The diapason closing full in man.

—JOHN DRYDEN[3]

This book explores the nature of Christian community by drawing upon the fertile synergy of theology and music.[4] It does not seek to offer a theological appraisal of music, but rather, through the metaphor of music, presents a theology of how Christians might seek to live together. It has no intention to theologize about music, but wants to engage in a theology of community through the metaphors of music.[5] So it is sympathetic to Aristotle's dictum that "midway between the unintelligible and the common place, it is metaphor which most produces knowledge."[6] It is hoped that using music in this way might "liberate our theology from some of its worst bad habits, and refresh it for the future."[7]

Arthur Koestler would call such an interaction between theology and music "a bisociative" methodology.[8] He argues that bringing together previously unrelated subjects (bi-sociation) often precipitates a "eureka act," which shows a familiar situation or event in a new light.[9] At its core this insight is the basis of "all creative activities, artistic originality, scientific study, even the good joke."[10]

In addition to the central imagery of music, this book will employ a number of other metaphorical images through which the nature of Christian community will be explored. It is hoped that the richness of metaphorical reflection, particularly when the metaphors are mixed, will provide new horizons of thought and experience.

3. Dryden, "Song for St. Cecilia's Day," 58.

4. In so doing, I affirm Jeremy Begbie's assertion that "music can serve to enrich and advance theology, extending our wisdom about God, God's relation to us and to the world at large." Like Begbie's work, I do not aim to offer a systematic theology of music, which situates it within a particular doctrinal environment. Begbie, *Theology, Music and Time*, 3ff.

5. Ibid., 4. Begbie develops Attali's assertion that "music is more than an object of study: it is a way of perceiving the world. . . . My intention here is thus . . . not only to theorise *about* music but to theorise *through* music." Attali, *Noise*, 4.

6. Aristotle, *Rhetoric*, book 3, 141b, as cited in McFague, *Metaphorical Theology*, 67.

7. Begbie, "Through Music: Sound Mix," in Begbie, *Beholding the Glory*, 139.

8. Koestler, *Act of Creation*, 35.

9. Ibid., 101ff.

10. Young, *Art of Performance*, 2. Francis Young is specifically commenting on Koestler's ideas.

As well as mixing various metaphors, the book will develop the idea of bisociation by bringing together the life and work of Dietrich Bonhoeffer and George MacLeod, two twentieth-century Christians who never met and yet shared a passion for Christian community. While separate attention has been given to both of these individuals in other places, no one has yet brought together their thinking on community. So the book is not an attempt to offer a comprehensive examination of Christian community nor indeed does it offer a complete comparative biography of Bonhoeffer and MacLeod, but it does hope to offer a fresh perspective on what it means to be a Christian living with others in today's world.

MUSIC, THEOLOGY, AND THE CHURCH

The bisociative relationship by which music is used to illuminate theology has been largely untested until recently and it remains so in examining the nature of Christian community.[11] This is because theologians have historically been more concerned with the moral nature of music and its effects on society than they have been in its potential as an explorative metaphor.[12] This is unusual given how throughout history communities have made music in a myriad of ways to reflect and express their experiences of celebration, anger, or lament. Music had a place in almost every activity and at almost every event in ancient Jewish life[13] and was included in the Temple and Synagogue. Early Christianity evolved out of Judaism and while direct

11. For examples of the bisociative relationship between music and theology see von Balthasar, *Truth is Symphonic*. Vern S. Poythress has similarly used the metaphor of a symphony to examine plurality in theology, Poythress, *Symphonic Theology*. Robert W. Jenson has drawn on Jonathan Edwards to reflect on the Trinitarian nature of God arguing that God is a melody, "And as there are three singers who take each their part . . . the melody is fugued." Jenson, *Triune God*, 236. Dietrich Bonhoeffer's allusion to "polyphonic living" is another attempt to think theologically through the metaphor of music and his work is central to this book. See letter dated May 20, 1944, in Bonhoeffer, *Letters and Papers*, 393–95. David F. Ford has reflected on this musical metaphor coined by Bonhoeffer in *Self and Salvation*, Chapter 10. David S. Cunningham has perhaps come closest in developing music as a metaphor for community living in his book, *These Three Are One*. See also Hans Küng and Karl Barth, who have both commented upon the vestiges of God to be found in the music of Mozart. Küng, *Mozart*; Barth, *Wolfgang Amadeus Mozart*; and the work of James Cone on the spirituality of the blues, in *Spirituals and the Blues*. June Boyce Tillman has helpfully explored the role of music in relational theology in "Even the Stones Cry Out," 153–78. More recently, see Crawford, *Theology as Improvisation*; and Benson, "Improvising like Jazz," in *Liturgy As a Way of Life*, 71–97.

12. See Cole, *Music and Morals*.

13. Wilson-Dickson, *Brief History of Christian Music*, 22ff.

musical connections are ambiguous, music quickly became an inherent part of worship in churches such as those at Colossae and Ephesus, where Paul exhorted the people to "sing psalms, hymns and spiritual songs."[14] While music played an active role in the early church, no one considered how it might be a resource through which a theology of Christian community might be articulated.[15] Indeed as the church evolved, music was viewed with some suspicion: attention habitually gravitated toward the ethical propriety of a particular instrument or performance. This suspicion may be because Genesis records Jubal, the ancestor of all who play the lyre and pipe, as being a descendant of the murderously sinful Cain.[16] However, it is more realistic to think that Christian hostility to music, especially instrumental music, came from its association with the debauched entertainments of Graeco-Roman Society (Jewish theology had often displayed open antagonism to music for this very reason).[17] But the embryonic church may not have followed the example of its Jewish cousin as readily as is often supposed. The first hint of a polemic against music did not appear until late in the second century.[18] Thereafter, the criticism grew in intensity throughout the third century, as evidenced in the writings of Tertullian (160–225) and Arnobius (d. 330), and it became commonplace in the fourth-century theology of John Chrysostom (345–407), Ambrose (340–397), and Augustine (354–430).[19] Chrysostom interpreted music as "sensual and pagan, obstructing our progress toward the real world of the spirit,"[20] and Augustine expressed

14. Eph 5:19 and Col 3:16, and other possible early hymnody in 1 Pet 1:3–5, 1 Tim 3:16, and Phil 2:6–11.

15. The classical world had reflected on the relationship of music and creation. Boethius (c. 480–524) recorded their thoughts in his work *De Institutione Musica.* This sixth-century work articulated a three-fold distinction of music: "*Musica Mundana*" (Music of the Spheres), which was produced by creation itself, "*Musica Humana*," which governed the relationship between body and soul, and finally, "*Musica Instrumentalis*" that was music as we know it. See Pickstock, "Ascending Numbers," 185–215.

16. Astley, Hone, and Savage, *Creative Chords*, xviii.

17. McKinnon notes Plato's objection to "many stringed" and "many keyed" musical instruments in the *Republic* (399), and cites Livy's (6, 7, 39) objection to women harpists at banquets as an undesirable luxury imported from Asia. He adds to these sources a comment from Rabbi Johanan which illustrates a Jewish suspicion of music: "Whoever drinks to the accompaniment of the four musical instruments brings five punishments to the world" (*Sotah* 48a), as cited in McKinnon, *Music in Early Christian Literature*, 2.

18. Ibid.

19. Ibid.

20. "In Tune with Heaven: The Report of the Archbishops' Commission on Church Music," as cited by Inge, "Power Praise," in Astley, Hone, and Savage, *Creative Chords*, 172.

deep concern about being taken up into the emotion of music.[21] But earlier church writers had been more sympathetic and even hinted at the possibility of doing theology through the metaphor of music. Ignatius (35–107) wrote in a letter to the Ephesians:

> Your justly respected clergy, who are a credit to God, are attuned to their bishop like the strings of a harp, and the result is a hymn of praise to Jesus Christ from minds that are in unison, and affections that are in harmony. Pray, then, come and join this choir, every one of you; let there be a whole symphony of minds in concert; take the tone all together from God, and sing aloud to the Father with one voice through Jesus Christ, so that He may hear you and know by your good works that you are indeed members of His Son's Body.[22]

Even Augustine, a theologian who so reflected patristic unease with music, fascinatingly compared the "unified diversity of the soul" with music. He reflected upon

> that marvelous creation of Archimedes . . . the hydraulis (*organum hydraulicum*)—with its many parts, sections, connections, passages—such a collection of sound, variety of tone (*commercia modorum*), array of pipes *(acies tibiarum)*—and yet it all constitutes a single entity. So too the air, expelled from below by the agitation of the water, is not thereby divided into parts because it is distributed in different places; rather, it is one in substance though diverse in function.[23]

These images of diversity and unity are a helpful metaphor for the nature of God and community, a metaphor that is adopted and modified later in this book. But such a metaphor was redundant to medieval theologians who were still concerned with whether developments such as Gregorian chant and polyphonic composition could claim the favor of God. In the sixteenth century, Luther (1483–1546) adopted a more positive approach

21. Inge, "Power Praise," in Astley, Hone, and Savage, *Creative Chords*, 172. See also Jordan, "Augustine on Music," 123–35. Augustine was equivocal on music: He reflects upon its metaphorical purposes in *De Trinitate* and in his *Confessions* compares the human ability to imagine a piece of music in one brief moment with God's knowledge of time, past, present, and future. Jordan, "Augustine on Music," 123.

22. Ignatius, "Epistle to the Ephesians," in Staniforth, *Early Christian Writings*, 62. See also Pseudo-Justin, "Hortatory Address to the Greeks," cited in McKinnon, *Music in Early Christian Literature*, 21.

23. Augustine, "De anima," XIV, 4, as cited in McKinnon, *Music in Early Christian Literature*, 45.

to music. He had "no use for cranks who despise music"[24] and argued that "next to the Word of God, music deserves the highest praise" because "whether you wish to comfort the sad, to terrify the happy, to encourage the despairing, to humble the proud, to calm the passionate, or to appease those full of hate . . . what more effective means than music could you find?"[25] Calvin was less accommodating. He feared anything that might distract the congregation from Scripture and felt that music remained "tainted by association with the unacceptable practices of the Roman Church or linked with singing and dancing. In the first case, one's soul was at risk; in the second, one's morals."[26] Insisting that only the psalms and one or two canticles were appropriate for worship, Calvin forbade harmony and banned instrumentation. In later years the church became a great patron of music, commissioning works from composers such as J. S. Bach (1685–1750), J. Haydn (1732–1809), and W. A. Mozart (1756–91). New styles of music were not without controversy but the disputations were rarely concerned with divine approval, neither did they preoccupy the minds of theologians. However, while the church appreciated how theology might endow musicians with material with which to work their skill, it remained inconceivable that the reverse could occur and music might furnish the theologian with a way to interpret God or Christian community.[27]

This position persisted into the congregational hymnody of the late seventeenth and eighteenth centuries when music was co-opted to bear the message of theology. Inspired by Isaac Watts (1674–1748), more than 250 different hymn books were published during the eighteenth century.[28] However, this was no uniting of equal disciplines. Music was important only as a bearer of doctrine. The hymns of Watts, John Wesley (1703–91), and his brother Charles (1707–88), made no attempt to engage in theological reflection through music; their purpose was to carry Christ's offer of salvation and to warn of the dangers of damnation. The contribution of these writers to hymnody is perhaps unsurpassed, even by the Victorians,[29] but music as a method of theological reflection remained redundant.

24. Bainton, *Here I Stand*, 341.

25. Martin Luther, *Luther's Works* 53:323, as cited in Begbie, *Resounding Truth*, 102.

26. Wilson-Dickson, *Brief History of Christian Music*, 101.

27. Viladesau, *Theology and the Arts*, 4. The exception is Jonathan Edwards who spoke of the eschatological perfection of creation as a "very complex tune, where respect is to be had to the proportion of a great many notes together." Edwards, "Miscellanies," 182, as cited in Jenson, *Triune God*, 235.

28. Wilson-Dickson, *Brief History of Christian Music*, 178.

29. For an insightful assessment of Victorian hymnody, see Bradley, *Abide With Me*, and Watson, *English Hymn*.

In time, music sought inspiration beyond the Christian narrative and with that the potential for a fecund bisociation faded. In the nineteenth century, Romantic painters, poets, and above all the makers of music came to be revered as, "the supreme discerners of transcendent truth."[30] So by the early twentieth century, theology and music rarely communicated: "The corridors of theology were not generally alive with the sound of music," and "apart from a few notable exceptions, twentieth-century theologians paid scant attention to the potential of music to explore theological themes."[31]

Recently, however, the potential of a fruitful relationship between theology and music has received renewed attention. Contemporary composers such as John Tavener (1944–2013) and Arvo Pärt (b. 1935) have written music that unashamedly explores theological themes to critical acclaim and widespread popularity.[32] Similarly Henryk Górecki's (1933–2010) "Symphony of Sorrowful Songs" draws inspiration from a prayer to Mary scratched on the wall of a Gestapo prison.[33] A different music but one that is equally bisociative of theology is the work of James MacMillan (b. 1959). MacMillan is by self-declaration, a "practicing but not pious" Roman Catholic[34] who believes that the more tranquil compositions of Tavener, Pärt and Górecki turn their back upon the "corporeal nature of man's humanity" and are lacking a "dialectic in the normal western sense."[35] That MacMillan's music contains more conflict and even violence reflects his deliberate theological position, and while he acknowledges a redemptive aspect to his music, he stresses how "it needs to have that conflict gone through and fought through before it is reached."[36]

30. Harding, *Gounod*, as cited in Wilson-Dickson, *Brief History of Christian Music*, 206.

31. Begbie, *Theology, Music and Time*, 3.

32. For instance, in John Tavener's "The Protecting Veil," the composer strives to capture some of what he considers to be the almost cosmic power of the Mother of God. The work commemorates the appearance of the Mother of God in a vision in the tenth century. She was seen spreading her veil as a protective shelter over the Christians in Constantinople who were under threat of Saracen invasion. The vision inspired the Greek Christians who repelled the Saracen army. Other works include, "Akathist of Thanksgiving," "The Annunciation," "We Shall See Him As He Is," and "The Myrrh-Bearer." Arvo Pärt's religious works include "St. John Passion" (1982), "Te Deum" (1984–86, rev. 1993) and "Litany" (1994). Works for SATB choir such as "Magnificat" (1989) and "The Beatitudes" (1990) have proved popular with choirs around the world.

33. Liner notes, Górecki, *Symphony No. 3, Op. 36*, Naxos CD 8.550822.

34. MacMillan, "Contemporaries of Christ" radio broadcast, March 15, 1994, noted in "Creation and the Composer: An Interview with James MacMillan," in Astley, Hone, and Savage, *Creative Chords*, 8.

35. Ibid., 16.

36. Ibid., 17.

THE METAPHOR OF POLYPHONY

One musical practice, in particular that of polyphony (literally sounding many notes at the same time), provides theology with a rich metaphor for exploring the nature of Christian community. For most of the first eight hundred years of Christian worship the music employed was monophonic, whether it took

> the form of a cantillated prayer of extreme simplicity or of an ornate Gradual for a solemn occasion. . . . A single line of melody, untainted by any accompaniment, was the most perfect and satisfying symbol for the unity of Christian believers.[37]

However, the advent of notation led to the development of polyphony: the simultaneous sounding of many interweaving melodies. In polyphonic music, more than one "melody" happens at any given time, overlapping and interweaving with one another over long periods of time.[38]

The Thomas Tallis motet "Spem in Alium" has forty different voices arranged in eight five-part choirs, all interweaving in counterpoint, exchanges of block harmony and massed outbursts.[39] As Begbie notes,

> Despite the sonic profusion, it never sounds "jammed" or crowded. There is a multiplicity without dissipation, togetherness without mutual overwhelming, each voice being enabled to become more fully itself. "As though being ourselves we're more capacious."[40]

Indeed not only might there be a variety of interweaving vocal melodies but in orchestral music different instrumentation might be assigned to particular melodies, calling forth different timbres that are attached to respective melodies. In the latter case, each is distinct, not only in their melody, but also in their particular sound. But these remain undivided in their character and purpose with neither denying the other their right of differential existence. So, a melody introduced by a solo horn does not prevent a countermelody of strings beneath it (the strings may themselves be polyphonic in nature, comprising violins, violas, cellos, and double basses), nor is anything "lost" when the solo theme is developed by three

---

37. Wilson-Dickson, *Brief History of Christian Music*, 75.

38. Ibid.

39. Tallis's work is itself a powerful synthesis of the established musical traditions of the time, together with emerging and experimental forms.

40. See Begbie, "Through Music: Sound Mix," in *Beholding the Glory*, 152. The final line is a reference to the poem "That in the End" by Micheal O'Siadhail.

further horns playing in harmony. The difference-in-unity extends when, perhaps, the strings share their multifaceted countermelody with a further polyphony of woodwind (oboes, clarinets, flutes, bassoons, etc.). It is entirely usual for such a symphonic piece to be additionally punctuated by percussion (triangle, cymbal, xylophone, side drum, and timpani) and be joined by the remaining brass (trumpets, trombones, and tubas).[41] Indeed it can work with each of three instruments working in different keys.[42] This is polyphony.

It can theoretically be either "harmonious" (i.e., attaining certain culturally conditioned aesthetic standards) or "dissonant" (displaying an apparent lack of agreement or tension between the notes). As Cunningham notes, the chief attribute of polyphony is, "Simultaneous, non-excluding difference: that is, more than one note is played at a time, and none of these notes is so dominant that it renders another mute."[43] Hence, polyphonic music permits and encourages individual difference, yet unites them in what might be deemed a community of melodies. Drawing on this metaphor provides a valuable insight for a theology of community and enables an examination of diverse melodies of belonging.

In early polyphonic music there was often a *cantus firmus* (literally the firm song), which was usually a preexisting melody such as a chorale tune around which the other countermelodies were then arranged. Kemp notes how, musically,

> the contrapuntal voice in a *cantus firmus* composition owes its existence to the Tenor upon which it is erected. . . . It is distinct from the Tenor. . . . If heard without the Tenor it would seem self-sufficient in motion, ambit and material; but its source of generation and control would remain the *cantus firmus*; it cannot operate beyond the ultimate "barrier" of the Tenor's dictates.[44]

The *cantus firmus* then lent its form to derivative melodies that fragmented, mirrored, echoed, and retextured the original melody in other voices. These

41. Hans Urs von Balthasar makes similar insights, drawing parallels with an orchestra who must be pluralist in order to unfold the wealth of the totality that resounds in the composer's mind. See von Balthasar, *Truth is Symphonic*, 7. Cunningham notes that "one of the words for a musical performance (*concert*) actually reflects this multiplicity (from *con+certare*, 'to act together')." Cunningham, *These Three Are One*, 127.

42. Gustav Holst's "Terzetto" is written for flute, oboe, and viola, with each instrument playing in a different key, although initially the composer himself was not quite sure about whether it was real music. See Holst, *Gustav Holst*, 114.

43. Cunningham, *These Three Are One*, 128.

44. Kemp, "Polyphonous Christian Community," 9.

countermelodies and harmonies could weave their way together with or even against one another, but as long as each remained in relation to the *cantus firmus*, the music could continue. This book will employ these metaphors of *cantus firmus* and polyphony to investigate the nature of Christian community: if Christ is conceived as the *cantus firmus* of all Christian living, then his "solid song" will be fragmented, mirrored, echoed, and retextured within a variety of people whose own diverse and individual melodies only find their unity, indeed their community, in Christ.

This musical metaphor of polyphony will bisociate with two major theological sources, both of which have their genesis in the early decades of the twentieth century. The first of these is the life of George MacLeod (1895–1991) and the work of the Iona Community that he founded. While MacLeod had a fine singing voice[45] and could accompany himself at the piano, he would never have considered himself a musician. Furthermore, while he was an inspirational preacher and a dedicated pastor he was no systematic theologian[46] and showed no predilection to theologize through music. He did, however, have a natural instinct for leadership and a longing for authentic Christian community. The Christian community he founded now comprises some three hundred members who are dispersed primarily throughout the UK but with others living around the world. Male and female, cleric and laity, for many years they have lived by a five-fold ecumenical rule of common discipleship:

1. Daily prayer and Bible-reading;

2. Sharing and accounting for the use of our money;

3. Planning and accounting for the use of our time;

4. Action for justice and peace in society; and

5. Meeting with and accounting to each other.[47]

Although MacLeod was too autocratic a leader to perceive the full polyphonic potential of the community in its early life, today men and

45. He sang in the chantry choir while at school at Winchester, and while at St. Cuthbert's Church in Edinburgh loved to sit at the piano and sing songs in the church's Mission Centre for the Poor. See Ferguson, *George MacLeod*, 88.

46. Indeed he would tease intellectuals, saying they were "someone who can hold a vital issue at arm's length for a life time." Ibid., 204.

47. *Iona Community Members' Prayer Book: 2014*. See also Galloway, *Living By the Rule*. In 2015 the rule was amended to a four-fold rule of daily prayer and reading the Bible, mutual sharing and accountability for the use of time and money, regular meeting together, and action for justice, peace, and the integrity of creation. See https://iona .org.uk/movement/the-rule.

women of differing races, socioeconomic backgrounds, sexual orientation, and Christian denominations have found their own individual melodies gathered in counterpoint around the vision of Christ they share.

The second source for this study draws upon the life and work of Dietrich Bonhoeffer (1906–45), the German pastor/theologian imprisoned and subsequently executed by the Nazi regime. Much of his work concerned the nature of Christian community[48] but he was also a talented pianist who loved music all his life. It was perhaps inevitable that in time his theological reflections would be informed by music and it is from his writing that the metaphor of polyphony is taken. MacLeod and Bonhoeffer never met, but both men believed in a new and polyphonic vision for Christian community.

GEORGE MACLEOD: FOUNDER OF THE IONA COMMUNITY

George MacLeod was born in Glasgow, on June 17, 1895, the third child in an upper-class Victorian family. His father came from a distinguished Scots ecclesiastical dynasty[49] but had become "a good accountant" rather than "a mediocre minister."[50] George inherited many of the family characteristics.

> The MacLeod house not only represented power in the Church of Scotland, but also a particular—and very influential—ethos. The distinctive MacLeod style was marked by attractiveness, tolerance, breadth, humour, and gaiety. Theologically it was broadly evangelical, inclusive and ecumenical. Politically it was sympathetic to the establishment, yet concerned for the poor. Combined with Celtic romanticism and poetry, skilled oratory, confidence in the presence of all ranks of people and a popular touch, the MacLeod style was bound to be a potent force for change in the Church.[51]

Church attendance was compulsory and religion was part of the family fabric, but at the core of family life was the aristocratic notion of gentlemanly duty, a concept summed up in Christmas 1901 when George (age 6)

---

48. See his doctoral thesis, *Sanctorum Communio*, and one of his most widely read books, *Life Together*, in which he reflects on the community of seminarians at Finkenwalde.

49. His ancestry contained five moderators of the Church of Scotland and a chaplain to Queen Victoria.

50. Ferguson, *George MacLeod*, 37.

51. Ibid., 36.

and his brother Norman (age 10) received from their father a scroll entitled "Do Your Duty." It read:

> Come wealth or want, come good or ill,
> Let young and old accept their part,
> And bow before the awful Will,
> And bear it with an honest heart.
> Who misses, or who wins the prize?
> Go, lose or conquer as you can;
> But if you fail or if you rise
> Be each, pray God, a gentleman.[52]

George's education at Winchester College reinforced this ethos, but the task of Winchester "was to train not just gentlemen, but leaders."[53] Thus, when George left to study law at Oxford, he knew that he was "not only born to rule but born to serve."[54] The opportunity came quicker than imagined: after his first year, war broke out and he signed up with the Argyll and Sutherland Highlanders.

The war revealed his skill of leadership and he was decorated twice for bravery. But it also affected him in two vital ways. He was impressed with the community spirit shared between officers and soldiers at the front and "having shared terrifying danger with such men, he could no longer simply accept the social assumptions he had taken for granted at home and at school."[55] Secondly, the war made him reconsider his faith. He wrote to his sister Ellen, "I have heard it said that a man comes out of this war with a very real religion or no religion at all. . . . Personally I think that any man who sees this war must come out with a very real religion or cut his throat."[56] Years later he recounted how when on leave he realized that he was "going to hell in a hurry" and so knelt down in a railway carriage and "surrendered his life to Christ."[57]

After the war he resolved to become a minister.[58] He studied in Edinburgh and then accepted a scholarship to Union Seminary, New York. There

---

52. Ibid., 43.

53. Ibid., 44.

54. Ibid., 50.

55. Ibid., 62.

56. A letter written from George to Ellen in 1917, as cited in ibid., 60.

57. Ronald Falconer, "The Kilt Beneath my Cassock," as cited in ibid., 72.

58. George's personal interest in the church predated this event. As a teenager he had visited the minister of St. Cuthbert's Church, Edinburgh, and questioned him about how well the churches were attended in the industrialized areas of the city. MacLeod would become an assistant minister there in 1926.

he met the man who shaped his future: Rev. P. B. (Tubby) Clayton. Clayton had been a chaplain in the war and established Toc H, a hostel that ministered to soldiers. Its motto was "abandon rank all ye who enter here" and after the war, survivors reconvened in an attempt to keep alive the trench-time spirit of cooperation among different classes. They met for ecumenical fellowship and initiated small communities for voluntary work. Clayton's energy and purpose impressed MacLeod and within a short time he had not only recruited the Scot as acting secretary for Toc H, but without either man knowing, had sung to him an overture of the Iona Community.

MacLeod returned to Edinburgh as the assistant minister to St. Giles Cathedral. In the overcrowded slums that surrounded the cathedral he was challenged by the gulf that existed between the "two nations" living on his doorstep: the rich and respectable classes and hard-pressed workers who thought that church was not "for the likes o' them."[59] It offended the ideal of a classless community he had known in the trenches and which many had hoped would shape the post-war reconstruction. He felt the church should take the lead in modeling such new forms of community life and began informal micro-communities modeled on Toc H fellowships.[60] A short time later, Clayton secured funding for a Toc H padre in Glasgow and offered the post to MacLeod. He relished the opportunity to join this self-proclaimed "aristocracy of comradeship."[61] The organization had a "hearty, practical simplicity about its life and fellowship"[62] and for MacLeod it embodied the future of Christian community. He loved the work, but all did not go well. A heated debate over segregated communion left MacLeod hurt and compelled him to leave the community he had hoped would be a model of ecumenical hospitality. He returned to Edinburgh and threw himself into the work with the poor around St. Cuthbert's Church. He also began a club for the "up and outs": young professionals who were as absent from church as their poor parish neighbors. MacLeod would no more abandon the middle class to an undemanding Christianity than he would ignore the condition of the poor. Then in 1930 he accepted a call to Govan Old Parish Church, Glasgow.[63]

59 Ferguson, *George MacLeod*, 86.

60. Ibid., 87.

61. Ibid.

62. Ibid., 88.

63. MacLeod had been invited to Govan six months previously, but thinking he still had work to complete in Edinburgh had recommended his friend Bruce Nicol. Nicol accepted, but within six months was dead of TB. It was perhaps with some guilt that MacLeod went to Govan and threw himself into the work. Furthermore, his ancestor, John MacLeod (1840–98) had been a popular community figure as minister of Govan

Here, he again experimented with the nature of Christian community. The church stood in the middle of one of the largest docklands in Britain, a place that the Great Depression had left silent and whose craftsmen had nothing profitable to do. Adjacent to the church was a community center given to the people by Lady Pearce, the widow of a wealthy shipbuilder. He refused the manse and moved into the Pearce Institute,[64] writing to his former congregation that "here was the chance of an experiment offered to one who has constantly referred to the need for such an experiment."[65]

In Govan he worked tirelessly in the parish and developed new approaches of structure and worship within the church.[66] But despite his industry, the poverty of Govan persisted and it all left him close to breaking point. While recuperating for some months in the Middle East, MacLeod attended a Russian Orthodox Easter Sunday service. There he encountered worship like he had never before experienced it and a renewed sense of the church as the corporate body of Christ. Ferguson comments:

> For George MacLeod, lukewarm, conventional Presbyterianism finally died in the Holy Land on Easter Sunday, 1933. The old structure of individual devotion and duty had cracked in the crucible that was Govan in the hungry thirties, and he knew in his heart of hearts that it could not be repaired by more work, or even by more faith. He needed, for his healing, a new way of *seeing*, and he found new vision in the midst of overwhelming, mysteriously beautiful worship. It was a vision which was personal, political and cosmic *all at the same time*, and it appealed to the Celt in him. Holiness had become wholeness had become holiness. It was as if the spiritual and the material fused in a never-to-be-forgotten rapturous moment of revelation. The rest of George MacLeod's life would consist in the acting out of this compelling vision, and Iona Abbey would in time become his theatre for the glory of God.[67]

He returned enlightened and empowered, telling his assistant that there was going to be in Govan a "community of the will of God." In uncompromising

for twenty-three years before his premature death in 1898. Ibid., Chapter 7 generally.

64. The P. I. as it had become known, not only provided a place for the unemployed to meet during the day, but it offered cheap food, together with facilities for reading and recreation. See ibid., 115.

65. Ibid., 112.

66. He radically reduced the numbers of parishioners on the roll, but increased the numbers attending and serving in leadership. He also encouraged the observance of the Calendar of the Christian Year.

67. Ibid., 125.

terms he proclaimed his intention to lead it: "That community I am going to make—with or without you—it's not going to be great fun, and it's going to be difficult. It's not going to be a miracle, but it's going to be real."[68]

MacLeod reimmersed himself in the congregation and in the parish. Its humor reminded him of the sociality of the trenches, but its poverty still frustrated him. A few miles from Govan, MacLeod found the ruins of Fingalton Mill and invited the unemployed laborers to rebuild it as a local holiday center. As the men worked with one another they shared their thoughts on matters both trivial and important: so was heard another overture to the founding of the Iona Community. But despite the success of Fingalton, MacLeod knew that the gospel demanded and the people longed for something more. To find it, MacLeod would have to leave Govan and travel to Iona.

He had spent holidays on Iona since childhood. It was rich in Christian history and symbolism. In 563, St. Columba founded a community of monks there,[69] and it became a center of work, worship, hospitality, and evangelism. Columba had been an aristocratic and single-minded leader of men who dedicated themselves to the mission of God. He was an icon of Scots Christianity. MacLeod found in this ancient monk not only a historical soul mate, but also an unimpeachable precedent for his experiment. The men were not unalike: Bradley notes that MacLeod "shared his predecessor's combination of deep prayerfulness and humility, imaginative insight and poetic flair and charismatic leadership qualities accompanied by a somewhat autocratic and dominant manner."[70] MacLeod shamelessly exploited his aristocratic contacts when seeking support, persuading friends in high places to part with their money "as much as Columba had persuaded kings and princes to give land and endowments for his monastic foundations."[71] It appears that for MacLeod at the heart of it all was the prophecy spoken by Columba shortly before his death:

> Iona of my heart, Iona of my love,
> Instead of monks' voices there shall be lowing of cattle:
> But ere the world comes to an end
> Iona shall be as it was.[72]

---

68. Ibid., 126.

69. The facts that precipitated the journey of Columba to Iona are now obscured by accretions of hagiography and are subject to much debate. What is certain is that Columba was of Royal Irish lineage and did found a monastery on Iona. For a more detailed treatment of St. Columba see Bradley, *Columba*, and Finlay, *Columba*.

70. Bradley, *Columba*, 102.

71. Ibid.

72. Ferguson, *George MacLeod*, 155.

With the gradual demise of Celtic Christianity the voices of monks did indeed give way to the lowing of cattle. In 1203 a Benedictine community had built a stone abbey on the site, but after the Reformation the decaying building was left to the cattle again. In 1899, the Duke of Argyll gifted the ruins to a public trust with a proviso that when the church was renovated it should be open to members of all Christian denominations. By 1910, the abbey church had been restored and MacLeod subsequently became a popular speaker at the many retreats conducted on the island.[73] The rebuilding of the other monastic buildings had often been discussed on such occasions, and MacLeod was not the only one with the idea, but he was the man who would make it happen.[74]

There are several versions of what finally motivated MacLeod to risk his audacious experiment, but clearly he was frustrated with the bias toward individual salvation offered from pulpits whose church life made little or no impact on the social problems people faced. He saw the restored abbey church with its ruined living quarters as a contemporary parable; here was a well-kept church surrounded by the ruins of a common life. It needed a counter-parable. MacLeod often retold the particular "kairos" moment.

> Firstly, one of our local Clydeside brilliants, a quasi-Communist who has smoked more of my cigarettes than any other man alive, suddenly burst into my room unexpectedly to proclaim, "You folk have got it: if only you knew that you had it, and if only you knew how to begin to say it." It was his certainty that rebuked me; his implied need that moved me. What in effect he said was, "You know you could save me and you know you aren't doing it."[75]

This was not a criticism of MacLeod, it was directed at all the clergy and at the church. MacLeod's response was the living counter-parable that combined the rebuilding of living quarters of Iona Abbey with training ministers to rebuild the common life of the nation's population. The otherwise

73. For a more complete history of the island see MacArthur, *Columba's Island*. For a critical assessment of the period directly concerning MacLeod and the early Iona Community see Chapter 14, 148–62.

74. David Russell, a paper mill owner and lover of Iona had talked with MacLeod about reconstructing the abbey buildings in 1931. The trustees of Iona decided not to proceed in the height of the Depression. Earlier, in 1926, an American group had wanted to found a Celtic College on the island. Even in 1904, the first appeal leaflet of the Iona Cathedral trust indicated their hope to restore the chapter house, the cloisters, and St. Oran's Chapel, as well as the church. Ibid.

75. MacLeod, *Speaking the Truth*, 13.

unemployed craftsmen would be put to the work of rebuilding while the ministers would assist them by serving as laborers. It was to be a

> "brotherhood within the Church of Scotland, of no permanent vows, into which men of such a mind could come for the first two or three years of their ministry." The first six months after leaving college would be spent in community life: they would then be ready "to be drafted out—still as members of the brotherhood—to the congested areas and the housing schemes where they would carry their ideas into practice."[76]

It would be "a micro-cosmic witness that 'Christianity works' not only on Sundays but on everyday of the week":[77] . . . "a tiny symbol that the thing can be done."[78]

MacLeod's personal commitment was intense. And he told his congregation that he could not remain with them, preaching risk and faith, if they knew that he had had the opportunity for such adventure, but had remained in "a much safer billet."[79] He told the Iona Trustees:

> For the purpose of its inception, I would myself be prepared to leave my present work at any time now and I would undertake to stand by the Experiment full time, resisting any conceivable inducements, for a term of five years. For such time during that period as I remain unmarried, I would offer my services without reward, but would ask for the payment of my essential expenses when travelling in the name of the Brotherhood.[80]

MacLeod had been seeking some such kind of fellowship ever since the war: Toc H, the Pearce Institute, and Fingalton Mill were all preliminary attempts to establish a "new, disciplined regiment trained and equipped for a new fight."[81] By July 1938, men had been recruited and sufficient funds were in

76. Ferguson, *Chasing the Wild Goose*, 51–52.

77. Iona Community, *Coracle*, no. 2, 20.

78. Ibid. MacLeod was to later find another living parable in the church of St. Nicolas in Liverpool. Before the war it had its back to the commerce of the River Mersey, to enter the church was to turn away from the hub of life. However, after it was bombed, a prefabricated hut was annexed to the ruins and turned to face the other way, ensuring that the surviving porch became the sanctuary and the massive doors became windows empty of stained glass that deliberately looked out on the business of the world. See MacLeod, *We Shall Rebuild*, 13, and Gardiner, "Worship in the Middle," 262–72.

79. Ferguson, *George MacLeod*, 164.

80. Cited in Ferguson, *Chasing the Wild Goose*, 53.

81. Ferguson, *George MacLeod*, 163. Ferguson notes how MacLeod drew not only on his experiences of the army, church, and Toc H, but was attracted by more experimental communities such as the Cotswold Bruderhof. And while MacLeod does not

place to begin.[82] Wooden huts were erected beside the ruins and as they met for worship on their first evening visitors and islanders joined them. The inclusion of these symbolized to the men that their new community must be lived within and for the concrete realities of the world.[83] However, the Community was not without conflict. It was almost as if they tried too hard to create community; ministers adopted the idealized image of a builder and the craftsmen were worse: "Thinking they were embarked on a religious work, they tried to discard their humanity."[84] In the ensuing arguments an important truth was affirmed: confession, forgiveness, and reconciliation were necessities for true community. These difficulties reflected the problems in the wider church and world: "how to live corporately, sharing life and its resources in a spirit of interdependence, while preserving the rights of the individual."[85]

The Community attracted criticism for being hapless romantics playing at being monks and were accused of being "half way towards Rome and half way towards Moscow."[86] MacLeod defended the project asserting that they only sought "to remain part of the world in which we find ourselves and yet not be of it. We have definitely barred the cloistered life."[87] He claimed the Community was

> an exceedingly calculated movement within the normal purpose of the Church. Poverty is not our aim, far less is the principle of celibacy involved. Those who come here will claim no "sacrifice"; we only claim a privilege to make perhaps the sacrifice of those who work in really difficult places a little less acute.[88]

The following year, in the face of European war and criticisms for the continuance of the experiment, MacLeod asserted that such a crisis demanded "not a battening of the hatches but rather a crowding on of more

---

mention Bonhoeffer's work at Finkenwalde, he was more than likely aware of it. Ibid., 152.

82. Characteristic of a man often long on energy and commitment but short on diplomacy, MacLeod had neglected to consult or even inform those living on the island of his intention. See MacArthur, Columba's Island, 148.

83. Iona Community, Coracle, no. 1, 6.

84. Ferguson, George MacLeod, 172.

85. Ferguson, Chasing the Wild Goose, 55.

86. Ibid., 56.

87. Iona Community, Coracle, no. 1, 12.

88. Iona Community, Coracle, no. 2, 18.

canvas. . . . The problem is not whether the Community should continue, but into what new channels it should regulate its forces."[89]

But the war changed everything. Few young ministers would wish to spend months on Iona while the hostilities in Europe continued, so while the craftsmen continued the rebuilding, their huts were also used as a retreat center for visiting clergy and laity. Thus, "round the tight, little community of full members the war brought another community, much larger, much looser, a very mixed assortment of men and women, old and young. It was indeterminate in limit. You could not say who belonged and who did not."[90] Iona became a place where people of differing denominations could come and learn discipleship and community living and, "once embarked on this road, there was no way back to the original simplicities of the Iona Community."[91] The young ordinands were then based in Edinburgh, and so, despite this war-time diversification, the Community still fulfilled its primary task of preparing ministers for urban parishes.[92] Such men had no ready answers for the problems they would encounter, but they could affirm a new way of finding solutions.

> Christ is a Person to be trusted, not a principle to be tested. The Church is a Movement, not a meeting house. The Faith is an Experience, not an exposition. Christians are Explorers, not map makers. And the New Social Order is not a blue print which someone must find quickly. It is a present Experience made possible at Bethlehem, offered on Calvary, and communicated at Pentecost.[93]

MacLeod seemed to know instinctively where the next step should be taken. Weekly courses on Iona were well subscribed and there were soon three thousand "Friends of the Community" supporting the work financially.[94] A group of minister associates was established to meet for prayer

89. Iona Community, *Coracle*, no. 3, 6.

90. Morton, *Iona Community*, 57.

91. Ferguson, *George MacLeod*, 185.

92. MacLeod knew that the ministers held no instant solution for the church or society and likened the Community to a "blind scout with one arm in a sling, and a gammy leg; it has unwittingly got over the hedge with its right leg and still has its gammy leg stuck in the old order of things." Ibid., 190.

93. Iona Community, *Coracle*, June 1942, as cited in Ferguson, *George MacLeod*, 204. For a more complete story of the Community's search for new solutions see Muir, *Outside the Safe Space*.

94. Many others were critical. The local Church of Scotland minister, Rev. Donald MacCuish, was wary of the developments and his Kirk Session complained to the Cathedral Trustees about the un-Presbyterian worship being conducted in the Abbey. See

and discussion and soon youth and women associates would follow. Ferguson notes that "these developments arose not because the Community planned them but because hungry people were looking for bread."[95]

In each successive year, the Iona Community commissioned more ministers to urban parishes. As they did so, the membership proved to be tenacious.[96] The original plan would have ensured a balance of artisans and ministers, with new ministers joining every two years. But it was quickly apparent that the ministers who had supported and befriended one another on Iona were now scattered throughout Scotland and wanted to continue their belonging in a more permanent community, albeit one that remained geographically dispersed. Ralph Morton notes that at this stage, "the members took the destiny of the Iona Community into their own hands."[97] They began by asking what it was that bound them together. On Iona it had been easily identifiable, living together in one hut, the communal sharing of work and worship and a common income of £50 per annum for each man. Away from Iona, their struggles to maintain some accountability to one another led to the creation of the Rule of Life that in its expanded form is now followed by its contemporary members.[98]

One final event would shape the embryonic Iona Community. In 1943, attendant on the Community's youth work on Mull, came a gift to the Church of Scotland of £20,000 per annum for seven years to establish experiments with young people along the lines of the Iona work. The money was used for a variety of causes but most importantly for the establishing of a center at 214 Clyde Street, Glasgow.[99] While the Abbey remained the iconic center of the Community, 214 Clyde Street became "its city counterpart."[100] Monica Stewart writes:

MacArthur, *Columba's Island*, 157. MacLeod's outspoken pacifism was deeply regarded as subversive and unpatriotic in a time of war. See Ferguson, *George MacLeod*, 190ff. Ministers who were Iona men were sometimes blacklisted when looking for a church. See Ferguson, *Chasing the Wild Goose*, 62.

95. Ibid.

96. While MacLeod intended the artisans to remain for "such periods as their labour was required" it was anticipated that the ministers would only serve within the "brotherhood" for two years. See Iona Community, *Coracle*, no. 36 (March 1960), 6, and Morton, *Iona Community*, 18.

97. Morton, *Iona Community*, 39.

98. See Appendix A. For further discussion see Galloway, *Living By the Rule*.

99. The story of the various projects is told in detail in Morton, *Iona Community*, 62ff, and in Muir, *Outside the Safe Space*.

100. See Morton, *Iona Community*, 71. Morton notes that Community House was not named "Iona Community House." The name "Community" was chosen to emphasize what it was trying to offer: "a place where men and women could meet and talk

> It is difficult to capture, in just a sentence or two, the richness
> and diversity of life within Community House! It became a
> centre of education for people of all ages; a place of worship;
> a cultural base where people experimented with art, drama,
> music and film; a place where people relaxed and shared meals
> together; a refuge for homeless folk; a place where people were
> encouraged to talk openly about religion and politics, and, of
> course, it was a home for those who lived there.[101]

Community House incarnated the idea of polyphony in community, a gathering of political, artistic, charitable, and religious melodies around an open hospitality, centered in Christ.

At the same time, the weeks held on Iona added to the richness of the Community witness. Such weeks were unlike any holiday: guests were expected to share in the daily chores as well as attend lectures and worship. Prayer and politics, work and worship and a weekly pilgrimage around the island were all vital to Christian community. Such weeks were intended to offer people a glimpse of Christian community: "This was—and is—the secret of Iona."[102]

MacLeod remained the leader until 1967 when he inherited a peerage. Throughout these years the deputy leader, Ralph Morton, once described as a "virtuoso of the second string,"[103] worked slowly and steadily to develop the structures of the community. Although MacLeod remained a formidable presence in the Community until his death in 1991, Ian Reid was given the immediate and unenviable task of being his successor. He quickly addressed the tensions members detected between life in the church, life in society, and the place of the Community. He wrote,

> The Community exists to help its members together to receive
> both vision and encouragement. At the present time there are
> those who, in obedience to Jesus, feel dissatisfied with the in-
> stitutional Church as it is. Some of them know that they must
> remain within the institutional Church trying to help it to be-
> come the kind of Church He wants. Others, still committed to
> Jesus, believe that they must work outside it. These two groups
> need one another.[104]

and, hopefully find community for themselves." Ibid., 67.

101. Stewart, *T. Ralph Morton*, 4. Ralph and Jenny Morton were the wardens. In 1951 Penry Jones joined them on staff at Community House and offered regular teaching on politics. See Morton, *Iona Community*, 76.

102. Ferguson, *Chasing the Wild Goose*, 72.

103. Ferguson, *George MacLeod*, 298.

104. Ian Reid, cited in Ferguson, *Chasing the Wild Goose*, 108.

In 1988, another leader, Ron Ferguson, would similarly argue,

> The need for a supportive network of people committed to radical spirituality and radical politics will grow, and it will require to operate within and outwith the institutional church. . . . God has provided resources for us beyond our limited imaginings. The resources are there for a purpose—building and rebuilding the common life.[105]

The inspiration behind MacLeod's vision of community was primarily clerical, male, and shaped by his military background and particular social conditioning. The Iona Community today acknowledges the debt owed to its founding father, but in its adulthood, has moved into an understanding of community that reveals an inclusive depth and breadth beyond the original vision of 1938. However, the emphasis firmly remains on building the common life.

DIETRICH BONHOEFFER: THEOLOGIAN OF POLYPHONY

Like MacLeod, Bonhoeffer was not only passionate about the nature of community but saw the great strength derived from life together. However, he knew that community did not simply mean living together or sharing common ideas but was about participating in the divine reality that God had already called into existence. Like the family in which he grew up, Bonhoeffer believed that community was a gathering together and a unity of diverse opinions and personalities.[106]

Dietrich was the elder twin to Sabine with whom he shared three elder brothers, two elder sisters, and one younger sister. The family has been described as cultured and humanistic, a place of "self-control . . . objectivity and balance."[107] Each member was expected to display the rationality and liberalism personified in their father Karl, a professor of psychiatry and neurology. But Dietrich inherited from his mother's family a love for both theology and music. His grandmother Clara von Hase loved to sing and had taken piano lessons from Franz Lizst. Her father had been an eminent

---

105. Ronald Ferguson, *Golden Jubilee Coracle*, 1988, cited in Shanks, *Iona—God's Energy*, 38.

106. Day argues that the views on Christian community Bonhoeffer articulates in *Sanctorum Communio* are no more than a description of his family. Day, *Dietrich Bonhoeffer*, 2. See also Rasmussen and Bethge, "Bonhoeffer's Family," 1.

107. See Bethge, *Bonhoeffer: An Illustrated Introduction*, 13. For biographical details pertaining to each family member see Leibholz-Bonhoeffer, *The Bonhoeffers*.

church historian who had once been imprisoned for subversive political activities, and her husband, Karl Alfred, was a professor of practical theology who had resigned as a chaplain to Emperor Wilhelm after a disagreement with the Kaiser.[108] But despite these ecclesiastical connections, Dietrich rarely attended church. His mother Paula had received a strongly Christian upbringing and had been connected with the Moravian brethren. She determined that Christian learning should be handed on to her children, but felt no need of the church to do so.[109] When religious ceremonies in the family required a clergyman, it was a family member, usually Karl Alfred von Hase, who presided. The children, however, were taught the Bible, learned hymns, and were offered grace before meals, as well as participating in evening prayers. In due course, they were baptized and confirmed. Paula governed their instruction in religion, but the remainder of their early education came from governesses Käthe and Maria Horn, who were dedicated followers of the Herrnhut community. While their spirituality was undoubtedly of secondary importance in the culture of family life, it would be foolish to disregard the influence that these "intelligent, humorous and beloved" women had on Dietrich.[110] Thus, there remained a Christian tone to family life without their feeling a need for any ecclesiastical guidance or participation in a community of faith. Yet, something of the church and a relationship in Christ would beckon to Bonhoeffer.

In his youth, Dietrich displayed a precocious musical talent, playing Mozart sonatas by the age of ten. When he was in the fifth form he composed a trio on Schubert's song, "*Gute Ruh*," which may have marked the beginnings of his desire to bring together music and theology.[111]

The Bonhoeffer children were encouraged to form their own opinions and to choose their own careers, while respecting the choices of those who differed from them. In this freedom of choice the teenage Dietrich devoted himself to theology. For all the familial tolerance, his decision was not well received. Paula accepted it, but with little enthusiasm. Karl had strong

---

108. Von Hase was imprisoned for a year for political radicalism. He later became a respected church historian. See Bethge, *Dietrich Bonhoeffer: A Biography*, 3–13. Karl Alfred objected to the Kaiser calling the common people a "pack of dogs." Ibid., 7.

109. See Bethge, *Bonhoeffer: An Illustrated Introduction*, 18.

110. Maria and Käthe joined the family six months after Dietrich and Sabine were born and Maria remained with them for seventeen years. See Bosanquet, *Life and Death*, 28ff.

111. Dietrich was not unique in the family in this regard. Bethge notes that Klaus later played the cello with "great sensitivity" and records how "none of his brothers or sisters ever wanted to miss the family musical evenings." Bethge, *Dietrich Bonhoeffer: A Biography*, 25.

misgivings but kept them to himself.[112] His brothers were less restrained, but Dietrich was a match to their criticism: Karl Friedrich thought that theology was redundant in a scientific world now coming of age, but Dietrich told him, "You may knock my block off, but I shall still believe in God."[113] Klaus condemned the church as an impotent and peripheral phenomenon and Dietrich retorted, "If the Church is feeble, I shall reform it!"[114]

His choice to study theology seems to have been influenced by the death of his brother Walter in World War I. It devastated the whole family. Paula moved into a neighbor's house for some weeks and was absent from family life for the ensuing year. Karl ceased to write the family annual memoirs for ten years. But Walter's death had an especially decisive effect on Dietrich. Until he was age twelve, he and Sabine had shared a bedroom and often conversed about death and eternal life.[115] Then, around the time of Walter's fatal wounding, Dietrich moved into a room of his own. Here, he struggled on his own to reflect on Walter's death.[116] He felt a deep loneliness at this time,[117] and it was then that he composed a cantata on the Psalmist's lament: "My soul is cast down within me." Like many others, in his grief Bonhoeffer had turned to both music and Christian faith. Sometime after Walter's death Dietrich tested a vocation in music by auditioning before Leonid Kreuzer, a virtuoso pianist. The outcome was indecisive but then, at age fifteen he began to study Hebrew and occasionally attended church accompanied by his mother.[118] After this, while music remained a constant presence, in Bonhoeffer's biography the references to it are incidental, as if his passion for it is constrained to leave room for the more important tasks

112. Karl Bonhoeffer felt his son would be wasting his abilities on a redundant profession but in a letter to Dietrich in 1934, he admitted that his preconception of a "quiet, uneventful minister's life" as he knew it from his Swabian uncles had been incorrect. Letter dated February 2, 1934, cited in Bethge, *Bonhoeffer: Exile and Martyr*, 43.

113. Bosanquet, *Life and Death*, 45.

114. Ibid.

115. Sabine recalls how Dietrich and she had previously meditated on eternity until they were dizzy and how, once separated, Dietrich would drum on the wall between them to remind her to "think of God." Sabine Leibholz, "Childhood and Home," in Zimmerman and Smith, *I Knew Dietrich Bonhoeffer*, 23–25.

116. Morris makes a compelling assertion that these meditations on death began in the period around their twelfth birthdays (February 1918) and continued through the period following April 1918 when their mother was absent from the house after hearing of Walter's death. Morris, *Bonhoeffer's Ethic of Discipleship*, 88ff.

117. Bethge suggests that it might be said that it "was because he was lonely that Bonhoeffer became a theologian, and because he became a theologian he was lonely." See Bethge, *Dietrich Bonhoeffer: A Biography*, 37.

118. Ibid.

of life. K. E. Morris speculates on that more important task and why it was theological. He argues that consciously or otherwise there was a bargain struck within the family when Walter died. The older brothers, whose careers were already chosen, would continue in the paternal world of science and law. In return, and with the hope of comfort to Paula, Dietrich would be allowed to pursue a future in the church.[119] There may even have been some hope that Dietrich's religious pursuits could bring healing to the family through the one enterprise that offered hope in death, namely Christianity. At this time, Dietrich was given Walter's Bible. In accepting it he may have been acknowledging that his would be the task of realizing the hope offered to a family fractured by death. "If the sting could be snatched from death, harmony in his childhood world could once again prevail."[120] None of this is to say that Walter's death or the family drove Bonhoeffer to be a theologian, but Bethge is certain that Dietrich's "childish spirit" not only responded to the event with a "fervent longing for the life beyond," but that he also had a strong, if unarticulated wish, to convey this faith to the others.[121]

Bonhoeffer was seventeen when he left home to study theology at Tübingen. The only lecturer who seems to have influenced him was Adolf Schlatter, whose unambiguous dedication to Scripture was formative in Bonhoeffer's theology, particularly his dedication to the Sermon on the Mount.[122] Of greater influence than Tübingen was the trip to Rome taken with his brother Klaus in 1924. There, Dietrich was captivated by the glory of the church. Easter Day in St. Peter's made him appreciate how "nationalistic, provincial and narrow-minded were the confines of his own church."[123] Until then his Christian education had been in the home and the academy. Now, "before his dazzled sight there blazed out the visible symbol of the Church Universal; the Church of Rome, the Church at the heart of the world. Without prejudice or

---

119. Morris, *Bonhoeffer's Ethic of Discipleship*, 82ff.

120. Ibid., 91. Morris speculates that this bargain was only settled in terms of his personal position when "Bonhoeffer joined his family in political resistance, it was the first time in his life that he had stood as a peer and an equal to his father and brothers. . . . Standing in quasi-identification with his dead brother Walter, he might also risk a wartime death. But his death, unlike Walter's would be the death of one who fights against war, not in a war. . . . Thus the constellation of events in the resistance paralleled those in the Bonhoeffer family of 1918 and allowed Dietrich to re-enact that primal drama—this time to break free of it. 131–32.

121. Bethge, *Dietrich Bonhoeffer: A Biography*, 38.

122. Rumscheidt has described the debt Bonhoeffer owes to Schattler, particularly on being accountable to church and Scripture and his knowledge of the Jewish culture of Jesus. See Rumscheidt, "The Formation of Bonhoeffer's Theology," in de Gruchy, *The Cambridge Companion to Dietrich Bonhoeffer*, 52.

123. Bethge, *Bonhoeffer: An Illustrated Introduction*, 34.

anxiety, Bonhoeffer gave himself up to this new experience."[124] He wrote in his diary, "I am beginning to understand the concept of 'church.'"[125] On the same trip he visited Africa where he noted,

> In Islam, everyday life and religion are not separated at all. Even in the Catholic church they are separated, for the most part. At home one just goes to church. When one returns a completely different kind of life begins.[126]

How life and religion could be manifest together in the church became the subject of Bonhoeffer's doctoral studies in Berlin under Reinhold Seeberg. Seeberg gave Bonhoeffer a strong Christocentrism and awakened an appreciation of the sociality of human existence.[127] The thesis, *Sanctorum Communio*, articulated a powerful sociality of church as "Christ existing as community" but below the capable theology lay a vivid description of his family before his brother's death. Subconsciously it seems that he was seeking for a way in which life and religion, the worlds of his father and mother, could be profitably united and heal his fractured family. As he worked on this thesis his longing for un-fragmented community compelled him to the fellowship of the church: teaching Sunday School and then a "Thursday Group," which not only discussed religious and political topics but also attended opera and concerts.

He pursued a career in the church, accepting a call to be an assistant pastor to a German congregation in Barcelona. While church and theology were the dominant concerns of his life at this time, still his interest in music did not wane. Before agreeing to go he asked whether there was a piano he could play and if there were an Opera House,[128] and he later recorded how much he enjoyed the concerts there.[129] On his return to teach in Berlin he befriended Franz Hildebrant, a young theologian who significantly shared Bonhoeffer's lively musicality.

As MacLeod before him, in 1930 Bonhoeffer accepted a scholarship to study at Union Seminary, New York. While there, he made a number of friendships, the first of which was Erwin Sutz, a Swiss student with whom he often played piano and debated doctrine.[130] He also enjoyed a significant

124. Bosanquet, *Life and Death of Dietrich Bonhoeffer*, 52.

125. Bonhoeffer, *Young Bonhoeffer*, 89.

126. Letter to his parents from Tripoli, April 9, 1924, in Bonhoeffer, *Young Bonhoeffer*, 118.

127. Bethge, *Dietrich Bonhoeffer: A Biography*, 70.

128. Ibid., 99.

129. Letter to Seeberg, July 20, 1928, cited Ibid., 101.

130. Erwin Sutz was a Swiss student who subsequently brought Bonhoeffer and

friendship with Albert F. Fisher, an African American who brought him to the Abyssinian Baptist Church in Harlem. Here he experienced and was appalled at America's racial segregation. But he was deeply impressed with the fervor of their worship, quickly acquiring a record collection of Negro Spirituals. Another friendship that developed at Union had no musical connection, but it is difficult to underestimate the influence of Jean Lasserre: he crucially shaped Bonhoeffer's views on pacifism and his interpretation of the Sermon on the Mount.[131]

When Bonhoeffer returned to Berlin, both Germany and he were changing. He saw that "an easily led citizenry was content to bask in the Teutonic pride that Hitler was proclaiming. . . . They sheltered, not in Jesus Christ, but under the political wings of Hitler's military might and Nazism's promise of unparalleled prosperity and national security."[132] Bonhoeffer experienced a deep personal transition, a "great liberation" in which it became clear that "the life of a servant of Jesus Christ should belong to the Church."[133] As Bethge interprets it, Bonhoeffer was moving from being a "theologian to a Christian."[134] As he did so, he quickly identified the threat of Hitler's Nazism and was immersed in the early stages of the Confessing Church and opposing Hitler's anti-Jewish legislation. But as Hitler's power grew, Bonhoeffer became frustrated by the lack of decisive opposition in the Confessing Church.[135] He left Germany to accept a pastorate in London.

Bonhoeffer was diligent in his responsibilities in London and worked tirelessly in ecumenical circles in opposing Nazism and promoting pacifism.[136] He also imported his Bechstein piano and used the manse as a rehearsal room for the parish music group and invited its youth group to listen to his large collection of gramophone records.[137] He was only there for eighteen months and in 1935, after a fact-finding tour of Christian communi-

---

Barth together. Ibid., 153.

131. Jean Lasserre was a pacifist who challenged Bonhoeffer on the commands against violence in the Sermon on the Mount.

132. Kelly, "Prayer and Righteous Action," in de Gruchy, *Cambridge Companion to Dietrich Bonhoeffer*, 247.

133. Cited in Bethge, *Bonhoeffer: An Illustrated Introduction*, 57.

134. Bethge's biography is subtitled *Theologian, Christian, Man for His Times*, indicating three phases of Bonhoeffer's life.

135. The church, in opposition, argued that a *status confessionis* was precipitated by Nazism, i.e., they represented a challenge to the fundamentals of faith to which the church must confess its opposition if it were to remain the church of the Gospel.

136. It was during his time in London that Bonhoeffer attended the Ecumenical Youth Conference at Fanö, Denmark, and spoke passionately on behalf of church opposition to the Nazi Regime.

137. Bethge, *Dietrich Bonhoeffer: A Biography*, 328.

ties, he returned to Germany to establish a new seminary for the Confessing Church.[138] It was here, at Finkenwalde, that Bonhoeffer experimented with the praxis of life together in Christian community. Work in the seminary brought together in one place all that had been preoccupying Bonhoeffer during the past few years. Here he could explore the praxis demanded from the Sermon on the Mount. He could experiment in a community that was rooted in spiritual disciplines and lived in service to one another, a group of men who might be witnesses to the power of passive resistance in a violent world.[139] But it was also a testament to balance in life. As well as rigorous study, Bonhoeffer reserved time for games and ensured the presence of two grand pianos in his impoverished college. He also placed his gramophone records, including his collection of Negro Spirituals at the disposal of all the students.[140] And while the emphasis of Finkenwalde was understandably biased to life in the church,[141] the students knew that their time in seclusion offered no escape from the increasing tensions in Germany. This time was an intensive period of preparation, the lessons of which they would soon have to practice within the dangerous world beyond. It should not come as a surprise that when Bonhoeffer wished to comment on this relationship of church and world beyond the seminary, he did so in a powerful and contextual bisociation of theology and music: "Only he who cries out for the Jews can sing the Gregorian chant."[142]

One final incident from the time at Finkenwalde is important for understanding a theologian who later came to practice his discourse through the metaphor of music. Johannes Goebel recounts being present when Bonhoeffer was improvising at the piano. He claimed,

> I asked him [Bonhoeffer] whether he had ever tried, or was trying, to compose anything. In a distinctly reserved tone he said he had stopped doing so since he had become a theologian, or

138. He contacted Bishop George Bell and arranged visits to Anglican seminaries and communities such as the Community of the Resurrection in Mirfield, the Society of the Sacred Mission at Kelham, and the Society of St. John the Evangelist in Oxford. See Julius Rieger, "Contacts With London," in Zimmermann and Smith, *I Knew Dietrich Bonhoeffer*, 97–98. He also visited the Quakers at Selly Oak. See Bethge, *Dietrich Bonhoeffer: A Biography*, 412.

139. See the proposal for a House of Brethren to the Council of the Evangelical Church of the Old Prussian Union, dated September 6, 1935, *Theological Education at Finkenwalde*, 95–99. Here the influence of Anglican Monasticism and conversations with Jean Lasserre are evident.

140. Bethge, *Dietrich Bonhoeffer: A Biography*, 427.

141. Much of the theological teaching and reflection was written up in his books *Discipleship* (1937) and *Life Together* (1939).

142. See Bethge, *Dietrich Bonhoeffer: A Biography*, 441.

something to the effect. This seems to me a typical trait of his nature. Bonhoeffer was a passionate preacher and theologian, as Bethge confirms. To sit down at an instrument and improvise or even compose—and not just play Mozart with exactitude . . . this can only be done in passion, and out of passion. Bonhoeffer cast this passion out of his life for the sake of the call to a greater "passion." This too is a contribution to the theme of "Call and Discipleship." That it was a "casting out" is quite clear to me from the picture which rises in my memory . . . while he was sitting at the piano something which I had not known in him and have never seen again, an expression of natural force, of something primeval, came over him, a Dietrich different from the one known to us. . . . It is strange that this should have been so preserved by my memory; this lightening up of a rudimentary "non-Bonhoeffer," and after that the short, harsh, sharp overcoming of himself, in the way he broke off his playing so suddenly, in his answer to my amiably condescending question implying such a subtle criticism of my curiosity, in the vigorous turning back to "work" to the "essential Bonhoeffer" . . . an overcoming of self which, in principle, had been accomplished long before. To him this may have been a trifle then, not worth mentioning. To me it remains a contribution to "sanctification," to "discipleship," and surely as such a precious memory.[143]

In much the same way as he broke off a romantic attachment to focus on the community at Finkenwalde,[144] it seems that Bonhoeffer gave up the childhood ambition of musical composition for the sake of unequivocal devotion to theology. Still, he could only conceive of theology and music as "either/ or choices" competing for his love and commitment. Perhaps he feared that a choice for music would have led him away from others down the path of "inner emigration"; an accusation he leveled at composers attending a Festival of church music in Berlin that year.[145] Only later does it appear that a

---

143. Goebel, "When He Sat Down at the Piano," in Zimmerman and Smith, *I Knew Dietrich Bonhoeffer*, 124–25.

144. Bonhoeffer reflected on this from prison saying, "I was once in love with a girl; she became a theologian, and our paths ran parallel for many years. . . . We didn't realize we loved each other. . . . Being totally committed to my work for the Church in the ensuing years, I thought it not only inevitable but right that I should forgo marriage altogether." Bonhoeffer and von Wedemeyer, *Love Letters from Cell 92*, 246. If Bonhoeffer knew this girl (Elizabeth Zinn) for eight years and since he was twenty-one, this places his decision to end things in 1935, as he returned to Germany to take his responsibilities at Zingst/Finkenwalde.

145. See Bethge, *Dietrich Bonhoeffer: A Biography*, 586.

metaphor of polyphony would enable him to overcome such dichotomized thinking.

In 1937 the Gestapo shut down Finkenwalde.[146] The following year, on the "Kristallnacht" of November 9, the Nazis destroyed Jewish shops and synagogues, killing ninety Jews and sending twenty thousand more to concentration camps. To Bonhoeffer's outrage there was no concerted opposition from the Confessing Church.[147] Things deteriorated in 1939 when hardly any pastor refused to sign an oath of loyalty to Hitler. Bonhoeffer's anxiety grew when conscription raised the possibility of having to fight in Hitler's army.[148]

Bonhoeffer was persuaded that a way around conscription was to accept an invitation to America. But within days he regretted it.

> I have come to the conclusion that I have made a mistake in coming to America. I must live through this difficult period of our national history with the Christian people of Germany. I will have no right to participate in the reconstruction of Christian life in Germany after the war if I do not share the trials of this time with my people. . . . Christians in Germany will face the terrible alternative of either willing the defeat of their nation in order that Christian civilization may survive, or willing the victory of their nation and thereby destroying our civilization. I know which of these alternatives I must choose; but I cannot make that choice in security.[149]

Within a few weeks of Bonhoeffer's return, Hitler invaded Poland. Bonhoeffer was forbidden to teach, publish, or preach. As his work for the Confessing Church became impossible, Bonhoeffer was increasingly taken into the confidence of a dissident group within Abwehr, German Military

---

146. Although the buildings closed, the work of training pastors for the Confessing Church continued for a few years through the *Sammelvikariate*, a "collective curacy" whereby students were nominally attached to obscure parishes as a cover for continuing to train them in small groups. See Bosanquet, *Life and Death of Dietrich Bonhoeffer*, 192; Bethge, "The Collective Pastorates 1938–1940," in *Dietrich Bonhoeffer: A Biography*, 587–678; and Schlingensiepen, *Dietrich Bonhoeffer*, 210–12.

147. Bonhoeffer wrote the date in his Bible and underlined the words of Ps 74:8, "they burned all the meeting places of God in the land." See Bethge, *Dietrich Bonhoeffer: A Biography*, 607.

148. There was no conscientious objection in Germany. With the Confessing Church in atrophy, the risk by their association was that his inevitable resistance would embarrass matters. See Clements, *Patriotism for Today*, Chapter 2, generally.

149. Letter to R. Niebuhr, June 1939, in Bonhoeffer, *Theological Education Underground*, 210.

Intelligence.[150] For the next four years, Bonhoeffer lived a double life, ostensibly using his international contacts to gather intelligence for the Nazis, but all the while risking imprisonment and death for his subversion of the Regime.

During this time he worked on what he hoped would be his magnum opus, *Ethics*, but in April 1943 he was arrested on suspicion of helping Jews escape to Switzerland.[151] It was just weeks after he had announced his engagement to Maria von Wedemeyer.

It was in prison that Bonhoeffer began to see music and theology not as rivals for his commitment but as companions: he began to sketch a bisociative method for doing theology through the metaphor of music. In his isolation, music evoked memories of happier times, often times of strong community. These recollections were a source of great encouragement to him, and through them, and news of recent family concerts, he felt connected to his friends and relatives.[152] He often recalled songs, psalms, and hymns learned and sung at Finkenwalde,[153] and there are frequent prison references to the Youth Hymn book, *Das Neues Lied*, and works by Heinrich

150. Earlier that year, Bonhoeffer had been approached by his brother-in-law Hans von Dohnanyi about an attempt by dissidents in *Abwehr*, the Justice Department, and the Army to overthrow Hitler.

151. Part of Bonhoeffer's double life in the German Resistance led to him participating in the "U7" venture; a scheme to help Jews over the Swiss border.

152. A letter from Karl Bonhoeffer on April 11, 1943, and Dietrich's reply on April 14, 1943, refer to a cantata organized by Dietrich for his father's birthday. A year later, he recalls how "the sight of all those children joining in the music making, will still be very present to us all this year, truly a great joy." See Letter dated April 23, 1944. Dietrich's letter to his parents May 4, 1943, speaks of his encouragement at receiving Bach cantatas and recites a song by Hugo Wolf. The song is repeated in his letter to Hans von Dohnanyi that same month. In November 1943 Bonhoeffer feels connected to the world beyond his cell because he knows that on Repentance Day his friends will be listening to Bach's "Mass in B Minor." It also brings to mind happier times of community when he first heard it as a student in Berlin. Letter dated November 17, 1943. Bonhoeffer's friends and family often reciprocated the music reflections. See letter from Bethge dated January 9, 1944, and from his father dated March 27, 1944. See Bonhoeffer, *Letters and Papers*, various.

153. On November 20, 1943, Bonhoeffer wrote comparing his cell with Finkenwalde saying, "I am lacking nothing—only missing all of you. I want to play the G minor sonata with you and sing Schütz, and hear you sing Pss 70 and 47." Letter dated November 20, 1943. The following week he wrote again saying, "Last night in bed I opened *Neues Lied* for the first time to the—"our"—Advent songs. There is scarcely any of them I can hum to myself without being reminded of Finkenwalde, Schlönwitz, and Sigurdshof." In the same letter he recalls and notates Altdorfer's "Nativity." Letter dated November 27–28, 1943. On his birthday in 1944 (February 4) he recalls Bethge's present of the D major violin concerto to him eight years previously when they were together in Finkenwalde. See Bonhoeffer, *Letters and Papers*, various.

Schütz[154] and Paul Gerhardt.[155] He laments not hearing a hymn sung in a year and adds that "it's strange how music, when one listens with the inner ear alone and gives oneself up to it utterly, can be almost more beautiful than when heard physically. It's purer, all the dross falls away, and it seems to take on a 'new body.'"[156]

However, in two crucial passages to which we shall return throughout this book, Bonhoeffer adopts music as a metaphor through which to engage in theological reflection. In a letter dated February 23, 1944, Bonhoeffer wrote to Bethge lamenting the fragmentariness of contemporary living.

> What matters, it seems to me, is whether one still sees, in this fragment of life that we have, what the whole was intended and designed to be, and of what material it is made. After all, there are such things as fragments that are only fit for the garbage heap (even a decent "hell" is too good for them), and others which remain meaningful for hundreds of years, because only God could perfect them, so they must remain fragments—I'm thinking, for example, of the *Art of the Fugue*. If our life is only the most remote reflection of such a fragment, in which, even for a short time, the various themes gradually accumulate and harmonize with one another and in which the great counterpoint is sustained from beginning to end—so that finally when they cease, all one can do is sing the chorale, "*Vor Deinem Thron tret' ich allhier*"—then it is not for us, either to complain about this fragmentary life of ours, but rather even to be glad of it.[157]

Here, Bonhoeffer considers the "exceptional prophetic possibility"[158] of the musical imagery of polyphony; how melody and countermelody might enable theological reflection on the increasingly fractured condition of modern humanity. Bonhoeffer argues that the *cantus firmus* for the Christian and their community is Jesus Christ, but that around him concrete living in

---

154. Bonhoeffer became aware of Heinrich Schütz, "the father of German Music" through Bethge during their time together in Finkenwalde. See Pangritz, "Point and Counterpoint," 30ff.

155. Letters dated November 22, 1943, and Advent IV, December 19, 1943, in Bonhoeffer, *Letters and Papers*, 190, 230.

156. Letter dated March 27, 1944, in Bonhoeffer, *Letters and Papers*, 332.

157. Letter dated February 23, 1944, in Bonhoeffer, *Letters and Papers*, 306. This passage is Bonhoeffer's personal lament that the turbulent politics of his time had prevented him completing his own great treatise *Ethics* and perhaps his "Outline for a Book."

158. Ford, "Polyphonic Living: Dietrich Bonhoeffer," in *Self and Salvation*, 254.

and for the world might exist in a variety of ways. Shortly before his execution Bonhoeffer returned to the image saying,

> God, the Eternal, wants to be loved with our whole heart, not to the detriment of earthly love or to diminish it, but as a sort of cantus firmus to which the other voices of life resound in counterpoint. One of these contrapuntal themes, which keep their *full independence* but are still related to the cantus firmus, is earthly love. . . . Where the cantus firmus is clear and distinct, a counterpoint can develop as mightily as it wants. The two are "undivided and yet distinct," as the Definition of the Chalcedon says, like the divine and human natures in Christ. Is that perhaps why we are so at home with polyphony in music, why it is important to us, because it is the musical image of this christological fact and thus also our *vita christiana*?[159]

Some sixty years after Bonhoeffer wrote this, philosophers and theologians have adopted the metaphor of "fragmentation" to characterize the social malaise of postmodernity.[160] Perhaps it was with prophetic wisdom that Bonhoeffer proposed the musical metaphor of melody and counterpoint to help theology respond to such fragmentation with polyphonic living.[161] Such living would allow for and even rejoice in the possibility of a community able to maintain difference within a unity assured by varying relatedness to the *cantus firmus* of Jesus Christ. While this book will suggest a new theological paradigm of polyphony through which to examine community and Christian discipleship it seeks only to offer a trajectory of purpose rather than a detailed analysis of application.

In Chapter 2, entitled "Mixing Metaphors and Making Melodies," the nature of metaphor as a methodology for examining Christian community is explored. It examines not only Bonhoeffer's metaphor of polyphony, but looks at how an understanding of the Christian community is best served through a polyphony of metaphors.[162] So while the musical metaphor of

159. Letter dated May 20, 1944, in Bonhoeffer, *Letters and Papers*, 394. Earlier, Bonhoeffer had hinted at the theme, instructing his godson nephew, "Music, as your parents understand and practice it, will bring you back from confusion to your clearest and purest self and perceptions, and from cares and sorrows to the underlying note of joy." Bonhoeffer, *Letters and Papers*, 385.

160. See below, Chapter 4, "Fragmented Epiphanies."

161. Begbie has sought to address postmodern fragmentation through a theology of the arts, including music. See Begbie, *Voicing Creation's Praise*.

162. Hans Urs von Balthasar adopts a similar metaphor and suggests that "in his revelation, God performs a symphony, and it is impossible to say which is richer: the seamless genius of his composition or the polyphonous orchestra of Creation that he has prepared to play it." See von Balthasar, *Truth is Symphonic*, 8.

polyphony remains at the core of the book, the ability and necessity for other metaphors to be woven around this foundational concept will be shown to be an integral part of the book's argument; namely, no individual metaphor can claim a singular sufficiency in articulating the complexities of Christian community.

Chapter 3, "Polyphonic Jesus: Cantus Firmus of Melody Making," will establish the polyphonic character of God through Christ, the *cantus firmus*. This chapter argues that a polyphonic Christ is expressed in the gospel narratives that bear witness to him as one *cantus firmus*. It will show that this polyphony of God can be detected through the Jewish Scriptures and forward throughout the remainder of the New Testament and the traditions of the church. The chapter explores the nature of a Christocentric community and how a polyphonic Christology affects ecclesiology. It will establish that the church ought to be the paradigmatic example of a polyphonic community, wherein the melodies of God are heard and proclaimed, but the people are in solidarity with the songs of an un-churched world. For a community to learn to do this the book suggests that it may adopt and adapt the early church practice of *Disciplina Arcani*, or the Discipline of the Secret.

Chapters 4, 5, and 6 examine, as additional melodies of community, the metaphorical imagery of "fragmented epiphanies," "worldly monasticism," and the concept of Christian community as a "colony of heaven." It is hoped that these metaphorical melodies might be creatively mixed around the *cantus firmus* of Christ, allowing the "sound" of the community to move from one theme to the next, changing in response to their solidarity with the changing world but yet still retaining the foundation of Christ's revelation.

Chapter 7, entitled "Performing the Discipline of Counterpoint," will concern the way in which Christ as the *cantus firmus* of polyphonic community living is shared responsibly within the church and world. The chapter begins by examining how the early church practiced the *Disciplina Arcani* through which they kept hidden from the pagan world the mysteries of the faithful such as Baptism, Eucharist, Lord's Prayer, and Creed. It will then argue that a twenty-first-century reappropriation of this practice, as the way in which the mysteries of Christ might be shared responsibly both in the church and world, offers the key to a Christocentric and polyphonic community.

Chapter 8, "Making Melodies in the Church: Three Movements," examines how some of the melodies of God are expressed with the life of the church, particularly its worship. Such an examination offers no attempt at articulating a complete or systematic framework for Christian worship. Neither does this particular examination aspire to represent the completion of any such endeavor. It is undoubtedly arbitrary in those aspects it chooses to examine in detail, and in those upon which it offers little comment, particularly the practices of Eucharist and Baptism. It has chosen to concentrate on those aspects of Christian worship that may be most readily appropriated in polyphonic form by all members of varying Christian denominations. Thus, while it has not directly addressed practices such as Baptism and Eucharist, it is hoped that the examinations that have been undertaken do provide a trajectory of thought that will illuminate a more far-reaching debate. The book therefore includes an exploration of the melodies of ecumenism within the church and the polyphony of Christian healing.

Chapter 9, entitled "Making Melodies in the World: Three Movements," affirms that the melodies of Christ are to be discerned beyond the boundaries of the church and asks how those who inhabit the polyphonic Christian community might responsibly share the *cantus firmus* of Christ's mystery with those people in the world whose lives may perform the music of peace, justice, and ecological integrity without acknowledging God as its source.

Chapter 10, "Cadenzas and Conclusions," acknowledges the limitations of the book, particularly with regard to mission, and offers some final reflections on the theology of community proposed.

CHAPTER 2

Mixing Metaphors
and Making Melodies

If someone concentrates his attention solely
on the metaphors used of God's majesty,
he abuses and misrepresents that majesty,
and thus errs
by means of those metaphors
with which God had clothed Himself for his benefit. . .

—ST. EPHREM[1]

Metaphors are an essential part of the way we grasp reality; in other
words, they yield real information, which cannot necessarily be
gained or understood in any other way.

—DAVE TOMLINSON[2]

[M]usic may on occasion speak of that which lies beyond it: not of
an undifferentiated and formless "transcendence," but of the God

---

1. A hymn by St. Ephrem. See Brock, "Introduction," in Saint Ephrem's *Hymns on Paradise*, 48, as cited in Holt, *Brief History of Christian Spirituality*, 52.

2. Tomlinson, *Post-Evangelical*, 93–94.

who enacts and speaks comfort and consolation on behalf of his
people and his world.

—FRANCIS WATSON[3]

[Metaphor] erupts at the surface of consciousness when the crust of
reality is too weak to support the status quo.

—DERRICK DE KERCKHOVE[4]

Hearing in each other harmonies of cross-purpose,
As though being ourselves we're more capacious.

—MICHEAL O'SIADHAIL[5]

SPEAKING METAPHORICALLY

The church has expressed the nature of Christian community in many and various ways throughout its 2000 years of history, often seeking to articulate its character through a variety of metaphors, many of which have been mixed together. This fact was acknowledged during Vatican II when the Council observed that the church had not been described "so much by verbal definitions as in the light of images."[6] The light of these images, or the sound of the melodies, in which their metaphors were mixed was considered preferable to ossifying definitions of verbal certitude. But that has made it difficult to arrive at one authoritative statement on the nature of the church or indeed to find one single paradigmatic metaphor of ecclesiastical choice. This is perhaps no bad thing, for it has allowed the church to perpetually describe itself afresh, often choosing imagery and mixing metaphors that are uniquely meaningful to a community's particular social context. In so doing the choice of metaphors expressed an

3. Watson, "Theology and Music," 462–63.

4. de Kerckhove, *Skin of Culture*, 169.

5. O'Siadhail, "That in the End," in *Our Double Time*, 96. Used with kind permission of Blood Axe Publications.

6. Weigel, "How is the Council Going?" 730, cited in Dulles, *Models of the Church*, 11.

essential part of how they grasped their reality as church. So when the early church community variously described themselves as the "body of Christ," or "the bride of Christ," or "a temple of living stones," or one of the many other New Testament descriptions they were expressing some fragment, albeit never the whole, of their central convictions of what it was to be "Christ existing in community."[7] There is precedent for such "biblical polyphony." Ricoeur noted that

> the naming of God, in the originary expressions of faith, is not simple but multiple . . . not a single tone, but polyphonic. The originary expressions of faith are complex forms of discourse as diverse as narrative, prophecies, laws, proverbs, prayers, hymns, liturgical formulas, and wisdom writings. As a whole, these forms of discourse name God. But they do so in various ways.[8]

If this were true of describing God, then it is also true for the naming of the church that God calls into being and that subsists as Christ existing as community. Any descriptions of church can best be understood as no more than a gathering together of partial expressions of God's encounter with the world. Time after time it is the church's task to gather together the fragments of God's revelatory melody. But as McFague notes, "the most that can be said is that some aspect or aspects of the God-world relationship are illuminated by this or that model in a fashion relevant to a particular time and place."[9] Interpreting the constant of God and of God's community is a "perennial task."[10] And it is one in which the community is compelled to speak metaphorically.

Finding such metaphors was a novel exercise for the early church. Jesus had rarely offered any metaphors for the community of disciples that gathered around him and the gospels reveal little of the nature of their group. He offered little teaching on the nature of the church that would follow him. He did, however, use the language of metaphor to speak frequently about the kingdom of heaven/God. It was, he said, like a mustard seed, a grain of yeast, or a pearl of great price. Or it might be like a fishing net, a wedding

7. Paul Minear listed ninety-six images for the church in his book, *Images of the Church in the New Testament*. See also Banks, *Paul's Idea of Community*.

8. Ricoeur, "Naming God," in *Figuring the Sacred*, 224. The musical imagery in biblical studies has been developed in Frances Young's *The Art of Performance*, where it is compared to various performances of one orchestral score. Rowan Williams similarly speaks of "contrapuntal elaborations, variations, even inversions" when re-reading scriptural texts, see Williams, "Postmodern Theology and the Judgment of the World," 93. See also Poythress, *Symphonic Theology*, and von Balthasar, *Truth is Symphonic*.

9. McFague, *Models of God*, 39.

10. Ibid., 41.

feast, or a farmer sowing seed. The Kingdom of God was undoubtedly fixed at the core of Jesus's mission, but he never described it directly, preferring to hint at it through this "bisociative" imagery. He relates the world of his listeners (images of farming, fishing, family, etc.) with the kingdom values of love, forgiveness, and justice. He expands this use of secular, nonreligious language to express the character of the kingdom in his teaching through parables.[11] In these stories of the kingdom, Jesus enables people to associate the familiar things of their world with the mysteries of heaven, but simultaneously he also reveals to them the dissimilarity between the values of their world and those of God. There is here a tension between what the kingdom is and what it is not; this tension is reflected by the often unexpected conclusion of each story, the unfamiliar "sting in the tail," which says the Kingdom of God is radically different to what is. This "is and is not" in the parables results from Jesus speaking metaphorically; that is to say, no one believed that the Kingdom of God was literally like any one of the images he offered, but they knew that the Kingdom of God was, and yet at the same time was not, a mustard seed, a grain of yeast, or a pearl of great price. This is the power of a metaphor, it always contains "the whisper 'it is and it is not.'"[12]

Literally the word means "meta" (transfer) and "pherin'" (to carry),[13] and may be understood as a figure of speech in which a word or phrase is applied to an object or action that it does not literally denote in order to imply a resemblance.[14] In Scripture it is an apposite vehicle to bring together heaven and earth. In due course, the gospel writers gathered together the metaphors invoked by Jesus and the early Christian communities wrestled with the "is and is not" of each: discerning its divine meaning for their context, and, from their many fragments, understanding the greater whole.

When first spoken by Jesus, and when shared within the new communities of post-resurrection people, the metaphors invoked were original and provocative, and their imagery was full of much implied resemblance. His use of metaphor provided glimpses of the reign of heaven with which he was familiar but which others had not fully witnessed. By associating the mystery of the Kingdom of God with the familiar world of their own experience, the bisociative tension, the "is" and the "is not" of the metaphors,

---

11. McFague acknowledges that parables are by no means the only form in the New Testament that deal with the kingdom but adds that "as the dominant genre of Jesus's teaching on the kingdom, they suggest some central, albeit indirect, clues to its reality." *Metaphorical Theology*, 14.

12. Ibid., 13.

13. See Soskice, *Metaphor and Religious Language*, 1.

14. Begbie examines how metaphor can be used in articulating a theology of the arts in Chapter 5 of *Voicing Creation's Praise*.

carried the transfer of God's alternative values into the world of the disciples and the early church community. Dulles even suggests that the "psychology of imagery" might enable this to speak to humanity existentially: in effect, God's image finding "an echo in the inarticulate depths of his [their] psyche."[15] This is the Psalmist's "deep calling unto deep," the mystery of God finding its image in humanity. If so, then this was a most adept way for Jesus to describe a "kingdom" that had come among them, and yet was not fully realized. The kingdom of heaven was, but it also was not yet. It is the unique blessing of a vibrant metaphor: to provide in one image the tension of the "now and not yet," to transfer the meaning of mystery of one through the familiarity of the other. It is why this book seeks to speak metaphorically in examining the character of Christian community.

DEAD METAPHORS

There is, however, the danger that any metaphor can lose power, that it can stagnate and die. In today's language there are ready examples of such "dead metaphors"; phrases such as the "neck of a bottle" or the "hands of a clock" that are so familiar as to have passed into common parlance. In these, the tension is lost: the image has died because the metaphor has become the thing itself.[16] This is the "substitution view of metaphor": a view much lamented by poet Micheal O'Siadhail.[17] He notes that most people have forgotten the subtle differences between the ancient tools of rhetoric—metaphor, irony, hyperbole, synecdoche, and metonymy[18]—and think of them only as "a sort of decoration to make our language high-flown."[19] He laments the poverty that such an undiscriminating approach to language has wrought, particularly this substitutionary perception of metaphor. By this he means simply that if the reader is conditioned to merely substitute "the thing itself" every

15. Dulles, *Models of the Church*, 12.

16. See Koestler, *The Act of Creation*. McFague notes that Koestler's extensive study of bisociative ideas, in which he detects the previously unnoticed similarities in two matrices of thought is not only the essence of discovery, but is "metaphor in its most obvious and brilliant form." See McFague, *Metaphorical Theology*, 36.

17. O'Siadhail, "Crosslight," in Ford and Stamps, eds., *Essentials of Christian Community*, 49–60. See also Black, *Models and Metaphors: Studies in Language and Philosophy*.

18. For a brief discussion of these see Fraser, "The interpretation of novel metaphors," in Ortony, ed., *Metaphor and Thought*, 2nd ed., 329–34 and Soskice, *Metaphor and Religious Language*, Chapter 3.

19. O'Siadhail, "Crosslight," in Ford and Stamps, eds., *Essentials of Christian Community*, 57.

time the metaphor is invoked, then the tension of "is and is not" is lost and the interplay between the known and the mystery is forgotten. The hands of the clock have become a thing in itself and the metaphor has collapsed.

This can happen in metaphors for the Christian community as well. For instance, the poem, "The Come-as-you-are Ceilidh" employs the traditional Gaelic gathering of people to sing, dance, and make merry as a metaphor for a Christian community.

> It's a Come-as-you-are kind of Ceilidh,
> beginning today around twelve;
> They'll be flinging and swinging
> to reels of redeeming
> where angels will shout
> to those inside and out
> The steps of the 'Now and Not Yet'
> over flashes of fiddles all dreaming
> of grace and abandon,
> Embraced in the rhythm
> of swing and be swung as they come
> as they are,
> to a come-as-you-are kind of Ceilidh
> whose promise sings clearly
> of loving more dearly
> than any have loved here before.[20]

The bisociation allows the reader to imagine the unknown mystery of the church community as being in some way like the welcoming and energetic celebration of the Ceilidh. But if the reader readily substitutes "Christian community" or "church" in the poem every time they read "The Come-as-you-are Ceilidh," then the "is and is not" vanishes and the thinking becomes literal. If this occurs with a religious metaphor, the image becomes idolatrous. For instance, if people can only conceive of the community of faith through the Pauline metaphor of the "family of God," but equate the church to their literal experience of family life along with the social conditioning and personal histories that may attach themselves thereto, then they will focus on the literal meaning of the finite medium rather than the reality of mystery beyond it to which the metaphor directs them. When people point to the "is" of the metaphor, declaring with certainty that they have fully grasped what was originally at best an attempt to describe the glimpse of a mystery, then the metaphor becomes the thing itself and hence idolatrous.

---

20. Gardiner, "Come-as-you-are Ceilidh."

What once seemed like a key becomes a lock by which their understanding of the mystery is controlled.[21]

Jesus seems to have been aware of the danger in which, for instance, any one metaphor for God might become "reified, petrified, and expanded so as not only to exclude other models but also to pretend to the status of definitions."[22] If any one metaphor for the kingdom were "canonized" with authoritative certainty, it could become idolatrous and dead. Wisely, he articulated a number of interpenetrating images that together mitigate against any one acquiring definitive status. By mixing metaphors for the kingdom together he kept alive the strength and fecundity of the reality beyond the "is" of metaphorical speech. As such, the metaphors were much more than idle linguistic decoration. They were one of the few methods by which he could tell humanity about those things of which they had no direct knowledge: he used imagery with which humanity were already familiar. As St. Ephrem wrote,

> Do not let your intellect
> be disturbed by mere names,
> for Paradise has simply clothed itself
> in terms that are akin to you;
> it is not because it is impoverished
> that it put on your imagery;
> rather, your nature is far too weak to be able
> to attain to its greatness,
> and its beauties are much diminished
> by being depicted in the pale colours
> with which you are familiar.[23]

The metaphor thus becomes unique in articulating that which may be said in no other way and to speak metaphorically becomes "a strategy of desperation not of decoration."[24] For the church it becomes the desperate method by which they can describe something of which they have had a glimpse, something that they cannot yet comprehend fully and yet of which they must speak. Such speech blurs the usual logical boundaries and uncovers new likenesses.[25] Eugene Peterson argues that live metaphor "does not so much define or label as it does expand, forcing the mind into participating

21. See Thiselton, *Language, Liturgy, and Meaning*, 25.

22. McFague, *Models of God*, 39.

23. See Brock, "Introduction," in Saint Ephrem's *Hymns on Paradise*, 25–32, as cited in Holt, *Brief History of Christian Spirituality*, 52–53.

24. McFague, *Models of God*, 33.

25. O'Siadhail, "Crosslight," 58.

action. . . . Metaphor keeps us from being spectators of language by forcing us to be participants in it."[26] It enables the Christian community to make tentative stabs at describing their unfolding participation in the reality of the Kingdom of God. It is a method as old as the church itself.

MIXING METAPHORS IN THE BIBLE

It is no surprise then that as the early Christian community attempted to describe the nature of the church, they struggled to express the mystery of their new reality and so chose to do so through a mix of metaphors. The Apostle Paul used a variety of metaphorical imagery to illustrate the characteristics of the *ekklesia*, the Greek word adopted to describe the Christian community.[27] They were not religious words, but everyday words infused with a new and potent religious significance. Paul frequently adopts an architectural metaphor; sometimes it is by referring to himself or other apostles as the "master builders" of local Christian communities[28] and on other occasions illustrating the interdependence of community members.[29] On occasion, Paul uses the particular metaphor of the Temple, drawing the community's attention to requirements to be holy.[30] He also speaks of communities of Christ being the foundation for the building of the church (1 Cor 3:10). This architectural imagery is also used by Peter who speaks of Christ as the "living stone," which the builders rejected, but which now forms the capstone for Christians being built into the spiritual house of the church (1 Pet 2:4–10). In the same way as Christ spoke of the Kingdom of God, using agricultural metaphors Paul also refers to the community as "a field"[31] and, most powerfully, as a "tree" in his description of the Gentile Church as branches engrafted to the root of Judaism.[32] Similarly, he uses domestic metaphors, referring to sin as the yeast that can work its way through the "dough"/church.[33] When Paul writes to Christians at Philippi claiming

26. Dawn and Peterson, *Unnecessary Pastor*, 70–71.

27. Originally this referred to the regular assembly of a city's citizens gathered to decide matters of mutual concern. Paul chose the word to distinguish it from the assembly of Jews, or the gatherings found in Hellenistic mystery cults. Banks, *Paul's Idea of Community*, 29.

28. 1 Cor 3:10–14; 2 Cor 10:8; Rom 15:20; Gal 2:18.

29. 1 Cor 14:5–12, 26; Rom 14:19; Col 2:7; Eph 4:16.

30. 1 Cor 3:16–17; 2 Cor 6:16; Eph 2:21–22.

31. 1 Cor 3:9.

32. Rom 11:17–24. See also Col 2:7 and Eph 3:17.

33. 1 Cor 5:6–7; Gal 5:9.

that they are a "colony of heaven,"[34] he deliberately employs language that they will associate with the privileges of citizenship recently conferred by Rome upon them. Banks rightly notes that one of the inadequacies of these metaphors is that they "lack the dynamic element characteristic of human and divine-human relationships,"[35] and significantly, Banks adds, "This leads Paul on several occasions to follow traditional practice and link or mix his metaphors so that the deficiencies of one may be remedied by the advantages of another."[36] So, too, Paul Minear argued that the "profuse mixing of metaphors" in the New Testament "reflects not the logical confusion" but "the theological vitality" of the early church.[37]

Clearly, no one metaphor may profess an entirety or eternity of understanding. The church is a mystery of which humanity can only offer fragments, pieces of the whole that will defy integration to one "single synthetic vision."[38] And so, "[In] order to do justice to the various aspects of the Church, as a complex reality, we must work simultaneously with different models . . . [keeping] several models in the air at once."[39] What is needed is a paradigm of church that not only permits but also celebrates the multiple descriptions of Christian community, acknowledging them to be each but a fragment of the greater whole, a paradigm that permits the mixing of metaphors, for this will reflect theological vitality. Of course, there is a danger of mixing metaphors. Mixed metaphors such as "clouded in a sea of controversy" can render the creative tension of the metaphor meaningless through their internal inconsistency. Examining the nature of Christian community requires a model within which to mix metaphors without losing the power of the bisociation. Here we see the rich potential in Bonhoeffer's musical metaphor of polyphony; the idea of many melodies mixing together, separate yet distinct, but grounded around the root theme or *cantus firmus*. Here we see both the fecundity of the metaphor of polyphony and the need for a polyphony of metaphor.

34. Phil 3:19–20. See more on this in Chapter 6.

35. Banks, *Paul's Idea of Community*, 48.

36. Ibid.

37. Minear, *Images of the Church in the New Testament*, 252.

38. Dulles, *Models of the Church*, 2.

39. Ibid.

THE METAPHOR OF POLYPHONY AND A
POLYPHONY OF METAPHOR

Bonhoeffer's metaphor of polyphony, which he believed gave life a "wholeness," provides for a multidimensionality of discipleship in a Christian's life, for the possibility of holding in tension a mix of illuminative and interpenetrating metaphors. His ability to bring together metaphors of a fragmentary life with "The Art of Fugue" allowed him to consider how a wealth of biographical themes might be welded into a harmony in which the diverse counterpoint is maintained from start to finish. Adopting this imagery of music is a compelling metaphor for our times. It need not be constrained to Bach and "The Art of Fugue" for the concept of polyphony is recognized throughout diverse forms of musical expression. Music also remains one of the few subjects capable of bearing the weight of the numinous in contemporary society. For Bonhoeffer, this metaphor of polyphony enabled him to conceive how to bring together the spiritual (loving God with our whole hearts) and the material (doing so in a way that strengthens that heart's love for the things of earth).[40] These two melodies were "undivided and yet distinct,"[41] like Christ in his "divine and human natures,"[42] and they, like their corollaries of church and world, could be intermixed throughout a lifelong performance that arose in response to Christ's *cantus firmus*. And when their *cantus firmus* is both clear and plain in the life of a Christian, then such contrapuntal melodies could be developed to sound "complete and full," so that each remains distinct in its own right but cannot "get out of tune or be cut adrift."[43] Only a polyphony of this kind, wrote Bonhoeffer, can give the assurance "that no disaster can befall [us] as long as the *cantus firmus* continues."[44]

However, despite the personal insight gained through this metaphor, Bonhoeffer did not make the subsequent leap to appreciate the value polyphony could bring to the "undivided yet distinct" nature of people in community. This is surprising for someone whose early theological reflection asserted that the church was "Christ existing as church-community."[45] For if Christ is then conceived not simply as the *cantus firmus* of an individual's polyphonic life, but as the *cantus firmus* of the Christian community, then

---

40. Letter dated May 20, 1944, in Bonhoeffer, *Letters and Papers*, 394.

41. Ibid.

42. Ibid.

43. Ibid.

44. Ibid.

45. Bonhoeffer, *Sanctorum Communio*, 121.

that "solid song" can be fragmented, mirrored, echoed and retextured within a variety of people. Their own diverse and individual melodies and metaphors will then find a unity in Christ existing as community. Such a polyphony of descriptive melodies can hear within each other "harmonies of cross-purpose" and in so doing become a more capacious community. Bonhoeffer's musical metaphor of polyphony can be transposed into a communal key.

It has remained only the sketch of a rich theological vision that regrettably Bonhoeffer was not granted the years to develop. Karl Barth criticized these theological thumbnails, claiming that Bonhoeffer was no more than "an impulsive visionary thinker who was suddenly seized by an idea to which he gave lively form, and then after a while he called a halt."[46] But what Barth criticized in Bonhoeffer, particularly the sketches of subjects such as "religionless Christianity,"[47] "a world-come-of-age," and "polyphonic living" were actually his most fecund thinking: namely a variety of interweaving metaphors, all of which must be sounded together if we are to better understand God and the church. Bonhoeffer was clear: if indeed all things hold together in Christ (Col 1:17) then Christ becomes the *cantus firmus* in whom the contrapuntal melodies of God, as revealed in the church and encountered in the world, are performed in bisociative tension.

Within each of these contrapuntal themes there may be contained a wealth of varying metaphors and harmonies that help illuminate the music of the Christian community. These harmonies might be "sung" simultaneously or at different times in history, but importantly, while each can be recognized as having Christ as their foundational *cantus firmus*, no one theme can dominate the others into the exclusion of muted silence. Polyphony enables a non-excluding difference in which none of the many notes may render another mute.[48] Hence, polyphonic music permits and encourages individual difference, yet unites them in what might be deemed a community of interweaving melodies. That Bonhoeffer's later theological reflections needed to employ a variety of metaphors and that his thinking was never systemized simply emphasizes the need to mix together new melodies and

46. Karl Barth, "From a Letter to Landessuperintendent P. W. Herrenbruck," in Smith, *World Come of Age*, 89–90. Almost an entire industry has developed in attempts to trace the unifying theme or root metaphor in Bonhoeffer's thought. However, D. H. Hopper argues that the inability of scholars to reach consensus on any root metaphor indicates that no such systematic coherence is there to be found. See Hopper, *Dissent on Bonhoeffer*, 27–28.

47. For a full analysis of Bonhoeffer's thought on the world-come-of-age, religionless Christianity and the nonreligious interpretation of life, see Wüstenberg, *Theology of Life*.

48. Cunningham, *These Three Are One*, 128.

live metaphors that help illuminate the mystery through which God reveals God's self in both the church and world.

It is on that premise that this book therefore employs not simply the central metaphor of polyphony, but also a polyphony of "new-ancient words."[49] This polyphony of new-ancients includes the metaphor of the church as a "colony of heaven" the concept of a "worldly monasticism" and the idea of the Christian community as a gathering place for the "fragmented epiphanies of God." In understanding each of these as a diverse melody of community united through the single metaphor of polyphony and mixed together around the *cantus firmus* of Christ, it is hoped to uncover new likenesses and helpful insights into the nature of the Christian community. In seeking such new metaphors there is no rejection of the traditional biblical imagery (indeed the first of them is taken from the Scriptures), but rather therein to ask the question: Do they offer a helpful perspective for a theology and praxis of Christian community today? But even if the answer to that question is affirmative, all such metaphorical description remains open to the charge of lying "somewhere between 'nonsense' and 'truth'" and as McFague has noted, any theology based upon them "will be open to the charge that it is closer to the first than the second."[50] Her point is well made, but she nevertheless asserts that the risk of such accusations must be taken. "No language about God [and by extension the community of God's people] is adequate and all of it is improper, new metaphors are not necessarily less inadequate or improper than old ones."[51] Hence, a new metaphor of polyphony and a new polyphony of metaphor is to be sought "not because such ways are necessarily better than received ways but because they cannot be ruled out as *not* better unless tried."[52] Such a search can only be enjoined with a recognition of the provisionality of its goal. Any better ways discovered must disavow any pretension to permanent universality, for in the words of Rowan Williams,

> in attempting to show the world a critical truth . . . we are dealing not with the "insertion" of definable blocks of material into a well-mapped territory where homes may be found for them, but with *events* of re-telling or re-working traditional narrative patterns in specific human interactions; an activity in which the Christian community is itself enlarged in understanding and

49. The phrase "new-ancient words" is taken from Jewish mysticism known as the "Kabbalah." See Matt, *Essential Kabbalah*, 1.

50. McFague, *Models of God*, 34.

51. Ibid., 35.

52. Ibid.

even in some sense evangelized . . . the Church needs both the
confidence that it has a gospel to preach, and the ability to see
that it cannot readily specify in advance how it will find words
for preaching in particular new circumstances.[53]

This shares with Bonhoeffer a realization that the traditional language employed for God and church must lose its power and be silenced[54] and hope
to be part of the process by which "people will once more be called to speak
the word of God in such a way that the world is changed and renewed."[55]
Bonhoeffer claimed that such a retelling would entail

a new language, perhaps quite nonreligious language, but liberating and redeeming like Jesus' language, so that people will
be alarmed and yet overcome by its power—the language of a
new righteousness and truth, a language proclaiming that God
makes peace with humankind and that God's kingdom is drawing near.[56]

The retelling of the traditional language for church will need to gather
to itself new metaphors that meaningfully bisociate an ancient, but now often barren, language with a lexis of reality relevant to twenty-first-century
contexts. This process will transform not only the language but the actual
nature of Christian community, drawing it into "a new kind of life and a
new identity," for as people are drawn into encounter with God, "they do
not receive an additional item called faith; their ordinary existence is not
re-organized, found wanting in specific respects and supplemented: it is
transfigured as a whole."[57] The metaphors employed, and how they are allowed to mix, play a vital part in shaping the community transfiguration.
For whether it occurs in the church or elsewhere in the world the metaphors
selected to describe reality in turn shape our understanding of reality. The
point is well made by Neil Postman. He argues that Marshall McLuhan's
famous aphorism "the medium is the message" is redundant now that the
medium has become an insidious metaphor. In critiquing the media in general and television in particular Postman argues,

53. Williams, "Judgment of the World," in *On Christian Theology*, 31.

54. Bonhoeffer, *Letters and Papers*, 390.

55. Ibid.

56. Ibid. Avery Dulles echoes this, claiming, "In times of rapid cultural change, such
as our own, a crisis of images is to be expected. Many traditional images lose their
former hold on people, while the new images have not yet had time to gain their full
power. The contemporary crisis of faith is, I believe, in very large part a crisis of images."
Dulles, *Models of the Church*, 13.

57. Williams, "Judgment of the World," in *On Christian Theology*, 41.

> A message denotes a specific, concrete statement about the world. But the forms of our media, including the symbols through which they permit conversation, do not make such statements. They are rather like metaphors, working by unobtrusive but powerful implication to enforce their special definitions of reality. Whether we are experiencing the world through the lens of speech or the printed word or the television camera, our media-metaphors classify the world for us, sequence it, frame it, enlarge it, reduce it, color it, argue a case for what the world is like.[58]

Thus, as we describe the Christian community through the metaphor of polyphony and with a polyphony of other metaphors, then the church will in turn perceive reality in a polyphonic paradigm. The point is reinforced by Stanley Hauerwas:

> We are as we come to see and as that seeing becomes enduring in our intentionality. We do not come to see, however, just by looking but by training our vision through the metaphors and symbols that constitute our central convictions. How we come to see therefore is a function of how we come to be since our seeing necessarily is determined by how our basic images are embodied by the self—i.e., in our character. . . . The moral life is not first a life of choice—decision is not king—but is rather woven from the notions that we use to see and to form the situations we confront.[59]

As long as it is acknowledged that, having chosen metaphors by which to describe the Christian community, we do so cognizant that such metaphors will precipitate a particular way of perceiving and defining God, humanity, and the church, then the ensuing task is clear: "theologians must think experimentally, must risk novel constructions in order to be theologians *for our time*."[60] The following chapters detail some such novel constructions in the hope of finding a better way through which to describe and participate in the Christian community. The polyphonic mix of metaphors proposed is no more than one model of a new theology of community. For the already noted reasons of necessitous provisionality the book does not aspire to be the dictum for a theology of community,[61] but rather it seeks to provoke a new understanding of God and the nature of the church.

58. Postman, *Amusing Ourselves to Death*, 10.
59. Hauerwas, *Vision and Virtue*, 2.
60. McFague, *Models of God*, 6.
61. The distinction relies on the comment of McFague, who understands the rich

CHAPTER 3

Polyphonic Jesus
Cantus Firmus of Melody Making

For Christ plays in ten thousand places,
Lovely in limbs, and lovely in eyes not his
To the Father through the features of men's faces.
—GERARD MANLEY HOPKINS[1]

Uniqueness need not be exclusive.
—W. PAUL JONES[2]

"Sing the song!" the heavens
seemed to cry. "We never
could have been without the

---

and diverse metaphors and concepts of the Bible as "models or exemplars *of* theology, rather than as dictums *for* theology." *Models of God*, 30.

1. Hopkins, "As Kingfishers Catch Fire," in *Complete Poems with Selected Prose*, 52.

2. Jones, *Trumpet at Full Moon*, inside cover.

melody that you alone can
sing."

—Calvin Miller[3]

Unity in multiplicity is the most commonplace problem facing all
philosophies and all our attempts to come to grips with daily life.
Theology should not act as if—all of a sudden, in the last twenty-
four hours—it had to bear the entire burden itself. Theology always
has the task of showing that the living God is free enough to utter
his most particular word in many languages.

—Hans Urs von Balthasar[4]

While theologians must undoubtedly risk novel constructions of vocabulary and image through which to describe the character of God and the Christian community, it is their word-wielding cousins, the poets, who often initiate such pioneering work. For it is poets who best distill life,[5] it is they whose "mother tongue" of metaphor gently stoops to testify to God's glory amidst a world of grey familiarity.[6] And it is in the words of such a poet, Gerard Manley Hopkins, that we glimpse a polyphonic Christ, one who "plays in ten thousand places, lovely in limbs and lovely in eyes not his, to the Father through the features of men's faces." The many melodies of this Christ are revealed in the faces and lives of numerous people who encounter one another in church and world and whose very being is an act of worship to the Father. Indeed, the melodies of Christ's revelation are not restricted to the realm of human creation, for "all things hold together in Christ,"[7] and so "the voice of the Lord thunders over the

---

3. Miller, *Singer Trilogy*, 12.

4. von Balthasar, *Truth is Symphonic*, 89.

5. Gwendolyn Brooks's assertion that "poetry is life distilled" became the title for a collection of her works, see Mootry and Smith, *Life Distilled*.

6. I am indebted to Kathy Galloway for drawing my attention to the Robert Browning poem, "The Ring and the Book," in which appears the line, "When testimony stoops to mother tongue." See "Testimony Stoops to Mother Tongue," in Galloway, *Walking in Darkness and Light*, 49–56.

7. Col 1:17.

mighty waters . . . and shakes the desert,"[8] while "the heavens declare the glory of God and the skies proclaim the work of his hands."[9]

While poets rightly perceive an immanent polyphony of revelation of Christ within creation, there is a deeper economy of polyphony located within his person. It is the task of the theologian to perceive how Christ is by his very nature polyphonic, precisely because God in God's own being is so.[10]

THE POLYPHONY OF CHRIST'S PERSON

Theologians have caught glimpses of this task, as their "contemplation of music" has led them into "the contemplation of the eternal."[11] Augustine's treatise, *De Musica*, sought to uncover the "vestiges left by the hand of the creator" in the material world of music.[12] Nicephorus of Constantinople (c. 758–829) spoke of singing that "venerable and thrice-illumined melody of theology," the Trisagion,[13] and Aquinas thought that music represented "the exaltation of the mind derived from things eternal bursting forth in sound."[14] Martin Luther greatly admired the choral works of the time in which the melody of Gregorian chant was elaborated with polyphonic counterpoint. He wrote,

> But when natural music is sharpened and polished by art, then one begins to see with amazement the great and perfect wisdom of God in his wonderful work of music, where one voice takes a simple part and around it sing three, four, or five other voices, leaping, springing round about, marvelously gracing the simple part, like a square dance in heaven with friendly bows, embracings, and hearty swinging of partners. He who does not find this an inexpressible miracle of the Lord is truly a clod and is not worthy to be considered a man.[15]

8. Ps 29:3.

9. Ps 19:1.

10. Rowan Williams is making a similar point when he speaks of "Different Christs." See "Different Christs: For a Theological College," in Williams, *Open to Judgment*, 105–11.

11. Jordan, "Augustine on Music," 130. See also Pickstock, "Ascending Numbers," 185.

12. Ibid., 124.

13. Uncited quotation in Pelikan, *Melody of Theology*, 167.

14. Thomas Aquinas, *Summa Theologiae*, cited in Shapiro, *Encyclopedia of Quotations*, 4. For a brief synopsis of Aquinas and music see Cole, *Music and Morals*, 68–81.

15. Martin Luther, *Weimar Ausgabe*, 368–73, cited in Bainton, *Here I Stand*, 343.

One especially imaginative work that reflects on the implications of hearing God through music and sound is by Nóirín Ní Riain. She has coined the phrase "theo-sony," the sound of God.[16] But it is David Cunningham who has most helpfully articulated a doctrine of a polyphonic God: a theology of the Trinity developed through the metaphors of music. He notes how the Christian claim that in God, "these three are one," purposely calls into question "the common assumption that oneness and difference are mutually exclusive categories."[17] If the existence of Christ the Son does not in any way exclude or reduce the presence of the Father or Holy Spirit in the Godhead, then all the Three-as-One act together, each distinctly different but all uniquely united.

The most appropriate metaphor for this Trinitarian phenomenon is the polyphony of music. Cunningham perceives in the Trinity a polyphony of persons, whose existential melodies demonstrate the perfect paradigm of non-excluding difference existing in unity,[18] i.e., more than one note is played at a time, and "none of these notes is so dominant that it renders another mute."[19] He goes on to assert that

> Christianity proclaims a polyphonic understanding of God—one in which *difference* provides an alternative to a monolithic homogeneity, yet without becoming a source of exclusion. Attention to any one of the Three does not imply a diminished role for the others; all three have their distinctive melodies, and all are "played" and "heard" simultaneously without damage to God's unity.[20]

Each member of this perichoretic unity participates in the life and music of the other, much as the different notes and melodies connect together in a performance of music. The Trinity is the mutual participation of Father, Son and Holy Spirit so that each partakes fully in the life of the others and so renders illegitimate any attempt to isolate them as individuals. Each dwells in and is indwelt by the others so that, as von Balthasar asserts, "eternal

---

16. This came to my attention through a BBC Radio 4 broadcast "The Sound of God," on October 27, 2003. My thanks to Norman Winter at the BBC for providing a CD of the broadcast, and to the University of Limerick, Ireland for a copy of Nóirín Ní Riain's thesis, "The Specificity of Christian Theosony: Towards a Theology of Listening." I am grateful to the author for her further comments.

17. Cunningham, *These Three Are One*, 127.

18. Ibid., 127ff.

19. Ibid., 128.

20. Ibid., 129.

Truth itself is symphonic."[21] Robert Jenson equally perceives that "God . . . is a melody. And as there are three singers . . . the melody is fugued. . . . There is nothing so capacious as a fugue."[22] If the one God found in the community of Trinity is by nature polyphonic, then each One of the Three is polyphonic too: the person of Christ, insofar as Christ may be isolated from the others, is then also polyphonic.

It is in Christ, the incarnation of the Word of God, that humanity encounters the most comprehensive performance of divine polyphony. Cunningham notes that "Christ bears witness to a God of harmonious flux and superabundant donation—a God in whom difference can exist without contradiction or confusion."[23] The most apparent contradiction and confusion that preoccupied the early church was that of Christ's simultaneous divine and human natures. To the ancient mind there was perhaps no more unlikely a concept than one in which deity and humanity were bound together as one. The two ought not to mix, even metaphorically. Yet the Council of Chalcedon (451) affirmed that Christ was complete in his deity and complete in his humanity. He was to be acknowledged in "two natures, without confusion, without change, without division, without separation, the difference of the natures being by no means removed because of the union, but the property of each nature being preserved and coalescing in one *prosopon* [person] and one *hupostasis* [subsistence]—not parted or divided into two *prosopa* [persons], but one and the same Son."[24] Søren Kierkegaard later called this twofold nature of Christ the "absolute paradox."[25] It is also the "Supreme Bisociation," the bringing together of divinity and humanity. In Christ the melodies of heaven and earth are performed in a unique polyphonic unity collapsing the former dualisms of spirit and matter into one unique fugue. Through him the purposes of heaven are performed.

When Bonhoeffer was in prison he was much taken with the similarities in form between the Christology of Chalcedon and the polyphony of fugue. His primary concern was not with the nature of Christ per se, but with the character of Christian living. He wrote,

---

21. von Balthasar, *Truth is Symphonic*, 12.

22. Jenson, *Triune God*, 236. The master of the Fugue was J. S. Bach. His mastery of polyphony as a vehicle through which the Divine was encountered earned him the title, "the fifth evangelist."

23. Cunningham, *These Three Are One*, 143.

24. Kelly, "Early Christian Doctrines," 340.

25. Kierkegaard, *Philosophical Fragments*, 46–67.

> Is that perhaps why we are so at home with polyphony in music,
> why it is important to us, because it is the musical image of this
> christological fact and thus also our *vita christiana?*[26]

Earlier, in his work on Christology, Bonhoeffer had asserted that it was not
only "useless to contemplate a Christ for himself, it is even godless."[27] Christ
was never Christ as Christ in himself but always in his relation to the world
and in his standing *pro me*.[28] Christ could only be thought of existentially,
i.e., in the church.[29] As von Balthasar has noted, "We cannot wrench Christ
loose from the Church, nor can we dismantle the Church to get to Christ. If
we really want to hear something intelligible, we are obliged to listen to the
entire polyphony of revelation."[30]

THE PURPOSE OF CHRIST'S POLYPHONY

The purpose of the polyphony of Christ is to call humanity into participative
performance with the melodies of divine being made known in the world.
It is a call to discipleship. As Hauerwas notes, "If Christian faith is from
start to finish a performance, it is so only because Christians worship a God
who is pure act, an eternally performing God."[31] For Bonhoeffer this was the
vital key in articulating a theology through which God could be acclaimed
in praxis as much as in dogma to be the Lord of the world and Lord of the
church. Doctrinally, of course, the church affirmed the boundarylessness of
Christ's Lordship over all. But in reality it had long detached the realm of
one from the other, affirming separate "spheres" of the spiritual and the temporal, spheres that were paralleled in the institutions of church and state. In
the classic Lutheran theology that Bonhoeffer inherited, each sphere/realm
was supposed to let the other proceed unhindered about its ordained business; neither was to interfere beyond its remit.[32] From an early age, perhaps

---

26. Letter dated May 20, 1944, in Bonhoeffer, *Letters and Papers*, 394. Earlier,
Bonhoeffer had hinted at the theme, instructing his godson nephew, "Music, as your
parents understand and practice it, will bring you back from confusion to your clearest
and purest self and perceptions, and from cares and sorrows to the underlying note of
joy." Ibid., 385.

27. Bonhoeffer, *Christ the Center*, 47. Translation preferred to that in "Lectures on
Christology," in Bonhoeffer, *Berlin*, 299–360.

28. Ibid.

29. Ibid.

30. von Balthasar, *Truth is Symphonic*, 11.

31. Hauerwas, *Performing the Faith*, 77.

32. In the 2005 edition of *Ethics* the German "*raum*" is translated as realm rather
than sphere. See 36.

due to fragmentation of his family life into similar realms, this dichotomy seems to have dissatisfied Bonhoeffer. As a student, he remarked upon the difference between this and Islam, particularly how in Islam, everyday life and religion were not kept separate as he had experienced life to be in the church.[33] Later, Bonhoeffer blamed this same dualism for the church's unwillingness to interfere in the politics of Germany under the Third Reich. It was while in prison for his own opposition to the Nazis that Bonhoeffer made the tentative connections between the pronouncements of Chalcedon, the world of political resistance and music, particularly Bach's "The Art of Fugue."[34] In the already noted letter from prison, he made the critical insight that Christ's divine and human natures are analogous to melody and countermelody in a fugue; each melody unique, but each inclusively interrelated, held together in polyphonous unity. He wrote,

> God, the Eternal, wants to be loved with our whole heart, not to the detriment of earthly love or to diminish it, but as a sort of cantus firmus to which the other melodies of life resound in counterpoint. One of these contrapuntal themes, which keep their *full independence* but are still related to the cantus firmus, is earthly love. .... Where the cantus firmus is clear and distinct, a counterpoint can develop as mightily as it wants. The two are "undivided and yet distinct," as the Definition of the Chalcedon says, like the divine and human natures in Christ.[35]

Bonhoeffer argues that the attraction and importance of polyphony in music might consist particularly in its being a reflection of the divine and human natures bisociated in the one person of Christ. His polyphony of heavenly *logos* and earthly incarnation was the music that Christ alone could sing. Music was a "vestige" of Christ left remaining in the world:[36]

33. Letter to his parents from Tripoli, May 9, 1924, in Bonhoeffer, *Young Bonhoeffer*, 118.

34. The opening melody was given to Bach by Frederick the Great. Bach composed a series of pieces in which the original theme was incorporated. They did so in a polyphony that included not only the repetition of the theme and dependent variations, but its reversal and inversion, its being slowed to half speed and doubled in meter. Bach understood his music theologically, seeking to address through music the nature of humanity's fallen state and the possibility of "redemption" in an equilibrium of music's horizontal (melodic) and vertical (harmonic) manifestations. Thus for Bach, postlapsarian humanity, having tasted the "delights and despair of harmonic duality," would no longer be "fulfilled in justly intoned monody." Bach's harmonic polyphony becomes a *demonstratio* of the workings of Christian grace more revealing than any theological text. See Mellers, *Bach and the Dance of God*, 36ff.

35. Letter dated May 20, 1944, in Bonhoeffer, *Letters and Papers*, 393–94.

36. The word "vestige" comes from the Latin *vestigium* meaning a footprint or

an eternal echo of the divine epiphany. Bonhoeffer could hardly have been aware that within the Welsh folk tradition there exists a most apposite echo of this Christological polyphony. In the practice of *Pennillion*, an instrumentalist, usually a harpist, begins to play a preexistent melody. The singer may begin at any point thereafter, not only adding extemporary words and an improvised melody, but also ensuring that the duo conclude the performance simultaneously. To participate in the music of Christ is to perceive how his belonging to heaven does not restrict his belonging on earth and how both "belongings" can be "sounded" simultaneously. To increase in deity does not reduce Christ's humanity, and to reduce his divinity does not increase his humanity. Christ exists with full divine freedom to act as he chooses, but he chooses to bind God's self to humanity, to be free not from them, but for them. Hauerwas suggests, "It may be that the Christian faith is 'primarily an account of divine action' and 'only secondarily an account of the believing subject.'"[37] "God is a performing God who has invited us to join in the performance that is God's life."[38] As such, to become Christ-like, for the individual and for the Christian community, is to acknowledge the human longing to live an authentically polyphonic life, to participate in the performance of God's melodies on earth as they play out in heaven while simultaneously belonging to each through their relationship in Christ.

But there is a second and more subtle polyphony within the person of Christ. If Christ, in whom resides the unique bisociation of heaven and earth, chooses to bind God's self to creation, then in this he becomes not only an active subject but is also a passive object. He is acted upon by humanity: nurtured by Mary and Joseph, rejected by his home town, betrayed by Judas, abandoned by the disciples, arrested by the Jewish leadership, tried by the Roman governor, and finally executed on Calvary. Cunningham suggests that this interplay of action and passion where Christ acts and is acted upon is also Christ's polyphony.[39] He notes three examples of this polyphony. First, with regard to the Law of God, Christ is simultaneously revealed as the one who offers humanity the gift of law, the one who liberates humanity from the law and the one who forgives humanity its transgressions against the law.[40] Likewise, the life of Christ reveals one in whom there exists the polyphony of complete power, willing obedience, and

---

mark. It has been adopted in Christian theology as *Vestigia Trinitatis*, illustrations or analogies of the Trinity found within the created order.

37. Hauerwas, *Performing the Faith*, 77.

38. Ibid.

39. Cunningham, *These Three Are One*, 143.

40. Ibid., 142–49.

genuine temptation.[41] Finally and most obviously in Christ's life, death and resurrection all concurrently occur in God: God acts (by raising Jesus); God is acted upon (by being raised); and God is the vehicle of the action (the Spirit in and through whom Christ is raised). All these are taken up into the polyphony of God and so into Christ who offers humanity the gift of eternal life. Cunningham argues that this claim, and the assertion that the life eternal will be one of embodied existence, can only be understood through "a 'musical' mode of thought,"[42] through the metaphor of polyphony in which "life and death, body, and soul can be 'sounded' simultaneously."[43]

THE POLYPHONY OF CHRIST'S COMMUNITY

It follows from this that a community based upon the polyphonic Christ will be polyphonic itself: a community as rooted in the melodies of the world as it is informed by music of heaven and a community in whom the two melodies are "fugued." It will also be a community of both action and passion: as much acted upon as acting. The love of God, experienced and expressed by such a community, will be concretized in their choosing to live the values of heaven and by binding themselves in solidarity with the earth, rejecting any flight from it that sought only to secure their own purity or salvation. In choosing to do so, the community will not only act as subjects, but will also engage with the vulnerabilities of being acted upon by the world. In being acted upon, the community are then challenged to respond in a Christ-like way. This is at the heart of Bonhoeffer's idea of *stellvertretung*, a concept best translated as "deputyship" or "vicarious responsible action."[44] This is primarily the "free initiative and responsibility for humanity that God takes in Jesus Christ; in God's becoming human, in the crucifixion and resurrection of Jesus Christ, God acts to reconcile and re-create humanity."[45] Bonhoeffer wrote that

> Jesus Christ is the very embodiment of the person who lives responsibly. He is not the individual who seeks to attain his own ethical perfection. Instead, he lives only as the one who in

41. Ibid., 149–51.

42. Ibid., 153.

43. Ibid.

44. The concept of *stellvertretung* is arguably the core around which the shifting emphasis in Bonhoeffer's life and work are arranged. See Gardiner, "Fragments and the Whole." See also Muller, "Bonhoeffer's Ethic of Responsibility" and Gestrich, "God Takes Our Place."

45. Green, "Editor's Introduction," in Bonhoeffer, *Ethics*, 12.

himself has taken on and bears the selves of all human beings.
. . . He indeed stands in the place of all human beings. . . . All
that human beings were supposed to live, do and suffer falls on
him.[46]

Christ is the "man for others," and so his church is the church "only
when it is there for others."[47] The Christian community is then called into a
life that consciously and responsibly is lived out of God's love for others and
within the reality of the world.

When this unique presence of the post-Ascension Christ was first revealed among believers, it noticeably did not unite them in monophonic
homogeneity, but rather revealed a rich polyphony of incarnation that has
been present in the church since its inception. Luke says it was in Antioch
that the disciples were first called Christians[48] and describes a diverse community made up of Jews (probably speaking Greek and Aramaic) and a
multiplicity of Gentiles. This community shared little commonality of race,
culture, or language.[49] What they claimed to have in common, the foundation of their unique and novel third race, the *genus tertium*,[50] was their
encounter with Christ.[51] The community was polyphonic and Christ was
fixed as their *cantus firmus*. Their encounter with him led them beyond
their existing boundaries of belonging and into the new phenomenon that
would be called church: a multiplicity of persons-in-community seeking to
become Christ-like.[52]

---

46. Bonhoeffer, *Ethics*, 231–32.

47. "Outline for a Book," in Bonhoeffer, *Letters and Papers*, 503.

48. Acts 11:26b.

49. While in a thoroughly Hellenistic city like Antioch Jews and Gentiles alike
would have spoken Greek, it is clear that such various "races" were forming a community of Christians whose identity was transcending former paradigms of belonging
through faith in Christ. See Towner, "Mission Practice and Theology Under Construction (Acts 18–20)," in Marshall and Peterson, *Witness to the Gospel*, 422.

50. Those gathered in the Circus of Carthage are reported as shouting out against
the Christians, "*Usque quo genus ertium*" / "How long must we endure this third race."
It was a term of derision used to refer to Christians, who were neither Graeco-Roman
nor Jews but a new race of people who defined their communal identity through belonging to Christ. See "Persecution," in Orr, *International Standard Bible*, 2327.

51. The name Christian is not likely to have been self-designated. It came from
those outside the group who would have regarded "Christ" as a proper name not laden
with meaning as a religio-political title.

52. Because Christians separated from Judaism they were no longer a tolerated section of Roman society, a *religio licita*, with its rites of privilege. See Barrett, *Critical and
Exegetical Commentary*, 548.

For the individual Christian and the community who seek to be Christ-like in the world, their task is to participate in the performance of the polyphonic melodies of Christ on earth as they are sung in heaven. And as with the nature of a jazz ensemble, the way in which any one improvised melody is performed in dialogue with the foundational progression of chords or melodic hook (the *cantus firmus*) can affect the direction of the music as a whole.[53] This is the polyphonic abundance of life: a life in which Christ remains at the beginning and the end and may be simultaneously present in every note, bar, and movement, and in every voice, as its core, generating infinite possibilities of action and passion. This does not deny the reality of cacophonic action or intentions, those whose noise seeks to deny, conceal, or silence the melodies of God. However, even the most virulent cacophony cannot overcome the persistent hope present in Christ's *cantus firmus*.

The content of such possibilities will depend much upon the context in which Christian disciples find themselves located. Neither every individual disciple nor every Christian community will manifest the polyphony of abundant living in identical ways and indeed some may find themselves in apparent tension or discord with others. But as von Balthasar notes, "Great music is always dramatic: there is a continual process of intensification, followed by a release of tension at a higher level. But dissonance is not the same as cacophony."[54] And while for a moment dissonance may exist in the melodies of the community, the church's affirmation has always been that in and through Christ as *cantus firmus* all melodies will, in the fulfillment of time, be resolved and reconciled. As the Christian community seeks to participate in this reconciling truth, they ought then to proleptically accommodate such internal tensions, becoming on earth a reflection of heaven's eternal polyphony. Indeed, the performance of polyphony should become the identifying mark of Christian discipleship. The church as "Christ existing as community" should be the people whose love and faithful obedience to God is concretized in their communal freedom to live for the world and in their service to others.

53. Holloway makes a similar connection in his references to "Ethical Jazz," in Holloway, *Godless Morality*, 21ff. In the past, Aquinas adopted analogous imagery in his theory of hermeneutics speaking of a "golden chain," or *catena aurea*, that bound together diverse elucidations of Scripture. See Aquinas, "Catena Aurea," cited in Cunningham, *These Three Are One*, 138. See also the "polyphonic" approaches to Scripture outlined in Fowl, *Theological Interpretation of Scripture*, 26ff, and improvisation as that which shapes character in Benson, "Improvising like Jazz," in *Liturgy As a Way of Life*, 71–98.

54. von Balthasar, *Truth is Symphonic*, 15.

PARTICIPATION AND PERFORMANCE IN CHRIST'S POLYPHONY

Whatever melody of service the Christian is called upon to perform within the world is already part of the polyphony of God in Christ, a part of the living exchange between Father, Son, and Spirit. Jenson notes that the Christian's enjoyment of God is that they are taken into this triune singing and are "allowed to double the parts."[55] The Christian community join their voices to those already performed in and through God. It is to this earthly doubling of the melodies of heaven that the community of God is called.

Von Balthasar argues that this participative calling has been present since the beginning: God has performed a cosmic symphony in which people have heard "the seamless genius" of the divine composition[56] and participated in the polyphonous orchestra of God's creation. Before Christ's incarnation this divine symphony could be heard by the people through the "ways God spoke of old to our fathers by the prophets" (Heb 1:1). But von Balthasar argues that it is only after the birth of Christ that the music can begin in earnest; the pre-incarnation orchestra have been merely "tuning up" and playing to themselves. However, while it must be true that the birth of Christ marks a critical development in what might be better described as God's "cosmic opera," it is insufficient to declare its overture as no more than a cacophonic humanity playing to themselves, even if somehow the tuning note of God is heard through all the mêlée. Too much of God has been revealed in these fragments of epiphany for them to be so easily dismissed. Too much has been learned of God through participation in this preemptory music. Its contrapuntal elaborations, variations, and inversions are now an integral part of the human whole. It is as Rowan Williams notes in a different regard:

> Rather like the simple theme given to Bach by Frederick the Great, that forms the core of The Art of Fugue. When we have listened to the whole of that extraordinary work, we cannot simply hear the original notes picked out by the King of Prussia as if nothing had happened. We can't avoid saying now: "*This* can be the source of *that*"—and that is a fact of some importance about the simple base motif.[57]

While the *cantus firmus* remains distinct it has already called into being melodies that shape the character of present participation. But here some

---

55. Jenson, *Triune God*, 235.

56. von Balthasar, *Truth is Symphonic*, 8.

57. Williams, "Postmodern Theology," 93ff.

further qualification is necessary: participation in this sense is not so much a participation in the performance of some task or other, even participation in the unfolding melodies of heaven, but rather, participation in *someone*, namely participation in the polyphonic person of Christ. Cunningham makes this point well in his discussion on Trinitarian perichoresis.[58] Each person of the Godhead dwells in and is indwelt by the others. Participation, when understood in the light of such relational considerations eschews its standard definition "to take part in," because such a designation suggests some activity in which one individual is joined by others to perform together. Cunningham's examination of participation rejects this idea and focuses on

> those instances in which we take part, not in some*thing*, but in some*one*—an *other*. For example, to "participate in the sufferings of another" is to make another's pain one's own . . .
>
> Similarly, if I ask you to "take part in" my life, I am asking for a very significant degree of emotional, physical, and spiritual intimacy.[59]

If the community is to perform the polyphony to which Christ calls them, then it must be a participative polyphony that takes part in the life of Christ and in the otherness of life in the world beyond the church.

Bonhoeffer captured something of this theology of participation: both the participation of Christ in the lives of others and the participation of the Christian community in the polyphonic life of Christ. His dictum that "Christ is the man for others" reveals his appreciation of Christ's willingness to participate in the pain and otherness of humanity, both generically through his incarnation (where he participates in all flesh) and the crucifixion (where he takes upon himself the sins of the world), but also by example in personal specifics such as his weeping over the death of Lazarus. Christ was the exemplar of one who participated with emotional, physical, and spiritual intimacy, in the "someone-otherness" of the world. Christ's bisociative participation in God and humanity is unique, but his place as the *cantus firmus* of the Christian community places upon it the privilege and responsibility of a relationship with God. There is, through Christ, an intimacy between God and the church community. Cunningham notes a number of biblical examples: Christ's encouragement to the disciples to pray to God *his* father as *their* father, together with numerous references to those who are called "children of God" or are understood to have been

58. Cunningham, *These Three Are One*, 166ff.
59. Ibid.

adopted and made co-heirs with Christ.[60] The church participates in the life of God through the person of Christ. Indeed, participation in Christ's suffering was at the core of repentance, "not thinking first of one's own needs, questions, sins, and fears but allowing oneself to be pulled into walking the path that Jesus walks, into the messianic event, in which Isa 53 is now being fulfilled!"[61] In this way, for Bonhoeffer, the suffering Christ completes the proto-melody of Isa 53. This is also seen in Bonhoeffer's reflections on Gethsemane. There, Christ's question to the disciples, "could you not stay awake with me one hour?" is for Bonhoeffer, "the opposite of everything a religious person expects from God. The human being is called upon to share in God's suffering at the hands of a godless world."[62] The theology is distilled in his poem, "Christians and Heathens."

> People go to God when they're in need,
> plead for help, pray for blessing and bread,
> for rescue from their sickness, guilt, and death.
> So do they all, all of them, Christian and heathens.
>
> People go to God when God's in need,
> find God poor, reviled, without shelter or bread,
> see God devoured by sin, weakness, and death.
> Christians stand by God in God's own pain.
>
> God goes to all people in their need,
> fills body and soul with God's own bread,
> goes for Christians and heathens to Calvary's death
> and forgives them both.[63]

Participation in the life of God is not to be considered arrogant presumption, for without daring to elevate humanity to the status of *sicut deus* the church must affirm that she shares in the unfolding purposes of Christ. Bonhoeffer is clear:

> Certainly, we are not Christ, nor are we called to redeem the
> world through our own deed and our own suffering; we are not
> to burden ourselves with impossible things and torture our-
> selves with not being able to bear them. We are not lords but

60. References for those named as the children of God include Matt 5:9; Luke 20:36; John 1:12; Rom 8:14–21; Gal 3:26; 1 John 3:1; and Rev 21:7. References to adoption include Rom 8:15, 23; and 9:4; Gal 4:5; and Eph 1:5.

61 See letter dated July 18, 1944, in Bonhoeffer, *Letters and Papers*, 480. Isa 53 refers to the suffering servant that Christian theology has traditionally interpreted as referring to Jesus.

62. Bonhoeffer, *Letters and Papers*, 480.

63. "Christians and Heathens," in Bonhoeffer, *Letters and Papers*, 460–61.

instruments in the hands of the Lord of history; we can truly share only in a limited measure in the suffering of others. We are not Christ, but if we want to be Christians, it means that we are to take part in Christ's greatness of heart, in the responsible action that in freedom lays hold of the hour and faces the danger, and in the true sympathy that springs forth not from fear but from Christ's freeing and redeeming love for all who suffer.[64]

The Christian community must participate in this "large-heartedness" of Christ, dwelling in and being indwelt by the performance of God's polyphony, doubling the parts in both the church and world. Participating in the church will mean believers being open to the changes brought upon them through their relationship with other Christians. This is a repeated theme in Bonhoeffer's consideration of Christian community, *Life Together*. There he writes that Christian community is "a reality created by God in Christ" in which believers "may participate"[65] and stresses the need for each person to be characterized by their service to others and bearing one another's burdens.[66] Here, "bearing the burden of the other means tolerating the reality of the other's creation by God—affirming it, and in bearing with it, breaking through to delight in it."[67]

Similarly, participating in and performing Christ's polyphony in the world does not simply mean an engagement with the world on monophonic terms dictated by the church (sing our melody or be damned for we will countenance no other) but, in much the same way as Christ was acted upon by earthly events, will mean that the Christian community displays not only a willingness to be in the world but an openness to let the songs of the church be shaped by the concerns and suffering of the world. Such an openness to the world undergirds the prayer of the Iona Community that "hidden things may be revealed . . . and new ways found to touch the hearts of all."[68] In these words there is an acceptance that the melodies of the church community will be shaped by subtleties in the *cantus firmus* that have been hitherto undetected. The same is also reflected in the Iona Community prayer:

> O Christ . . . wield well your tools in the workshop of your world,
> so that we who come rough-hewn to your bench
> may here be fashioned to a truer beauty of your hand.[69]

---

64. "After Ten Years," in ibid., 49.
65. Bonhoeffer, *Life Together*, 38.
66. Ibid., 98–101.
67. Ibid., 101.
68. See Iona Community, *Iona Abbey Worship Book*, 19–20.
69. Ibid.

Again, there is an acceptance of the potential for personal and corporate refashioning through the community's presence in and being acted upon by the world. The Christian community can only be the church when the performance of its melodies is open to perpetual modulation through their participation in the Christ who is the human—one who lives for others.

The concept of performance also merits some consideration. It is a metaphor that has attracted increasing attention in the area of biblical interpretation, but its parallel fecundity seems not to have been readily appreciated in theologies of Christian community. Nicholas Lash argues that the performance of a musical score might provide a helpful analogous paradigm for biblical interpretation,[70] suggesting that a full interpretation of a piece of music required more than the ability to read the notes or play the instruments. Nor was it sufficient to know the sociohistoric context of the composer and their composition. While these things were important, Lash argued that the central interpretative action was the performance, which was a matter not just of technical proficiency but necessitated a creative fidelity to allow the score to come alive once more for the community of conductor, orchestra, and audience.[71]

Bonhoeffer has been singled out as an archetypal "performer of Scripture," one whose life displayed a close relation between the reading and biographical embodiment of the Bible.[72] But Scripture is but one witness (albeit a vital one) to the *cantus firmus* that has invited participative performance since the beginning of time. While not at all disagreeing with the assertion of Bonhoeffer as an exemplary performer of Scripture, it is more helpful to understand him as a participative performer of the divine polyphony. He understood that performance necessitated being acted upon as much as acting on others, to listen as much as to be heard: he knew what it was to participate in the human community of faith and the divine polyphony of Christ. Lash agrees that in the end, the "fundamental form of the *Christian* interpretation of Scripture" comes through the performed "life, activity and

---

70. Barton's article "New Testament Interpretation as Performance" cites Lash as the first to draw the analogy between interpreting music and Scripture. See Barton, "New Testament Interpretation as Performance," 180. In 1982, Lash published an article entitled "Performing the Scriptures," reprinted in Lash, *Theology on the Way to Emmaus*, 37–46. Giles argues that the debate over performing music with the authentic instruments of the time is a preoccupation not with history, but with novelty, and draws parallels with the authentic performance of Scripture. Giles, "Performing Theology Authentically," in Astley, *Creative Chords*, 76–88.

71. Lash, "Performing the Scriptures," 40ff.

72. See Fowl and Jones, *Reading in Communion*, Chapter 6; and Hauerwas, *Performing the Faith*, 75–109.

organization of the believing community."[73] Critically though, he adds that it is not "the *script* that is 'holy,' but the people: the company who perform the script."[74]

But even this recognition of the importance of the faith community does not go far enough, for people participated in performing God's song before the script was ever written, the performance predates the script, even the Hebrew Scriptures. It is the script that bears witness to the participative performance of God's music. What the community performs is not the written script but their participation in and with God, the music that existed from before notation. As Lash writes elsewhere, "The practice of Christian faith is not, in the last resort, a matter of interpreting, in our time and place, an ancient text. It is, or seeks to be, the faithful 'rendering' of those events, of those patterns of human action, decisions, and suffering, to which the text bears original witness."[75] In other words, reinterpreting a performance of the melodies of divine epiphany and human testimony for a contemporary context.

Invoking the metaphor of performance should not permit any notion of "play-acting," taking on "a role" rather than becoming "transformed into a different kind of person or a different kind of community."[76] That would fail to grasp "the risk and radical contingency, the open-endedness . . . of the performance being given."[77] Such a "radical contingency" in performing the polyphony of God is vital because the participative performance of the Christian community can never constitute the whole of the music, for its melodies are constantly reinformed by the otherness of the world and the eternity of Christ's *cantus firmus*. The music heard within the midst of human community inevitably calls to them from beyond the boundaries of their context and beckons them further toward eschatological fulfillment. As von Balthasar has noted,

> The world cannot get an overall view of its own pluralism, for the unity has never lain in the world either formerly or now. But the purpose of its pluralism is this: not to refuse to enter into the unity that lies in God and is imparted by him, but symphonically

73. Lash, "Performing the Scriptures," in *Theology on the Way to Emmaus*, 42.

74. Ibid.

75. Lash, "What Might Martyrdom Mean?" in *Theology on the Way to Emmaus*, 90.

76. Barton accepts but distinguishes the significant and valid place of play acting as "a symbolic communicative enterprise . . . of culture" and play-acting Scripture which can help people "'find themselves' in the biblical text." Barton, "New Testament Interpretation as Performance," 189.

77. Loughlin, "Telling God's Story: Bible, Church and Narrative Theology," 134, as cited in Barton, "New Testament Interpretation as Performance," 189.

to get in tune with one another and give allegiance to the transcendent unity.[78]

The listening community will need to be open to the possibility of a renewing and evolving plurality within the communal unity made possible through Christ. Milbank argues that this means

> the freedom of people and groups to be different, not just to be functions of a fixed consensus, yet at the same time it totally refuses *indifference*; a peaceful, united, secure community implies *absolute* consensus, and yet, where difference is acknowledged, this is no agreement in an idea, or something once and for all achieved, but a consensus that is only in and through the interrelations of community itself, and a consensus that moves and "changes": *a concentus musicus.*[79]

Christian discipleship is then the responsibility and willingness of individuals and communities to move into a participative performance of the countermelodies, which is based on Christ's *cantus firmus*. The variety of such countermelody can be heard in and through the life-music of the Christian saints, canonized or otherwise. Their performances still resonate within the polyphony of the Christian community and while the church might regularly remember the exemplary melodies of canonized individuals, the deepest countermelodies are perhaps heard in the assured presence of the Church Triumphant within the life of the Church Militant. This real presence of the Communion of Saints was a distinguishing mark of the Celtic Christianity that often inspired MacLeod and the Iona Community. In these traditions, members of the church militant invoked the aid of saints triumphant in much the same way as assistance might be sought from a pastor, friend, or family member[80] or an old song might be performed and interpreted afresh.

Performing these melodies of God also necessitates a personal and corporate discipline or *askesis* through which transfiguring practices can be regularly revisited. This repeated balance of the "life alone" and the "life together"[81] is very similar to how an ensemble musician must simultane-

78. von Balthasar, *Truth is Symphonic*, 9.

79. Milbank, "Postmodern Critical Augustinianism," 228.

80. A collection of such prayers and hymns enjoying a resurgent popularity in recent times is the *Carmina Gadelica*. See Carmichael, *Carmina Gadelica*, 373. Just how ancient a pedigree can be afforded to the *Carmina Gadelica* is debatable but they clearly reflect a spirituality in which the communion of saints was a present reality. See Bradley, *Celtic Way*, Chapter 2; see also Sheldrake, *Living Between Worlds*, Chapter 4.

81. Bonhoeffer devotes a chapter to each of these disciplines in his book *Life*

ously develop personal and interpersonal disciplines (individual practice and corporate rehearsal) to participate in a public performance. So if we consider the Christian's responsibility to participate in the performance of the divine melody of mercy, L. Gregory Jones argues that it requires "a habit" of forgiveness that must be "practiced over time within the disciplines of Christian community."[82] The repeated practice of forgiveness enables the Christian as an individual and in community to hear again with clarity the compelling song of God, Christ as *cantus firmus*, rising above the activities of both church and world. The regular repetition of the Eucharist is one such important moment through which the community can hear repeated the melody of divine grace.[83] And in that relistening God reveals to the community, individually and corporately, the appropriate countermelodies to be performed within the polyphonic particularities of their context.

Some of the tensions found within the creative polyphonies of world and Christ are explored in the works of W. Paul Jones. He posits five "theological worlds" that are inhabited by Christians. Each is normally present in any given Christian community as its members respond to the "multiform Christ event." Through this event, Christ is encountered as a guide or a liberator, model-friend or redeemer, or as a suffering companion. Each of the worlds premised on these fragments appears mysteriously "as a composite confession of multiple and converging metaphors," each seeking to "heal the uncommonly diverse wounds of the world."[84] He, too, adopts a musical metaphor: asserting that none of his posited worlds has a claim on "reality in toto," but that their multiplicity "resembles a fugue, permitting little tolerance for a cheap pluralism of easy choices. Such an invitation is to play in *counterpoint* . . . establishing all five [worlds] as alternatives, insisting upon each as a viable and legitimate place in which to set up housekeeping."[85]

At no point in these worlds would the fragmented epiphanies of Christ be confused with his full and eternal richness, but each moment of revelatory encounter and the world it calls into being would be derived from and connected to the *cantus firmus*. What emerge in each "world" are not only differing perceptions of humanity and self-identity but also varying understandings of atonement.[86] Thus as well as the roles of Christ noted

---

Together and warns "whoever cannot be alone should beware of community. Whoever cannot stand being in community should beware of being alone." *Life Together*, 83.

82. Jones, *Embodying Forgiveness*, 163.

83. Begbie draws attention to the practice of Eucharistic repetition through the metaphor of music in "Play it (Again)," 56–64, and *Theology, Music, and Time*, 155–75.

84. Jones, *Worlds Within a Congregation*, 37, and Jones, *Theological Worlds*, 19.

85. Jones, *Theological Worlds*, 44.

86. I am indebted to Nancy Cocks, a former warden of the MacLeod Centre on

above, atonement is experienced as revelation (love shows us the true way), victory (love takes our place), affirmation (love fills and heals emptiness), propitiation (love forgives offence), and reversal (love outlasts suffering). Again, the goals of salvation are also diverse: the purpose of Christ's mission may be variously understood as one of home coming, justice, and freedom, wholeness and belonging, new birth and reconciliation, or survival and integrity. None of these worlds are exclusive to the others, and, indeed, one of the strengths of Jones's typography is that it remains fluid, adaptive to the varying narratives of an individual's evolving biography.

Jones's approach is then preferable to personality typographies, many of which suggest a "polyphony" of personality type within the humanity of Christ.[87] For instance, Stephen Barton detects four distinct spiritualities of Christ that attach to each of the gospels.[88] While he does insist that each portrait lacks the richness of all four taken together, the danger with such typologies is their tendency to become prescriptive rather than descriptive. Others have sought to assess the Jesus of each of the gospels in terms of personality typologies such as Myers-Briggs.[89] Jones's model specifically allows for movement between and within an individual depending on the presenting dilemmas and their contrasting resolutions. Thus, it admits the possibility that individuals and communities may simultaneously occupy a number of worlds, each world possessed of their own particular melody, but each still addressed by the *cantus firmus* of Christ who appears in "fragmented epiphanies" to the world and church. More than simply tolerating such difference it must become the irresistible option that the Christian community affirm gratefully. Thus, "rather than seeing diversity as an anaemic reduction

---

Iona, for introducing me to the work of W. Paul Jones.

87. Of these, the Myers-Briggs indicator is probably the most popular, although recently the Enneagram is being adopted widely. For helpful discussions on Myers-Briggs, see Thomson, *Personality Type*; Baab, *Personality Type in Congregations*; and Goldsmith, *Knowing Me, Knowing You*.

88. Barton, *Spirituality of the Gospels*, 147. Barton draws on Robert Morgan's analogy of a "biblical paint box." See Morgan, "Hermeneutical Significance of Four Gospels," in Mays, *Interpreting the Gospels*, 41–54. They suggest that there is always the possibility of delighting in the variety of colors out of which the reader draws images of faith. One of the weaknesses in the analogy is that it is not possible for colors to simultaneously exist in the same place in the way that polyphony sound can. It is more difficult to conceive of communal participation and performance within this model.

89. See Allen, "Brief History of Christian Devotion," 18. However, within all people there is a polyphony of personality choices and Jesus had open to him the full extent of possibilities that can be found in each person. So it was that Jesus seemed to know how to respond appropriately for each context and person he encountered.

of the theological task, it is a rediscovery of how the church once came into being, and how its heritage is a continuation."[90] To do so, says Jones,

> what is needed . . . is passionate conviction within a Christianity authentically variegated. . . . Such an effort would have as its goal a transforming faith that is without inflexible content, and a diversity of content without the indifference bred of relativism. . . . The goal could only be expressed paradoxically as "open conviction," "formed passion," [and] "disciplined freedom."[91]

In the following chapters a diversity of metaphors and apparent paradoxes are considered with the intention of moving toward a theology of Christian community that is authentically variegated.

90. Jones, *Worlds Within a Congregation*, 17.
91. Ibid., 25.

CHAPTER 4

Fragmented Epiphanies

Everything beckons to us to perceive it,
murmurs at every turn "Remember me!"
A day we passed, too busy to receive it,
Will yet unlock us all its treasury.

—RAINER MARIA RILKE[1]

Things fall apart; the centre cannot hold;
Mere anarchy is loosed upon the world . . .

—W. B. YEATS[2]

Having noted how the polyphonic Christ might be discovered playing in "ten thousand places,"[3] attention is now given to three descriptors by which those countermelodies of human participation in Christ's performance may be explored: fragmented epiphanies, worldly monasticism, and the colony of heaven. No one descriptor is exclusive and, indeed, each in itself may be thought of as but one melody sounding in harmony with the others, metaphors that may be mixed with integrity.

---

1. Maria Rilke, "Untitled," in *Later Poems*, 128.
2. Yeats, "The Second Coming," in *Selected Poems*, 60.
3. Hopkins, "As Kingfishers Catch Fire," in *Complete Poems*, 52.

The first of these metaphors is that of the epiphanal melody. God's epiphany, the divine disclosure to the world, comes from heaven upon the earth like phrases of music, echoing the rich polyphony of Christ. Gerard Manley Hopkins noted that the purpose of all creation is to be what it already is, in and through God's eye. He wrote,

> As kingfishers catch fire, dragonflies draw flame;
> As tumbled over rim in roundy wells
> Stones ring; like each tucked string tells, each hung bell's
> Bow swung finds tongue to fling out broad its name;
> Each mortal thing does one thing and the same: . . .
> Acts in God's eye what in God's eye he is—[4]

To act "in God's eye what in God's eye he is," may be transposed from a visual to an aural metaphor: to be in God's ear the melody that God already hears for us. The purpose of humanity is to play out these melodies that God hears in the reality of the world. As the polyphony of Christ is so performed, moments of epiphanal revelation emerge within the common life of participating people. Emily Dickinson called such moments "bulletins from immortality"[5] and George MacLeod spoke of them as "the glory in the grey."[6] They are occasions of the numinous[7] when materiality flashes with a glory scarce its own[8] and God's "*mysterium, tremendum et fascinans*" invites humanity to participate in the divine polyphony.[9] In such moments people are not taken up and out of this world into some ethereal seventh heaven. Rather, having participated in the polyphony of Christ they attain an awareness of his *cantus firmus* that permeates their otherwise everyday experience. They, and their common life, are transfigured into reality as God perceives and sustains them. In such moments, humanity hears itself and the world as God hears them. People perceive the particularity of their melody. They recognize its relation to the *cantus firmus*, to others and its place within the polyphony of God's creation. John V. Taylor described this as an experience of the ordinary "seen through the context of an otherness

---

4. Ibid.

5. Dickinson, "Bulletins from Immorality," in *Complete Poems*, 401.

6. MacLeod, "The Glory in the Grey," in *Whole Earth Shall Cry Glory*, 13–14.

7. Otto, *Idea of the Holy*, 7.

8. The allusion is to Wordsworth, "The Prelude, Book V," line 629.

9. "*Mysterium tremendum et fascinans*" is the phrase Rudolf Otto uses to describe the mystery of God who is totally other to humanity (*mysterium*), the awesomeness of the divine (*tremendum*), and the fascination and attraction humanity exhibits toward God (*fascinans*). See Otto, *Idea of the Holy*, 12–40.

which enfolds them all and lies with them all."[10] The twentieth-century theologian and poet, Thomas Merton, described an epiphanal moment in Louisville, Kentucky.

> At the corner of Fourth and Walnut, in the center of the shopping district, I was suddenly overwhelmed with the realization that I loved all those people, that they were mine and I theirs, that we could not be alien to one another even though we were total strangers. . . . I have the immense joy of being *man*, a member of a race in which God Himself became incarnate. As if the sorrows and stupidities of the human condition could overwhelm me, now I realize what we all are. And if only everybody could realize this! But it cannot be explained. There is no way of telling people that they are all walking around shining like the sun.[11]

For Merton, this is clearly a moment of heaven's melody breaking in upon the world. But such moments are just that: moments. They are only pieces of a greater whole: fragments of the divine epiphany and glimpses of heaven's polyphony. The Christian only ever has a fragment of the whole. So while every person may hear something of the *cantus firmus* and experience the richness of their own counterpoint, they can never hear the totality of music as it was in the beginning and will be in the end. It is not given for any human to hear the bars that heralded creation's birth, nor to guess at the chords that will conclude existence on this side of the eschaton. That is both the privilege and the burden of finite humanity. They are privileged to be cognizant of their place in the music: they know that they come after the beginning and appear before the end. But it is their burden to also know that there is a music that they can only hear in part. The condition of being human is that they can only ever participate in the performance of the middle fragments: it is to be limited and conscious of the limitation. The Genesis narrative claims that these limits were established in Eden where humanity was created in the image of God.

This image was not an *analogia entis*, something "like God" that humans possessed. Rather, it was located in the relationship of humanity to each other, creation and God. According to the biblical narrative, this societal relationship established Adam and Eve as created beings with a proper and limited place within creation. But in the Fall, Adam and Eve sought to reach beyond their limits, becoming *sicut deus*, like God. In this, they became self-referent fragments, acting out of their own knowledge rather

---

10. Taylor, *Christ-Like God*, 25.

11. Merton, *Conjectures of a Guilty Bystander*, 156–57.

than being in relationship with the whole that God established for them.[12] Sin is that choice to become a self-referent fragment separate from the God-addressed whole. Each fragment sets up boundaries to denote its distance from the whole, each separation blocks off the patterns that connect body and spirit, humanity and nature.[13]

Since the Fall, sinful humanity has both resisted and despised the burden of this limitation and has sought to overcome the fragmented nature of their existence. As *sicut deus*, they have acted out of their own resources and ever hungered after the unity located in the divine whole. But because humanity is made in the image of God they remain uniquely perceptive to the numinous and to the unity that exists beyond them. This perception of a greater whole that lies beyond them, but which only echoes in their midst, serves to remind them that they are not God and were driven from the garden precisely to prevent them becoming like God. And so, humanity is both attracted to the melodies of the numinous while at the same time being repelled by the boundary established by the *cantus firmus*. These fragments are not revealed to humanity so that they may presume to fashion them into the whole and so again grasp after divinity. For God is not a finite whole, the fragments of whom might be arranged together. Each fragment speaks of the wholeness of God, but the wholeness is a mystery into which humanity is drawn to participate. The fragments are gathered together to inspire a communal vision of reality that participates in the performance of divinely ordained countermelodies. To be Christian is to accept the privilege and the burden of being human before God. It is to accept the limitations of the human performance and to live in humble affirmation that "the whole" is always both before them, beyond them, and yet present with them in the fragments revealed within their midst.

The tension between this attraction to the melodies of God and the denial of the limits established by Christ's *cantus firmus* is played out in contemporary western civilization between the homogenizing forces of globalization and the fragmentation experienced within the postmodern condition. These forces influence the Christian community. As transnational corporations seek to homogenize the global marketplace, they fashion the identity of the world in their own unifying image. They, *sicut deus*, aspire to mimic the unity of the divine. But the rejection of the limits placed upon the

12. "Imago dei—humankind in the image of God in being for God and the neighbor, in its original creatureliness and limitedness; sicut deus—humankind similar to God in knowing-out-of-its-own-self about good and evil, in having no limit and acting out-of-its-own-resources, in its aseity, in its being alone." Bonhoeffer, *Creation and Fall*, 113.

13. See Grey, *Beyond the Dark Night*, 38.

individual through encounters with the other has led to the deification of the self and to social and personal fragmentation. As each person becomes increasingly intent on composing and performing the one tune, their tune, few are willing to listen to others or to listen in community. Fewer still wish to be addressed by the *cantus firmus*. In such conditions the tension is not one of the "person versus community, but personal community and massified individualism."[14] Personal community is established when distinct melodies are woven together into a polyphonic whole. It is made possible in the Christian community that acknowledges the limits set upon them by the otherness of Christ's *cantus firmus* and the differing melodies that are called to sound in "ten thousand people and places." Mass individualism can only ever beget a self-referent cacophony that knows little of such otherness or community.

In the context of postmodernity's mass individualism many wonder if polyphony can hold cacophony at bay. Yeats's insight: "Things fall apart, the centre cannot hold" has become a popular diagnosis for the *zeitgeist* of postmodern society. Fragmentation has been turned into a metaphor of choice in much political, philosophical and theological discussion.[15] Grenz and Franke inform us that "We are living in the midst of a widespread fragmentation and perhaps even disintegration that appears to be affecting all dimensions of Western culture, including the theological enterprise."[16] So where once Paul Tillich lamented that the "foundations had been shaken"[17] Mary Grey now asserts that "*there simply are no foundations any more!*"[18] They are fractured and fragmented and the very endeavor of their reassembly is discredited. Postmodern theorists reject universal foundations, arguing that interpreting the world by imposing upon it some undergirding explanation or metanarrative is not only historically calamitous, but is also morally suspect.[19] For them, such foundationalism can only exist when a dominant group suppresses or discredits dissenting voices of otherness. As

14. See Day, *Dietrich Bonhoeffer on Christian Community and Common Sense*, 12–13.

15. See Rasmussen, *Moral Fragments and Moral Community*; Woodhead, "Theology and the Fragmentation of the Self"; Lakeland, *Postmodernity*; MacIntyre, *After Virtue*; Grey, *Epiphanies of Grace*; and Grey, "Shaking of the Foundations—Again!"

16. Grenz and Franke, *Beyond Foundationalism*, 4.

17. Tillich, *Shaking of the Foundations*.

18. Grey, "Shaking of the Foundations—Again!," 2.

19. Lyotard, expressly refers to the postmodern "incredulity towards meta-narratives," in *The Postmodern Condition*, xxiv, where, as Steiner Kvale notes, "we pass judgment on truth, beauty and justice without criteria for the judgments." Kvale, *Psychology and Postmodernism*, 33.

such, postmodernity is too humble to forbid and too weak to banish the foundational excesses of modernity's hubris, yet its criticism means that the truth for any given community becomes no more than the truth constructed by them. In this brave new era, everything that has provided the foundations for western society in the last four hundred years (from philosophy and economics to physics and theology) appears to be dismantled, critiqued, and left fractured, seemingly beyond the possibility of any meaningful re-assembly. Even in science the bedrock Cartesian and Newtonian physics has shifted under Einstein's theory of relativity and the very foundations of science have started to move. And in the midst of such dislocation, science has also turned to metaphor and to music. The physicist and astronomer, Chet Raymo, has commented on the evolving scientific paradigm: "we find ourselves awash in a sea of cosmic music—surging, billowing, animating, never at rest."[20] If there is still a center, can it hold?

The contemporary church rarely regards this process of fragmentation positively. Most Christianity is affirming of some form of foundationalism and perceives the phenomena of fragmentation as both a cause and effect of the contemporary decline of Christianity in the West and its waning influence in the world. It is perceived as a rejection of Christ's *cantus firmus*. But this negative appraisal of fragmentation is not fully merited. It is possible to hold to Christ as *cantus firmus* and yet engage positively with the metaphor of fragmentation. The realities of fragmentation in no way debar the Christian community from making claims that assert a universal character in which God is acknowledged as the ground of all truth.[21] Christ is the *cantus firmus* in which every fragment holds together.

One of the difficulties in understanding fragmentation is that the historical foundations, whose demise the church often laments, owe more to the Enlightenment agenda of Copernicus, Galileo, Bacon, and Descartes than they do to the epiphanies of God appearing in the world. In the sixteenth century, the move from the premodern to the modern worldview was based upon the supposition that epistemology guaranteed ontology. In other words, there existed one single, foundational mode of representation that if it were uncovered, would provide the rational secular basis for all subsequent human belief and action. As science took upon itself the mantle of responsibility to provide that one foundation, Christianity challenged its

20. Raymo, "Skeptics and True Believers," 193, cited in Mayne, *Learning to Dance,* 57.

21. Grenz and Franke posit a "chastened rationality" by which foundationalism is rejected and Christian theology is reinterpreted as a variety of local and specific positions that are held together by the "family resemblance" of Trinity, community, and eschatology. See Grenz and Franke, *Beyond Foundationalism,* 25.

claim over ownership of the epistemological bedrock. It is true that post-Constantinian Christendom had ensured a strong relationship between religious belief and public policy, but no homogenized foundation had ever truly been achieved and in truth, it had never been the church's proper task. The task of the Christian community had not been to establish foundations for the world, but to participate in the performance of Christ's polyphony as it was played out in ten thousand pieces. Granted, the polyphony was stronger as the fragments of epiphany were gathered together, but establishing a foundation and assembling the whole always exceeded the human purpose.

The performing of this polyphony has never been anything other than a persistent encounter of divine epiphanies and a gathering together of their fragments. Even in its most monolithic moments, the church has always been comprised of various people and communities who appear to have heard the *cantus firmus*, but who bore witness to differing revelations of God's presence. In the beginning, each personal encounter with the incarnate Christ was a unique fragment that the disciples brought together in community so to better understand its meaning and to participate in performing its purpose. At Pentecost, people heard the message of God spoken in their own tongues. There was present on that day both the unifying mystery of God encountered and the fragments of language expressed in diversity. Indeed, James D. G. Dunn notes that from its inception Christianity knew no uniform concept of orthodoxy at all, contending that the stream of first-century Christianity was broad, with "many currents and crosscurrents running in it, and that its banks crumbled away at many points."[22] Dunn argues that the early church was in fact a multiplicity of contextually relevant expressions of encounter with and longing for God[23] and that their common strand was the affirmed unity between Jesus the man, and Jesus the exalted one.[24] Each early-church community was an epiphanal fragment of the Christ's polyphony, identifiable only by its relationship to the *cantus firmus*. What they also shared in common were the tensions that existed between being a disciple of Christ and a citizen of the state.

Under the Emperor Constantine that tension changed. After his conversion, the subversive Christianity of a *religio illicita* became the faith of the establishment,[25] the church became the bearer of civilizing culture, and the emperor quickly moved to resolve perpetuating divisive theological acrimonies at the Council of Nicaea in 325. He moved toward a monophonic

22. Dunn, *Unity and Diversity*, 4.
23. Ibid., Chapters 2–5.
24. Ibid., 371.
25. Strictly this did not come into being until 380.

Christendom in which membership of the church and of civil society was almost identical. But as he did so the "conditions of church membership, which had once been stringent, became accommodating."[26] The formation of Christendom as a societal paradigm began to collapse the bisociative tensions that were essential to the Christians "being in the world but not of it."

But no sooner had this homogenization of the fragments been established than a fresh and counter-cultural epiphany was heard through the melodies of St. Antony and the phenomenon of monasticism. Monasticism was a radical response to the secularizing church, and Eoin de Bhaldraithe notes Cassian's observation that it was not long before monastic renunciation rather than baptism became the great divide of the human race.[27] Here was a fresh epiphany, the introduction of another melody in counterpoint to Constantine's desired monophony. A number of new and diverse countermelodies were performed within the emerging monasticism. In adding their music to that of the established church, they continued the rhythmic tensions that existed between the centrifugal forces of worldly order and the prophetic epiphanies of heaven that erupted in their midst. While some sought to preserve the fragments of the past, weaving toward a homogenized whole, others sought to continue the journey through fresh epiphanies and new melodies. Over time the tension of this rhythm threaded its way into the very existence of Christian community. To be Christian was to perpetually move between order and prophecy. In time, the prophetic epiphany of monasticism moved toward domesticated order and was duly brought "under the roof of the institutional church."[28] The Rule of St. Benedict became a standardized guide for religious life.

Yet, in the British Isles, the fragments of epiphany found in the Celtic churches differed substantially from their European counterparts. And in time, fresh revelations arose both within and outside the institutional church in Europe; movements such as the Waldenses in the twelfth century and the Mendicant orders such as the Franciscans and Dominicans in the following century. Added to these was a flourishing polyphony of mysticism in the fourteenth century as seen in Meister Eckhart, Catherine of Sienna, and others in the Rhineland, and, in England, Richard Rolle, Julian of Norwich, and Margery Kemp. All these were fresh epiphanal fragments of the melodies of heaven performed on earth. The contrapuntal melodies introduced by mystics were not always appreciated nor welcomed at the time. Nor were the themes that came from reformers such as Wyclif and

---

26. de Bhaldraithe, "Early Christian Features," 153.

27. Ibid., 166.

28. Lawrence, *Medieval Monasticism*, 17.

Hus. In the fourteenth and early fifteenth centuries, such melodies were declared heretical but the music they performed only anticipated the fresh themes that would flourish under Luther, Zwingli, Calvin, Cranmer, and the Anabaptists in the sixteenth century. Each was but a new epiphany and a fragment of the whole. Each led the church into new experiences of God. However, the mistaken assumption of each was that their fragment of epiphany was the whole: each beginning as a prophet but ending up as a policeman.[29]

A myriad of post-reformation developments, from the Puritans to Pentecostalism could all illustrate this same point; namely, the church has perpetually been renewed and reformed through fresh epiphanal encounters of Christ in which they were encouraged to participate in his polyphony. But each epiphany has been no more than a proleptic fragment, an echo of the whole. As people have participated in these fragments of God's polyphony, they have ever sought to bring their particular epiphany into harmony with what has historically come to pass and what is anticipated in eschatological fulfillment.

Thus, rather than bemoan the fragmentariness of life, these Christians have sought to rejoice in the possibility of participating in fragments of God's epiphany and in the fact that they, in community, can perform the pieces in a rich and present harmony. Bonhoeffer understood this when he wrote,

> What matters, it seems to me, is whether one still sees, in this fragment of life that we have, what the whole was intended and designed to be, and of what material it is made. After all, there are such things as fragments that are only fit for the garbage heap (even a decent "hell" is too good for them), and others which remain meaningful for hundreds of years, because only God could perfect them, so they must remain fragments—I'm thinking, for example, of the *Art of the Fugue*. If our life is only the most remote reflection of such a fragment, in which, even for a short time, the various themes gradually accumulate and harmonize with one another and in which the great counterpoint is sustained from beginning to end—so that finally, when they cease, all one can do is sing the chorale "*Vor Deinem Thron tret' ich allhier*"—then it is not for us, either, to complain about this fragmentary life of ours, but rather even to be glad of it.[30]

29. Uncited reference, attributed to Newman in Finney, *Fading Splendour*, ix.

30. Bonhoeffer, *Letters and Papers*, 306.

Living polyphonically enables the Christian and their community to maintain multiple differences within a unity assured through a common connection to the *cantus firmus*, Jesus Christ. This rescues people from the tyranny of their isolating, self-referential fragment and calls them into belonging with a polyphony of otherness. Of course, the totality of the heavenly fugue, in its eschatological fulfillment, remains beyond the limits of fallen humanity. But the unifying ground bass and echoes of the harmonies continue to be encountered in God's fragmented epiphanies. So these fragments ought not to be despised. They are to be celebrated, for it is from them that it is possible to discern how the whole music of heaven is arranged and planned, and of what material it consists. As Brueggemann notes, the Christian task is "the voicing of a lot of little pieces out of which people can put life together in fresh configurations."[31] In gathering the fragments together, the church deepens its communal participation in the performance of Christ's polyphony and establishes Christ in the world. In so doing it establishes a location and a people in whom others can experience a healing of their brokenness: "*gathering the fragments* must be part of the process of redemption and healing."[32] Mary Grey makes this point by drawing on the Jewish tradition of *tikkun olam*. She argues that the social and personal fragmentation of the former foundations that is experienced in postmodern society is expressed by the Kabbalistic story of sin, understood as the broken fragments of the vessels of creation. Redemption, conversely, is seen as gathering the fragments together, as *tikkun olam*, or cosmic repair, creating whatever wholeness is possible.[33] Reinterpreting this within the Christian community means that all the fragments are gathered around Christ's *cantus firmus* in a process of reentering the polyphony, becoming the melody that God hears for each person. This move toward wholeness, while at the same time accepting the necessary responsibility to remain a countermelody to the *cantus firmus*, gives people the voice and the place to sing their melody with confidence. If Christ remains acknowledged as the *cantus firmus* then fragmentation need not mean the end of all cohesion. The Christian community becomes the place in which the fragments of Christ's epiphany can be gathered together and they can become the people in and through whom his melodies are performed.

It is important that in gathering these fragments the Christian community remain open to the fresh epiphanies. Alasdair MacIntyre has imagined a society where people live only with fragments of a once coherent

---

31. Brueggemann, *Texts Under Negotiation*, 20.

32. Grey, *Beyond the Dark Night*, 34.

33. Ibid., 42.

morality. In such a place he seeks "another—[though] doubtless very differ-ent—St. Benedict"[34] who will help reconstruct "local forms of community within which civility and the intellectual and moral life can be sustained through the new dark ages which are already upon us."[35] The image is a powerful one, not least because MacIntyre acknowledges that his chosen archetypal gatherer of this fractured morality was also open to new frag-ments of epiphany. That Benedict's monasticism played a great role in pre-serving Christianity and the fragments of other cultures through "the Dark Ages" is beyond doubt. However, Benedict's monasticism was concerned with more than simply gathering up the pieces of the past, he turned aside from the task of shoring up the civility of the Roman *imperium* to construct "new forms of community within which the moral life could be sustained."[36] Christian Monasticism, therefore, sought to participate in the fresh frag-ments of epiphany, to sing a new song along with the older melodies. "The Lord had yet more light and truth, to break forth from his word."[37]

If this is true, then rather than having to "get used to a world of mul-tiple realities"[38] as Walter Truett Anderson suggests of postmodernity, it is more accurate to suggest that the Christian community will have to live in a world made up of multiple fragments of reality, fragments of the reality that is Christ's polyphonic whole. Thus, reality for the Christian community must be the way in which Christ takes form in the world. For Christ's *cantus firmus* underpins all of creation: "through him all things were made, with-out him nothing was made that has been made," and "no one can lay any foundation other than the one already laid, which is Jesus Christ."[39] Christ is then the "Real One" and as such, "he is the origin, essence and goal of all reality."[40] In Christ, the reality of God enters the reality of material existence. As such, questions of truth and reality are made concrete in the question, "how Christ may take form among us today and here."[41] Bonhoeffer was in no doubt as to how Christ took such form. "The church is the place where Jesus Christ's taking form is proclaimed and where it happens."[42] The

34. MacIntyre, *After Virtue*, 263.

35. Ibid.

36. Ibid.

37. See John Robinson speaking to English Puritan Pilgrims as they departed for the "New World." See Young, *Chronicles of the Pilgrim Fathers*, 87. MacLeod is often quoted as using a similar phrase: "Follow the Light you have and pray for more light."

38. Anderson, *Fontana Postmodernism Reader*, 6.

39. John 1:3 and 1 Cor 3:11.

40. Bonhoeffer, *Ethics*, 263.

41. Ibid., 99.

42. Ibid., 102.

Christian community is that part of the world in which Christ has taken form: it is the earthly locus in which people have chosen to participate in the performance of Christ's polyphony. The purpose of such participation is not to turn the world into the Kingdom of God by imposing upon humanity a Christian foundationalism that owes more to Constantinian imperialism than to the humble servanthood of Christ.

Perhaps the greatest service postmodern fragmentation has offered to the Christian community is to have broken the Constantinian linkage between religion and society. Bonhoeffer correctly noted that the time when people could be told everything "with words—whether with theological or with pious words—is past, as is the age of inwardness and of conscience, and that means the age of religion altogether.[43] In this new era of a religionless world, the church was no longer required to explain itself to the world: not through claims of foundationalism nor by somehow reserving a place for God, even a *deus ex machina*, in its midst. Free of the Constantinian linkage, the church could return to interpreting the world before Christ. Its purpose was not to change the world into itself but to allow the world to be the world, a world over which Christ still remained as Lord. This brings the world into a new self-understanding: showing that it is indeed godless, and in so doing, bringing it closer both to God's judgment and God's grace. The church must, for its own sake and for the sake of the world, recognize its own finitude. Its theology must be "suitably humble in its claims, repenting of its imperialist claims for universal truth, resisting foreclosure, creating a flexible discourse, ready not only to dialogue but to be continually under criticism, and judgement."[44] Yet it must also participate in the countermelodies that Christ calls into being through them in the world. The task of the Christian community is simply to play the next notes of the music as they are revealed. The church becomes a people in which God's melodies are gathered not primarily for the sake of the world but for the sake of the church. In this way the church can truly be the people of God, i.e., that bit of a lost and godless world, which is qualified by God's revealing, gracious Word, fully present in the world and really the presence of God. Only when the church is the church, the gatherer and performer of Christ's fragmented epiphanies, can she be of service to the world. Only then will the fragments of epiphany be

---

43. Letter dated April 30, 1944, in Bonhoeffer, *Letters and Papers*, 362.

44. Grey, "Shaking of the Foundations—Again!," 3. Stephen Pattison suggests that Christian theology can no longer pretend "to ultimacy or depend upon the dominance of the grand, unified narrative." He adds that if it shows "proper humility and egalitarianism" it may be able to contribute "theological fragments of insight and wisdom" to public debate, helping both individuals and society to flourish. See Pattison, "Public Theology," 57–76.

gathered in an "authentically redemptive manner,"[45] only then can the community participate in the melodies of Christ's salvation, and as Adrienne Rich says,

> Cast my lot with those
> who age after age, perversely,
>
> with no extraordinary power,
> reconstitute the world."[46]

The work of George MacLeod on Iona may be understood as a physical manifestation of this metaphor. He sought to reconstitute the world and rebuild the fragments of the common life around Christ. Years before he began his experiment, the abbey church had been rebuilt. But the buildings of the common life remained in ruins: left lying in fragments. This was MacLeod's parable in stone: Churches were busy and in good repair, but their witness was monophonic. They were not affecting the wider polyphony of the common life wherein communities and individuals were falling apart. MacLeod argued:

> It is the week-day life of men [people] that lies in ruins. The economic structure—the industrial, the international—these are the grave concerns bereft today of Spirit. These are the places where men [people] have to live and move and have their being—and the roof of them is falling in![47]

Yet Christ was Lord of that ruined world as much as he was Lord of the church. What was needed was a gathering together of the pieces: a bringing together of the worlds of work and worship around the *cantus firmus* of the Christ. What was needed was a community in which clergy and craftsmen could weave into polyphonic harmony the melodies of epiphany experienced by both.

Iona became the place in which these fragments were gathered. It was "a tiny symbol that the thing can be done."[48] And indeed much of the members' time would be spent literally gathering stones together to reconstruct the ruined buildings. MacLeod was well aware that the rebuilding had been embarked on partly for its own sake, but also as a symbol of the church building itself up again with "modern material on an old foundation."[49] In

---

45. Grey, *Beyond the Dark Night*, 35.

46. Rich, "Natural Resources," in *Dream of a Common Language*, 67.

47. Ferguson, *Chasing the Wild Goose*, 61.

48. Iona Community, *Coracle*, no. 2, 20.

49. Sermon by George MacLeod, cited in Ferguson, *Chasing the Wild Goose*, 61.

so doing, they would discover the fragment-gathering nature of community living. Even as they brought wood and stone together to reconstruct the buildings, so ministers and laity together learned from each other's experiences of Christ in church and world.

But for all their gathering of epiphanal melodies on Iona, members were soon scattered again. Just as grain is gathered into one Eucharistic loaf and then scattered among the people, the aim of the Iona Community was that each minister should spend twenty-one months out of twenty-four in one of the difficult parishes of Scotland. The aim of gathering them together on Iona was not to take them out of their situation but rather to listen to the differing melodies in which each was called to participate and weave together a polyphony that would sustain them all. In the preface to his book, *We Shall Rebuild*, MacLeod reflected that it was "*what to do there*, in the modern situation, that alone draws us together for a very short period on the Island, to set our compass and intensively experience in Work and Worship the Redeemed Community that we would preach."[50]

The gathering together of ancient stones and modern materials in the rebuilding of the abbey became a living metaphor for the rebuilding of the common life with which the church was charged. The Iona Community was to be "a laboratory of cooperative living,"[51] a living countersign in which the members hoped to discover more of the church's place within the world.

And as new members gathered year by year and as associates, pilgrims, and even tourists added their melodies to those fragments already gathered, so they brought together fresh expressions of Christ existing as a community, new counterpoints to an established *cantus firmus*. And as they returned to the contexts of their common life, they took with them new melodies through which they might participate in performing fragments of Christ's epiphanal polyphony. Rasmussen argues that in our increasingly mobile world this is exactly what may be needed: communities of moral character with multilayered interactions among its people, communities where "traditions and rituals are developed and preserved, skills are learned and utilized, discipline is expected and nurtured, and fidelity and accountability to community members is practiced."[52] Such communities can gather in and send forth members with ease because while strong dimensions of belonging and loyalty are necessary, "not everyone need know everyone

---

50. MacLeod, *We Shall Rebuild*, 5.

51. Iona Community, *Coracle*, no. 1, 3.

52. Rasmussen, *Moral Fragments*, 127.

else," as long as each feels a "sense of personal presence and contribution."[53] He concludes,

> Not all members need hold all purposes in common nor act as a unit on every matter. But there must be an overlapping of members' interests, a "community" of interests. The community is not simply each individual member's interests writ large; rather, collective interests draw the individual beyond the place she or he started and into a network of open response and responsibility. [54]

Shanks comments in similar terms with regard to the island center work of the Iona Community:

> We stand, as a global community, at a place of enormous possibility and also of overwhelming threat. In it all, our island's work is a tiny fragment in the multiple purposes of God. But what is so important is that it *is* a fragment and in its own particular way is recovering social holiness and a recognition that the fate of the soul is the fate of our social order.[55]

As MacLeod himself admitted in the Iona Community at the end of the rebuilding of the abbey, this is a challenge.

> We must find the techniques of the devotional life adequate to the make-up and needs of Modern Man. If all we have built is a shell, we shall deserve to be shelved. By grace alone, signs are not wanting that this will in fact be our next Building Project.[56]

The "technique," or perhaps more accurately the melody that will sustain such a devotional life is to be found in a new monasticism, a worldly monasticism.

---

53. Ibid., 128.

54. Ibid., 129.

55. Shanks, *Iona—God's Energy*, 220.

56. MacLeod, *We Shall Rebuild*, vi.

CHAPTER 5

Worldly Monasticism

Since my early youth I have seen myself as a monk, but one without
a monastery, or at least without walls other than those of the entire
planet. And even these, it seemed to me, had to be transcended—
probably by immanence—without a habit, or at least without
vestments other than those worn by the human family.

—RAIMUNDO PANIKKAR[1]

The monk proposed to himself no great or systematic work beyond
that of saving his soul. What he did more than this was the accident
of the hour.

—CARDINAL NEWMAN[2]

The Christian is not a *homo religiosus* but simply a human being, in
the same way that Jesus was a human being—in contrast, perhaps,
to John the Baptist. I do not mean the shallow and banal this-
worldliness of the enlightened, the bustling, the comfortable, or the

1. Panikkar, *Blessed Simplicity*, 6.
2. Newman, *Church of the Fathers*, 452–53.

lascivious, but the profound this-worldliness that shows discipline
and includes the ever-present knowledge of death and resurrection.

—DIETRICH BONHOEFFER[3]

We need a whole spectrum of models of what the Wild Hope of
God might look like as expressed in communities that are clearly at
counterpoint to the dominant culture.

—TOM SINE[4]

My prayer is not that you take them out of the world
but that you protect them from the evil one.

—JOHN 17:15

The idea of "worldly monasticism" might appear to be an oxymoron.
The perceived character of monasticism is usually one in which
the world is specifically rejected so that the monk may pursue the
cloistered perfection of their soul. It would seem impossible to pursue this
monastic aim and simultaneously be fully present in the world. Yet, the tensions inherent to this apparent contradiction are those same tensions that
are bisociated in Christ: he who was both human and divine, belonging to
heaven and yet fully present on the earth. As such, these are the tensions
that are necessarily reflected within the reality of the Christian community
as they seek to participate in performing the polyphony of Christ. In bisociating monasticism and worldliness, we find a further insight and another
metaphor into how the church might become the polyphonic community
of Christ.

This revisitation of the monastic life as an inspiration for the wider
church is no new idea. Bonhoeffer spoke compellingly of the need for "a
new type of monasticism, which has nothing in common with the old but a
life of uncompromising discipleship, following Christ according to the Sermon on the Mount."[5] MacLeod specifically rejected the suggestion that the

---

3. Bonhoeffer, *Letters and Papers*, 485.

4. Sine, *Wild Hope*, 281.

5. Letter to Karl Friedrich, dated January 14, 1935, in Bonhoeffer, *London*, 285.

Iona Community was pursuing "the cloistered life,"[6] but consciously placed the iconic center of his experiment in Christian community on the site of both a Celtic and Benedictine monastery. Richard Mouw has argued that the church would benefit from a "remonasticization" that called all Christians to a clearer and more radical witness,[7] as has John Stott[8] and Eugene Peterson, who argue for "monasteries without walls" wherein "an imagination large enough to contain all of life, all worship and work as prayer [is] set in a structure (*askesis*) adequate to the actual conditions in which it is lived out."[9] Tom Sine suggests that "the only way any of us at any age can hope to be successful in reordering our lives and begin to flesh out something of God's future is in community,"[10] and that "a return to a radical idea of Christian community is essential to the renewal and the survival of a vital church in the Western nations."[11] He concludes that what is needed are "interim models of community that don't require a lifelong or common-purse commitment . . . or necessitate relocating into communities of poverty. . . . We need to develop 'enclaves of the future.'"[12]

In recent years this has been reflected in the rise of what is often referred to as the "new monasticism." This development was front page news for *The Christian Century* on October 18, 2005, when Jason Byassee attributed the idea largely to the reflections contained in Jonathan R. Wilson's book, *Living Faithfully in a Fragmented World: Lessons for the Church from MacIntyre's After Virtue.*[13] There have been a number of initiatives and publications emerging under this new monastic theme, notably Jonathan Wilson-Hartgrove's *New Monasticism: What It Has to Say to Today's Church, School(s) for Conversion: 12 Marks of a New Monasticism*, as well as Graham Cray, Ian Mobsby, and Aaron Kennedy's *New Monasticism as a Fresh Expression of Church.*[14]

---

6. MacLeod wrote, "One of the great purposes of the Iona Community is to experiment with a project that shall steadfastly remain part of the world in which we find ourselves and yet not be of it. We have definitely barred the cloistered life." Iona Community, *Coracle*, no. 1, 12.

7. Mouw, as cited in Sine, *Wild Hope*, 280.

8. Uncited reference, in ibid.

9. Peterson, *Under the Unpredictable Plant*, 98–99.

10. Sine, *Wild Hope*, 278.

11. Ibid., 280.

12. Ibid., 281. I am also grateful to Ray Simpson for conversations on this topic. See also Simpson, *Pilgrim Way*.

13. See *The Christian Century* 122 (October 18, 2005), and Wilson, *Living Faithfully*.

14. Wilson-Hartgrove, *New Monasticism*; and *School(s) for Conversion*. See also Cray, Mobsby, and Kennedy, *New Monasticism*; Adams, *Cave, Refectory, Road*; and

These and other instances of new monasticism all envision a community in which the devotional disciplines that nurtured the radical spirituality of traditional monks are reinterpreted so that the Christian community can participate in the performance of the melodies of God in the midst of contemporary society.[15] But here, in choosing to name it a worldly monasticism, it is hoped to invoke a deliberate tension and bisociation that reflects the praxis and spirituality of such communities. This will adopt the best of ancient disciplines, many of which retain rich value in contemporary society, but clothe them in no vestments "other than those worn by the human family" and inhabit a monastery "without walls other than those of the entire planet."[16] Its purpose is to nurture Christians who practice a this-worldly holiness, for as Bonhoeffer noted, "one only learns to have faith by living in the full this-worldliness of life," by living fully in "the midst of life's tasks, questions, successes and failures, experiences and perplexities."[17]

But traditionally, the church and particularly monasticism have not valued the idea of worldliness. Concerns with the material, the earthly, the here and now have been perceived as being entered into at the expense of the transcendent, the heavenly, and the here-after. The world has been predominantly understood as the antithesis of the church's purpose, namely the development of the spiritual. The dualism that puts spirit and matter in opposition to one another rather than bisociating them as they are found together in Christ is in no small amount due to the influence of Neoplatonic and Gnostic thought in early Christianity.[18]

Grimley and Wooding, *Living the Hours*. See also Markofski, *New Monasticism and the Transformation of American Evangelicalism*; and Mobsby and Berry, *New Monastic Handbook*. Mobsby and Berry helpfully identify fourteen interweaving features that, while not unique to new monasticism, are indicative of it. Mobsby and Berry, *New Monastic Handbook*, 4.

15. For Wilson-Hartgrove, these include relocation to the abandoned places of Empire, sharing economic resources with community members and the needy, offering hospitality to the stranger and lament for racial divisions along with the active pursuit of a just reconciliation. It also focuses on humble submission to Christ's body, the church, intentional formation with the Rule of the Community, and the nurturing of a common life among members of intentional community. There is also specific support for celibate singles and monogamous married couples and their children and a determination to live geographically close to community members who share a common rule of life. There is a commitment to care for the creation and support local economies along with work in peacemaking and conflict resolution. Finally, there is commitment to a disciplined contemplative life. *School(s) for Conversion*.

16. Panikkar, *Blessed Simplicity*, 6.

17. Letter dated July 21, 1944, in Bonhoeffer, *Letters and Papers*, 486.

18. A third influence, Stoicism, was also important, particularly its concept of *apatheia*, which tried to control the inclinations of nature through a renunciation of the

The first source of this dualism came from Neoplatonism. Its main protagonist, Plotinus (204–270), argued that all objective existence was but the self-expression of a transcendent and inherently contemplative deity that he called "the Unity" or "the One."[19] From this immaterial and impersonal "One" everything overflows; moving out and down in graded states of being. First, the One begets its own image, the *nous*, which in turn begets the *psyche* (world-soul).[20] It is from the psyche that all physical matter is derived. Each new level of being, awareness, and value strives to return to the primal unity of the One through a contemplative negation that, by removing all the non-essentials to material existence, leads to ecstatic union. Thus, while the descent of a soul into a material form is not intrinsically evil, the ultimate purpose of all materiality is an inward journey of self-discovery and reuniting with the One.[21] This philosophy shaped the early Christian concept of the world, elevating the experience of the individual soul to the status of an actualization of a divine form. Hence, Origen argued that the soul nearest to God was a soul for whom the highest good was the knowledge of his own self,[22] and St. Antony argued that the life of a Christian monk was a "constant struggle for self-knowledge, self-purification and through these, the return of the soul to unity with God, in whose image it was created."[23] Retreat from the world and isolated contemplation of the self/soul was the pathway to the One, a praxis that is summed up by the monk Arsenius, who declared, "I cannot live with God, if I live with people."[24]

Gnosticism was the second great influence on how Christianity understood materiality.[25] It claimed to impart a special knowledge of God and redemption, the possession of which enlightened the initiated and guaranteed the salvation of their souls. At its core was "a cluster of systems" generally representing a "commitment to the fundamental unreliability of the empirical environment and of the god responsible for it."[26] Gnosticism operated

---

world.

19. O'Meara, *Plotinus*, 54ff.

20. Ibid., 60–69.

21. Ibid., 100–110.

22. See Mark Edwards, "Christ or Plato? Origen on Revelation and Anthropology," in Ayres and Jones, *Christian Origins*, 11–25.

23. Rubenson, "The Letters of St. Antony: Monasticism and the Making of a Saint," cited in Dunn, *Emergence of Monasticism*, 4.

24. B. Ward, *The Sayings of the Desert Fathers*, 9, cited by de Bhaldraithe, "Early Christian Features," 164.

25. See Burton-Christie, *Word in the Desert*, 37.

26. Williams, "Defining Heresy," 324. See also Grant, "Gnostic Spirituality," in McGinn, Meyendorff, and Leclercq, *Christian Spirituality*, 44–60.

with a rigid dichotomy that set the spiritual condition in opposition to the material world. Matter was understood to be intrinsically evil and Gnostics sought to escape "from everything except the self" in their quest for spiritual enlightenment.[27]

To the adherents of Neoplatonism and Gnosticism, the idea of God becoming human and the spirit condescending to material existence was inconceivable. Their world-renouncing critiques affected an embryonic Christianity that displayed bewildering inconsistencies in its stance toward material reality:[28] was it an evil from which the spirit longed for liberation or was it a blessing that should be celebrated? Should they submit to earthly authorities or separate themselves entirely from society? Such inconsistencies were born in the Christian struggle to live the gospel paradox, what the Epistle to Diognetus called being "alien citizens."[29] While they participated in the earthly society around them, they confessed that their conduct was guided by their citizenship in the coming kingdom of heaven. This paradox of "alien citizenship" was a common and defining metaphor for the early church, but it was a balance that Christians found difficult to define in theory or to perform in practice. Tertullian claimed that Christians were an integral part of his society, "people who are living among you, eating the same food, wearing the same attire, having the same habits, under the same necessities of existence,"[30] and indeed praying for the well-being of the Empire, "because in God's providence it has been ordained to restrain evil."[31] However, he also insisted that Christians ought to break all ties with a world totally corrupted by idolatry.[32] Conversely, Clement believed that Christians ought to live "in the city as in a desert."[33] He also went on to assert that a Christian's citizenship was this-worldly, requiring a restructuring of the earthly Empire.

This restructuring became the avowed purpose of the Imperial Christianity initiated by Constantine in 313 and established in 389 under Emperor Theodosius: all non-Christian worship was forbidden by the state.

27. Lee, *Against the Protestant Gnostics*, 9–10.

28. See Greer, *Broken Lights*, 142ff.

29. The Epistle to Diognetus refers to Christians as "residents at home in their own countries. . . . They take their full part as citizens, but they also submit to anything and everything as if they were aliens. For them, any foreign country is a homeland, and any homeland a foreign country." Epistle to Diognetus 5.4; cited in Greer, *Broken Lights*, 141.

30. Tertullian, "Apology," 42, cited in ibid., 143.

31. Tertullian, "Apology," 32, 39, cited in ibid.

32. Greer, *Broken Lights*, 144.

33. Clement of Alexandria, "The Stromata," 7.12, cited in ibid., 145.

The church welcomed such a move after long periods of suspicion and persecution. But in making Christianity a legal requirement of Imperial citizenship, the hitherto distinctly "alien" character of Christian citizenship was jeopardized, compromised, and lost.[34] The once stringent conditions of church membership were "reduced drastically in order to accommodate all people."[35] David Knowles suggests that

> the Christian church became what it has in a large measure re-mained ever since, a large body in which a few are exceptionally observant and devout, while many are sincere believers without any pretension to fervour, and a sizeable number, perhaps even a majority, are either on their way to losing the faith, or retain it in spite of a life which neither obeys in all respects the commands of Christ nor shares in the devotional and sacramental life of the church with regularity. Under such conditions there has always occurred a revolt of some or many against what seems to them prevailing laxity.[36]

Monasticism was the first significant revolt against such secularized laxity. Those who embraced the life of a religious, both men and women, were anxious to maintain their status as alien citizens believing that even under a baptized emperor, the Empire and the Kingdom of God were far from synonymous.[37] But their objections resulted in them spurning not just the worldliness that they felt had infected the church, but all contact with the world.

ST. ANTONY AND THE DEVELOPMENT OF MONASTICISM

The etymology of monasticism comes from the Greek "μονοσ"/monos, which means alone/solitary. Monks fled the world to be alone with God.

---

34. Augustine believed that the church could survive without state approval. He describes the "City of God" as a "pilgrim among the wicked" that was rooted in the "stability of (its) eternal resting place." In the East, however, Constantine and his successors ruled over both church and world, understanding their vocation to make the people of their kingdom fit for that of God. See Williams, *Christian Spirituality*, 90.

35. de Bhaldraithe, "Early Christian Features," 154.

36. Knowles, *Christian Monasticism*, 12. Workman agrees, saying, "The stalwart Christians whom Diocletian had killed had been replaced by a mixed multitude of time-servers and half-converted pagans." Workman, *Evolution of the Monastic Ideal*, 6.

37. See Williams, *Christian Spirituality*, 91–92; and Swan, *Forgotten Desert Mothers*.

Their emergence has various suggested origins[38] and certainly not everyone who fled the world did so from spiritual motivations. Some fled persecution or to avoid the discharge of ruinous civic obligations.[39] But certainly after the Constantinian settlement there was a dramatic increase in the monastic movement as many Christians sought a radical and demanding discipleship.[40]

Much monastic development was inspired by the example of St. Antony. In 271, Antony had already renounced his claims to earthly wealth and sought instruction in the spiritual life. Initially, he dwelt in solitude among the tombs outside his village. Later, he retreated into the desert,[41] where thousands of women and men followed his example hoping to isolate themselves from anything that would distract them from the conquest of sensuality and union with God.[42] Gradually, as the empire of Christendom was established, the former tensions dissipated. Christians either accepted the idealism of the new dispensation in which God's kingdom and Constantine's empire were seen as one, or they renounced the world and the church of its empire. No one imagined bisociating the two.

After Athanasius wrote *The Life of St. Antony* in the fourth century, the ascetic life of the solitary became popularized as *the* choice of life for the committed Christian. Undoubtedly, this crystallized values long held in solution within the church, but the deepening dichotomy between radicalism and compromise[43] forced people to choose between one monophony and the other. And so despite a tradition that God revealed to Antony that in the city he has a spiritual equal, an ordinary layman living no less in sacrificial poverty and humility,[44] there was no suggested polyphony in which monastic disciplines might be practiced in relation with the world. Nor was

38. See Dunn, *Emergence of Monasticism*, 1–2; Burton-Christie, *Word in the Desert*, 36ff; and Chitty, *Desert a City*, 2–16.

39. Greer, *Broken Lights*, 108; and Dunn, *Emergence of Monasticism*, 2.

40. Constantine makes an easy scapegoat for lax standards in the church, but corruption was already deeply rooted in a Christian community by the time of the Council of Elvira (c. 300). See Workman, *Evolution of the Monastic Ideal*, 6, fn. 2.

41. It is unclear if Antony went there to battle the forces of evil and the flesh or seeking solitude and silence. See Hall, *Doctrine and Practice*, 174.

42. See Lawrence, *Medieval Monasticism*, 2.

43. Ford draws on Bonhoeffer to assert that a false choice arose in early monasticism between a "wrong radicalism" and a "wrong compromise." Monasticism chose a wrong radicalism that sought the ultimacy of God without an appreciation of the penultimacy of the world, while Imperial Christianity adopted a wrong compromise, celebrating the penultimate without acknowledging the priority of the ultimate. The responsible action required the bisociation the two poles of choice. Ford, *Self and Salvation*, 247.

44. Cited in Williams, *Christian Spirituality*, 97.

the material world conceived as a place redeemed in Christ and pregnant with epiphany. Monastic lives remained too conscious of themselves to seek the redemption of the world or the purification of the church;[45] their world-renouncing disciplines were undertaken for the spiritual condition of the individual. Thus, St. Antony exhorted monks,

> Just as fish die if they remain on dry land so monks, remaining away from their cells, or dwelling with men of the world, lose their determination to persevere in solitary prayer.[46]

So even as hermits began to gather in communities, each monk remained diligently separate from the others. If the community had an Abbot or Abbess, his or her counsel usually reinforced that of Abbot Allois. "Except a man shall say in his heart, I alone and God are in this world, he shall not find peace."[47] A rigorous asceticism of poverty, fasting and all night vigils were adopted to help each monk conquer the distractions of the world, the body, and the self and lead him to enlightenment. While not denying the importance of a religious vocation devoted to a life of prayer and discernment, historically it may be argued that at times the monastic vision was myopic, failing to see the world beyond itself.

Such world-renouncing individualism remained a dominant theme even as a more communal monasticism evolved. Gradually, solitaries realized that their souls could be saved from seduction and deceit only if they allowed for the presence of others who might be prepared to "undertake a drastic surgery upon the fantasizing and dominating self."[48] Communal monasticism was founded by St. Pachomius (c. 292–346). His monks shared common accommodation, prayer, and manual labor. One of the strengths of such community was the way in which its members "could sustain one another in their ascesis."[49] Community was needed, but only to perfect the individual's salvation. So while the products of their labor were sold in the market-place they remained primarily committed to withdrawing from the world and perfecting their souls.[50] Communal monasticism developed further under St. Basil (329–379). As Bishop of Caesarea, Basil later became a social reformer, but he nevertheless perpetuated the monastic antithesis to

---

45. See Workman, *Evolution of the Monastic Ideal*, 12.

46. Cited in Merton, *Wisdom of the Desert*, 32.

47. See "Apophthegmata Patrum," as cited in Lawrence, *Medieval Monasticism*, 6. The most eccentric withdrawal from the world came from Simon Stylites who lived on top of a pillar for forty-seven years.

48. Williams, *Christian Spirituality*, 98.

49. Dunn, *Emergence of Monasticism*, 27.

50. Ibid., 32.

the world. For him, the defect in the solitary life was not its negative attitude to the world but that, by definition, it provided no opportunity to fulfill the Christian commandment to love one's neighbor. "If you live alone, whose feet will you wash?"[51] The question was how a monk was to learn to perfect patience without the irritation of other people around them who might upset or resist them. This limited approach to community monasticism was later reinforced by John Cassian who stressed the monks' need for "'imperturbable peace' and 'uninterrupted prayer', the *nous* flying home to God."[52]

St. Benedict (c. 480–547) synthesized the wisdom of Basil, Cassian, and others[53] to become "the patriarch and founder of all institutes of western monachism."[54] His Rule balanced simplicity and practicality, bringing together spiritual development with the earthiness of manual labor, but while he claimed to speak of what is common, universal, and basic to all Christians, his Rule was written for and practiced by monks, not the wider church.[55] Indeed, while Benedictine monasticism as an institution was often involved in the affairs of the world, Benedict himself had taken pains to ensure that monks remained isolated from the outside world, appointing a door-keeper to minimize contact with visitors and giving the abbot charge of all contact with the outside world.[56] Too much can be made of the differences between this continental monasticism and that practiced by the Celtic monks living in the British Isles. Benedictine monasticism was not unconnected to the affairs of the world. And yet, while the penitential Celts could be as austere as any of their continental cousins, overall, their monasticism was much more interwoven with the high political intrigues of their time and the struggles of ordinary people. They were free to marry and travel in the world and did so often. Their monasteries were integrated with local communities. Significantly, Iona was one of the centers of this Celtic monasticism, but in time it was forced to retreat by the homogenizing practices established at the Synod of Whitby in 664.[57]

---

51. "Regulae Fusius Tactatae, Interrogatio VII," cited in Lawrence, *Medieval Monasticism*, 10. While Basil did not reject the vocation of a hermit he did regard the solitary as a less perfect fulfillment of the gospel.

52. "Cassian Collationes," 9.2, cited in Williams, *Christian Spirituality*, 101.

53. See "Rule of St. Benedict," in Chadwick, *Library of Western Classics*, 291–337.

54. Knowles, *Christian Monasticism*, 33.

55. That it is now a rich source for "common Christians" does not negate the point.

56. See Rule 53, Rule 56, and Rule 66, in Chadwick, *Library of Western Classics*. See also Dunn, *Emergence of Monasticism*, 124–25.

57. See Bradley, *Celtic Way*, 24–25; and *Celtic Christianity*, 25ff; and Sheldrake, *Living Between Worlds*, 12.

Benedictine monasticism was effectively universal by 818, but the monks were becoming increasingly preoccupied with spiritual concerns and less involved in the manual labor that Benedict so valued. Periods of reform from Cluny and through the Carthusians and Cistercian Orders sought to return to the original tenets of Benedict,[58] but in so doing unquestioningly retained its characteristics of a world-denouncing elite. Pope Urban II spoke of this dichotomy between church and monastery as if it were explicit in the gospel. "From the beginning the Church has always offered two types of life to her children: one to aid the insufficiency of the weak, the other to bring to perfection the goodness of the strong."[59] But by the twelfth and thirteenth centuries the laity was less satisfied with clerical authority and the wealth of ecclesiastical bodies. At this time the friars evolved as a movement that renounced the pivotal monastic principle of personal holiness nurtured in isolation in favor of a ministry to the world.[60] Gerald Arbuckle notes,

> This did not downgrade the importance of holiness, but it was to be seen now as a requirement for effective ministry to others. The friars abandoned the geographical isolation of monasteries and enclosure in order to minister especially to the new urban populations. They developed a passion for the ministry of preaching and the simplicity of the gospel: there were to be no spiritual elites in the Church, but all were called to holiness in whatever state they were living.[61]

While this brought radical discipleship out of the monastery and into the world, such prophetic movements faced a constant struggle with the forces of ecclesiastical order that seemed capable of only imagining such disciplines within traditional monasticism. For instance, the movement begun by Francis of Assisi (1182–1226) embraced voluntary poverty and sought to minister to the poor, not as many monasteries had done, from the strength of their enclosures, but to live in vulnerability among them. The world was their cloister. But while Francis captured the imagination of the people, after his death the movement became a predominantly clerical community. Parallel "second order" communities, such as the "Poor Clares" and

58. See Lawrence, *Medieval Monasticism*, Chapter 9; Knowles, *Christian Monasticism*, Chapters 8 and 12.

59. In Lozano, "Discipleship: Towards an Understanding of Religious Life," cited in Arbuckle, *From Chaos to Mission*, 20. Other movements, such as the Dominicans, replaced the elitism of monasticism with that of a celibate and mendicant clergy, again leaving Christendom with the impression that costly discipleship remained the reserve of someone other than themselves.

60. Ibid., 17.

61. Ibid.

the Beguines,[62] were similarly unable to withstand the ecclesiastical pressure to place radical discipleship within a traditional cloistered life.[63] A similar fate befell the Brethren of the Common Life, a fourteenth-century lay movement for men and women, begun by Geert de Groote. As well as embracing poverty, they practiced a life of communal prayer, individual meditation, and self-examination. However, they took no formal vows and rejected the mendicant lifestyle. Members continued to ply their trade (most often book production) to supply their meager needs, and while clergy were welcomed they were afforded equal status with others. In short, they sought to incarnate that elusive vision of living in the world but not being of it.[64] Again, such a communal group attracted the critical suspicions of the ecclesiastical establishment and after his death a more traditionally monastic community with permanent vows evolved. But they did for a while manifest the possibility of communities whose monastery was the urban neighborhood.

In Ralph Morton's reflections on the early Iona Community he quotes directly from the Brethren of the Common Life. "We are not members of an Order, but religious men trying to live in the world."[65] But a vision for a worldly monasticism found little resonance in the reformations taking place in the sixteenth century. Protestantism was ill-disposed to any form of vowed life. Luther and Calvin condemned it as an attempt at self-justification before God,[66] and monastic communities all but disappeared from the Lutheran and Reformed traditions until the mid-twentieth century.[67] Monasticism did continue in Roman Catholicism but perpetuated its otherworldly and elitist characteristics. The Jesuit movement developed a spirituality that affirmed that God was to be found in all things, not just in prayer

---

62. See Arbuckle, *From Chaos to Mission*, 26–27.

63. Clare Offreduccio joined Francis in 1212 and established a parallel community of women, but by 1219 they were obliged to accept a Rule and convent property imposed from the ecclesiastical hierarchy. See Rausch, *Radical Christian Communities*, 79ff. A "third order" was added for laypeople seeking to follow the example of St. Francis in 1289.

64. See Lawrence, *Medieval Monasticism*, 284ff.

65. Morton, *Iona Community*, 86.

66. See Biot, *Rise of Protestant Monasticism*, 7–46. Pietistic movements did grow out of Lutheranism in the seventeenth century and formed communities such as the Moravians and Herrnhutt.

67. Biot distinguishes Protestantism from Roman Catholicism, and Anglicanism, which proved more fertile for monasticism. Ibid., 5. He notes a cenobitic revival in the mid-twentieth century and specifically mentions Iona. Ibid., 105.

or the solitude of their rooms.[68] Their "world-affirming" spirituality[69] had a new asceticism that was not dependent on self-imposed austerities, but on the "rigors and hardship imposed by total dedication to an ideal of ministry in the world of ordinary people."[70] But even this perpetuated the concept of an itinerant Christian elite taking on a role on behalf of the wider church. As long as Christendom remained, the dichotomy seemed unavoidable.

Yet there are fragments of the divine melodies found within the history of monasticism that can nurture a non-elitist community with an anticipation of meeting God in the world. These fragments of epiphany can be reclaimed and performed in ways that affirm a bisociation of heaven and earth in its *cantus firmus*. They can be forged into a new monasticism that esteems worldly presence and earthly engagement. For while traditional monasticism envisioned discipleship as something practiced in freedom *from the world*, what is needed are communities that enable every Christian to live a polyphonic life that is *within* the world and *in freedom for* the world.[71]

Such an endeavor must refute a negative appraisal of the world. MacLeod often did so with a story of the electric slot machine. In funfairs there was a machine in which a person would place a coin and then hold on to a brass bar for as long as they could stand the machine's increasing voltage. MacLeod noted that if a person were properly insulated, by standing on some india-rubber or other insulating material, then the electricity had no effect, not because the machine was faulty but because the person was not earthed. He then described the incarnation as God's choosing to be earthed and argued for the church to be the extension of that incarnation.[72] The Iona Community was his attempt to incarnate such an extension, barring the cloistered life and seeking steadfastly to remain part of the world in which they found themselves and yet not be of it.[73]

Being part of the world, but not of it, was Bonhoeffer's intention for Finkenwalde. He had been impressed by the disciplines of Christian communities in England but longed for a community nurtured for worldly engagement. He wrote to Karl Friedrich,

---

68. Ignatius, "Constitutions," 228, cited in John O'Malley, "Early Jesuit Spirituality: Spain and Italy," in Dupré and Saliers, *Christian Spirituality*, 7.

69. O'Malley, "Early Jesuit Spirituality," in Dupré and Saliers, *Christian Spirituality*, 8.

70. Ibid.

71. Bonhoeffer states that God is free not "from" human beings but "for" them. Bonhoeffer, *Act and Being*, 90–91.

72. MacLeod, *We Shall Rebuild*, 92.

73. Iona Community, *Coracle*, no. 1, 12.

The restoration of the church must surely depend on a new kind of new monasticism, which has nothing in common with the old but a life of uncompromising discipleship, following Christ according to the Sermon on the Mount. I believe the time has come to gather people together and do this.[74]

Finkenwalde was not to be a retreat from the world. Christians belonged "not in the seclusion of a cloistered life but in the midst of enemies. There they find their mission, their work."[75] And it was not to be a community of the elite. The cost of discipleship learned in the community was to be available to the whole church. Bonhoeffer argued that in the past,

the expansion of Christianity and the increasing secularization of the church caused the awareness of costly grace to be gradually lost. The world was Christianized; grace became common property of a Christian world. It could be had cheaply. But the Roman church did keep a remnant of that original awareness. It was decisive that monasticism did not separate from the church and that the church had the good sense to tolerate monasticism. Here, on the boundary of the church, was the place where the awareness that grace is costly and that grace includes discipleship was preserved. . . . Monastic life thus became a living protest against the secularization of Christianity, against the cheapening of grace.[76]

But, continued Bonhoeffer,

because the church tolerated this protest and did not permit it to build up into a final explosion, the church relativized it. It even gained from the protest a justification for its own secular life. For now monastic life became the extraordinary achievement of individuals, to which the majority of church members need not be obligated. . . . The mistake was that monasticism essentially distanced itself from what is Christian by permitting its way to become the extraordinary achievement of a few, thereby claiming a special meritoriousness for itself.[77]

---

74. Letter to Karl Friedrich, dated January 14, 1935, in Bonhoeffer, *London*, 285.

75. Bonhoeffer, *Life Together*, 27.

76. Bonhoeffer, *Discipleship*, 46–47.

77. Ibid., 47. A similar analysis is found in Rausch, *Radical Christian Communities*, 187ff.

Finkenwalde was to be a place of deep inward concentration for service beyond its boundaries, not a secluded *collegium pietatis*[78] that could claim a "special meritoriousness" for itself. But while the seminary experimented with the potential of a new monasticism, Bonhoeffer's understanding of worldliness during this period was predominately negative. While his world was not one to be renounced and forgotten, it was one with which Christians were "to engage . . . in a frontal assault,"[79] "conquering territory for Christ."[80] He argued that the Finkenwalde community must follow Luther's example and return to the world, not because the world merited affirmation, but because Luther's action in rejecting a specialized monastic endeavor represented "the sharpest attack that had been launched on the world since early Christianity."[81] "What had been practiced in the special, easier circumstances of the monastic life as a special accomplishment now had become what was necessary and commanded for every Christian in the world."[82]

This antithesis to the world had not always been so clear to Bonhoeffer, nor did it prove to be long lived. His youthful theology contained an oscillating mix of positive and negative attitudes to worldliness,[83] but he had consistently believed that the church was not a consecrated sanctuary, but the world, called by God to God and anyone who would abandon the earth and flee her present distress lost their sustaining connection with the eternal and mysterious forces of God.[84] At Finkenwalde he was less optimistic about finding God in the world and portrayed the Christian community as "a sealed train passing through foreign territory."[85] At that time the world was dominated by Nazism and so it is perhaps "not surprising that in many of Bonhoeffer's assessments of the world, anything that could encourage

78. See Bonhoeffer, *Life Together*, 45.

79. Bonhoeffer, *Discipleship*, 244.

80. The language from this, page 260 of the 1959 SCM edition of *Cost of Discipleship*, is rendered less aggressively in the new edition. "The church-community has a very real impact on the life of the world. It gains space for Christ." See, Bonhoeffer, *Discipleship*, 236. While he later distanced himself from negative views of worldliness he still stood by what he had written. See letter dated July 21, 1944, in Bonhoeffer, *Letters and Papers*, 486.

81. Bonhoeffer, *Discipleship*, 48.

82. Ibid.

83. See Feil, *Theology of Dietrich Bonhoeffer*, 99ff.

84. "Basic Questions of a Christian Ethic," in Bonhoeffer, *Barcelona, Berlin, New York*, 377–78.

85. Bonhoeffer, *Discipleship*, 260. The allusion is to Lenin passing through Germany on his way from Switzerland to Russia in 1917, but also to the sealed trains travelling through the "Polish corridor" to East Prussia during the 1920s.

church leaders in their facile incensing of the Nazi altar was avoided in favour of a more counter-cultural perspective."[86]

However, even at this time there are fragments of a more positive appreciation of the world. He spoke of Christians who are so certain of their "heavenly citizenship"[87] that they are truly free to "live in the world without losing themselves in it."[88] But this was only possible in the world. While the goal of early monasticism was to know and to be known by God, it often became an exercise in discovering the true self. This goal can only be realized through a series of encounters with the otherness of God, and the otherness of the world, with creation in general and people in particular.[89] Each fresh encounter brings into sharp relief the new boundaries of the other's otherness and the boundary of a person's own self. For the individual to exist at all, Bonhoeffer argues that such "'others' must necessarily be there."[90] The otherness of every human encountered becomes "an image of the divine You."[91] Thus, Christians do not simply need other Christians to be the bearers of Christ's otherness, but the community of the whole world becomes this epiphanal bearer. Responding to Christ's *cantus firmus* with countermelodies of integrity requires "a properly orientated individuality and a genuinely responding relation."[92] This results in a conformity to Christ which is forged amidst these "dual moments of individuality and relation."[93] Such conformation to Christ can neither be an autonomous self-constitution nor a heteronymous imposition. And while monasticism rightly encouraged its adherents to pursue personal holiness by becoming more like Christ, its error was in understanding Christ-likeness as requiring separation from people and the otherness of the world. Christ is revealed in the world of which he remained both Lord and Savior. Within the Iona

86. Editor's introduction to Bonhoeffer, *Discipleship*, 16. But see also Willmer's argument that Bonhoeffer's *Discipleship* and *Life Together* should not be thought of as political resistance literature. Willmer, "Costly Discipleship," 173.

87. The phrase "heavenly citizenship," with its distinct echoes of Phil 3:20 is the translation offered by the 1959 edition of *Cost of Discipleship*, 47. In the more recent translation by Green and Kraus, the rendering "heavenly home" is less evocative. See Bonhoeffer, *Discipleship*, 55.

88. Ibid.

89. See Alistair McFadyen's helpful imagery of the sedimentation of historical relations whereby "persons are a manifestation of their relations, formed through though not simply reducible to them." McFadyen, *Call to Personhood*, 40.

90. These assertions from Chapter 2 of *Sanctorum Communio* remain at the core of Bonhoeffer's thinking throughout his life. Bonhoeffer, *Sanctorum Communio*, 51ff.

91. Ibid., 55.

92. McFadyen, *Call to Personhood*, 58.

93. Ibid., 59.

Community, similar thinking was developing, particularly under the influence of John Macmurray's philosophy of persons in relation.[94] He claimed that human life was inherently a common life and that the freedom offered to humanity in Christ is then the freedom from false and inwardly focused relationships, perhaps especially for the religious self that is preoccupied with personal and spiritual perfection.[95]

ENCOUNTERING EPIPHANIES IN THE WORLD

Bonhoeffer adopted a more positive theology of the world in the final years of his life. This may have been in some part due to his work with *Abwehr*, beyond the immediate boundaries of the church. In *Ethics* he refutes the Christendom dichotomy of secular and spiritual, and argues that Christ is the "one place in the world [where] God and humankind [are] at one."[96] Christ is Lord of the world as much as the church and might be revealed in each. This is a new understanding of worldliness; all creation carries in it the possibility of epiphany and a potential performance of the melodies of Christ. In such Christianity, the humanity of the world is not only affirmed as being its fellow humanity, but is understood as the "sacrament of our encounter with God."[97] Within this sacrament, Christians ought not to try and be more spiritual than God himself by seeking to flee the world, because it is in Christ that we see God and the world in one.[98] The world that God loves is affirmed, not as an ideal world with a perfect humanity upon it, but the real world, as it is, and as Christ is present in it. The church, Christ existing as community, is no longer understood as a religious community of worshippers of Christ, "but Christ who has taken form among human beings."[99] It is "nothing but that piece of humanity where Christ really has taken form,"[100] and so does not exist "in order to fight with the world for a piece of its territory, but precisely to testify to the world that it is still the world."[101] In Christ, the reality of God meets the reality of the world and allows us to

94. Macmurray, *Persons in Relation*, 28ff.

95. Ralph Morton notes Macmurray's importance to the early Iona Community, particularly his thought in *Clue to History*, in Morton, *Iona Community*, 54.

96. The quotation comes from a letter to Theodor Litt, cited in Feil, *Theology of Dietrich Bonhoeffer*, 139.

97. See Gorringe, *Discerning Spirit*, 74.

98. Bonhoeffer, *Ethics*, 82.

99. Ibid., 96.

100. Ibid., 97.

101. Ibid., 63.

share and participate in the melodies performed in that encounter. Thus, the task for the "worldly monastic" is to live before Jesus Christ in whom the world and God have come together, avoiding the misguided radicalism of the other-worldly isolation at the expense of this-worldly encounter and escaping the errant compromise of a this-worldly life lived bereft of any heavenly character.[102] In this understanding of the world it is a false choice to be asked to ally oneself to either the world or Christ, because that forces people to abandon one pole of the essential bisociation, either the reality of Christ or that of the world.[103] Rather, Bonhoeffer's worldliness asserts that, in Christ, there can be only one realm: in Christ the world is offered "the possibility of partaking in the reality of God and the reality of the world at the same time," but not in the one without the other.[104] As MacLeod asserted, "In the light of the Incarnation, nothing is secular," but added that we need to "handle each paper token of the seeming secular and hold it till we see its true value in the light of the glorified humanity."[105] This engaged process is vital for community because as Gorringe notes,

> There is no pure meeting with the Thou. . . . [T]here are only meetings mediated through the awkwardness of families, places of work, schools, churches, across sexual, racial and class divides, full of tensions, dislikes and misunderstandings.[106]

He adds,

> When community is understood in terms of this *process* then it becomes "sacramental" in the Augustinian sense of being a means or channel of "grace," a mediator of the forgiving, healing, restorative power of God.[107]

In *Letters and Papers from Prison*, Bonhoeffer developed his understanding of the world further arguing that worldly/human love and heavenly/divine love cannot and should not be either collapsed into one nor kept apart from each other because together they are undivided and yet

102. See Ford, *Self and Salvation*, 247.

103. Bonhoeffer argues that if forced to choose between "wanting Christ without the world or the world without Christ," humanity either deceives itself or tries to stand in both realms at once and thereby becomes people in eternal conflict. See Bonhoeffer, *Ethics*, 58.

104. Ibid., 55.

105. MacLeod, *Only One Way Left*, 161.

106. Gorringe, *Discerning Spirit*, 79.

107. Ibid.

distinct, they are "the polyphony of life."[108] That which is of heaven does not injure or weaken that which is in the world, but rather provides the *cantus firmus* around which the melodies of a fully earthly life may be gathered in counterpoint.[109] In an illuminating letter to Bethge he asserts this positive theology of worldliness:

> Redemption now means being redeemed out of sorrows, hard-ships, anxieties, and longings, out of sin and death, in a better life beyond. But should this really be the essence of the proc-lamation of Christ in the Gospels and Paul? I dispute this. The Christian hope of resurrection is different from the mythologi-cal in that it refers people to their life on earth in a wholly new way, and more sharply than the OT. Unlike believers in the redemption myths, Christians do not have an ultimate escape route out of their earthly tasks and difficulties into eternity. Like Christ ("My God . . . why have you forsaken me?"), they have to drink the cup of earthly life to the last drop, and only when they do this is the Crucified and Risen One with them, and they are crucified and resurrected with Christ. This-worldliness must not be abolished ahead of its time.[110]

Here, Bonhoeffer replaces Christianity's aversion to the world with a critique of religiosity and a positive theology of worldliness. He does so by reasserting the balance of heaven and earth that is uniquely found in Christ. The task of the Christian is to learn how to responsibly participate in per-forming these melodies of Christ in the world.

George MacLeod had come to similar conclusions in 1948. He asked,

> What really is the gospel?
>
> Is it really the declaration of a spiritual world over against a ma-terial world?
>
> Is it really that this physical world is a vale of woe, and we must keep our spirits clean so as to bear up in it and finally find free-dom in heaven?
>
> Is it that this material world is doomed to destruction, but there is a way of escape even in this life, and happy are they that find it?

---

108. Letter dated May 20, 1944, in Bonhoeffer, *Letters and Papers*, 394.
109. Ibid.
110. Letter dated June 27, 1944, in ibid., 447–48.

Is it that the physical, the earthly, is of very passing account whether it be physical bodies, or physics or bodies-politic, and that matter does not matter, while spirit matters everything?

I just cannot find it in the Bible. What I find in the Bible—which differentiates our faith from all other world religions—is precisely that *God is to be found in the material.* And that He came to redeem man, soul and body. The Gospel claims the key to all material issues is to be found in the mystery that Christ came in a body, and healed bodies and fed bodies, and that he died in a body, and rose in a body: to save man body and soul.[111]

The Christian community must therefore adopt an accountable communal discipline that embraces the worldliness of life and calls it into relationship with heaven. And if the Christian community is to offer plausible structures in which such discipleship can happen then as Andrew Walker notes, it will require something akin to "the monastery, the religious community and the sect."[112]

In the pre-Constantinian church, such discipline began in the catechumenate, a discipleship program that socialized pagans into the alternative values of gospel living. It was often analogized through the Greek concept of "askesis," a term employed for the training of athletes.[113] A spiritual askesis nurtured Christians in resisting the original temptation to place themselves in the center of existence. Communities who resist this temptation affirm Christ at the center of their church and world, in their work and their worship.[114] Peterson argues that "the most conspicuous construction of a workable *askesis* is the monastery."[115] And while he is writing primarily in terms of a discipline for pastors, only a slight variation of vocabulary is needed to render his reflections applicable to all Christians. He writes, "Pastors are not monks and do not live in monasteries," but "the only substantial difference between the monk's monastery and the pastor's parish is that the

111. MacLeod, Sermon, "The Church in the Modern World," cited in Ferguson, *Daily Readings*, 60.

112. Walker, *Telling the Story*, 190. Walker is clear that this need not necessitate exclusivism, social separatism or retreat. See 191ff.

113. See 1 Cor 9:24–27; Phil 3:12–15; 2 Tim 2:1–13; and Heb 12:1.

114. Michael Riddell argues that the church's inability to resist cultural pressures such as individualism and consumerism is due in large measure to failures in worship and community. He argues that if a community is to be Christian then it must be a community of resistance. See Riddell, *Threshold of the Future*, 154–55.

115. Peterson, *Under the Unpredictable Plant*, 98. To the "pastor's parish" we might simply add the Christian's place of daily activity.

monastery has walls and the parish does not."[116] But, continues Peterson, "walls are not the critical factor in either praying or not praying. What is critical is an imagination large enough to contain all of life, all worship and work as prayer, set in a structure (*askesis*) adequate to the actual conditions in which it is lived out."[117] Peterson's imagery of a "monastery without walls" echoes Pannikar's idea of the "monk to all the earth" and assumes that the disciplines of monasticism can be reconfigured in a this-worldly way. For as Nicholas Lash noted,

> If, in thirteenth-century Italy, you wandered around in a coarse brown gown, with a cord round your middle, your 'social location' was clear: your dress said that you were one of the poor. If, in twentieth-century Cambridge, you wander around in a coarse brown gown, with a cord round your middle, your social location is curious: your dress now says, not that you are one of the poor, but that you are some kind of oddity in the business of "religion." Your dress now declares, not your solidarity with the poor, but your amiable eccentricity.[118]

But the monastic vocation, if understood as a universal archetype for the longings of all humanity, means that the values of monasticism can be and ought to be adopted by all people, not simply a religious elite.

The three disciplines of western monasticism were the vows of poverty, chastity, and obedience,[119] understood as the responses to "worldly" values of money, sex, and power.[120] Property was forsaken through poverty, sex was renounced in celibacy and personal will was relinquished in obedience. As H. A. Williams noted in a Cambridge sermon,

> Most of you will probably have preconceived notions of what poverty, chastity and obedience mean. If so, you will almost certainly regard them as negative, kill-joy qualities by which tight-arsed old maids of both sexes try to stifle the life which is in you. Poverty, chastity and obedience, it is true, have sometimes, perhaps often, been presented in those terms because they have misused as weapons against life by those who have been too cowardly (only they think it too virtuous) to go out and

116. Ibid., 98.

117. Ibid., 98–99.

118. Lash, *Theology on the Way*, 54.

119. To this is often added the vow of stability. In the Benedictine tradition the vow of stability has accompanied those of obedience, and *conversatio morum* (a vow of openness to ongoing conversion).

120. See Foster, *Money, Sex and Power*, 2–12.

try to get a life. But it would be a pity to allow poverty, chastity and obedience to remain the illegitimate preserves of cowardly stay-at-homes, and to conclude that there was nothing more to them than those craven caricatures. For, properly understood, they are the breath of life itself.[121]

These vows need not be the traditional "no" spoken against a world perceived as evil. They can be enjoined to heaven's emphatic "yes" to the world in Christ and his calling to the church to live as alien citizens.[122] Then any "no" that is spoken is only uttered in the name of a greater "yes" for this-worldliness. Diarmuid O'Murchu is critical of the destructive reductionism and supercilious perfectionism that has virtually stripped the traditional vows "of all sense of global and earthly engagement."[123] He proposes their reappraisal within a framework that affirms the greater "yes" to the world. He writes that,

> Those called to live the vowed life are the recipients of a vocation that belongs to *all* God's people, even to those who have no explicit faith in God . . . to live out more deeply the values that all people yearn for . . . values . . . which relate to the human search for meaning.[124]

Christians accepting the responsibility of performing the melodies of these vows would then not regard themselves from a religious point of view, as specially favored, but rather as belonging wholly to the world. They would be calling the world to realize its true worldliness, understanding the world, as Bonhoeffer suggested, better than it understands itself.[125] They would do so in a new polyphony of poverty, chastity, and obedience that was reinterpreted for the world, an *askesis* that could be practiced by those who do not choose to live in a permanent residential community, who have jobs and receive income from them, who are sexually active, who have to make decisions amidst the this-worldliness of life.

The traditional vows offer a suitable access point to such an *askesis*. They arose in direct response to abuses of money, sex, and power in Christendom. Such abuse was usually a male preserve and it is clear that through the centuries many women appreciated the vows for different reasons. Their

121. Williams, *Poverty, Chastity and Obedience*, 36–37.

122. The point is reiterated in specific reference to reinterpreting the monastic vows by O'Murchu, *Poverty, Celibacy and Obedience*, 13ff.

123. Ibid., 68.

124. Ibid., 15–16.

125. Letter dated June 8, 1944, in Bonhoeffer, *Letters and Papers*, 428.

understanding of poverty, chastity, and obedience cannot be simply elided with male interpretations: for many the vowed life offered liberation from patriarchy. However, as Richard Foster notes, these issues are inseparably intertwined throughout history and were often made manifest as power. Sex is used to acquire money and power, and power is often called "the best aphrodisiac."[126] These are the false-gods of this world; expressions of "the Powers" that dominate the world and stand in opposition to the Reign of God.[127] They need to be unmasked as such, named, engaged, and redeemed to their true purpose under the Lordship of Christ.[128] To do so, Foster suggests that the traditional vows be developed into disciplines of simplicity, fidelity, and service.[129] In a similar, but more radical endeavor, O'Murchu begins by changing the preposition of monastic choice from "of" (vows of poverty, of chastity, and of obedience) in favor of vows "for."[130] Echoing the insight of Bonhoeffer's dictum that God is not *free from* the world but *free for* the world,[131] O'Murchu argues that "of" is a word that indicates how something is defined in terms of its boundaries (a glass of water) whereas the word "for" has "echoes of freedom, creativity, initiative, possibility, exploration, search and the expansion of horizons."[132] It denotes "movement, action, growth, change and possibility, but not necessarily an eventual outcome."[133] It is a move away from a set of clear cut boundaries (no wealth, no sex, no self-determination) to more open and engaged values that explore discipleship within and before the world. Living the *askesis* of such a life is quite a different invitation to keeping vows. As O'Murchu notes, keeping vows implies a holiness and individual salvation that remains at a distance from the world, whereas living the vows implies "engagement with the issues of real life."[134]

Thus, rather than a vow of poverty, which sought to detach itself from the this-worldliness of property, the Christian community might adopt a new vow for mutual sustainability in the face of global consumerism.[135] Such

---

126. Foster, *Money, Sex and Power*, 2.

127. See Keller, *Counterfeit Gods*.

128. See Wink, *Naming the Powers*. Wink does not specifically identify money, sex and power as "the Powers," of his work, but the way in which these three issues integrate around idolatrous values to form a system of domination fits with his analysis.

129. See Foster, *Money, Sex and Power*, Chapters 5, 9, and 13.

130. O'Murchu, *Poverty, Celibacy and Obedience*, 28ff.

131. Bonhoeffer, *Act and Being*, 90–91.

132. O'Murchu, *Poverty, Celibacy and Obedience*, 29.

133. Ibid.

134. Ibid., 37.

135. Ibid., 65ff.

a vow would accept the responsibility for handling personal and collective wealth conscious of both the blessings and dangers of that activity,[136] acknowledging that the poverty of traditional monasticism might be achieved but still leave an individual imprisoned by nostalgia or envy.[137] This *askesis* will probe the ethics and extent of personal and corporate ownership, not just of money, but of other material resources as well. In developing this *askesis* the community affirms the tensions between the negative and the positive characteristics of wealth in the Bible and seeks to be present in the world that handles money without being controlled by it. As a positive value lived in and for the world, this affirms that Christ is Lord of all the (limited) resources of the world.[138] As such, the Christian concern should not be about losing or acquiring these resources for themselves but ensuring that they are used for the benefit of all people.

In the mid-1980s, John Bell, Graham Maule, and voluntary staff of the Iona Community experimented with such an *askesis*.[139] They lived among the socially marginalized as mini-communities known as Columban Youth Houses. They lived in solidarity with the poor, living in the same accommodation, queuing on the same dole lines, with hopes of the same jobs. They sought to live less materialistic, simpler lives. In the midst of this they reflected:

> It has been our own repeated experience that when we give up notions of ourselves as the "givers" to the poor and get close enough to be receivers from them, two things happen. One is that the poor discover that a value is being put on their lives . . . the other . . . is that we realize the poverty of our own experience, limited as it has been by the constraints of wealth.[140]

The vow of chastity/celibacy has for centuries fallen prey to that dualism that implied that spiritual growth and bodily pleasure, particularly in sexual intercourse, were incompatible. But Christ is Lord of body and spirit and offers an abundance of life in both. Both O'Murchu and Foster propose new disciplines of fidelity in human relationships, sexual or otherwise. Both

---

136. See Foster, *Money, Sex and Power*, Chapters 2 and 3.

137. Williams makes the point that I may own nothing and yet "spend a great deal of my time either being jealous of people more affluent than myself, or lamenting the days when I was more affluent than I am now, and this would block rather than promote my growth into human selfhood." Williams, *Poverty, Chastity and Obedience*, 39–40.

138. Williams argues that "perhaps one of the greatest blessings God has bestowed upon this earth . . . is to have made its resources limited." Williams, *Poverty, Chastity and Obedience*, 38.

139. Bell and Maule, *Poverty, Chastity, Obedience*.

140. Ibid., 10.

note how the sexual act is rapidly usurping the place of God in the world by seeing itself as the purported center of human experience. This has focused humanity inwards, on the satisfaction of the individual's experience, worshipping at altars of performance and conquest, but divorced from any relational context.

While this imagery may accord with the predatory sexual activity of some men and women in the West in the twenty-first century, it is not necessarily how others, in particular how many women, now and in preceding centuries will have experienced sex. However, it is still true that in a worldly monasticism, a vow for relational fidelity would place others at the center of the human experience and thus, in otherness, find a locus for Christ. A commitment to such relational fidelity does not require the traditional celibacy. "All believers—whether male or female, whether single, married, divorced, widowed or remarried—are called to fidelity in their sexual relationships."[141] Reinterpreting the vow of celibacy in terms of related faithfulness also moves the consideration away from purely sexual matters and into faithfulness to the calling placed by God upon an individual or a community.

In this endeavor there is the need for emotional and intellectual chastity as well as its physical expression.[142] The first is concerned with Christians being faithful to their emotions, not being ruled by them but being honest about them before God and the world. The second is concerned with fidelity to our minds' ability to discern truth and authenticity. The language of Christianity must then be faithful to the world in which it is spoken and to the eternal God of whom it speaks. Bonhoeffer was aware that the church of his time had cheapened its ancient language of "reconciliation and redemption" and thus earlier words "must lose their power, be silenced."[143] What was needed was a fidelity to language, history, and present context.

The Columban Houses also reflected on what chastity meant in a worldly context. They agreed that the focus on sexual practice was an unhealthy narrowing of a discipline that was applicable to all of life.[144] They embarked upon a reassessment of the priorities revealed in their fidelity to themselves, others and God. This precipitated a deepening of personal relationships but also brought about job sharing or giving up work altogether, for others it meant deciding not to drive a car, or resolving to share their

141. Foster, *Money, Sex and Power*, 150.

142. Williams, *Poverty, Chastity and Obedience*, 55.

143. "Thoughts on the Day of Baptism of D.W.R.," May 1944, in Bonhoeffer, *Letters and Papers*, 389.

144. Bell and Maule note, "Why Chastity should be invariably connected with sex and sex alone is something of mystery." See *Poverty, Chastity, Obedience*, 11ff.

special skills or insights. For all it meant a review of leisure time, not always because they had too much of it, but because many had none.[145]

The vow of obedience stands in stark contrast to the lust for power that pervades the world from playgrounds to the UN and from transnational corporations to church leadership. Power is routinely misused so that instead of sharing strengths that enable people to live abundant lives it is used to divide and conquer. So endemic is this that Foster comments, "The very idea of somebody—anybody—having any kind of say in our lives runs so counter to everything in our society that anger and even hostility is our almost automatic response."[146] What is then required is an *askesis* that nurtures an alternative and Christ-centered obedience as the automatic response. The monastic vow of obedience was designed to reveal the monk's desire to exemplify a Christ-like laying down of self-will, emptying him or herself and becoming an obedient servant.[147] However, the obedience revealed in Jesus was not the result of a divine diktat from the Father, but was the collaborative result of freely made decisions within the life of the Trinity. To construe Christ's obedience without acknowledging the collaboration in God misunderstands how and why God became flesh. Christ gave himself to the world because of love, not out of blind submission or required service. The traditional vow of obedience risks missing this distinction. Monasticism did not replace the societal hierarchies of Christendom with a communal structure of service but rather retreated from the world and then replicated its power structures within the monastery. Bonhoeffer believed that voluntary service to one another, bearing others in their freedom, could take the place of the vow of obedience.[148] In the post-resurrection world, obedience ceases to be about submitting our will to a higher authority, "but about exploring and proffering ever new ways to engage responsibly, collaboratively, and creatively with the issues of power and powerlessness that we encounter in daily life."[149] "Obedience" becomes a discipline for "mutual collaboration"[150] with God, humanity, and creation.

In reinterpreting obedience for a this-worldly context, the Columban Houses affirmed the communal nature of their faithfulness to God. Its mutual accountability was in contrast to the prevailing individualism of contemporary society. The praxis was unpacked in each micro-community

---

145. Ibid., 15–16.

146. Foster, *Money, Sex and Power*, 10.

147. See Phil 2:1–11. See Chapters 5 and 68 of the *Rule of Benedict*.

148. Benedict, *Life Together*, 100ff.

149. See O'Murchu, *Poverty, Celibacy and Obedience*, 16.

150. Ibid., 88ff.

where four people shared a common space, domestic tasks, local responsibilities, church activity, devotional life, and personal development.[151] This
placed privacy in a communal environment and challenged each person
to accept responsibility for others. It meant having to admit their failures
in obedience to God and to others. That in turn meant taking seriously
the promise of forgiveness declared by God and the community each day.
Critically, they came to realize that no community would ever be perfect.
Bonhoeffer also realized the impossibility of perfection in community. As
he wrote from Finkenwalde,

> On innumerable occasions a whole Christian community has
> been shattered because it has lived on the basis of a wishful im-
> age. . . . But God's grace quickly frustrates all such dreams. A
> great disillusionment with others, with Christians in general
> and, if we are fortunate, with ourselves, is bound to overwhelm
> us as surely as God desires to lead us to an understanding of
> genuine Christian community. By sheer grace God will not
> permit us to live in a dream world even for a few weeks and
> to abandon ourselves to those blissful experiences and exalted
> moods that sweep over us like a wave of rapture . . .
>
> Only that community which enters into the experience of
> this great disillusionment with all its unpleasant and evil ap-
> pearances begins to be what it should be in God's sight, begins
> to grasp in faith the promise that is given to it. The sooner this
> moment of disillusionment comes over the individual and the
> community, the better for both.[152]

Those living in the Columban Houses took no vows of poverty, chastity, or obedience, but they did try and live the values behind those vows
in and for the world.[153] In their own context they captured something of
the essence of Bonhoeffer's hope for the church of the future, sharing "in
the worldly tasks of life in the community—not dominating but helping

151. There are strong parallels here with the more recent praxis of "12 marks of
a new monasticism" recounted by Jonathan Wilson-Hartgrove and the Rutba House
Community. See Wilson-Hartgrove, *New Monasticism*. The twelve marks of their new
monastic living are noted above. See also Mobsby and Berry, *New Monastic Handbook*,
4.

152. Bonhoeffer, *Life Together*, 35. Kathy Galloway recalls a similar event in a housing scheme in Edinburgh. With the worshiping community in disarray there came a
critical moment when they realized they must live with "the community we actually
had and not with our agenda for community." See Galloway, "Put Your Hand in My
Side," 14.

153. The nomenclature indicates how these projects owed their origin to the
disciplines of St. Columba. See Adomnan, *Life of St. Columba*.

and serving,"[154] and never underestimating "the significance of human example."[155] They were hidden in the midst of the world, with nothing to distinguish them or their home from the surrounding culture except the nature of their living, which was shaped by a rhythm of regular worship, reflection, and involvement in projects within the wider community.

This type of worldly *askesis* is incorporated in various ways in the disciplines of the Iona Community, particularly in their reinterpretation of stability. This lay at the core of Benedictine monasticism. It required the monk to commit to the same place and community for the remainder of their life. This was designed to empower the life of continual conversion and offered a communal accountability to that process. The holiness envisaged by Benedict is inseparable from the common life with others as governed by the Rule; thus the workshop of Rule and Common Life becomes the very stability of the community.

The Iona Community share such a vision as part of their daily office, but extend the boundaries of the workshop beyond their neo-monastic community to include the presence and handling of these tools within the world. The prayer says,

> O Christ, the Master Carpenter, who at the last through wood and nails, purchased our whole salvation, wield well your tools in the workshop of your world, so that we who come rough hewn to your bench may here be fashioned to a truer beauty of your hand.[156]

In this way the community becomes the workshop wherein Christians learn to handle the tools of spiritual *askesis*, and as Rowan Williams notes, for the seasoned worker such tools become the "extension of the hand,"[157] and the performance of a worldly *askesis* becomes for the Christian "an extension of their bodies and words that they no longer notice."[158]

Accountability remains important in a this-worldly expression of new monasticism. Bonhoeffer emphasized the need for each member to bear the burden of the other by "tolerating the reality of the other's creation by God—affirming it, and in bearing with it, breaking through to delight in

---

154. "Outline for a Book," in Bonhoeffer, *Letters and Papers*, 503.

155. Ibid.

156. Iona Community, *Iona Abbey Worship Book*, 19.

157. The allusion to the seasoned worker comes from Simone Weil. See Williams, "God's Workshop." http://rowanwilliams.archbishopofcanterbury.org/articles.php/654 /shaping-holy-lives-a-conference-on-benedictine-spirituality.

158. Ibid.

it."[159] He acknowledged that there were times when the community must "admonish one another to go the way Christ bids [them] to go."[160] For "nothing can be more cruel than that leniency which abandons others to their sin" and "nothing can be more compassionate than that severe reprimand which calls another Christian in one's community back from the path of sin."[161] But valuable as such bearing one another is, few people in today's mobile world seek such accountability in a traditional monastic community. However, a community Rule such as that practiced by the members of the Iona Community can provide a stabilizing *askesis* appropriate for a this-worldly discipleship. Members find a stability in their practice of a common *askesis* provided through the Rule. Indeed, Norman Shanks, a former leader of the Iona Community, draws specific attention to the attraction exercised by the Community's Rule in offering members the "possibility of discipline in highly pressurised lives."[162] In such a community not all members express their *askesis* in an identical fashion, for there will be a polyphony of as many countermelodies as there are personalities and contexts of expression. But still, there is a unity through the Rule.

The goal of Iona members is not the traditional vowed life itself, or indeed the purity of the Rule, but the performance of a polyphonic counterpoint that bears witness in the world as to how the church and world might be if Christ were allowed to truly take form within it. From the beginning MacLeod argued that the Iona Community was

> an exceedingly calculated movement within the normal purpose of the Church. Poverty is not our aim, far less is the principle of Celibacy involved. Those who come here will claim no "sacrifice"; we only claim a privilege to make perhaps the sacrifice of those who work in really difficult places a little less acute.[163]

And a mark of the community's "worldliness" was detected from the beginning.

> Evening Worship on that first night in the half light of a dying day was our first confirmation that the thing would go on. Some folk from the island, visitors and residents, came and by their presence there symbolised, from its very inception, the truth

---

159. Bonhoeffer, *Life Together*, 101.

160. Ibid., 104.

161. Ibid., 105.

162. Shanks, *Iona—God's Energy*, 65.

163. Iona Community, *Coracle*, no. 2, 18.

that this was no "community apart" but an experiment within the world community as it is.[164]

Although Iona members have never taken vows of poverty, chastity or obedience, they have in the Rule a common and worldly discipline that seeks to express the values of simplicity, fidelity, and service and to do so in a way that reveals how "work and worship, prayer and politics, sacred and secular" are all one under the Lordship of Christ.

As noted earlier, the Rule begins with a commitment to daily devotions, requiring Bible reading, prayer, and intercession for named community members, areas of concern and countries around the world. The same prayers are included in the morning worship on Iona.

The second melody of the Rule deals with accountability in personal economics. MacLeod and the community knew how easy it was for the church to preach about the responsible use of money. They also knew how difficult it was to achieve and how easy it was to avoid examination by others. In 1943, Lex Miller developed an economic discipline in which members committed to give 5 percent of their income to the church and 5 percent to the community. An alternative devised by Jenny Morton was later implemented[165] and the current economic discipline involves an agreement of individual "baseline commitments, special circumstances and expenses," after which the accountability can be as rigorous and flexible as those involved choose to make it. However, Miller's early work precipitated many searching discussions concerning personal finance and his influence has meant that the community has never disregarded their accountability to one another.

A third "melody" of the Rule is a member's commitment to account for their use of time. This began in the conversations between the first men to work on the abbey reconstruction. The clergy conceded that unlike the craftsmen they were accountable to no one as to how they spent their day. Lazy ministers might delude themselves as to their industry while a workaholic pastor could leave no time for relaxation. The remedy was a discipline of accountability in which members are to plan their time in such a way that proper weighting is given, not simply to work, but equally to leisure, to time for family, to developing skills, or acquiring new ones, to worship and devotion, to voluntary work—and to sleep![166]

164. Iona Community, *Coracle*, no. 1, 6.

165. Ralph Morton subsequently wrote a book in which he explained the necessity for some economic discipline to be adopted in the church. See *Household of Faith*, 114ff.

166. See Appendix A, *"Rule of the Iona Community."* This is in effect a "chastity of time."

The importance of this *askesis* was noted by Ralph Morton:

> But the determining factors in any discipline, especially for a group of men [*sic*] who have not given up their individual responsibilities in family, work and society, are the use of time and money. We see this from the two unanswerable excuses that people give: "I haven't the time" and "I can't afford it." For time and material possessions are the only things that are ours to use. Our use of them determines how we live. In a convent or a religious order use of time and money is taken care of. In secular life they are matters of thoughtless convention or of every-day decision. In the discipline of a society like the Iona Community they must always remain central and matter for unending discussion.[167]

Attendant on this accountability was the discipline of meeting together in local family groups and together in plenary. The family groups (comprising between seven and fourteen people) usually meet monthly and each year the whole community meets for weekend plenary sessions and a "community week" on Iona. Additionally, at the beginning of each year members return a "with-us" card indicating their ongoing commitment to follow the Rule, together with a personal assessment of how they have maintained their discipline in the previous year.

In 1966, the Rule was expanded to include a commitment to work for peace and, as the community realized that one could not be achieved without the other, it soon amended the Rule further to reflect a need to work for justice in the world. This is the most detailed aspect of the Rule and while it strives to offer a comprehensive praxis, its most arresting provision remains the statement that "our act of commitment on justice and peace is . . . a point of departure. It will remain no more than a pious hope (and a false witness) unless we seek, separately and together, to put it into practice."[168] Norman Shanks comments that "it is this commitment that in many people's eyes gives the community its distinctiveness, in not just believing that peace and

---

167. See Morton, *Iona Community*, 44–45.

168. See Appendix A, "Rule of the Iona Community." For a detailed and personal reflection on the nature of the Iona Community Rule see Galloway, *Living By the Rule*. Tellingly here, Kathy Galloway cites with approval the comments made by fellow community member Alison Swinfen, "The Rule is, for us, a source of freedom and, in its outworking, contains something of our prophetic edge. It is not so much that I keep the Rule, as that the Rule keeps me." Galloway, *Living By the Rule*, 23. The Rule was updated in 2015, see Appendix A.

justice are 'good things' but being prepared, within a framework of mutual accountability, to do something about it."[169]

The Rule, which addresses both the spiritual and the worldly, enables the community to live out the tensions of alien citizenship in the church and world. In so doing, the community becomes akin to a colony of heaven in the world, a metaphor that itself requires further investigation.

169. Shanks, *Iona—God's Energy*, 69.

Chapter 6

The Colony of Heaven

But we are a colony of heaven, and we wait for the Savior
who comes from heaven, Lord Jesus Christ.

—Phil 3:20[1]

Like Ulysses bound to the mast, Christians are freed from the lethal
effects of the old songs of custom and idolatry and able to join in the
harmony of the New Song, the harmony that ordered Creation and
now brings the order of Redemption.

—Rowan A. Greer[2]

For if we are set upon being citizens here,
we shall be so neither here nor there
but if we continue to be sojourners,
and live in such wise as sojourners ought to live in,
we shall enjoy the freedom of citizens both here and there.

—John Chrysostom[3]

1. Moffatt, *The Bible: James Moffatt Translation*, 293.

2. Greer, *Broken Light and Mended Lives*, 146–47.

3. Homily 16 on 2 Cor, in "A Select Library of Nicene and Post-Nicene Fathers of
the Christian Church," cited in Greer, *Broken Light and Mended Lives*, 154.

The books or the music in which we thought the beauty was located
will betray us if we trust to them; it was not *in* them, it only came
through them, and what came through them was longing. . . . If they
are mistaken for the thing itself, they turn into dumb idols, breaking
the hearts of their worshippers. For they are not the thing itself;
they are only the scent of a flower we have not found, the echo of
a tune we have not heard, news from a country we have never yet
visited. . . . Heaven is, by definition, outside our experience, but all
intelligible descriptions must be of things within our experience.

—C. S. LEWIS[4]

A further metaphor through which the character of Christian community might be understood is that of the "colony of heaven."
Again this metaphor makes no claim to exclusivity and asks only
that it be mixed with the other melodies of investigation adopted so far
and gathered around Christ's polyphonic *cantus firmus*. But the colony of
heaven does invoke an image of how the Kingdom of God may be located
upon the earth, how Christ is bisociated on earth as he is in heaven, how the
church participates in the melodies of God amidst the world.

THE BIBLICAL COLONY

The idea of the church as a colony of heaven is noted in the New Testament,
but despite this authority, it has not often captured the imagination of the
historical Christian community. It seems to have been invoked first by Paul
in his letter to the Philippians. There he exhorts the church that "if they
have any encouragement from being united with Christ," then they should
regard themselves as "a colony of heaven."[5] Most English translations render
this as an encouragement for the church there to consider "their citizenship
to be in heaven," but Paul chooses the Greek word *politeuma* to describe
this "citizenship relationship" between the earthly Christian community
and their belonging to heaven. The word is not used elsewhere in the New
Testament and while the translation of it into English as "citizenship" or

4. Lewis, *Weight of Glory*, 30–31, 33.

5. Phil 3:20, in Moffatt, *The Bible: James Moffatt Translation*, 293. The tension of
Christians as being alien citizens in the world is widely expressed in the writings of the
early church. See John 17:11–19; Rom 13:1–8; 1 Cor 5:9–13; Gal 4:26; Heb 12:22–24;
and 1 Pet 2:11–17. And see Greer, *Broken Light and Mended Lives*, 141ff.

"commonwealth" is accurate it does not capture the contextual richness of Paul's deliberate choice of vocabulary.[6] His use of *politeuma* is an appropriation of a term that owes its origins to the language of the sociopolitics of the Roman Empire. The political imagery was deliberate;[7] *politeuma* was used to describe an outlying colony of Rome. Philippi was such a colony,[8] an *ius italicum*.[9] The populations of such "colony cities" were not made up of conquered peoples but instead housed Roman citizens, often retired soldiers who had, through service, earned their citizenship.[10] There were similar outposts of "Little Rome" established throughout the empire and their purpose was to establish centers of Roman custom and law. J. C. Carlile notes that

> the colonists . . . reproduced the social order, the religion and all that came in their train as they existed in imperial Rome. The colony was a witness to something greater than itself. It was but a fragment, but it represented the whole. It possessed an importance not simply for what it was, but that for which it stood.[11]

If we think of each of the Roman colonies as a distinct refrain, we can see how it was possible to discern from them the symphony of the empire

6. Ketcherside notes various attempts to render *politeuma* as "empire," "realm," "common life," "free citizens of heaven," and "form of government," but concludes that none is as satisfactory as "colony of heaven." Ketcherside, *Colony of Heaven*, 135. Carlile cites Dr. MacLaren as first suggesting that *politeuma* might best be understood as "colony" and credits Moffatt's translation with giving "play to the sanctified imagination, without which accurate translation is impossible" to render it a colony of heaven. See Carlile, *Colony of Heaven*, 1–2. See also Banks, *Paul's Idea of Community*, 39–41.

7. See Kraus, *Community of the Spirit*, 88–89.

8. See Acts 16:12. Barth disputes the translation of *politeuma* as a colony and draws on the translation of the verb *politeuesthai* in Phil 1:27 to translate 3:20 as citizenship in heaven. Barth, *Epistle to the Philippians*, 114. Martin notes possible alternatives but suggests that Paul is "consciously reflecting on the civic statutes of Philippi as a Roman colony." Martin, *New Century Bible Commentary*, 147.

9. *Ius italicum* was the highest legal privilege obtainable by any provincial municipality and extended to its citizens identical rights and privileges to those born in the imperial capital. See Hawthorne, *Philippians*, 170.

10. A city of foreigners who were adopted under the standard of Rome after being subjugated was called a *municipium*, not a *colonia*. Philippi, a colony, was composed principally of Roman citizens, primarily military men and their families, who were transplanted to protect and defend the interests of Rome. See Martin, *New Century Bible Commentary*, 147.

11. Carlile, *Colony of Heaven*, 3. William Barclay makes the same point, "The great characteristic of these Roman colonies was that, wherever they were, they remained fragments of Rome. . . . No matter where they were . . . these colonies remained unshakably and unalterably Roman." Barclay, *Letters to Philippians*, 85–86.

and the character of its *cantus firmus*. By referring to the Philippian church as a "colony of heaven," Paul encouraged the Christians at Philippi to draw positive parallels between the kingdom of heaven and the empire. They were encouraged to participate in the performance of customs and freedoms that came not from Rome, but from heaven through Jesus Christ. As an alien colony, they were "mandated to carry out the instructions of the home [i.e., heavenly] government" and, as with other colonies, this would often place them "in tension and even open conflict with purely secular loyalties, methods and goals."[12] The authority for the colony did not come from the surrounding culture but from heaven. Colony living was a conscious witness to something both among and beyond itself: the kingdom of heaven that had come among them in Christ and which paradoxically was yet to be fulfilled in the Parousia.[13] The Christian colony would confess the "now and not yet" character of living in but not being of the dominantly pagan world. So while the Roman colony maintained the *Pax Romana* in anticipation of receiving the emperor, Paul encourages the Philippian Christians to analogous tasks: to propagate the peace and justice of heaven in anticipation of the return of Christ.

In adopting the metaphor of a colony, Paul may also have been drawing parallels to those who were part of the Jewish diaspora scattered throughout Asia who were granted permission by the Romans to live

> a more or less independent existence as small colonies surrounded by ethnologically different populations. He [Paul] knew that the Jews made up their πολιτεύματα wherever they settled and that they were permitted to live according to their own laws and follow their own religious practices.[14]

Stanley Hauerwas and William Willimon refer to Paul's colonial metaphor and draw specific lessons for the Christian community from its Jewish cousins in dispersion. These "resident aliens" had to learn how to "stake out a living on someone else's turf," singing Zion's songs "in a land that didn't know Zion's God."[15] Hauerwas and Willimon develop the imagery arguing that

12. See Kraus, *Community of the Spirit*, 99.

13. The phrase "colony of heaven" draws Christian community into an eschatological awareness that they belong "both to a heavenly Church that is permanently in session and to a local Church that, though it meets regularly, is intermittent in character." Banks, *Paul's Idea of Community*, 41.

14. Hawthorne, *Philippians*, 171.

15. Hauerwas and Willimon, *Resident Aliens*, 11–12.

a colony is a beachhead, an outpost, an island of one culture
in the middle of another, a place where the values of home are
reiterated and passed on to the young, a place where the distinctive language and life-style of the resident aliens are lovingly
nurtured and reinforced.[16]

However, Paul wants to make a definite theological distinction between the historical Jewish and the evolving Christian colonies. Hawthorne
asserts:

Paul believed that these Jews, irrespective of what they themselves might have speculated about themselves, belonged only
to colonies that were linked to Palestinian Jerusalem, earthbound, time-bound colonies without any enduring quality. By
contrast, he says that Christians are a colony of heaven, living
here on earth, to be sure, but belonging to a heavenly city that
is enduring.[17]

So if Paul did have Jewish colonies in mind when writing to Philippi,
then he would have been keen to distance the church from Jews who already
thought of themselves as "a heavenly community on earth" with no need for
any "future hope."[18] In effect, by selecting the term "colony of heaven," Paul
specifically refutes any influence of those who might wish to collapse the
bisociative and eschatological tensions of living in the "now and not yet,"
a tension that should in fact characterize the Christian colony. The citizens
of Philippi knew that while the colony must remain distinctively Roman,
it would nonetheless have to engage with the surrounding culture. Carlile
argues that Paul's image of the church as colony will not tolerate a separatist
ekklesia but rather notes that those in the colony are called to

a strenuous life, challenging the world for an ideal which had
never been attained. They were the representatives of another
order, the citizens of a better country, whose business it was not
to flee from the sinful world, but to introduce into it a new way
of life—a higher social state.[19]

Hauerwas and Willimon agree, but warn:

To be resident but alien is a formula for loneliness that few of
us can sustain. Indeed, it is almost impossible to minister alone

16. Ibid., 12.

17. Hawthorne, *Philippians*, 171.

18. Martin, *New Century Bible Commentary*, 147.

19. Carlile, *Colony of Heaven*, 2.

because our loneliness can too quickly turn into self-righteous-
ness or self-hate. Christians can survive only by supporting one
another through the countless small acts through which we tell
one another we are not alone, that God is with us.[20]

It is to counter the isolation of ministering alone that Christians are
called to belong in community, through small acts of encouragement to
be together in the colony of heaven made manifest on earth. In the midst
of a contemporary western culture that is not always attuned to melodies
of God's kingdom, the existence of the colony gives a place of belonging
wherein Christ's melodies may be repeated and affirmed.

COLONIES AT FINKENWALDE AND IONA

In an early radio broadcast, MacLeod specifically chose the image of the
Christian colony to describe what he had been attempting on Iona with his
experimental community.[21] In his book *We Shall Rebuild*, he argued that
"this or that local congregation . . . is an embassy in an alien land, representing the dictates of the King to whose heavenly court we already belong."
He continued, "Like this world's embassies, which used to be built actually
on soil carried from the home country, our very church buildings are, so
to say, built on heavenly soil."[22] Bonhoeffer similarly said, "Here on earth,
the church-community lives in a foreign land. It is a colony of strangers far
from home."[23] He understood this to be central to the character of the Finkenwalde community, which he described as a "peculiar people"[24]—people
who "cannot conform to the world because their concern is the [peculiar]
perisson,"[25] the extraordinary life that is found only in Christ.

While Bonhoeffer worked on the nature of community at Finkenwalde
and MacLeod experimented with similar aims on Iona, they both recognized that the Christian colony was not so much about the place as it was
about the people. The community exists whether its members are gathered
together or scattered apart because each individual belongs to Christ and
participates in performing his polyphony. In each individual fragment,
something of the greater whole and of its *cantus firmus* can be discerned.

20. Hauerwas and Willimon, *Resident Aliens*, 12–13.

21. MacLeod, "Abundant Life," 126.

22. MacLeod, *We Shall Rebuild*, 29.

23. Bonhoeffer, *Discipleship*, 250.

24. Ibid., 144.

25. Ibid.

The colony has no fixed abode but the melodies of its people can, for a time, be gathered in one place; its purpose being to offer to God's people an outpost of heaven in the world. Gathering in this outpost brings into one space the fragmented epiphanies of Christ that each person has encountered in their mix of work and worship. The colony is an earthbound locus in which the fragments of Christ's epiphany come together as one.

There is an undoubted strength to be found in such a gathering. Together, its people share in the "alien righteousness" of Jesus Christ and participate and perform the melodies of Christian discipleship. The melodies of such alien righteousness do not transform humanity into the divine, but do take them up into the polyphony of the Christ who became human, and so enable them to be transformed into the fullness of human community.[26] The benefit of gathering these melodies in the colony were readily apparent to Bonhoeffer who joined with the Psalmist in proclaiming, "How very good and pleasant it is when kindred live together in unity."[27] However, the people who gather into the Christian colony do not do so simply to experience the unmediated joy of being together, or to escape there from the hazards of the world. The colony is established so that Christ may be known in the people, strengthening their hearts and minds, enabling them to participate in the melodies of heaven through times of isolation, vulnerability, and attack. Such times are not only inevitable, but are an inherent part of being Christian. As Christ lives in the midst of the world, so Christians do not belong "in the seclusion of a cloistered life," but ought to be found "in the midst of enemies."[28]

At the seminary in Finkenwalde, Bonhoeffer and the students knew firsthand about living amidst the enemy and how difficult it was to sing the Lord's song in the foreign land of the Nazi regime. The Confessing Church was already under attack from the Third Reich and the support of the community was vital if Christians were to continue to perform the polyphony of Christ after they left the seminary. Finkenwalde was to be a colony in which the melodies of heaven were reinforced. Bonhoeffer organized "retreats" uniting the incoming seminarians with those who had just finished.[29] He did so with the deliberate hope "of influencing the spirit of the new candidates from the outset."[30] He dedicated a chapter of *Life Together* to the prac-

---

26. See Bonhoeffer, *Ethics*, 96.

27. Ps 133:1, as cited in Bonhoeffer, *Life Together*, 27.

28. Bonhoeffer, *Life Together*, 27.

29. He organized five such retreats between April 1936 and June 1938. See Bethge, *Dietrich Bonhoeffer: A Biography*, 518.

30. Ibid., 517.

tice of living with others and bearing their burdens and sent regular letters to those who had left to enter ordained ministry. Even they were expected to gather together again. To be absent from the seminary's reunion was almost inexcusable. Bonhoeffer wrote, "I probably don't need to remind you that we committed ourselves to this meeting when we left one another. . . . Whoever thinks he doesn't need to attend, please write me immediately so I can convince him that he does have to come."[31]

The colony of Finkenwalde was always about preparing Christians to sing the melodies of God beyond its boundaries and in vicarious solidarity (*stellverter*) for the world. Bonhoeffer reminded his students that the Christian could not take for granted the privilege of living among other Christians, but even when scattered they would remain held together in Jesus Christ alone, "having become one because they remember *him* in the distant lands, spread out among the unbelievers."[32] And as Christ had acted vicariously toward humanity and granted us an "alien righteousness,"[33] so too the church, his body, was to continue to act vicariously on behalf of others; to do as a colony of people upon the earth as it is done by God in heaven.

The colony of the Iona Community served the same purpose. MacLeod reflected that, for them, it was what was done in the city parishes, in the modern situation, that drew them together for a period on the island, "to set our compass and intensively experience in Work and Worship the Redeemed Community that we would preach."[34] So while during the summer months they celebrated how "good and pleasant it was to live together in unity," for the rest of the year the community was geographically fragmented, each member detached from the others as lone voices seeking to perform the melodies of the colony in "alien" parishes.

But the members were no idealized body of men living out a wishful image. They quickly experienced what Bonhoeffer refers to in *Life Together* as "the great disillusionment,"[35] that moment which shatters each person's imagined perfections of a community. Such "disillusionment" enables the members of a community to leave behind the dream of idealism and enter the reality that God is calling into being. The members of Iona became part of a true community as much in the communal nature of their disagreements

---

31. Ibid.

32. Bonhoeffer, *Life Together*, 28.

33. Bonhoeffer specifically refers to an "alien righteousness," that comes from "outside of us (extra nos)." *Life Together*, 31, fn. 10.

34. MacLeod, *We Shall Rebuild*, 5.

35. Bonhoeffer, *Life Together*, 35.

as in their prayers.[36] Many of those disagreements were between its founder and the capable men who joined him in his experiment. MacLeod's idealism dominated the community in the early years and his dreams of uniting everyone behind "a demanding common task" (usually one of his discerning) had to be balanced with the gentle and deeper reflection of Ralph Morton.

> For we are not trying to build community. We can never do that. God sets us in community and it is man's sin that he is always breaking it. God has set us in inescapable community, in our family, in our neighbourhood, in all the relationships with others that life brings.[37]

Christian community is not an ideal to be realized, but rather a "reality created by God in Christ in which [the people] may participate."[38]

The reality of participating in the performance of the music of community into which God had already called them remained the task of the colony members even as they were scattered throughout the parishes of Scotland. Each was an ambassador of Christ, a performer of his melodies and a member of the Christian colony. Years after founding the Iona Community, MacLeod specifically invoked the metaphor of the "colony of heaven" to explicate his thoughts on the experiment.

> Now (in earthly parable) we know the duty of an ambassador; it is to represent the King, to care for his nationals and to spread his country's ideals in a foreign land. Equally we know the peculiar vantage of an embassy in foreign lands. It is recognised as a piece of British ground: the foreigner cannot enter it: it is an island of home in the midst of an alien people. . . . We are a colony of heaven; in the world but not of it; pledged to be the ambassadors of Christ.[39]

---

36. Bonhoeffer criticized those who demand that their idealized community be fulfilled by God, others and by themselves as if their visionary ideal binds the people together. Bonhoeffer, *Life Together*, 36. It would not be inappropriate to suggest that these criticisms could, on occasion, be leveled at MacLeod. For all his vision, determination and pastoral sensitivity, MacLeod was undeniably autocratic and could quickly run roughshod over the opinions of others. The first member to leave the community informed MacLeod that he should have called it "I own a Community." See Ferguson, *Chasing the Wild Goose*, 63. John Harvey, a former leader of the Iona Community and warden of the abbey has noted in correspondence with the writer that he also, on occasion, fell victim to the dangers of imposing his "personal blueprint for community" upon others.

37. Morton, *Household of Faith*, 122.

38. Bonhoeffer, *Life Together*, 38.

39. MacLeod, "Abundant Life," 126.

Sustaining the melodies of the colony needed times of reflection and refreshment: occasions when the people might gather together the fragmented melodies of Christ's revelation in the life of world and church. These were the times in which epiphanal melodies could be listened to, affirmed, and participation in the purposes of God discerned. They facilitated accountability and encouragement in discipleship, acknowledging that it is only in this gathered colony of others that the epiphanal fragments could be woven into a polyphony of life that renews and sustains the members for their life as ambassadors of heaven engaging with the world.

Both Bonhoeffer and MacLeod realized the paradigm of Christendom was in decline. Institutional churches of the West had imagined themselves not as a colony of resident aliens amidst a foreign land, but as co-rulers of the world, in cooperation with the benign power of states, co-governing a world of two kingdoms. But the state no longer welcomed the church and the church had too easily acceded ground to secularism, accepting their role to be concerned with piety not politics. There was, as Bonhoeffer said, "little ground under their feet."[40] The *cultus* of Christendom had been rendered faulty "by the shifting of the subsoil of this evolving world"[41] and as Karl Barth noted, what the world needed was "not to be confirmed and strengthened by another variation of its own way, but to be pointed beyond it in unambiguous practice."[42]

It was the task of the colony to stand in deputyship for the world, in "unreserved participation in its situation"[43] and in unambiguous performance of heaven's polyphony to direct the world toward its *cantus firmus*. But to do so there was a desperate need for some new theologically firm ground on which such a truly heavenly colony might be built. The Christian community needed to rediscover the *cantus firmus*, upon which his peculiar people might participate in the polyphony of Christ, performing the Lord's song in an alien land. The Christian colony was divinely created through God's revelatory action in Jesus Christ, concretely existing as a community located in humanity, with an ethical responsibility to be a realization of the will of God. It is both a means to an end and an end to itself: it exists to do God's will, while at the same time, is in itself a performance of that

---

40. Bonhoeffer, *Letters and Papers*, 38.

41. George MacLeod, in a private paper to the Iona Cathedral trustees in 1938, cited in Ferguson, *Chasing the Wild Goose*, 52.

42. Barth, *Church Dogmatics* 4.3.2, 779.

43. Ibid., 773ff. Bonhoeffer wrote that "since we know ourselves to be accepted and borne within the humanity of Jesus, our new humanity now also consists in bearing the troubles and sins of all others. The incarnate one transforms his disciples into brothers and sisters of all human beings." Bonhoeffer, *Discipleship*, 285.

will: a perpetual and ontological epiphany of earth participating in heaven's polyphony.

There is, of course, a danger that members of the Christian colony will misunderstand the purposes of heaven and seek to collapse the bisociative tension between heaven and earth, the "now and the not yet," hoping to make concrete and audible on the earth the extraordinary melodies of heaven. The jeopardy in this is that the Christian community then establishes boundaries that separate themselves from the world, boundaries that it must guard and protect. In detaching from the world the Christian community ceases to be a faithful witness to the world and can no longer act in vicarious responsibility for its people. In refusing to accept the tensions that exist in Christ's bisociative belonging in heaven and the world, they absent themselves from both and are no longer aliens at all. The colony can no longer offer the fullness of life to the world because it is no longer relationally amidst its people. As Ketcherside notes, "There is a difference in 'the life of the church' and the community of the Life."[44] The Christian colony can be no more than that "part of humanity in which Christ has really taken form."[45] As Bonhoeffer concluded in his *Ethics*,

> In Christ we are invited to participate in the reality of God and the reality of the world at the same time, the one not without the other. The reality of God is disclosed only as it places me completely into the reality of the world. But I find the reality of the world always already borne, accepted and reconciled in the reality of God.[46]

Participating in the life of the Christian colony is then "the essential preliminary to Christian conduct . . . [because it] enlivens the meaning of the two great duties that are demanded of Christians—our duty to God, and our duty to our neighbor."[47] Both duties are melodies that interact around the community's confession of Christ as the *cantus firmus*, both of the church and of the world. "The Church becomes the home of the colony of heaven; the embassy building of the King of Kings; the earthly home of God: and we, as ambassadors of Christ, assemble there from our work in the world, to proclaim our allegiance; to receive fresh instructions; and to go out into the alien world more conscious of our real citizenship."[48]

---

44. Ketcherside, *Colony of Heaven*, 8.

45. Bonhoeffer, *Ethics*, 97.

46. Ibid., 55.

47. MacLeod, "Abundant Life," 127.

48. Ibid., 128.

CONFESSING CHRIST IN THE COLONY

For Bonhoeffer, the idea of the church as a confessing people was a vital one. It was because of his confession of Christ that, in 1933, he was at the forefront of opposition to Nazi legislation that excluded those of Jewish descent from public office. He was among the first to realize that a church that excluded the Jews could no longer be the church:[49] its boundaried exclusivity rendered illegitimate any claim it may have had to be a genuine colony of heaven. In July 1933, on the morning of church elections in which the *Deutsche Christen* took control of key ecclesiastical positions, Bonhoeffer preached about the rock against which the gates of hell could not prevail and exhorted: "'but you, my church, confess, confess, confess.' . . . Christ alone is your Lord; by his grace alone you live, just as you are. Christ is building."[50] In the critical time of September 1933, when many of the delegates at the General Synod of the Prussian Church appeared in Nazi uniforms and had endorsed the Aryan legislation, Bonhoeffer wrote to Barth seeking advice concerning a *status confessionis* in Germany.[51] Barth had previously argued that if the church were to adopt the Aryan clause it would cease to be a Christian church. Bonhoeffer was sure that the Aryan incursions had precipitated a *status confessionis*: a point at which Christians must confess their allegiance to Christ and their separation from the Nazi apostasy. Although Barth counseled that Bonhoeffer and others should wait until they were expelled, this marked the beginning of the Confessing Church in Germany.

And, drawing on the experience of that Confessing Church, John Howard Yoder has made a powerful argument for the *status confessionis* to represent a new and radical norm for the church.[52] Yoder claimed that while the early church was a confessing one, two other forms of church evolved under the Constantinian framework, namely the "activist church" and the "conversionist church." Neither of these are an adequate witness to a people who seek to be a colony of heaven. Significantly, Hauerwas and Willimon draw on Yoder's work for their own reflections on the church as a colony of resident aliens.[53] They note that the activist form of church is "more concerned with the building of a better society than with the reformation of the church," hoping to glorify God through the "humanization of social structures" and encouraging its members to "join in movements for justice

49. See Bethge, *Dietrich Bonhoeffer: A Biography*, 272ff.

50. Sermon, July 23, 1933, in Bonhoeffer, *Berlin*, 481.

51. Letter to Karl Barth, September 9, 1933, in Bonhoeffer, *Berlin*, 164–65.

52. Yoder, "A People in the World," in Garrett, *Concept of the Believers' Church*, 252–83.

53. Hauerwas and Willimon, *Resident Aliens*, 45.

wherever they find them."[54] They distinguish this from the conversionist form of church which, they suggest, argues that "no amount of tinkering with the structures of society will counter the effects of human sin. . . . The sphere of political action is shifted . . . from without to within, from society to the individual soul."[55] But, "[b]ecause this church works only for inward change, it has no alternative social ethic or social structure of its own to offer the world" and degenerates into "a religiously glorified conservatism."[56]

In reflecting on the nature of the Christian community as a colony of heaven, Hauerwas and Willimon argue for a confessing form of church. This would not be "a synthesis of the other two approaches . . . [but] rather . . . is a radical alternative . . . that finds its main political task to lie, not in the personal transformation of individual hearts or the modification of society, but rather in the congregation's determination to worship Christ in all things."[57] As Barth similarly argued, Christ awakens them as a community to confess him and gives himself to be known by the community so they may confess him.[58]

In a critical passage, Hauerwas and Willimon continue,

> The confessing church, like the conversionist church, also calls people to conversion, but it depicts that conversion as a long process of being baptismally engrafted into a new people, an alternative *polis*, a countercultural social structure called church. It seeks to influence the world by being the church, that is, by being something the world is not and can never be, lacking the gift of faith and vision, which is ours in Christ. . . . [It] seeks the *visible* church . . . in which people are faithful to their promises, love their enemies, tell the truth, honor the poor, suffer for righteousness, and thereby testify to the amazing community-creating power of God. The confessing church has no interest in withdrawing from the world, but is not surprised when its witness evokes hostility from the world. . . . This church knows that its most credible form of witness (and the most "effective" thing it can do for the world) is the actual creation of a living, breathing, visible community of faith.[59]

---

54. Ibid., 44–45.
55. Ibid., 45.
56. Ibid.
57. Ibid.
58. See Barth, *Church Dogmatics* 4.3.2, 796.
59. Hauerwas and Willimon, *Resident Aliens*, 46–47.

To be a colony of heaven, the Christian community must confess Christ and participate in the performance of the polyphonic life he calls into being. For as MacLeod suggested, "The Christian does not primarily look at the world with its myriad problems, but concentrates on appreciating the man Christ Jesus. Only by appreciating Him . . . will we see the world in a true perspective . . . and to determine every action from His viewpoint."[60]

THE PROBLEM WITH THE COLONY

No one metaphor is ever sufficient to describe the Christian community, and a colony of heaven is no exception. The negative associations that the word "colony" shares with historical imperialism leave it weakened and even discredited among many. For the members of former colonies of nation states, the term can evoke memories of personal and cultural abuse through the wholesale imposition on them of an alien culture. (There was similar resentment on occasions from the indigenous islanders to the way in which MacLeod and the expanding "Iona Community" sought to colonize the island community.)[61] And however clearly we may articulate the difference between geopolitical colonization and the diametric theology of a community who seeks only a place for themselves within a dominant culture that will always be alien to them, the negative historical associations will remain.

Moreover, Hauerwas and Willimon are right to note further unease with the metaphor when they say, "To be a colony implies that God's people settle in, stake out a claim, build fences, and guard their turf."[62] They rightly fear that if the church thinks in this way then it implies that the church is "somehow satisfied with [their] little corner of the world, [their] little cultivated garden of spirituality or introspection, or whatever crumbs are left after the wider society has used reason, science, politics, or whatever other dominant means it has of making sense of itself."[63] Such an entrenched community, primarily concerned with preserving its boundaries can never be the colony of heaven. It cannot reserve some special place for God over and against the world. There can be no place to which it can withdraw from the world, rather it must become that piece of the world "where Christ's taking

---

60. MacLeod, "Abundant Life," 125.

61. For an assessment of relations between George MacLeod, the community and the islanders see Muir, *Outside the Safe Place*, 92ff.

62. Hauerwas and Willimon, *Resident Aliens*, 51.

63. Ibid.

form is proclaimed and where it happens."[64] The only boundary that separates the colony from the world is that which the world creates by refusing to listen to and participate in the melodies of God.

So when Bonhoeffer argued that whoever knowingly separated themselves from the Confessing Church also separated themselves from salvation,[65] it was not with the ambition of determining their boundaries. Rather, this asserts that when Christ takes form in the world, there is the colony of heaven. Those who do not wish to participate in its melodies draw boundaries against it from outside. To suggest that "outside the Church there is no salvation" can only be construed as sectarian or exclusivist if predicated on Constantinian presumptions. These are that the church should, as activists, change the world into being a place that is in agreement with itself, or, as conversionists, retreat from the world. But as Hauerwas notes, if the church is faithful, then she always exists on foreign or alien ground.[66] It will always point the world to the polyphony of Christ that is present in the midst of the now and calls to them from the beyond of the not yet. The purpose of the colony is to invite the world to root itself in the *cantus firmus* of Christ and participate in the performance of his polyphony of life.

The colony cannot remain static. The Christ whom they confess is "the beyond in their midst,"[67] he is "a fast God" . . . always leaving just as they arrive.[68] As in the gospels, he is always on the move, a peripatetic pilgrim, whose every end is a new beginning,[69] and whose disciples were physically, mentally, and spiritually trying to keep up with him. The incarnated Christ claimed that foxes had holes and birds of the air had nests, but the Son of Man had no place to lay his head.[70] His disciples likewise became a nomad community with "the beyond" at their center. And a colony whose center is always "beyond" it, cannot stake out a claim, build fences, and guard their turf. This colony of heaven, this city of God, is a nomad city . . . the *civitas Dei peregrina*.[71] The colony will be in perpetual pilgrimage. Christ will be

---

64. Bonhoeffer, *Ethics*, 102. This is effectively a restatement of the theology of *Sanctorum Communio.*

65. "Essay and Discussion on Church Communion," in Bonhoeffer, *Theological Education at Finkenwalde*, 675ff.

66. Hauerwas, *After Christendom*, 18.

67. Letter to Bethge, April 30, 1944, in Bonhoeffer, *Letters and Papers*, 367.

68. The phrase is adopted from R. S. Thomas, "Pilgrimages," in Thomas, *Collected Poems*, 364.

69. The allusion is to T. S. Eliot, "Four Quartets: Little Gidding, V," in Eliot, *Collected Poems*, 208.

70. See Matt 8:20.

71. Augustine referred to Christians as the *civitas Dei peregrina*, the City of God on

their center, but will simultaneously call them beyond the borders of their own experience and existence.

Such a colony can propose no permanence of melody for itself. It can have no long-term strategies for participating in the performance of Christ's polyphony because the concept of strategy "postulates a place that can be delimited as its *own* and serve as the base from which relations with an *exteriority* composed of targets or threats . . . can be managed."[72] For pilgrims, there can be no boundaried location, any sense of place must reflect the life of a people caught up in a perpetual rhythm of arriving and leaving. The colony disavows any ambition of permanent settlement. Hauerwas's work on the Christian colony notes with approval Michel de Certeau's distinction between strategy and tactics in this regard.[73] De Certeau argues that tactics are actions determined by the absence of a proper locus, where there is "no delineation of exteriority" that "provides it with the condition necessary for autonomy. The space of the tactic is the space of the other. Thus, it must play on and with the terrain imposed on it and organized by the law of a foreign power . . . a tactic is an art of the weak."[74] However, while the analysis offered by de Certeau is helpful in challenging the Christian colony to operate without a permanent geographic locus, the distinction only takes us so far. The colony is a people informed of heaven's strategy, but they perceive it only as through a glass darkly and are informed only in part.[75] Nevertheless, fragments of heaven's great apotheosis find a place in the melodies of time and space. In this way, heaven does possess a strategy, a longing for its will to be done on earth, for a day to come when "at the name of Jesus every knee should bow, in heaven and on earth and under the earth and every tongue confess that Jesus Christ is Lord, to the glory of God the Father."[76] The establishing of the kingdom of heaven is not the responsibility of the earthly colony. However, the colony is required to share the fragmented epiphanies of heaven's melody in the here and now. The colony responds tactically to participate in the performance of heaven's strategy. Only in Christ's *cantus firmus* are these melodies held in tension. The colony therefore exists as aliens who do not seek a place for themselves, but hope to reveal to the

Pilgrimage among the ungodly. See Dyson, *Augustine*, xx; and Greer, *Broken Lights and Mended Lives*, 67ff.

72. de Certeau, *Practice of Everyday Life*, 36.

73. Hauerwas, *After Christendom*, 17ff.

74. Ibid., 37.

75. 1 Cor 13:9–12.

76. Phil 2:10–11.

world the reality of itself wherein Christ has taken form. In this way the colony

> does not have a sight, or walls, or gates. It is not, like Rome, an *asylum* constituted by the "protection" offered by the dominating class over a dominated, in the face of an external enemy. . . . Instead of a peace "achieved" through the abandonment of the losers, a subordination of the potential rivals and resistance to enemies, the church provides a genuine peace by its memory of all the victims, its equal concern for all of its citizens and its self-exposed offering of reconciliation to enemies.[77]

The place of the Christian colony is its people. There is no fortified position, be it theological or geographical, to which one may point and say "there is the colony of heaven." The locus for heaven's epiphany is the people who share in the performance of Christ's polyphony and it cannot be restricted to any land, mountain, temple, or other building. As humanity understands it, revelation comes primarily to people and through one person, Jesus Christ in particular. It is through their relationship with that person that the people of God become the place of God in the world.[78]

And yet, as citizens of the colony come together, they do so in a geographical space: as the fragments of epiphany are shared between the community, they are gathered in a particular location. Over time this gathering space of the people becomes invested with a sense of place. Walter Brueggemann argues that

> place is space that has historical meanings, where some things have happened that are now remembered and that provide continuity and identity across generations. Place is space in which important words have been spoken that have established identity, defined vocation and envisioned destiny. . . . Whereas pursuit of space may be a flight from history, a yearning for a place is a decision to enter history with an identifiable people in an identifiable pilgrimage.[79]

A place, then, serves as a reminder of where the epiphanies of heaven have been manifest on earth. A theology that takes seriously the incarnation of Christ into spatially and temporally specific contexts must afford due import to an understanding of place. When there is an occasion of human

77. John Milbank, *Theology and Social Theory*, cited in Hauerwas, *After Christendom*, 22.

78. This point is made by Sheldrake, *Spaces for the Sacred*, 37.

79. Brueggemann, *Land*, 4. See also Sheldrake, *Spaces for the Sacred*, 7, and his consideration of "'Place' and Human Identity," in *Spirituality and Theology*, 165ff.

participation in the performance of Christ's polyphony a space becomes a place: it becomes the "home of being"[80] where people learn to be fully present to God, to themselves, and to the world. Such places are where the Christian colony is most keenly aware of the *cantus firmus* and of the contrapuntal melodies in which they are invited to participate in church and world. They become "holy sites," often because of their association with a particular person or community. But their existence and attraction generate a tension for the colony. How does a pilgrim colony honor place without returning to boundaries that encourage the community to settle in, stake out a claim, and guard their turf?

If the community is continuing to participate in the performance of Christ's polyphony in a given place, then they and the "hallowed" place will display two important characteristics: first, both it and the people gathered there will be possessed of a certain liminality, and second, they will be renewed in their sense of journey and pilgrimage.

THE LIMINAL COLONY

Holy places are revered because of their associations with people and events in which the boundaries of heaven and earth draw close together and the fragmented epiphanies of God can be heard most clearly. Perhaps no people group was so fascinated by this liminal encounter than the Celts who occupied parts of the British Isles from the fourth to tenth centuries. Among them was St. Columba, the founder of the first monastic site on Iona. The Celts had an extraordinary sense that "'the other-world,' of saints, the dead, angels, demons and God was close at hand."[81] The liminal edges between these worlds enveloped these people who had a keen awareness of the persistent "presence and protection of God."[82] Nonetheless, particular locations were considered to have a special quality of liminality. Their pagan ancestors had displayed a keen sense of the boundaries between the worlds of the material and the spiritual and often erected standing stones as the *axis mundi*, a linkage between the realm of the now and that of the beyond. When the Celts embraced Christianity, the practice of using stones evolved into standing crosses that symbolized not only the locus of contact between heaven and earth, but also the place of Christ as the center and source out of which all blessings would flow. The crosses were often a focal point around

---

80. Heidegger once claimed that "place is the house of being," cited in Sheldrake, *Spaces for the Sacred*, 7.

81. Sheldrake, *Living Between Worlds*, 46.

82. Bradley, *Celtic Way*, 31.

which the people gathered for worship and affirmed that Christ took form among them. Many such crosses were located in the midst of a monastic community.

Ian Bradley has recently adopted the image of a colony of heaven to specifically describe these ancient Celtic monastic sites.[83] He asserts that the metaphor powerfully conveys "the thin dividing line between the physical and the spiritual and the need to establish on earth places which speak of heaven."[84] Such places are where the world becomes as it should be and at the same time, reveal the world as it is in reality. For the Celtic Christians, such as the monks on Iona, their community was just that: a colony of the world as it should be and a microcosm of the whole of society. So, while these monastic sites were physically enclosed, their boundary vellum was not established in order to shelter monks *from* the world, but to mark out an area that was to be regarded as the colony of heaven, existing *for* the world. It was a "privileged space within which a particular vision of the world could be lived out";[85] a place wherein people participated in the performance of the polyphony of Christ. In such a place there existed

> anticipations of paradise in which the forces of division, violence and evil were excluded. Wild beasts were tamed and nature was regulated. The privileges of Adam and Eve in Eden, received from God but lost in the Fall, were reclaimed.
>
> The living out of this vision of an alternative world involved all the people who were brought within the enclosed space. It was not something that concerned merely the "professional" ascetics. The Columbanian tradition, for example, believed that all people were called from birth to the experience of contemplation. So, "monastic" enclosures were places of spiritual experience and of non-violence and also places of education, wisdom and art. Within the enclosures there took place, ideally

83. Ian Bradley adds a cautionary note, arguing that "because virtually all of our sources for this period, both written and archaeological, tend to come from monasteries, there is a danger of over emphasizing its monastic character. We know virtually nothing of the Christian life that took place outside the monasteries, but that does not mean it did not exist or was insignificant." Nevertheless he adds, "Even among revisionist historians there is a general consensus that the *monasterium* was the key ecclesiastical institution in the British Isles until the development of parish churches and territorial dioceses in the aftermath of the Norman conquest." Bradley, *Colonies of Heaven*, 2–3.

84. Ibid., x–xi.

85. Sheldrake, *Living Between Worlds*, 39.

speaking, an integration of all elements of human life, as well as all classes of human society.[86]

Such places were open and inclusive of the surrounding society, which understood the colony to be "*the* way of being Church."[87] They socialized their members into coherent vision and praxis. This contrasts favorably with medieval and post-medieval monasticism of Europe whose boundaries were perceived "as a means of protecting 'spiritual persons' from everyone else."[88] The boundaries of these communities were seen as the demarcation point for those retreating from the world, a view that is depicted graphically in Victor Hugo's *Les Misérables* and theologically critiqued by Bonhoeffer in *Discipleship*.[89] Hugo's novel refers to "the cloister filled with the black effulgence of death . . . mouths closed, brains walled up, so many hapless intellects incarcerated in the dungeons of eternal vows."[90] This is undoubtedly a negative caricature of monasticism that gives no credit to the genuinely deep spirituality of the cloister or to the charitable initiatives undertaken by such monastics. However, it does reflect a prevalent public (mis)conception of monasticism that Bonhoeffer also censures. He criticizes communities that distanced themselves from what was truly Christian by exalting the extraordinary achievement of the few and allowing the "humble work of discipleship" to become "the meritorious work of the holy ones."[91] When the colony so excludes the world from its presence, then it ceases to be the colony of Christ. For if, as Gorringe suggests, "a non-engaged God is no God"[92] then a non-engaged colony is no colony of God. God is free not *from* the world but free *for* the world,[93] and as such, the colony of God's heaven must exist as the *stellverter* for humanity, to be free to act in deputyship for the world. It must be present in and to the world. The Celtic enclosures were consciously "planted on earth to point as a sign and harbinger of the kingdom that was

---

86. Ibid.

87. Ibid., 31.

88. Ibid., 39–40.

89. Bonhoeffer, *Discipleship*, 46ff.

90. Hugo, *Les Misérables*, as cited in Bradley, *Colonies of Heaven*, 42. A similar sentiment was expressed by Milton, who wrote, "I cannot praise a fugitive and cloistered virtue, unexercised and unbreathed, that never sallies out and seeks her adversary, but shrinks out of the race where the immortal garland is to be run for, not without dust and heat." John Milton "*Areopagitica*," ii, 68, cited in Workman, *Evolution of the Monastic Ideal*, 337.

91. Bonhoeffer, *Discipleship*, 47.

92. Gorringe, *Discerning Spirit*, 1.

93. Bonhoeffer, *Act and Being*, 90–91.

yet to come."[94] These were proleptic epiphanies of redeemed relationships whose colony was open to all and whose boundary paradoxically became a new center. Bonhoeffer's Christology reflects a similar understanding.

> Where this structure can be demonstrated, it provides the theological proof that Christ's incidental appearance in space and time is his manner of existing as a person, as the risen Lord. Where does he stand? For me, he stands there in my place, where I should be standing. He stands there because I cannot, that is, he stands at the boundary of my existence and nevertheless in my place. This is an expression of the fact that I am separated, by a boundary that I cannot cross, from the self that I ought to be. This boundary lies between my old self and my new self, that is, in the center between myself and me. As the limit, Christ is at the same time the center that I have regained. . . . Christ is not the center that we can see is here but rather that center according to our faith. In the fallen world, however, the center is at the same time the boundary.[95]

Christ now stands where the world should stand but cannot. He stands within the colony and in the new center of heaven-redeemed relationships made proleptically present on earth. The heavenly colony exists to be as the world should be but cannot. These colonies are "thin places" as MacLeod once described Iona, places where the line between creator and creation is "gossamer thin"[96] and the tension between the now and the not yet is palpable. In such places the melodies of heaven and earth can be heard in clear polyphony and the *cantus firmus* is distinct. Everything within the boundary of such places is caught up into Christ's capacious "boundarylessness," where all things are reconciled to God through Christ and all boundaries collapse into Christ who is found both at the edge and in the center. As such, the reality of the colony made possible through Christ is different from what we think of as natural communities, because as Rowan Williams notes, the Christian community is one whose limits are "at the same time the ultimate natural 'limits'—'the ends of the earth.' *The world we inhabit* is the potential scope of the community that is created by relation to Jesus."[97] It is a boundaryless reality and Christ's presence at its center means that he is also its limit and accordingly the judgment of humanity. But he is also the beginning of

94. Bradley, *Colonies of Heaven*, 19.

95. "Lectures on Christology," in Bonhoeffer, *Berlin*, 324.

96. "A Veil Thin as Gossamer," in MacLeod, *Whole Earth Shall Cry Glory*, 60.

97. Williams, *On Christian Theology*, 231.

its new existence, its new center.[98] Indeed, in the colony humanity can learn to perceive themselves to be a border location. Here they cease to be the perpetual self-referent center of existential investigation, but instead accept their creatureliness, affirming their limits and the unending Otherness of the Creator God who addresses them through Christ's epiphanal revelation. Here, humanity must accept the liminality of its own creaturely existence, and the fact that the boundaries of such existence are located in and through Christ who also is their center. This leads the colony into a new reality. For as Bonhoeffer notes,

> Jesus Christ does not encounter reality as someone who is foreign to it. Instead, it is he who alone bore and experienced in his own body the essence of the real, and who spoke out of knowledge of the real like no other human being on earth. . . . As the Real One he is the origin, essence and goal of all reality. . . .
>
> Action in accordance with Christ is in accord with reality because it allows the world to be world and reckons with the world as world, while at the same time never forgetting that the world is loved, judged, and reconciled in Jesus Christ by God.[99]

This new reality of colony and world is as open and capacious as a fugue but it remains one in which the *cantus firmus* is clear. And Christ's *cantus firmus* beckons the colony to journey beyond itself and into pilgrimage toward a new reality of the fullness of humanity.

THE PILGRIM COLONY

The Celtic tradition within Iona not only helps us to understand the liminality of colony, but also the journeying *civitas Dei peregrine*. The epic journey was an important aspect of the Celtic pre-Christian tradition,[100] and pilgrimage was a favorite metaphor for how they later expressed a dynamic aspect of Christian discipleship.

As it has evolved, the term pilgrimage implies a deliberate journey to and from a place perceived to be sacred on account of its association with an epiphanal event. However, for the Celts, pilgrimage was "first and foremost an inner state of mind expressed in outward terms in a life of physical

---

98. See "Lectures on Christology," in Bonhoeffer, *Berlin*, 325.

99. Bonhoeffer, *Ethics*, 263–64.

100. For instance "The Voyage of Mael Duin," in Geddes and Grosset, *Celtic Mythology*, 198ff. See a retelling in Scott, *Celtic Odyssey*.

exile and journeying."[101] As the risk of genuine martyrdom declined, Celtic monks often sought a life of "white martyrdom," a commitment to extreme asceticism, often involving a journey of permanent exile from their home.[102] This deliberate forsaking of home was sometimes undertaken as a penalty for some sin committed,[103] but more commonly was understood to be a way of bearing witness to Christ and discovering what St. Columbanus[104] sometimes called one's "place of resurrection."[105] This concept of resurrection and place evokes a particularly earthed spirituality, one in which Christ might take form in the pilgrim or the pilgrim community.[106] Bradley argues that despite a certain strain of unworldliness in Celts such as Columbanus, his understanding of Christians as "colonists of heaven" demanded full engagement with the life of earth.[107] Celtic Christians were a people "unable and careless to know where the secular began and the religious ended"[108] and easily integrated the world of heaven with the daily vicissitudes of earthly life.[109] Not only did they disavow a world dichotomized into the material and spiritual, but they also knew the dangers of overly individualized discipleship. While the Celtic saints often spent time in solitude, the need for an *anamcara* (soul-friend)[110] in the life-journey meant that even exilic pil-

101. Bradley, *Colonies of Heaven*, 200.

102. "Red martyrdom" was understood to be dying for one's faith. The "green martyrdom" of the penitentials required a life of austere inner discipline, penance, fasting, labor, and physically demanding prayer. See O'Laoghaire, "Celtic Spirituality," in Jones, Wainright, and Yarnold, *Study of Spirituality*, 221.

103. A classic example of penance is Columba, who is traditionally understood to have been banished from Ireland for his part in the battle of Cul Drebene. His arrival on Iona may, however, be as much political as penitential. See Bradley, *Columba*.

104. Columbanus is not to be confused with St. Columba. Columbanus was born in Ireland in 540 and was ordained in 572. In 591 he left Ireland and travelled to Gaul, Switzerland, and Bobbio in Italy where he died in 615.

105. Columbanus, "Sermon 8," cited in de Waal, *World Made Whole*, 54.

106. Occasionally, Columbanus came close to pietistic elitism when he spoke of remaining disentangled from earthly desires. See ibid.

107. Bradley, *Colonies of Heaven*, 201.

108. Carmichael, "Carmina Gadelica," xxxiii, cited in Bradley, *Celtic Way*, 37.

109. "Caim prayers," with which the Celtic Christian would draw an area of God's protection around themselves, are especially illustrative of this. The most famous is St. Patrick's Breastplate, but good examples may also be found in Carmichael, *Carmina Gadelica*, 344.

110. *Anamcara* literally means "soul friend," the person to whom you could reveal the hidden intimacies of your life. Anamchairdeas was "an act of recognition and belonging . . . cutting across all convention and category." O'Donohue, *Anam Cara*, 16. Its significance to the Celtic Christians can be summed up in the phrase variously attributed: "a person without a soul friend is like a body without a head." Cited in Bradley,

grimages were often taken communally, in effect travelling as a mini-colony. Blessings were thought to be received, not only by those on pilgrimage, but also by those who remained behind and any communities visited along the journey. Thus, while there were occasions of personal separation, there was also support and communal responsibility.[111] Thus, Bradley notes that "for all its lonely isolation and painful penitential character, pilgrimage, like other aspects of Celtic Christianity, was also a matter of balance and rhythm."[112] According to Columbanus, "Every day you depart and every day you return."[113] Such pilgrims carried the *cantus firmus* of Christ, their center, with them and every day it called them to participate in melodies of departure and return, the now and not yet of heaven and earth.[114]

This motif of departure and return is strongly represented in the later medieval idea of pilgrimage, wherein pilgrims left home to travel to a holy site seeking a blessing and then returned. This, too, has import for contemporary considerations of the colony of heaven. Bradley notes how the revival of journeying to sacred places has been one of the most "striking and surprising religious movements of recent years."[115] He is rightly critical of some aspects of this "spiritual tourism"[116] and it is true that on occasions the phenomena has led some communities away from their vocation in Christian socialization and into becoming "booth keepers in an emporium of transcendence."[117] However, that notwithstanding, Bradley argues,

> we should not perhaps be too censorious about this mushroom-
> ing new branch of the package tourist industry. They are, after
> all, blurring the lines between tourism and pilgrimage and en-
> couraging those who may be literally attracted by the lure of

---

Celtic Way, 73.

111. While the motivation behind Columba's peregrination is disputed it is clear that a group of 12 monks travelled with him. See Adomnan of Iona, *Life of St. Columba*, 19.

112. Bradley, *Colonies of Heaven*, 204.

113. *Sancti Columbani Opera*, 85, cited in Bradley, *Colonies of Heaven*, 201.

114. Even though Celtic pilgrims did not always consider the possibility of return-ing home, a rhythm of departing and returning, or more accurately gathering and scat-tering remained present in their practice of pilgrimage. Monks would often stop in an area to be near and serve people. In doing so they would establish another community from which in time another group would depart.

115. Bradley, *Colonies of Heaven*, 212.

116. In particular he criticizes their focus on seeking spiritual highs from one par-ticular visit rather than "cultivating a lifelong spirit of exile and finding one's desert place of resurrection." Ibid., 216.

117. The phrase is taken from Catherine L. Albanese, "Forum," as cited in Rasmus-sen, *Moral Fragments, Moral Community*, 103.

the holy place and the romantic destination to think about their lives and the inner journey which was at the heart of the Celtic understanding of pilgrimage.[118]

In this revival of pilgrimage, there is the potential for people to depart from their own particularity and journey to a place where they encounter and participate in a community that celebrates the melodies of liminality and the rhythms of pilgrimage.[119] In order to arrive at the center they must go the way of the boundary's edge. If having then gathered for a time, and learned to be fully present to heaven and earth in that place, they may then scatter and return to their own particularities, taking with them, something of the art of participating in Christ's polyphony.

This journey into place particularly resonates with the rootless character of the postmodern condition and the many people who now dwell in what Marc Augé calls "non place": these locations do not integrate with a past and in them no true community is possible.[120] Such non-places precipitate a "fragmentation of awareness that leads to incoherence in relation to 'the world.'"[121] Amidst such ontological dislocation, the rhythm of departure and return enables colonies of heaven to facilitate an encounter with the reality of place. This offers the pilgrim a community, a place, in which they might learn to live, fully present to the now, but informed and inspired by all that is not yet. The art and the rhythm continue with them in their journey back. So as Michel de Certeau has commented,

> Both elements, the place and the departure, are interrelated, because it is the withdrawal from a place that allows one to recognise the enclosure implicit in the initial position, and as a result it is this limited field which makes possible a further

118. Bradley, *Colonies of Heaven*, 216.

119. Macmurray notes the importance of the "rhythm of withdrawal and return" to individual and communal development. He argues that a person's rhythm of withdrawal and return to "the Other" (including occasions when the Other withdraws specifically "for the sake of the return," throwing the person back upon themselves) constitutes the universal and necessary pattern of personal development. See Macmurray, *Persons in Relation*, 86–105.

120. Augé draws on the imagery of polyphony in his articulation of place, as that which connects to the past. He cites the reflection of Jean Starobinski: "the possibility of a polyphony in which the virtually infinite interlacing of destinies, actions, thoughts and reminiscences would rest on a bass line that chimed the hours of the terrestrial day, and marked the position that used to be (and could still be) occupied there by ancient ritual." Starobinski, "Les cheminées et les clochers," as cited in Augé, *Non-places*, 75.

121. Sheldrake, *Spaces for the Sacred*, 8.

investigation. Boundaries are the place of the Christian work, and their displacements are the result of this work.[122]

Iona is well equipped to take on the mantle of being such a place. It incorporates both the Celtic, medieval, and contemporary understandings of pilgrimage. It is in fact a living metaphor for such an endeavor; the ancient Celtic site was specifically chosen to be the place where the medieval Benedictine buildings were built. The presence of the contemporary Iona Community similarly indicates a desire to build something connected to these histories but yet still be altogether new. MacLeod gathered the early community together to learn how to participate in the polyphony of Christ and then to scatter again, returning to their urban parishes. He instinctively discerned what Sheldrake suggests is essential for a good theology of place: "a balance between God's revelation in the particular and a sense that God's place ultimately escapes the boundaries of the localized. . . . Place is both *this, here and now*, and at the same time more than 'this,' a pointer to 'elsewhere.'"[123] MacLeod knew that "thin places," like Iona, enabled such a balance to flourish. In such a colony of place, realms of work and worship, the secular and the sacred, of church life and common life would gather around the Christ into one polyphonic experience of reality and symbolism. The Christian colony on Iona was to be a symphony of gathering and scattering and gathering again. Each movement brought together new fragments of God's epiphany, each fragment bearing witness to the whole around the *cantus firmus*.[124] This dialectic movement continues to be affirmed through the Iona liturgy in which members affirm, "Gathered and scattered, God is with us."[125]

Because of the changes of direction forced upon the community during World War II, Iona became a colony for more than the few apprentices handpicked by MacLeod. As hundreds visited the island on retreat, laypeople learned of the character of the colony and many wanted to join. The community proceeded pragmatically but was left with having to discern what the rich diversity of new members meant for a community whose effective purpose until then had been ministerial formation. Ralph Morton

122. de Certeau, "How is Christianity Thinkable Today?" in Ward, *Postmodern God*, 139. See also Sheldrake, *Spaces for the Sacred*, 31–32.

123. Sheldrake, *Spaces for the Sacred*, 30.

124. This is similar to the religio-cultural movement of orientation, disorientation, and new orientation detected in the psalms by Walter Brueggemann, where he argues that the Psalter displays a movement of personal and national reimagining of God and the people's relationship with the divine. See Brueggemann, *Message of the Psalms*, 19ff.

125. "An Act of Prayer," in Iona Community, *Iona Community Members' Prayer Book*, 8.

perceived the potential for Iona to nurture the whole people of God into colonies of heaven.[126]

Many others who did not seek to become members of the community still returned home having heard something of the melodies performed within a colony of heaven. Guests would have shared their own fragments of epiphany, the abbey had become a boundaryless boundary, a reconciling place, where guests and members heard the echo of heaven's music not yet heard. The place and the community began to understand themselves as a gatherer of epiphanies and as a departure point for pilgrims to return to their world infused with a deeper reality of life in all its fullness. Having learned to participate in the melodies of God on Iona, they began to nurture the art of performing the polyphony of life in whatever space or place they found themselves.

Indeed even day-tourists can be touched by the place of Iona. Bradley notes that for many of the tourists who go there every year,

> the few hours spent on Columba's island may not differ from a visit to any other ancient monument or historic site. . . . Yet most visitors can hardly be left unaware of the Iona Community's presence and its lively Christian witness and concern for contemporary issues. Those going into the Abbey are quite likely to find it adorned with banners and posters drawing attention to some campaign for peace and justice. . . . It is impossible to eat or drink at the café opposite the Abbey without being made aware of the issues of fair trade and environmental sustainability.[127]

And it is not coincidental that the time in which Iona draws tourists, guests, residents, and members together most is on the weekly pilgrimage around the island. This seven-mile walk is more than a guided trip around the island, it is a "peripatetic act of worship,"[128] involving shared conversations and short periods of silence and a picnic meal. The six-hour walk is punctuated with stops for prayer, song, and brief meditation at places of historic and religious significance. Norman Shanks comments that

> the Pilgrimage is at the heart of the Iona experience not only because of its timing in the middle of the week—often indeed at

126. Ronald Ferguson describes Morton's insight as "how to mobilize and train the whole people of God for mission, and how to train ordained men for this kind of enabling ministry." Ferguson, *Chasing the Wild Goose*, 81.

127. Bradley, *Colonies of Heaven*, 217. Although the café is no longer open (it now houses the Iona Community shop), the point was well made at the time and remains apposite in all other respects.

128. Shanks, *Iona—God's Energy*, 93.

a critical point in the programme when some of the novelty has worn off and people are starting to ask difficult questions! The Pilgrimage is also an integrated and integrating embodiment of the Community's understanding of and approach to spirituality—described before as "an energising kind of connectedness." . . . It affords opportunities, within a framework of worship and sharing, for reflecting and exploring, for discussing new ideas and old, for forging and deepening relationships, for discerning and engaging with the struggles of the world and the purposes and promises of God, for looking to the future as the journey goes on.[129]

At the heart of the pilgrimage are fragments of the bisociation of heaven and earth, the now and the not yet, what Emily Dickinson called "the beautiful but bleak condition" of wonder: "not precisely Knowing and not precisely Knowing not."[130] This is the proleptic mystery of the melodies of heaven breaking into earth. This eschatological aspect is strong within the Celtic tradition and Bradley insists that it is the central key to understanding not only pilgrimage, but the metaphor of the colony of heaven.[131] He writes,

> We are brought back to the notion of colonies of heaven. . . . Christians inhabit the in-between times, living in a perpetual Advent state, waiting and hoping for the glory of God to be revealed. Unfulfilled as this condition of "not yetness" may be, it is also suffused with those glimpses of glory that we already have in our sacramental world so thinly divided from the world to come.[132]

On Iona, and with the community, pilgrims encounter in the Christian colony, fragments of Christ's boundaryless polyphony and therein learn to participate in its performance. It becomes a place where people proleptically practice the eternal melodies of heaven in the here and now. It is a place from which the *cantus firmus* beckons people to share not only in the fragments of epiphany they have listened to so far, but to enter into the echo of a polyphony they have not yet fully heard.

A former warden of the abbey sums it up in poetry:

"A place of hope,"

129. Ibid., 96–97.

130. "Wonder—is not precisely Knowing," in Dickinson, *Complete Poems*, 577.

131. In this he acknowledges being influenced by the PhD thesis of James Bruce, "The Nature and Function of the Marvellous in Adomnan's Life of Columba," now published as *Prophecy, Miracles, Angels, and Heavenly Light?*

132. Bradley, *Colonies of Heaven*, 241–42.

they say:
and in their thousands
they journey, year by year,
to this tiny island
on the margins of Europe.
Sunswept and windswept,
yet always deeply
a place of transformation.
A sacred spot on earth:
a pilgrim's place
of light and shadow
energy and challenge.
We need you, Iona,
with your alternative vision,
with your ever-present questions
your often uncomfortable silence.
For you are a place of prayer,
of Christ's abiding:
waving a rainbow of meaning
through the endless busyness of our days,
holding together the frayed threads
of our fleeting devotion,
opening a path for healing
and for peace.
Not momentary healing
nor easy faith,
but struggle, commitment,
and an ongoing conversion
are your gifts for our
broken yet beautiful lives.[133]

133. Millar, *Iona Prayer Book*, 67–68. Reproduced with the kind permission of Canterbury Press.

CHAPTER 7

Performing the Discipline of Counterpoint

"Back to devotionalism" would be as fatal as if our agricultural community went "back to the land" by selling their tractor and yoking bullocks to the plough. As it must be forward to the land, so it must be forward to the new devotionalism: or rather the recovery of primitive holiness. The key is in a serious re-view of the challenge of the Incarnation.

—GEORGE MACLEOD[1]

Everything begins in Mysticism and ends in Politics.

—CHARLES PEGUY[2]

The "religious act" is always something partial, whereas "faith" is something whole and involves one's whole life. Jesus calls not to a

---

1. MacLeod, *Only One Way Left*, 152.
2. Charles Peguy, un-cited reference, in ibid., vi.

new religion, but to life . . . participating in God's powerlessness in the world.

—DIETRICH BONHOEFFER[3]

One of the greatest difficulties for a community seeking to be a colony of heaven on earth is maintaining the tension of being in the world, but not of it. As the church seeks to belong in the world and express its solidarity with it, it faces the danger of becoming indistinguishable from it. The result being that the melody of the gospel appears to be lost in the cacophony of fallen life. If this happens, the fear of those within the colony is that the melodies of God will be lost from the world. Hence, at times they try to protect what they believe to be the gospel melody. Their fear of losing the melodies of God is fueled by the mistaken belief that they have heard and possessed the complete symphony of God. In reality, they, like those before them, have only ever heard a fragment. For some, this desire to protect the gospel leads them to separate the colony from the world, and indeed from other expressions of the Christian community. In extreme form, claims to the exclusive right to perform the polyphony of Christ lead such communities into religious and inward looking isolationism and the condemnation of other melodies.

But these extremes of being indistinguishable from the world or living in isolationism arise out of the false premise that the call to alien citizenship upon the life of Christians requires them to struggle between these two competing realms. However, if Christ's regal anthem sounds within both realms, then the Christian is no longer to think in terms of two realms. This means Christians must learn to celebrate the counterpoint God calls into being in all places of creation. The church needs to sing this counterpoint in ways that invite the world to participate in a deeper awareness of Christ as *cantus firmus* and to encounter the fragments of melody into which they are called. This means that Christians and their communities are to perpetually seek to find harmonies of Christ in others. In so doing, they discover that in Christ all things are reconciled to God[4] and the boundaries of existence are eternally transcended.

There are many examples of this boundary crossing in the life and ministry of Jesus. According to Luke, his manifesto of mission was initially proclaimed on the Sabbath within "the realm of the religious" before the synagogue congregation. This was the announcement of "good news to the

3. Bonhoeffer, *Letters and Papers*, 482.

4. Col 1:20.

poor, release to the captives, recovery of sight to the blind and to let the oppressed go free and proclaim the year of the Lord's favor."[5] The reality of this was revealed in his willingness to befriend the marginalized; lepers, women, Gentiles, and include them in the polyphony of the kingdom of heaven on earth. This transcendence of boundaries was offered to all people on earth through Christ's work upon the cross. At the foot of a cross erected at the behest of the religious realm, it was a "worldly" Roman centurion who recognized the crucified one as creation's *cantus firmus*. In the cry of dereliction the separation of God from God[6] is revealed, and the paradox of being in the world but not of it is made known.[7] At the cross the boundary that separated the holy of holies from the world was rent in two and, three days later, the boundary that had appeared to separate life from death was overcome in the resurrection.

The early Christian church struggled to come to terms with the mystery of Christ, and, as has been noted, with being a colony of heaven. In the communities of the New Testament, the performance of Christ's regal anthem increasingly became associated with the peculiar practices of the colony: Baptism, Eucharist, the Lord's Prayer, etc. In the face of persecution and the potential corrupting influence of the pagan world, these practices were conducted in secret. It was this private discipline that enabled them to live with the tensions of alien citizenship: to be present to the empire while belonging to the Christian colony. In order to protect these mysteries, New Testament communities were encouraged only to share their content and meaning with the initiated. At this time it was important and proper that these melodies were rehearsed within the colony and not performed to a public who were unprepared for the profundity of the music. While the story of Jesus was proclaimed in word and deed and people were urged to listen and respond, the deeper mysteries of discipleship were not to be regarded lightly. Hence, the gospel writers said, "To you has been given the secret of the kingdom of God, but for those outside, everything comes in parables" and "do not give what is holy to dogs; and do not throw your pearls before swine or they will trample them underfoot."[8] The understanding of this practice can also be seen in the words of Paul's first letter to the colony at Corinth.

5. Luke 4:16–19.

6. See further Fiddes, *Past Event*, 218, and *Creative Suffering of God*, 163.

7. As Moltmann argues, "The cross was an event between God and God. It was a deep division in God himself, insofar as God abandoned God and contradicted himself, and at the same time a unity in God insofar as God was one with God who corresponded to himself." Moltmann, *Crucified God*, 244.

8. Mark 4:11, and Matt 7:6.

> Yet among the mature we do speak wisdom, though it is not a
> wisdom of this age or of the rulers of this age, who are doomed
> to perish. But we speak God's wisdom, secret and hidden, which
> God decreed before the ages for our glory. None of the rulers of
> this age understood this; for if they had, they would not have
> crucified the Lord of glory.[9]

The early church began to practice a discipline over the mysteries of
the faith that meant that they kept a qualified silence before the world until
such matters could be spoken of responsibly.[10] This did not mean that they
were concealing Christ from the world; rather, until the appropriate time
had come, a discipline was needed that enabled the Christian to live in and
for the world as a citizen of heaven but which spoke to the world only as
a participant of their secular estate. This concern for an appropriate time
and place in which the Christian could declare in words the contrapuntal
melodies of Christ ran consistently through the early church. The discipline
is evidenced in the writings of Tertullian, Origen, Basil, Ambrose, Gregory
of Nazianzus, Jerome, Chrysostom, Augustine, Innocent I, and Cyril of Alexandria.[11] The first Christians developed such a discipline not least because
careless talk could cost them and others their lives. Romans were suspicious
of anyone who threatened the safety of the empire by refusing to worship
their gods. Care had to be taken by Christians to protect the people and the
unique practices of the faith. Thus, when Chrysostom wrote to Pope Innocent I over an act of irreverence in Constantinople, he stated clearly that
"the most holy blood of Christ was spilt."[12] However, Palladius, reporting
the same incident in a book intended for a readership beyond that of the
church, provides a more vague reference: "They overturned the symbols."[13]
It was not appropriate to speak of the mystery of the Eucharist before the
world. In the same way Cyril of Jerusalem declared, "Should a catechumen
ask, what the teachers have said, tell nothing to a stranger; for we deliver to
thee a mystery. . . . See thou let out nothing; not that what is said is not worth
telling, but because the ear that hears does not deserve to hear it."[14]

---

9. 1 Cor 2:6–8.

10. See Phillips, *Form of Christ in the World*, 229ff.

11. Matthews, "Responsible Sharing of the Mystery," 115.

12. "Correspondence of St. Chrysostom with the Bishop of Rome," in Schaff, *Work of St. John Chrysostom*, 311.

13. Barnes, "Discipline of the Secret," *Catholic Encyclopedia*, http://www.newadvent.org/cathen/05032a.htm.

14. St. Cyril of Jerusalem, "Catechetical Lectures," in Telfer, *Cyril of Jerusalem*, 72.

The development of this Discipline of the Secret or *Disciplina Arcani*[15] was not, however, simply a response to the threat of persecution in the early church. It was also a response to the dangers of Neoplatonism and Gnosticism. Not only did such philosophies deny the incarnate Christ in their continual affirmation of the split between the spiritual and the material, but they claimed an intellectual elitism for the initiated that was rejected by the early church. There are obvious and inherent difficulties in finding evidence for any secret practiced by a community, but it does seem that the *arcanum* of the early church was more strictly enforced immediately after the cessation of persecutions rather than at their height. It seems likely that this was in response to these philosophies that undermined the incarnation and the potential for creation to bear the revelation of God. Barnes argues that it is

> probable enough that the discipline was growing more strict all through the second and third centuries on account of the pressure of persecution, and that, when persecution was at last relaxed, the need for reserve was felt at first, while the Church was still surrounded by hostile Paganism, to be increased rather than diminished.[16]

Thus, during the fifth century, as Christendom was becoming more firmly established, Cyril of Alexandria still could tell a class of catechumens,

> These mysteries, which the Church now explains to thee who art passing out of the class of Catechumens, it is not the custom to explain to heathen. For to a heathen we do not explain the mysteries . . . but many things we often speak in a veiled way, that the believers who know may understand and they who know not may get no hurt.[17]

The catechumenate was a formal initiation program, normally lasting three years, through which people were gradually guided into a deeper understanding of Christianity. Catechumens would be present in the regular liturgy, but would not share in the mysteries of faith. There was both doctrinal and practical training throughout an initiation period, and individuals were assessed as to their worthiness to share in the deeper mysteries such as Baptism and Eucharist. The institution of a catechumenate reveals a church

15. In German, Bonhoeffer referred to the practice as the *arkandisziplin*, but Williams notes that this term can be misleading, precipitating English translations that tend to describe it as the pious counterpart to his ideas on worldliness. See Matthews, "Responsible Sharing of the Mystery," 125, endnote 3.

16. Barnes, "Discipline of the Secret."

17. Cyril of Alexandria, "Catech. vi, 29," cited in Matthews, "Responsible Sharing of the Mystery," 115.

community conscious of their responsibilities. Here were a people who took their discipleship seriously and courageously laid down clear conditions for those who wanted to become her members.[18] But in contrast to the mystery religions of the time, the discipline was not an elitist privilege whereby the baptized lorded their knowledge over the catechumenate and unbelievers. Harmless notes how Augustine was bothered by any such divisions in his congregation and used every opportunity to encourage his listeners to be baptized and enter the community of the faithful. When the baptized shouted in affirming response to one of his sermons, Augustine replied, "Those of you who have cheered have understood; but, you who have understood, bear with me a little longer for the sake of those who have not, that I may open it up to them."[19]

However, as Christendom expanded to include the people of the empire and the threat of paganism retreated, the mysteries became public knowledge. As this occurred, the perceived need for a Discipline of the Secret disappeared. Under Constantine, the mysteries of committed discipleship became profane. Apathy and religious banality gradually infected the church, reducing the polyphony of alien citizenship to a drone of comfortable convention. The mysteries of a radical performance of Christ were relocated in the monasteries that, largely and erroneously, accepted a place of isolation from the world. The church had nothing to conceal from unbelievers because everyone was now understood to believe. Since then, argues Georg Huntemann, "the established church and arcane discipline have been mutually exclusive."[20] In a strict understanding of how the early church practiced the Discipline of the Secret, Huntemann is correct. There is no way to return these mysteries of the Christian church to secrecy. They became known and are now publicly well documented.

While the mysteries may now be well established, there continues to be a need for a Discipline that the Christian colony practices in secret: a Discipline of Counterpoint. That is, there needs to be a responsible sharing of the mysteries within the Christian community, an opportunity for the colony to bring together fragments of epiphany and rehearse the polyphony revealed in their gathering. This is an important practice for a community that claims that its authority comes from heaven but is simultaneously engaged with God, who is in the world. The importance of such a Discipline in Christian community inspired MacLeod and the Iona Community and

---

18. See Matthews, "Responsible Sharing of the Mystery," 114–17.

19. Augustine, Sermon, 335 a.2., in *Sermones Obras Completas de San Agustin*, cited in Harmless, *Augustine and the Catechumenate*, 170.

20. Huntemann, *Other Bonhoeffer*, 109.

shaped the practices of Bonhoeffer and the Finkenwalde seminarians. For Bonhoeffer the need for a Discipline occupied his mind, especially in his later years, as he sought to collapse the traditional Christendom dichotomy of two separate spheres or realms.[21] He articulated a theology that affirmed how all reality was taken up into Christ's Lordship and sought an accompanying praxis of discipleship. At the core of his response was what he identified as the Discipline of the Secret.

Bonhoeffer earnestly sought a Discipline by which he and the community at Finkenwalde might reclaim the alien citizenship possessed by the early church and reappropriate it for his time. So although he refers to it only briefly in his writings, commentators agree that it was central to his theological orientation. It was at the heart of the praxis of discipleship he sought to introduce to the colony of worldly monasticism, and it remains instructive for how contemporary Christian communities might participate in the performance of the polyphonic Christ.

In Finkenwalde, under Bonhoeffer's leadership, the seminarians sought ways to maintain the practices of word, sacrament and community untainted by the heresies of Nazism and ecclesiological complacency. Bonhoeffer had a negative theology of the world at this time. So, it is not surprising that the Discipline was used to enable Christians to share the mysteries primarily within the community of faith and in so doing they did battle with a pernicious world. But in time, as Bonhoeffer's theology of world expanded, he came to understand the Discipline not simply as something which protected the mysteries of faith *from* the world, but which enabled the community of faith to responsibly perform the mystery of God's melodies *for* the world, in and before the secular community. Was there a this-worldly way of affirming the polyphonic Christ in a world that seemed to have outgrown the comforts of religion? To this end, he posed the question:

> What does a church, a congregation, a sermon, a liturgy, a Christian life, mean in a religionless world? How do we speak about God—without religion, that is, without the temporally conditioned presuppositions of metaphysics, the inner life, and so on? . . . How can we be Εκ-κλησια, those who are called out, without understanding ourselves religiously as privileged, but instead seeing ourselves as belonging wholly to the world? Christ would then no longer be the object of religion, but something else entirely, truly lord of the world. But what does that mean? In a religionless situation, what do ritual [Kultus] and prayer mean? Is this where the "arcane discipline" [Arkandisziplin] or the

---

21. Bonhoeffer, *Ethics*, 62–63, 73–74.

difference (which you've heard about from me before) between
the penultimate and the ultimate, have new significance?[22]

Bonhoeffer clearly believed in the importance of reappropriating the
Discipline of the Secret while seeking to remain within established Lutheranism. He could not have been suggesting a return to the Secret as it was
once practiced, but clearly saw something within it that suggested to him
the possibility of a renewed and renewing faith. In much the same way,
MacLeod sought to form the Iona Community as a disciplined brotherhood
within the established Church of Scotland, and did so seeking to address
the threats posed to institutional Christianity in his particular context. Mac-
Leod's vision paralleled Bonhoeffer's conviction that there was scope for the
established church and a Discipline to sound together in a new polyphony
that affirmed the bisociating Christ in church and world. A new discipline
of worldly monasticism could arise within the church and be present in the
world affirming the greatest mystery of all: the polyphonic Christ was the
cantus firmus for all reality.

So while Bonhoeffer argued that "an 'arcane discipline' must be re-
established, through which the mysteries of the Christian faith are sheltered
against profanation,"[23] the subject of the Discipline was no longer as the
early church perceived it to be: the mysteries of Baptism, Eucharist, etc.
Now the mystery is, as it always should have been, the performance of the
polyphonic Christ in the church and world. Andreas Pangritz follows Hanfried Müller to insist that "the concept of 'arcane' undergoes a change in
Bonhoeffer in comparison to its meaning in the ancient church."[24] Christ
is now to be affirmed not as the object of religion but really Lord of the
world. Accordingly, rather than focus on the ancient particulars of the
Discipline, what Bonhoeffer valued was safeguarding the integrity of the
church community against pagan corruption. What was necessary was the
church's affirmation of Christ as *cantus firmus* and their continuing participation in the performance of the countermelodies he called into being,
countermelodies that would sound in both the church and world. Hence, to
appreciate the value Bonhoeffer found in the Discipline of the Secret, "it is
not enough simply to take over the dictionary definition of 'arcane'; rather,
attention has to be paid to the contrapuntal context in which the '*cantus
firmus*' rings out."[25] It is a Discipline of Counterpoint. For each community

22. Letter dated April 30, 1944, in Bonhoeffer, *Letters and Papers*, 364–65.

23. Letter dated May 5, 1944, in Bonhoeffer, *Letters and Papers*, 373.

24. Hanfried Müller, "Von der Kirche zur Welt," 393, cited in Pangritz, *Karl Barth*,
5.

25. Pangritz, *Karl Barth*, 5.

these counterpoints may differ. The context in which MacLeod sought "a serious re-view of the challenge of the Incarnation"[26] was not identical to the context in which Bonhoeffer affirmed that it was only in Christ that we are invited to participate "in the reality of God and the reality of the world at the same time, the one not without the other."[27] Yet the purpose of the Discipline remains the same: to participate in performing the polyphony of Christ in both church and world.

The contrapuntal context in which Bonhoeffer operated was one in which the unique claim of Christ to be both Lord of heaven and earth, was under physical threat from the Nazi empire, theological threat from the Reich Church and the spiritual threat of falling for a cheapened grace. In place of the Kingdom of God that transcended the boundaries of otherness came the thousand year Reich, intent on the exclusion of any non-Ayran. Their physical persecution of any opposition resulted in Bonhoeffer's execution. The threat of heretical corruption came through the Reich Church's belief in the German nation as a second source of revelation. The Confessing Church at Barmen repudiated as "false doctrine" the claim that there were areas of life that would not belong to Jesus Christ but to other lords, but ten years later, they seemed gripped by a third and final threat, a preoccupation with their own security. They sheltered behind a corrupted Lutheranism in which they acceded the ground of public affairs to the state, seeking to preserve for themselves some private sphere of spiritual activity beyond the world of politics.

For Bonhoeffer, the integrity of the church was at stake; the authenticity of a colony of heaven depended on the performance of the mystery of the incarnation, which for him was the way in which Christ took form in the world. This Christological *cantus firmus* could not be sublimated into doctrinal discussions but must be made concretely manifest. This was and is the mystery of the Christian faith. Bonhoeffer argued that the concrete incarnation of Christ in time and space was "the holy mystery, which theology was instituted to preserve and protect."[28] But when he asked where that mystery was being shared amidst his world, "who is Christ actually for us today?"[29] he could find increasingly few examples of "humanity being remade and redeemed as a result of God's creative grace."[30] The Reich Church

26. MacLeod, *Only One Way Left*, 152.

27. Bonhoeffer, *Ethics*, 55.

28. Finkenwalde Circular Letter, "Meditation on Christmas, December 1939," in Bonhoeffer, *Theological Education Underground*, 529.

29. Letter dated April 30, 1944, in Bonhoeffer, *Letters and Papers*, 362.

30. See Green, "Human Sociality and Christian Community," 121.

was apostate and the Confessing Church had compromised the place of Christ in the world. Bonhoeffer concluded that the mystery of the incarnate Christ was disappearing from view.[31] In response, Bonhoeffer first sought to protect the mystery from his godless context because, as he argued in 1937, "for the sake of the sacred, for the sake of sinners and for the sake of the church-community, the sacred should be protected against being given away cheaply."[32] The melodies of Christ needed to be performed authentically in the church community and the Discipline was the Secret by which Christians participated in the polyphony.

Increasingly, Bonhoeffer became convinced that while the church could never abandon their responsibility to perform the melodies of Christ within the church, neither could they separate their ultimate identity in Christ from their penultimate solidarity with Christ who was present in the world. Bonhoeffer perceived how the true Christian identity entrusted to the church had been squandered by their failure to engage the mystery of the polyphonic Christ with a religionless world now seemingly come-of-age.

When Bonhoeffer referred to his context as a world-come-of-age he did not mean that the world had reached a moral maturity: this was clearly untrue given his imprisonment by a totalitarian regime involved in global warfare and mass genocide. But what it did mean was that humanity had attained its majority (i.e., it was independent in thought and was responsible for its own actions). Humanity was no longer dependent on God as a *deus ex machina* or the "omnipotent stop gap" explanation of religion, adopted when human knowledge reached its limit. In this world-come-of-age Bonhoeffer perceived that "the age when we could tell people that with words—whether with theological or with pious words—is past, as is the age of inwardness and of conscience."[33] The time of religion was over. Bonhoeffer welcomed this end. He followed Barth's technical critique of religion,[34] namely that everything religious was a human attempt to reach beyond themselves and their ordained boundaries, and engage in an exercise in self-justification before God. Religion was identified as being those practices that dichotomized reality into the secular and sacred, a position that was denied in the biblical affirmation that all reality was reconciled to God

---

31. "Outline for a Book," in Bonhoeffer, *Letters and Papers*, 500.

32. "Power of the Keys and Church Discipline," in Bonhoeffer, *Theological Education at Finkenwalde*, 828.

33. Letter dated April 30, 1944, in Bonhoeffer, *Letters and Papers*, 362.

34. For an appraisal of Bonhoeffer's theology of religion see Wüstenberg, *Theology of Life*; Plant and Wüstenberg, *Religion, Religionlessness and Contemporary Western Culture*; and Pugh, *Religionless Christianity*.

in Christ. Bonhoeffer posited the possibility for a religionless Christianity. As Dumas sums up the differences,

> Religious Christianity unrealizes, provincializes, interiorizes, and makes Jesus remote. A nonreligious Christianity realizes, universalizes, and makes Jesus public and present, at once extraordinary and hidden.[35]

Bonhoeffer rejected the dichotomized reality of privatized religion in favor of a religionless epoch in which the church admitted that "everything gets along without 'God' and does so just as well as before."[36] He argued that the church could no longer be honest to themselves unless they recognized that they had to live in the world *"etsi deus non daretur"* (as if there were no God) but "before God!"[37] The Christian community then must engage in a discipline whose ambition was the opposite of religion; it must respect the world and then seek to relate it to God. Not so much to explain God to the world (religion) but to explain the world to God's people. Worship in word, sacrament, and community was not being replaced by worldly *caritas*. Bonhoeffer hoped that the Discipline would still enable the Christian community to "preserve and foster those practices and conventions that constitute the Church as a distinctive polity in the midst of a world caught in the throes of arrested adolescence."[38] This nonreligious interpretation would not precipitate a loss of identity for the Christian community; indeed, on the contrary, this was precisely what was to be retaken. A religionless Christianity would accept the world on its terms, but it would still seek to be authentically Christian in such a context. Bonhoeffer put the questions so sharply because he believed "the church would soon face a new possibility itself to be a real Christian community."[39]

So it was that religionless Christianity, or more specifically Bonhoeffer's search for a nonreligious interpretation of biblical and theological concepts, was not simply a search for a more relevant language with which to talk to the world about Christ. Indeed, Bonhoeffer seems to have wanted to make it more difficult to speak of Christ, but to ensure that when such conversations began that they were full of meaning for the world.[40] As

35. Dumas, "Religion and Reality in the Work of Bonhoeffer," in Klassen, *Bonhoeffer Legacy*, 266–67.

36. Letter dated June 8, 1944, in Bonhoeffer, *Letters and Papers*, 426.

37. See Letter dated July 16, 1944, in Bonhoeffer, *Letters and Papers*, 478.

38. Harvey, "Body Politic of Christ," 312.

39. Day, "Conviviality and Common Sense: The Meaning of Christian Community for Dietrich Bonhoeffer," in Klassen, *Bonhoeffer Legacy*, 225.

40. Rowan Williams asserts that in the *Letters and Papers from Prison*, Bonhoeffer

L. Gregory Jones notes with accuracy, "Bonhoeffer's 'new' language . . . is not so much 'new' as it is radically purified and renewed through the arcane discipline."[41] He clearly hoped that the Discipline would be the *askesis* by which traditional Christian doctrines such as reconciliation and redemption would enable the church to once again speak meaningfully and with integrity of Christ to a world-come-of-age. And what doctrine could not be interpreted nonreligiously was to be allowed to remain as it was, of enduring value within the Christian community, but retained by them in secret. To express it beyond the colony would violate the maturity of the world and profane the concepts themselves. They would speak of a Christ who refused to inhabit the peripheries of life to which liberal theology and scientific rationalism had conspired to relegate him. And in so doing, the Discipline protected the world from violation by religion and acquired the important function of protecting Christianity from lapsing into religion.[42]

This Discipline of Counterpoint is essentially an attempt to return Christ to the center of living, to make Christ Lord of the religionless world that has come-of-age as well as the church. This is a Christianity that collapses all attempts of humanity to think in bipolar terms of secular and sacred, because such a "static distinction between one domain [*Bereich*] as belonging to the devil and another as belonging to Christ denies the reality that God has reconciled the whole world with himself in Christ."[43]

> As long as Christ and the world are conceived as two realms [*Räume*], bumping against and repelling each other, we are left with only with the following options. Giving up on reality as a whole, either we place ourselves in one of the two realms, wanting Christ without the world, or the world without Christ—and in both these cases we deceive ourselves. Or we try to stand in the two realms at the same time, thereby becoming people in eternal conflict. . . . There are not two realities, but *only one reality*, and that is God's reality revealed in Christ in the reality of the world.[44]

Under this reality, Christians find God and the world reconciled. Their worldliness does not divide them from Christ, and their Christianity does

---

was not seeking to make religious language easier but rather hoped "to make it more difficult to talk about God." See Williams, "Bonhoeffer: the Sixties and After," 1.

41. Jones, *Embodying Forgiveness*, 30, fn. 71.

42. See Bethge, *Dietrich Bonhoeffer: A Biography*, 883.

43. Bonhoeffer, *Ethics*, 66.

44. Ibid., 57–58.

not divide them from the world. Rather, because they belong wholly to Christ, they belong wholly to the world.

The danger for a Christian colony is that establishing solidarity with the world through such a Discipline abandons the very ground that has been won, reestablishing boundaries that were supposed to have been transcended in Christ. If there is a community practicing the Discipline of Counterpoint and affirming Christ as Lord of all, how can they remain in solidarity with those for whom such things remain unknown? The solidarity seemingly collapses. Kenneth Surin makes this point in regard to Bonhoeffer's appropriation of the Discipline of the Secret. He claims that those who seek to affirm their participation in a divine solidarity with the world through the Discipline simply cannot "retain their identity as members of the *corpus Christi* in a world that has effectively extirpated the charismatic basis of this membership."[45] Additionally, he argues that those who maintain the Discipline cannot then fully identify with the profane world as the full nature of the world's disenchantment is concealed from them. These are valid criticisms if we accept the social rationalization that directs Surin's argument. But by Surin's own admission, this same rationalism has left the world "weary of life" leaving them a choice of "a stoical and sober acceptance of things as they are, or else a flight into religion."[46] Neither of these options seems palatable: the world is clearly not as it ought be, but no flight into religion will resolve that. Surin's ideological preclusion of any involvement of the truly transcendental leaves him righteously critical, but in the end dissatisfied with life. Conversely, it is exactly because the colony of true worldliness derives its ultimate meaning from the heavenly beyond that those who practice its Discipline avoid a flight into religion and can work within the world through self-interpreting acts of justice. Christ continues to break into human reality from beyond and stand in its center, between the old existence and the new. Within that boundary, and at its rediscovered center, is a boundarylessness that eludes the world. This is the mystery that must be shared with the world. In a reversal of Bonhoeffer's famous dictum, here, it is the other world of heaven that cannot be abolished ahead of its time.[47]

So Bethge admits, "No one can deny that *arcanum* ('mystery') separates, and that *disciplina* distinguishes."[48] Its people remain distinctively

---

45. Surin, "*Contempus Mundi*," 396.

46. Ibid., 395.

47. Bonhoeffer famously asserted that "this-worldliness must not be abolished ahead of its time." Letter dated June 27, 1944, in Bonhoeffer, *Letters and Papers*, 448.

48. Bethge, *Dietrich Bonhoeffer: A Biography*, 883.

different from the world and there is "probably no way of constructing a safeguard against a new boundary, unless the safeguard would come from the real and present Christ himself, who is our sole concern in the dealing with the *arcanum*."[49] Bethge offers a possible resolution to this boundary dilemma: "By worldliness Bonhoeffer testifies to Christ as the real one, and by the arcane discipline as the present one. Worldliness and arcane discipline 'are correlated attitudes of the Christian resulting from the presence of the real one.'"[50] This seeming paradox derives from the essential bisociation we find in Christ's divinity and humanity. The Discipline creates a Christological identity within which there are no boundaries between church and world. Within its boundary resides the only space in which divisions are transcended and all reality is taken up into the undivided whole of Christ.[51] It is in such a space that the community affirms that religious boundaries are untenable for the Christian colony. "There is no real Christian existence outside the reality of the world and no real worldliness outside the reality of Jesus Christ."[52] The believing community then becomes the concrete manifestation of Christ through an identity that is created and sustained by the practice of the Discipline. If, as Ray Anderson suggests, "the normative character of the ontic relationship is not to *find* Christ concretely, but to *be* Christ concretely in the world, the problem is resolved"[53] as the Christian moves "out of his 'secret place', where he knows Christ as community, and *becomes* Christ in the world."[54] Thus the Discipline "must complete itself in worldliness, not by becoming worldly, nor merely 'nonreligious', but by taking the place of Christ in the world."[55]

Even as Christians gather to rehearse a Discipline of Counterpoint, and perhaps especially at that time, they bring with them the fragments of their epiphanal encounters with Christ in the world and a nonreligious interpretation of them. This is important, for if a nonreligious interpretation of the world and the Discipline do not mutually correct each other, then the Discipline lapses into a ghetto of "liturgical monasticism," and nonreligious worldliness becomes no more than "a boulevard," preoccupied

---

49. Ibid.

50. Meier, "Weltlichkeit und Arkandisziplin bei Dietrich Bonhoeffer," cited in Bethge, *Dietrich Bonhoeffer: A Biography*, 883.

51. See Bonhoeffer, *Ethics*, 62.

52. Ibid., 61.

53. Anderson, *Historical Transcendence*, 96.

54. Ibid., 97.

55. Ibid.

with intellectual games.[56] Those who follow the Discipline begin to have realized within themselves the boundaryless way of living that comes of being Christ-like. Their identity is this paradox: their distinguishing character exists only so that barriers of privilege should be transcended. It is through the Discipline that Christ takes hold of the Christian colony and leads them back into the world to greet him there in the ten thousand faces of humanity.

This leads us back to Bonhoeffer's idea of polyphonic living and the Discipline as a practical *cantus firmus* to life. Bonhoeffer posits Christ as the central source and limit of the contrapuntal themes of life. In his lectures on Christology Bonhoeffer asserted that Christ stands on the boundary of human existence and yet at its center. Christ is

> between my old self and my new self, that is, in the center between myself and me. As the limit, Christ is at the same time the center that I have regained. As boundary, the boundary can only be seen from its other side, outside the limit. Thus it is important that we human beings, in recognizing that our limit is in Christ, at the same time see that in this limit we have found our new center.[57]

The Discipline then keeps the colony centered on Jesus as the *cantus firmus*, enabling them to become Christ existing as religionless community in the world. This is genuine transcendence, humanity directed by Christ toward God and the world, in all its fragmented dimensions, at the same time. Members of the colony "accommodate God and the whole world within us. . . . Life isn't pushed back into a single dimension, but is kept, multidimensional, polyphonic."[58] This allows for the stability of the Christ "beyond" to remain concrete in the multidimensional and fluid "midst" of reality and enables the participative performance of the counterpoint of life found in Christ. Participating in this performance of Christ not only enables the colony to transcend false boundaries but, by recentering humanity in Christ, the Discipline preserves the ordained limits between humanity and God. Indeed, Paul Ballard argues it will also be the means whereby the specific relationship between heaven and the world is articulated.[59] In its concealment, the Discipline enables the colony to keep the distinction between this world and the realm beyond. The church is not dissolved into the world, but lives in solidarity with it, sharing in its action for justice. The church's identity as colony is affirmed in its gathering for worship, which becomes

56. See Bethge, *Dietrich Bonhoeffer: A Biography*, 884.

57. "Lectures on Christology," in Bonhoeffer, *Berlin*, 324.

58. Letter dated May 29, 1944, in Bonhoeffer, *Letters and Papers*, 405.

59. See Ballard, "Worship in a Secular World," 33.

not an escape from worldly tasks and difficulties, but a retreat for the world that then sends the Christian back "to drink the cup of earthly life to the last drop."[60] The contrapuntal lines of action, if heard without the *cantus firmus*, are what the world hears of the melodies of Christ. They may sound complete in themselves, but yet they could not operate without connection to the *cantus firmus* and indeed they invite the world to listen for him.

Clearly the Discipline is not the pious counter-balance to worldly, nonreligious Christianity. Rather worldly Christianity is an important implication of a disciplined participation in the performance of the melodies of Christ. It is the dialectical movement between the twin poles of worship and solidarity with the world that provides the vital key to participating in the performance of Christ's polyphony. Bonhoeffer's hope was that this movement not only prevents either pole eliding into the other but also acts against any dualistic tendencies for Christianity to dichotomize into pietism or activism. While Bethge himself seems to have remained dissatisfied with his own formulations on this subject, he notes how "he never considered the dissolution of one in favor of the other."[61]

The provisionality of practicing the Discipline is an inherent part of its very character. Bonhoeffer anticipated a "melting pot" period of transition in which the Discipline would help the Christian community move into a nonreligious and worldly discipleship, and warned against emerging too quickly from the process. Ballard warns that this provisional aspect of the Discipline "must be taken seriously: first against panic and desperation to find instant solutions to our problems, or to hail each new (and valuable) experiment as the longed for answer; and secondly against despair, to resignation that all that is left is wilderness."[62] However, he also notes that it would be wrong to see the Discipline as no more than a "temporary expedient."[63] Its practice in varying forms will remain an essential key to performing the polyphony of Christ as Lord of heaven and earth. Those who seek to practice the Discipline of Counterpoint will be cognizant of their performance of the melodies of Christ in the church and also aware of the ways in which this music is connected yet different to that heard and performed within the world. While the two cannot exist in isolation, for the purposes of clarity the two realms must be examined in their own particularity.

The first arena in which Christians may seek to perform the polyphony of Discipline is inside the boundary of the Christian colony. They will do

---

60. Letter dated June 27, 1944, in Bonhoeffer, *Letters and Papers*, 448.

61. Bethge, *Dietrich Bonhoeffer: A Biography*, 884.

62. Ballard, "Worship in a Secular World," 35.

63. Ibid.

so through practices such as a sermon, a liturgy, worship, and prayer. Bonhoeffer never envisioned the church without these traditional practices. He advocated religionless Christianity precisely to preserve their unique value over and against religious profanation. Religionless Christianity was thus never intended to become churchless Christianity: the goal was a radically purified and renewed church whose practice of the Discipline of the Secret forged them into a distinctive community whose deeds in the world interpreted themselves. But the inspiration for these deeds was to remain a secret affair; it was not to be flaunted triumphantly before the world or forced upon its uncomprehending people. But the colony remained a place for worship. Bonhoeffer practiced regular prayer, meditation on Scripture, and hymns. His last action with others was to conduct a worship service, albeit only after his fellow prisoners had insisted on it. Thus, concludes Rasmussen, "Cultus counted for Bonhoeffer in his life and thought, in his last days, and for the future he envisioned."[64] Perhaps more importantly this reveals the significance of his practice of the Discipline: it was only after the prisoners had heard something of the *cantus firmus* in the counterpoint of his actions that he acceded to share with them his understanding of the mystery of Christ. This, too, was a gathering of fragmented epiphanies, a revelation of the suffering God for whom no boundaries existed. For Bonhoeffer, only a suffering God could help.[65]

In a world of ecclesiastical compromise such nonreligious worship with the crucified Christ in its center will not be welcomed by everyone. Indeed, it is not those initiated into the church through Baptism, but those initiated in Christ through suffering, who are invited to gather. It may be the established church that will be the strongest opponent of the rediscovery of Christianity in its nonreligious roots and it will fight to save a space for itself and its god. Bonhoeffer criticizes such responses as pointless, ignoble, and unchristian. Pointless because it is an attempt "to put a person who has become an adult back into puberty, that is, to make people dependent on a lot of things on which they in fact no longer depend, to shove them into problems that in fact are no longer problems for them."[66] It is ignoble because it attempts to "exploit people's weakness for alien purposes to which they have not consented freely."[67] Finally, it is unchristian because "it confuses Christ

64. Rasmussen, "Worship in a World Come of Age," 269.

65. See Letter dated July 16, 1944, in Bonhoeffer, *Letters and Papers*, 479.

66. Letter dated June 8, 1944, in Bonhoeffer, *Letters and Papers*, 427.

67. Ibid.

with a particular stage of human religiousness, namely, with a human law."[68] Rasmussen declares,

> Arcane discipline means that worship in a world-come-of-age is . . . only for small groups of clearly committed Christians who comprise an intense community on the basis of their intense loyalty to Christ; and their expression of the meaning of that loyalty as members of the one Body is communicated with one another in worship, but not to and with all. Worship as arcane discipline is not for the streets, the posters, the media, or the masses. It is certainly not Hollywood Bowl and drive-in Easter sunrise services, nor Sunday East Room exercises in American civil religion, nor Astrodome rallies of religiosity. It is not bumper-sticker and slick-paper Christianity. If Bonhoeffer were to have his way, the church would begin by giving up its property for the sake of the needy, would be devout in its practice of disciplines and demanding in its stipulations for participation. It would be a poor and apparently powerless church that would dispense costly grace, rather than a rich and privileged church that would offer only cheap grace.[69]

Ballard provides a powerful summary of the performance of the Discipline when he writes, "The Christian presence in the world should not be seen in terms of the sanctuary or 'going to church' as the primary activity, but as a community whose inner life is nourished in secret."[70]

If the first arena for the performance of the Discipline is the Christian colony, then the second is that of "worldly solidarity" or deputyship. This theme of deputyship or *stellvertretung* (literally standing in the place of another) is a unifying thread in all of Bonhoeffer's work and is "the opposite of everything a religious person expects from God . . . to share in God's suffering at the hands of a godless world."[71] Its roots can be found in the early theology of *Sanctorum Communio*,[72] but are perhaps most powerfully articulated in the later poetry from prison where he writes,

> People go to God when God's in need,
> find God poor, reviled, without shelter or bread,
> see God devoured by sin, weakness and death.

68. Ibid.

69. Rasmussen, "Worship in a World Come of Age," 278.

70. Ballard, "Worship in a Secular World," 31.

71. Letter dated July 18, 1944, in Bonhoeffer, *Letters and Papers*, 480.

72. See especially the subsection entitled "Ethical Collective Persons," in Bonhoeffer, *Sanctorum Communio*, 118–20.

Christians stand by God in God's own pain.[73]

Rasmussen suggests that this means "groups of Christians operating rather incognito in the world, making common cause with the non-Christian and the nonreligious, all without ecclesiastical and theological pretence and qualification."[74] As the Christian participates in the performance of Christ in the world they discover blessing (in no longer thinking that they need to be more pious than the worldly Christ) along with suffering (as they give themselves into the service of others and discover what it means to stand by God in his time of need) and also strength (as Christ equips them for the melodies they are called to perform).[75] And the further the Christian community moves from their religious notions of God, the closer they come to participating in this blessing, suffering, and the strength of Christ, being caught up into his polyphonic purposes. In other words, it is in singing songs of protest and freedom, songs that are not readily identified with the church, or the realm of the religious, that the Christian participates in the performance of Christ.

The Rule of the Iona Community in its initial form was not a conscious attempt to reinterpret the Discipline of the Secret. Even now, as it has evolved, it cannot be directly equated with a performance of the mystery of the polyphonic Christ. However, the Rule does seek to enable its members to live in the world while not being of it. An examination of the disciplines of the Iona Community reveals some indication of how the practice of such a Discipline of Counterpoint might appear in a contemporary context. For instance, part of the Community Rule deals with the commitment to work for justice and peace and affirms their decision that as individual members and family groups they will engage in forms of "political witness and action, prayerfully and thoughtfully, to promote just and peaceful social, political and economic structures."[76] For members, this part of the Rule is a point of departure, the place from which members of the colony launch themselves into worldly solidarity. Some will engage in such action through the church or other faith-based organizations, but many others will do so as part of "secular" groups, such as local councils, political parties, the Campaign for Nuclear Disarmament, the Campaign Against Arms Trade, or the coalition to Make Poverty History. Much of this work is hidden in the world in the sense that those who engage in such righteous action make no overt claim to be acting in the name of God, but do so, before God, as if God did not

73. "Christians and Heathens," in Bonhoeffer, *Letters and Papers*, 461.

74. Rasmussen, "Worship in a World Come of Age," 279.

75. See Kuhns, *In Pursuit of Dietrich Bonhoeffer*, 209ff.

76. See Appendix A, "Rule of the Iona Community."

exist. These are deeds that interpret themselves, melodies that are performed before the world, with the world, and for the sake of a better world.[77]

There is then within the Christian community an acknowledged dialectic between the melodies that occur in worship within the boundary of the colony and those which are sung beyond it, in solidarity with the world. The *cantus firmus* underpins them both and the fragmented epiphanies of counterpoint that Christ calls into existence may be encountered in either realm. Performing Christ's full polyphony requires the community to gather together the fragments into one realm, under one Lord, so that each informs the other. Prayer and work for justice form a counterpoint to Christ's *cantus firmus*. Bethge seems to have understood this when he wrote,

> "Doing the just thing among men" keeps praying from escaping into self-sufficient piety, and praying keeps the doing of the just thing from self-righteousness. Second, doing of the just thing keeps praying from that hypocrisy which the children of the world have discovered in the pious at all times, and praying keeps the doing of justice from the fanaticized ideologizing which makes those who work for change most of the time bad representatives of their own cause. Third, doing the just thing keeps praying from pessimism, which is not faith, and praying keeps doing of the just thing from resignation, which is not Christian either. And fourth, doing keeps praying within the reality of this earth, and praying keeps doing justice in line with the truth of the Gospel.[78]

This dialectic is performed in the Iona Community through regular gatherings of the membership, both in community week on Iona and on other occasions around the UK for plenary discussions. But, perhaps more importantly, this discipline is practiced in the smaller and more accountable family groups. It is here that the fragments of Christ from world and worship are brought together. Their meeting for worship and accountability in these groups is important, because the members realize that for all MacLeod's contention that community was formed by the "demanding common task" in reality, "the most vulnerable element, and usually the first to go, is not shared action but the constant holding of the other in love and respect."[79] It is through the discipline of accountability to one another of their performance of the Rule that the Lordship of Christ in church and world is

---

77. Aspects of these melodies of worldly solidarity are explored in more detail in Chapter 9.

78. Bethge, *Prayer and Righteous Action*, 26–27.

79. Ford, "Prayer and Righteous Action," 344.

affirmed, not simply in the words of pious hope, but in reality. Many church fellowships remain entrenched in Christendom and an understanding of reality as existing in two distinct realms. The discipline practiced by the Iona Community enables their members to remain as a colony of heaven within the church as much as in the world, slowly working for change. As the closing responses for Iona family groups, the liturgy affirms,

> In work and worship
> God is with us
> Gathered and scattered
> God is with us
> Now and always
> God is with us.[80]

The Discipline of performing the polyphony of Christ requires that the Christian community gather together, bringing to worship what melodies they have learned of Christ in their solidarity with the world. But it also requires a commitment to allow themselves to be scattered back into that world, performing the polyphony of Christ to a cacophonic humanity. The world is hence invited to listen to the music and, if they desire, to participate in its performance. As they do so, the world hears within itself echoes of the *cantus firmus* and begins to discover Christ for themselves and in themselves.

---

80. Iona Community, *Iona Community Members' Prayer Book*, 3.

CHAPTER 8

Making Melodies in the Church

Three Movements

FIRST MOVEMENT: POLYPHONIC WORSHIP

The regular, continual pattern of gathering for worship may be
viewed as the church's rehearsal. Worship thus becomes a kind of
performance before the performance, a preparation beforehand for
whatever witness the church might be called upon to give.

—STANLEY HAUERWAS[1]

I think prayer does change us. Our convictions, our activities, our
perspectives on our fellow humans, the nature of life, the nature of
God, can be radically altered through giving up time to prayer. And
it is the same with music. I think our perspectives are fundamentally
changed through the power of music. There is an analogy there, and
I think it is because they are from the same source: we are talking
about the same thing.

—JAMES MACMILLAN[2]

1. Hauerwas, *Performing the Faith*, 98.
2. MacMillan, "Sound of Heart," 18.

And if music is the most fundamentally contemplative of the arts, it is *not* because it takes us into the timeless but because it obliges us to rethink time: it is no longer time for action, achievement, dominion and power, not even time for acquiring ideas. . . . It is simply time for feeding upon reality; quite precisely like that patient openness to God that is religious contemplation.

—ROWAN WILLIAMS[3]

Worship is "an exasperatingly difficult word to pin down" and determining what makes such human behavior particularly Christian can be even more complex.[4] There are, for instance, many practices of worship that Christians share with other faiths; namely, an annual cycle of symbolic events, dedicated space and buildings, prayer, singing, and the reading of Holy Scriptures, all of which take on a particular identity when done within a Muslim, Jewish, Christian, or other paradigm. There are practices, particularly Eucharist and Baptism, that are definitively Christian, but are celebrated by the church in diverse ways.[5] What makes this diverse worship uniquely Christian is its consciously Christological center.[6] Christ is the *cantus firmus* of each practice. Christian worship is humanity's response to the perceived understanding of God's fragment of self-revelation in Christ. Thus, as a whole, and as separate practices, expressions of Christian worship should reflect the polyphonic nature of Christ.

The church does not have a reputation for a polyphony of worship. Each denominational division of the church has historically tended toward a monophonic homogenization that dismissed variant worship practices. In such a paradigm every move toward "oneness" in worship is understood as a distancing from "differentiation" and vice versa. A particularly conspicuous instance of this is in what North Americans have labeled the "worship wars."[7] These "wars" are examples of conflict between those with a more conservative, traditional, and usually more liturgical approach to worship and those advocating a more contemporary and/or charismatic style of

3. Williams, "Keeping Time," in *Open to Judgment*, 248.

4. White, *Introduction to Christian Worship*, 21.

5. Not all Christian tradition celebrates the Eucharist. For a comprehensive review of the diversity of practice see Jones, *Study of Liturgy*, 184–338.

6. See White, *Introduction to Christian Worship*, 25ff.

7. See York, *America's Worship Wars*.

service.[8] Christians have been urged to choose between one "camp" or the other and often congregations have split with acrimony.

Ironically, given the central metaphor of this book, many of the battles in the worship wars have been fought over the nature of singing and music, its style and instrumentation in the church.[9] This is not surprising, because of all ways that Christians worship, singing together is perhaps the most genuinely communal. As Eleanor Kreider notes, "Singing is something we do together. We agree on the tune, the pitch and the speed. Everyone, from the youngest to the oldest, can take part. Of all the things we do in worship, singing is the most genuinely corporate."[10] And notable attempts have been made to find a "third way" through the zero-sum dichotomies of America's worship wars. In particular, Robert E. Webber[11] has argued for what he terms "blended worship," and Thomas G. Long has articulated nine characteristics of congregations who have successfully united traditional and contemporary worship.[12] But there is lacking in these works a sufficiently robust foundational theology on which to construct worship that genuinely bisociates unity and difference. For instance, Webber's thesis is clear, "Worshipping churches respect their own tradition, are in dialogue with the worship traditions of other churches, and draw from the church's worship practices throughout history."[13] His context has been the competing traditions of North American worship wars: the liturgical tradition, the traditional Protestants, the creative/contemporary model and the praise and worship/charismatic tradition. But his laudable proposals for "blended worship" can leave the impression that it is a pragmatic solution to an embarrassing conflict rather than a direct response to a revealed understanding of the nature of God. It is the metaphor and the theology of polyphony that rises to the challenge of this otherwise unmet task.[14]

8. Rather than being the subject of theological reflection these battles have often been decided by a synthesis of zero-sum logic, democracy and free market philosophy: victory has gone to that which attracts the most "consumers" of worship.

9. For a summary of conflicts over music styles in worship see York, *America's Worship Wars*. For a discussion of conflict over language see Kenneson, *Worship Wars*, 72–75.

10. Kreider, *Enter His Gates*, 59.

11. Webber, *Blended Worship*; and *Planning Blended Worship*.

12. Long, *Beyond the Worship Wars*. These are "an experience of mystery, practicing hospitality, recovering a sense of drama, excellence and eclecticism in music, creatively adapting the worship space, connecting worship to mission, encouraging worshippers to develop a range of worship responses, moving towards a joyous festival as worship concludes and employing strong gifted leaders."

13. Webber, *Blended Worship*, 3.

14. Hawn suggests that a more appropriate metaphor can be drawn from the

Polyphonic worship will gather into a single unity the differing worship practices of the past, the present, and the future.[15] It begins with the past, acknowledging the debt owed by the contemporary community of faith to the historical communion of saints. It is their worship, their liturgy, and their hymnody that has kept alive the story of salvation and nurtured the church since the days of Christ and his first disciples. Polyphonic worship will discern that while some of their practices may be no longer relevant to contemporary this-worldly worship, the wealth contained in these traditions cannot be quickly relegated to books of history. Polyphonic worship will search the past and treasure what of its history still speaks to the world and church in the present. It will acknowledge that the best of the past may need to be recontextualized for the present and it will work at such a task.

Gathering the fragments of what has gone before and rearranging them for a new time and place is a classic mark of today's postmodern culture. Musical examples are legion, but might include Jacques Loussier's jazz reinterpretation of Bach, Jan Garbarek's fusion of saxophone with the medieval choral sound of the Hilliard Ensemble, Enigma's synthesis of 1990s pop music with Gregorian chant, and the deliberate cultural fusions of bands such as Afro Celt Sound System.[16] To carry the past with them, but to reimagine it for the journey, is also a process incarnate in the biography of worship in the Iona Community.[17] MacLeod was always clear that the Iona Community was not the resurrection of a dream of the past, Celtic or Benedictine. It was an experiment for today and one that was always conscious of the future. It was a "'John the Baptist' movement": singing songs in the

---

polyrhythms of a West African drumming ensemble. Hawn, *Gather Into One*, 273. Hawn specifically rejects the images of "unison singing," "harmonic blending," and "contrapuntal complexity" because they are "essentially Western terms that describe the priorities of Euro-North American musical traditions." *Gather Into One*, 272. Hawn's criticism is well made but it lacks a compelling locus for a Christological center such as that offered in the imagery of the *cantus firmus*. The same metaphor of polyrhythm is adopted by Taylor, "Polyrhythm in Worship," in Blout and Tisdale, *Making Room at the Table*, 108–28.

15. See also the discussion on "multi-voiced worship" in Murray and Murray Williams, *Multi-voiced Church*, 43–62; and Kreider and Kreider, *Worship and Mission After Christendom*, 73–120.

16. Jacques Loussier, *The Very Best of Bach* (CD, BMG, 2000); Jan Garbarek and the Hilliard Ensemble, *Officium* (CD, ECM, 1994); Enigma, *MCMXC a.D.* (CD, Virgin, 1991). Afro Celt Sound System combines African and Celtic traditional music with pop technology and dance rhythms. See Afro Celt Sound System, *Sound Magic*, vol. 1 (CD, Real World Records, 1996).

17. For an appreciation of how MacLeod and the early Iona Community understood worship see Muir, *Outside the Safe Place*, 204–40.

desert, crying out to make smooth the rough places of the world, and calling others to prepare for a new coming of the Lord.[18]

Given Bonhoeffer's reflections on theology, community, and music, one might have expected the worship in Finkenwalde to have displayed some polyphonic characteristics. He was, in fact, strongly critical of the students singing in parts. He may have been following the example of early church fathers such as Clement of Alexandria,[19] who understood unison song as symbolic of the unity found in Christ. He certainly notes that unison singing avoided conflict and competition in music. There was, he believed,

> no place in the worship service where vanity and bad taste can so assert themselves as in the singing.... The improvised second part that . . . kills both the words and the sound . . . the bass or the alto voices that must call everybody's attention to their astonishing range . . . the solo voice that drowns out everything else . . . [and] those who will not join in the singing because they are particularly moody or nursing hurt feelings.[20]

While Bonhoeffer's reasons for singing in unison are laudable, he failed to address the fact that musical conflict in worship has, at its root, a refusal to recognize the unique unity and diversity that exists within the polyphonic Christ. Such conflict represents a lack of theological imagination in our conception of the Christ. The polyphonic singing of one song is a concrete expression of that truth. As Cunningham points out, modern theology has interpreted oneness and difference as a zero-sum game, and

> to set these two categories against one another is to force Christian theology to work against itself: the more one argues in favor of difference, the less one is committed, it seems, to a specifically Christian identity. And on the other hand (according to this way of thinking), the more one seeks to merge everything into a single, undifferentiated whole, the more remote one's theology

18. MacLeod referred to Iona as a "'John the Baptist' movement," cited in Ferguson, *Chasing the Wild Goose*, 68.

19. Clement of Alexandria wrote, "We want to strive so that we, the many, may be brought together into one love, according to the union of the essential unity . . . The union of many, which the divine harmony has called forth out of a medley of sounds and divisions becomes one symphony, following the one leader of the choir and teacher, the Word, resting in that same truth and crying out 'Abba Father.'" Clement of Alexandria, *Protrepticus*, 9, cited in Hawn, *Gather Into One*, xvi.

20. Bonhoeffer, *Life Together*, 67. On Iona, young abbey musician Ian MacKenzie took Bonhoeffer's thinking seriously and literally, arguing that there should be no harmony singing in worship, as it detracted from the unity of the congregation. See various reflections on this in Muir, *Outside the Safe Place*, 222–35.

becomes from the obvious differences that mark the world in which we dwell.[21]

There is, therefore, a need to discover a polyphonic practice of worship in which diverse melodies of the church remain rooted in the *cantus firmus* of Christ but learn to complement rather than compete with one another. Indeed, despite these comments from Bonhoeffer, in other ways a distinctive polyphony is apparent during the time in Finkenwalde. While there he insisted that it is not the voice of the individual but "the voice of the church" that should be heard in song and that all true singing together served to "widen [the] spiritual horizon" of the community.[22] This enabled gathered communities of faith to recognize their membership of the wider Christian church on earth[23] and the need to stand in solidarity with suffering brothers and sisters in Christ. Thus, in Finkenwalde, he taught students the Negro Spirituals he had sung in Harlem and spoke of the struggles out of which they were born. His eclectic adoption of worshipping practices from beyond his Lutheran tradition, disciplines such as confession and meditation, clearly mark him as one who was instinctively moving toward what was in essence polyphonic worship: a gathering of worshipping fragments around a *cantus firmus* of the Discipline of Counterpoint. But it also brought criticism from some, including Karl Barth, who believed that he was leading his seminarians down the road to Roman Catholicism.[24]

George MacLeod was similarly accused of leading the Iona Community to Rome because of his equally eclectic approach to worship. He was criticized for his adoption of non-Presbyterian practices such as twice daily services that employed candles and liturgical responses,[25] and his weekly celebration of communion in the community.[26] But MacLeod was a man with a passion for worship. The celebration of Easter he experienced in the Russian Orthodox Church in Jerusalem captivated his imagination. He was overwhelmed by the combination of "action, mystery and theatre" and by the way "the spiritual and the material fused in a never-to-be-forgotten

21. Cunningham, *These Three Are One*, 270.

22. Bonhoeffer, *Life Together*, 68.

23. Ibid.

24. Barth wrote expressing concern at the "indefinable odour of the eros and pathos of the cloister." See Bosanquet, *Life and Death of Dietrich Bonhoeffer*, 159.

25. Although such practices are common now, at the time innovations from other denominations, especially Roman Catholicism were regarded with suspicion in Scots Presbyterianism.

26. Many of the practices adopted by MacLeod were (or at least were represented by him as) being firmly located within the history of his own reformed tradition or that of the "Celtic Church" of yesteryear.

rapturous moment of revelation."[27] This was worship that reflected the bisociation of heaven and this-worldliness in its Christological center; this was worship that appealed to the personal, the political, and the cosmic in MacLeod.[28] It was an epiphanal fragment that would inspire him for the rest of his life and it particularly enthused the worship of the colony of heaven he founded on Iona. In time, Iona Abbey became the theater in which this compelling vision of God's glory was often expressed.

Returning to Scotland in 1933, an enlivened MacLeod had argued that the reformed scheme of private and public worship was increasingly redundant and in need of a new experiment that would "infuse with the Christian spirit every department of life."[29] He wrote,

> Is the truth not that the old cultus has splendidly served its day and generation; it is our modern environment that has rendered it outmoded. It is not the old Reformation timbers that are in criticism, it is that they survive from a day of wooden houses. It is not the building of the old channels that has rendered them faulty, but the shifting of the subsoil of this evolving world.[30]

MacLeod instinctively appreciated that the infusion of the Christian spirit in all of life must be grounded in the relation of heaven and earth that was located in the Christ. It was the way of Columba and the Celtic church. It was the experiment that was needed for his time. And so it was with the specific intention of embodying a spirituality that broke down the barriers between everyday life and language and the life of the worshipping community that the first members of the Iona Community arrived to rebuild the medieval abbey.[31] In time, the Iona Community would incarnate a multiplicity of practice that illustrates the idea of polyphonic worship. MacLeod realized that worship must unite the realms of heaven and earth. He argued that

> the key to all material issues is to be found in the mystery that Christ came in a body, and healed bodies and fed bodies, and that he died in a body and rose in a body, to save man body and soul.[32]

27. Ferguson, *George MacLeod*, 125.

28. Ibid.

29. Ferguson, *Chasing the Wild Goose*, 53.

30. Ibid., 52.

31. See Galloway, "Worship of the Iona Community," 222.

32. MacLeod, "Church in the Modern World," cited in Ferguson, *Daily Readings*, 60.

The worship must be this-worldly. It will seek out the "hidden things" of heaven that are yet to be revealed on earth and the new ways that might be discovered to "touch the lives of all."[33] Thus, the concerns of a this-worldly discipleship, matters such as peace, justice, racism, economics, and ecology must find a place in the worship of the church.

There will be a wide number of people involved in such worship. If in Christ there is "neither Jew nor Greek, slave nor free, male nor female," if all are "one in Christ Jesus,"[34] then polyphonic worship will be inclusive of people, not only in who might be permitted to participate in worship, but in how and with whom it is planned and facilitated. There will be united around one *cantus firmus* the differences of people lay and ordained, male and female, married and single, rich and poor, gay and straight, young, old, and middle aged. Bonhoeffer's Finkenwalde community was an exclusive brotherhood of unmarried clergy from a particular denomination. The early Iona Community reflected a similar exclusivity[35] but with one notable exception: it was deliberately devised to place clergy and laity in community with one another.[36] From the beginning the craftsmen participated in daily worship in the abbey and their presence was vital. "Time and time again," wrote MacLeod, "we [ministers] were reminded that artisans are better men than parsons—not just at their jobs but at piercing through by instinct to those real issues which mental acrobatics so often utterly confuse."[37]

In time, the community expanded to include other interested lay-people from a wide range of socioeconomic backgrounds. They were not craftsmen and did not have the time to spend three months rebuilding the abbey, but they were in sympathy with the work of the community. Despite its reputation for social justice the community remained an all-male pre-serve until 1969 when Dr. Nancy Brash became the first woman member.

33. "Prayer for the Iona Community," in Iona Community, *Iona Abbey Worship Book*, 19–20.

34. See Gal 3:28.

35. The first community members were all male, single, and belonged to the Church of Scotland. For an overview of how the relationship between the Iona Community and women changed over the years see Muir, *Outside the Safe Place*, 126–49.

36. It must be acknowledged that its main purpose focused on educating the ministers in a this-worldly discipleship and some artisans felt that they were no more than "audio-visual aids for the training of ministers." See Ferguson, *Chasing the Wild Goose*, 80. For an overview of the relationship between clergy and craftsmen see Muir, *Outside the Safe Place*, 151–80.

37. MacLeod, cited in Ferguson, *Chasing the Wild Goose*, 55. While the craftsmen participated in worship, it was led by the clergy, with MacLeod believing that each vocation had their expertise and that the richness of a community was found in their balance.

The inclusion of women into the community only came because of female persistence and the delay does not represent one of the community's finer hours of inclusion.[38] Its current membership is almost half female and it has had its first female leader, Kathy Galloway.

Today, the planning and facilitating of worship in the abbey mostly involves women and men who are not actually members, but who work in the abbey on behalf of the Iona Community. They come from a variety of countries, races, and Christian traditions, and are part of the residents' group or have volunteered to work on the island for a few months. Every week it will also include a number of guests staying at the abbey and MacLeod centers. Few of these people have any theological training or are ordained. Indeed, as Kathy Galloway notes, "The worship is as likely to be led by a 20-year-old volunteer cook as by the warden."[39] And everyone will be encouraged to participate in the worship, returning the idea of "the liturgy" to its original meaning, the work of the people.

A recognition of difference will also require the community of faith to reflect upon their generational differences; the varying needs and gifts of people at different stages of life. Hawn is right to argue that "the bright voices of children and changing timbres of young persons should be just as common as the softer voices of senior adults."[40] But this is a particular challenge with regard to children. As Cunningham notes, "Children tend to be the first victims of an excessive quest for homogeneity in the worship service,"[41] and making space for the melodies of children means more than carving out a particular niche for them in the service. "It also requires adults to rethink their own expectations about the worship service, and to recognize that—if it is to be an act of the whole Body—it will require all members to accept the 'otherness' of the other members."[42]

"Otherness" is a key concept in the polyphony of ritual that is also to be found in this worship. All worship has within it certain prescribed and symbolic actions that mark epiphanal points in the story of the community and/or enable its people to manage change. Some of these rituals will be familiar "common rites" that affirm the community culture and enable the personal and communal flux endemic of the human condition to encounter an epiphanal fragment of divine order. Within the church, these

38. See Ferguson, *Chasing the Wild Goose*, 112–13. For various reflections on this from women connected with the Iona Community in the early days see Muir, *Outside the Safe Place*, 126–49.

39. Galloway, "Worship of the Iona Community," 225.

40. Hawn, *Gather Into One*, 274.

41. Cunningham, *These Three Are One*, 279.

42. Ibid., 280.

are moments like Baptism, weddings, or funerals, rites whose particular words and symbolic actions "are a special kind of doorway into a new stage of life."[43] They may also include regular moments of worship such as reciting the Lord's Prayer, the Creed, and celebrating Eucharist. These "common rites" are properly understood as epiphanal fragments, and are regarded as sacred. Within the worship life of the Iona Community the daily responses contained in the weekly cycle of morning liturgy (especially the daily prayer of confession, intercession for members, and the community prayer) mark such occasions. So, too, the weekly rhythm of services dedicated to welcome, quiet, justice and peace, prayers for healing, acts of commitment, and communion. The monthly cycle of psalms, the annual community week gathering, and the hallowing service for new members also mark important common rites.

However, polyphonic worship will also include "innovative rites," actions that speak to the community of an "otherness" that draws the community beyond its normative paradigms of belonging and commitment. The evening services in the abbey are more open to such innovative rites. Thus, while there exists a set liturgy for the various evening services (the common rite) there is within that a large degree of freedom for creative expression. For instance, the liturgy for the service of welcome leaves a space for "signs of welcome," in which guests and staff are invited to greet one another, but the sign may change every week.[44] Similarly, in the service for justice and peace, after the reading of Scripture, provision is made for the readings to be "highlighted by other expressions of the Word, such as other readings, newspaper reports, drama, poetry, testimonies, comment and chants,"[45] and the response to the Word may include a symbolic action in which the people are invited to "declare their engagement with the concern" by, for instance, "lighting candles, placing stones, ringing a bell, planting seeds or writing."[46] The evening service of commitment is usually planned and led by guests who will draw from their own wealth of experience and the issues discussed in their week. This openness allows for the innovation of "the other" to enter the worship.

Such innovative rites may be divided into those of comfort and those of disturbance. Innovative rites of comfort may be those designed to bring assurance and reorientation in times of disorientation. Alternatively, innovation may be designed as an opportunity to deliberately disturb the people

---

43. Grainger, *Message of the Rite*, 45.

44. *Iona Abbey Worship Book*, 57.

45. Ibid., 73.

46. Ibid., 74.

beyond the comfortable orientation of their common rites into some new commitment of discipleship. Two brief examples may illustrate the point. In a service held immediately after the events in America on September 11, 2001, the congregation were in a season of shocked disorientation and needed both to express their grief over those who had died and their solidarity with those working in the ongoing emergency relief operation. At the front of the church were placed newspaper pictures of the disaster and a large pile of unwashed stones. As a song of lament was sung, people were invited to come and move the stones, in solidarity with the rescuers who were still at that time removing rubble from Ground Zero. As they did so they were further invited to build the stones into a cairn of remembrance for those who had died. After this, a prayer of assurance was offered. This was both a comfort to disturbed people and an opportunity for them to move beyond disorientation. Contrastingly, in a service of commitment entitled "Pushing the Boat Out," the sermon challenged the people to a risky faith on the basis of Jesus's words to his disciples to push the boat into deeper water.[47] As they arrived, the people were given a picture of a boat tied to the jetty and in a subsequent action of response they were invited to come forward to a small dinghy placed near the communion table and from there exchange their picture for one of a boat in full sail which they could take home.

Of course, in other responses the symbolic action may itself be polyvalent, allowing for different members of the congregation to respond according to their own context of personal orientation, disorientation, or reorientation. In this way the same action may be comforting to one and disturbing to another. And if appropriate a number of different symbolic actions may be offered at separate "stations" located around the one worship space so that many people may be enabled to respond in different ways at the same time.[48]

This raises questions over a polyphony of space in worship; can many things happen simultaneously in the same space without distraction and chaos? Musically, if one note is played and a second and a third is added, each occupies the same "audio space," but each is heard distinct from the other. So, in polyphony the different melodies are united, but distinct. Cunningham cites the medieval cathedral as an architectural incarnation of the

47. See Luke 5:1–11.

48. One service entitled "Down to Earth" focused on the gospel and ecology and based around the Parable of the Four Soils (Luke 8:4–15). People were asked to reflect on which soil most represented their response to issues of climate change. Seeds were available at four different "stations" and people were invited to take a seed from their particular station and plant it in good soil.

musical metaphor. He notes how its architecture of side chapels, foyers, and aisles enables

> a beehive of activity, in which many people are doing many different things at once. In the midst of their diverse activities, they are held together by their common focus on Christian worship and the Christian life. They do all meet under the one roof; but their activities are many and various, and no one seems particularly concerned that other people, in other parts of this great room, may not be doing the same thing. Rather than being distracted by this great swell of activity, people seem to thrive in it, and to concentrate their attention all the more fully on their own particular acts of participation in the Christian life.[49]

This does not require a modern replication of such medieval constructions, not least because they often reflected an unhealthy separation of people and clergy, but worship space should reflect the polyphonic character of the Christ who is worshipped. But it is not always the case. James White notes that "church architecture not only reflects the ways Christians worship but architecture also shapes worship or not uncommonly, misshapes it,"[50] and while he admits that the church could "worship only with difficulty without buildings," he adds, "often we worship with difficulty because of them."[51] Theology and church architecture have consistently influenced one another through the centuries[52] and usually interact around the varying arrangements of six different liturgical spaces and three or four liturgical centers from which worship is enabled.[53] But usually the congregational focus has united in one space and center at one time. Rarely has the arrangement of church space sought to reflect the plurality that is revealed in the polyphonic Christ.[54] Graham Maule, one of the facilitators in the Iona Community's Wild Goose Worship Group has a particular interest in this

---

49. Cunningham, *These Three Are One*, 272.

50. White, *Introduction to Christian Worship*, 89.

51. Ibid., 90.

52. For a comprehensive review see Hammond, *Towards a Church Architecture*. See also Kilde, *Sacred Power, Sacred Space*; and Giles, *Re-pitching the Tent*.

53. See White, *Introduction to Christian Worship*, 93ff. These are: a gathering space, a movement space, congregational space, a choir/music space, a baptismal space, and an altar/communion table space. The main liturgical centers are a baptismal font/pool, a pulpit, an altar/communion table.

54. Cunningham argues that the tendency to reduce each space in church architecture to only one activity (particularly what happens in the "sanctuary") is connected to a failure to transpose Trinitarian values into concrete worshipping practice. See Cunningham, *These Three Are One*, 274–78.

area, having originally trained as an architect. He argues that much of a congregation's difficulty in worship comes from the restricting architecture of the building.[55] His thinking has provoked the creative polyphonic use of space in events like "Last Night Out" and in the less flexible arena of Iona Abbey.[56] The creative and multiple uses of available space have brought rich rewards in forms of worship that have been truly polyphonic. If the church architecture were designed upon a theology of a polyphonic Christ then new possibilities for building design and worship planning would unfold.[57]

If the Christ worshipped is both Lord of church and world then considerations of space cannot be limited to ecclesiastical buildings. If a single note is played upon a piano, the note fills the whole of the audible space; there is no holy space reserved for sound any more than there is some arena from which the note is absent. Christ's *cantus firmus* fills the whole of creation. So, Christian theology affirms the church as the gathering of believers, not the building but a congregation that can occur in diverse venues such as a dining room, a hospital, or in an open field.[58] If those believers are Christ existing as a community, and Christ is not only polyphonic but a boundaryless epiphany of heaven, then reflection will be needed on how worship might reflect the claim that Christ is Lord of all space. This might involve worship being deliberately located in ways that transcend traditional boundaries of sacred space. Acts of worship may be held in pubs[59] or shopping centers or places of public significance. Or it might involve acts of worship that occur without buildings at all. For instance, on Iona, worship has been held around the standing stone cross[60] and in events like the Christian arts festival called Greenbelt, ten thousand people have shared Eucharist in a field.[61] Outside worship has also formed an integral part of some acts of political resistance. A good example is the regular protest outside the

55. The author first heard these comments made by Graham Maule during a plenary on church architecture at the Third Iona School of Music, August 1997.

56. "Last Night Out" is now known as "Holy City," see http://www.holycity-glasgow .co.uk.

57. See Giles, *Re-pitching the Tent*; and Green, "Build my Church," 27–36.

58. Debuyst, "Architectural Setting," in Davies, *New Dictionary of Liturgy*, 26.

59. One of the longstanding examples of this is "Holy Joes," a group of Christians who met in the basement of a London Pub. See http://www.smallfire.org/holyjoespage1 .html. For examples of other alternative worship spaces see http://www.alternativewor ship.org; and Riddell, Pierson, and Kirkpatrick, *Prodigal Project*.

60. This is how Celtic Christians may have worshipped. The crosses acted not only as a gathering point for congregations but the biblical stories carved into them would be used as teaching aids.

61. See http://www.greenbelt.org.uk.

Faslane Nuclear Submarine Base.[62] Outside worship may also incorporate public acts of procession and pilgrimage. For instance, on Good Friday on Iona there may be a public procession through the Stations of the Cross from the center of the village to the abbey church. Every week the pilgrimage journeys around the island stopping for reflection, song, and prayer at various points of significance.

The prayers of the community at worship will also allow for diversity, such as an open time for spoken prayer, opportunity for silent prayer and meditation, body prayer, praying with icons, praying with the psalms, and sensory prayer. Space for silence is particularly important in a frenetic world that offers little room for reflection on their relationship with others or God. Such quiet space is necessary if Christians are to hear the melodies of heaven[63] and listen with discernment to their performance in the world as God hears it. So any one act of polyphonic worship may include a combination of this diversity of practice along with spoken prayers that may be liturgical, prayers written for that particular event, and/or extempore prayer. Indeed, extempore prayer may afford the polyphonic opportunity for the community to pray simultaneously as a number of smaller groups. But in any event, all such prayers should be those of the community and not simply those personal to the individual. Bonhoeffer wrote that even extemporaneous prayer should not be "the chaotic outburst of a human heart, but the prayer of an internally ordered community."[64]

Bonhoeffer was correct. Often, prayer within the Christian community is erroneously understood as being at its best when it begins with the individual and when it is both personal and spontaneous, a sharing of one's private hopes and fears with God. This fails to realize that first and foremost prayer is a response to God and so should begin with God rather than with the individual. If it begins with the individual and the sounds of human desire, then it risks drowning out any epiphanal fragments of heaven's song that may seek to draw near. Humanity dare not so risk or presume to address God first with a song of its own making for true prayer is not concerned

---

62. In Galloway's *The Pattern of Our Days* there is an adaptation of the act of worship held outside the Faslane Base on October 27, 1986. See Galloway, *Pattern of Our Days*, 69–73.

63. Indeed, even in heaven there is a silence kept (Rev 8:1). Muers takes this verse as a beginning for her theological work on a responsible and listening silence. Muers, *Keeping God's Silence*. The Sunday evening service in Iona Abbey is traditionally one of silence.

64. Bonhoeffer, *Life Together*, 70. Bonhoeffer placed the responsibility for such prayer on one person, the *Hausvater*, to safeguard prayer from "the wrong kind of scrutiny and from false subjectivity," but he admitted that it placed an unexpected responsibility on that individual. Bonhoeffer, *Life Together*, 69.

with revealing or attaining human desires, it is about learning to participate in all that God wishes for them. Prayer leads the praying person(s) to discover their part and to participate in the mysterious symphony of the company of heaven, the communion of saints, angels, and archangels. It is only the melodies of heaven that can lead humanity into the revelation of God's purposes. As such, there can never be any truly "private prayer" because any individual prayer is only ever but a part of this greater communal music. It is in this way that the individual or community of faith participates in the unfolding melodies of heaven. Christians participate in the melodies of God by first learning in an internally ordered community how to listen and sing the melodies of heaven. Prayer then is a disciplined response, a response that is taught. This is not to suggest that heaven remains resolutely deaf to the well-intentioned prayers of an untutored but sincere heart. Grace will find a space for such prayer in the symphony of heaven. But it is to argue that prayer, when understood as the discernment of heaven's melodies for the people of God, necessitates disciplined instruction.

That the melody of prayer is a tutored discipline should come as no surprise. After all, it was the first disciples who asked Jesus to teach them to pray.[65] In doing so, they acknowledged that discerning the melodies of heaven required a rehearsing discipline. In this way, Christ increasingly became the ground bass of their own being. The disciples sensed that they could only learn this from Christ. And similarly, through the centuries when people have sought to pray they have apprenticed themselves to those who have themselves distinctly heard the song of Christ. But any such masters of prayer can in the end only direct the novice pray-er beyond themselves and into the company of Christ; encouraging an attentiveness to the *cantus firmus*. In the Christian community, this ground bass of Christ is sounded most clearly through the reading of the Scriptures. It is there that the song of Christ addresses the community of faith. And so those seeking to learn the discipline of praying with Christ may best begin by praying with the Scriptures. Down through the centuries, when the Christian community has sought to pray through the words of Scripture, as steps to find their way to God, they have looked for instruction from the Bible's own book of prayer: the Book of Psalms. This is not to claim, in some pre-critical fashion, that the psalms must be read with an overt Christological agenda,[66] but is to

---

65. This point is made in Bonhoeffer, *Life Together*, 155; and see Luke 11:1.

66. Such pre-critical readings of the psalter do not take account of the psalms within the context of the life and worship of Ancient Israel. However, this does not necessarily render their discussions inferior for as Bell notes, the "Word of God is too profound to have its depths unlocked only by intellectual analysis." See Bell, "Battering the Babies Heads." See also Bell, "The Lost Tradition of Lament," in *Composing Music for Worship*,

suggest that if Christ was in God, the Word within the words that constitute the Scriptures, then we might expect a prefiguring fragment of him in the words of the psalms in much the same way as an overture may hint at the themes which will be later developed in an opera.[67] In this way, "the words that come from God will be the steps on which we find our way to God."[68]

The psalms are epiphanal fragments of heaven's melody that lead the Christian into the discipline of prayer. Their words were the prayer book of Jesus and were often found upon his lips. But before that they were, of course, the prayers of David and of others. In both they become the Word of God in Scripture. When the psalms are prayed by a polyphonic Jesus, he who is the living bisociation of humanity and divinity, the human words of David simultaneously become the Divine Word, spoken to the community of faith. And likewise, when the community of faith pray along with the words of Scripture, then through Christ, God's Word becomes again a human word, placing the fullness of human experience before God.[69] The psalms become not only the melody of God that heaven wishes the human community to hear, but also and simultaneously the music of humanity that God longs to hear voiced from the community: it is the Word of Christ, and the church is Christ existing as community. Immersed in their words the Christian community finds an *askesis* of learning that helps them attune the experiences of this world to music in the key of God: to pray with Christ and sing in harmony with his *cantus firmus*. In this way, the psalms have become for the Christian community a vast repertoire of the melodies of God,[70] and the regular incorporation of them into the worship of the people becomes the one rehearsal hall in which their melody is learned.[71] It is only through

104-16, particularly 111–14. Walter Brueggemann argues that while critical analysis aids a faithful hearing of the psalms he is equally assured that many "pre-critical" works provide a perceptive power and vitality to their understanding. See Brueggemann, *Message of the Psalms*, 16, fn. 2.

67. The analogy is borrowed from Bell, "Battering the Babies Heads."

68. Bonhoeffer, *Life Together*, 156.

69. This is essentially the argument proposed by Bonhoeffer in *Life Together*, 157.

70. A cursory eavesdrop on many a church prayer meeting will reveal how the language of the psalms has found its way into the language of prayer via hymnody and contemporary worship songs. Despite recent interest in rediscovering the place of lament in worship, whether the breadth and depth of human experience that is found in the psalms is adequately represented in contemporary hymnody is doubtful.

71. Ambrose thought of the psalms as a "gymnasium for the spiritual athlete." See "Explanatio psalmorum," xii, as cited in Wells and Van Neste, *Forgotten Songs*, 11. It is for this reason that the psalms have played a vital role on the daily office of many monastic communities. They continue to play this role within the new "this-worldly monasticism" of the Iona Community, being afforded a specific place within family group worship and in the morning worship in the Abbey. See Iona Community, *Iona*

learning to rehearse the sounds of the psalms that the minds of Christians have learned to sound in harmony with the music of heaven their voices repeat.[72]

Prayer in this way is akin to those who learn to play music by ear.[73] The musician first learns to play because they hear and are attracted by the music that has already been played. They then learn to participate in that music through an *askesis* of repeating, developing, and improvising upon what others have played to them. So the Christian community learns to sing to God because God has first sung to them, and in repeating the music of God, God's children learn to sing with God. By repeating God's own music, the community of faith begins to pray with and to God.[74]

Bonhoeffer tried to tutor his students in Finkenwalde to this end. He encouraged the praying of the psalms both in the corporate times of morning and evening worship and in solitude. He was convinced that a truly Christian community developed a prayerful relationship with God by praying through the Scriptures, particularly the psalms. He approvingly quoted Luther to the effect that other prayers seemed bloodless when compared to the "juice, the strength, the passion, the fire" of the psalms[75] and wrote, "Whoever has begun to pray the Psalter earnestly and regularly, will 'soon take leave' of those other, light and personal 'little devotional prayers.'"[76] This was true of Bonhoeffer's own prayers. Often, it was through the psalms that he not only encountered the presence of God in life but made connections between God's Word and the events of his time. Bethge illustrates this when commenting on the many marginal notes Bonhoeffer made in his Bible. The most poignant example refers to Psalm 74. Beside verse eight, "They said in their hearts, 'We will crush them completely!' They burned every place where God was worshipped in the land," Bonhoeffer wrote the date, November 9, 1938, the occasion of Crystal Night, when synagogues were burned, Jewish shops and houses attacked, and Jews were assaulted.[77]

Abbey Worship Book, 212–57.

72. This is a paraphrase of the Rule of St. Benedict in which the saint suggests that the psalms enable the mind to echo in harmony with the voice. See Rule 19, "The Rule of St. Benedict," in Chadwick, *Western Asceticism*, 309.

73. The analogy also works with those who learn to play music "by sight" except in that instance they learn to participate in what other musicians have written down, not what is being performed.

74. This is a development of the analogy Bonhoeffer uses in *Life Together*, 156.

75. Ibid., 161.

76. Ibid.

77. See Bethge, *Dietrich Bonhoeffer: A Biography*, 607. Later (in November 1938) he again reflected on the plight of the Jews through Scripture in a circular letter to

Significantly, he then added, "That leads deeply into prayer."[78] Later, from prison he would write to his parents, "I read the Psalms daily, as I have done for years. There is no other book that I know and love as much."[79]

For Bonhoeffer, the psalms were the prayers of Jesus Christ, the one who "stands in our place and prays for us . . . [who] knows us better than we know ourselves and was truly human for our sake."[80] The psalms become the prayer of Bonhoeffer and the prayers of the community of faith because they are, *ab initio*, the prayers of Christ. Thus, Bonhoeffer concludes,

> Who prays the Psalter? David (Solomon, Asaph, etc.) prays. Christ prays. We pray. We who pray are, first of all, the whole community of faith in which alone the entire richness of the Psalter can be prayed. But those who pray are also, finally, all individuals insofar as they have a part in Christ and in their congregation and share in the praying of their prayer. David, Christ, the congregation, I myself—wherever we consider all these things with one another, we become aware of the wonderful path that God follows in order to teach us to pray.[81]

If the Christian community is praying with and to Christ, hearing the melodies of heaven through the psalms as prayed within their midst, then their prayers will inevitably direct them back into this world to which God has chosen to bind God's self. They draw the Christian community back into the real world, "outside the camp," and as MacLeod said,

> Outside holiness.
> Out to where soldiers gamble
> and thieves curse,
> and nations clash
> at the cross-roads of the world.[82]

And the psalms further encourage a this-worldly discipleship of prayer by employing a melody of language that is drawn directly from the

---

Finkenwalde graduates. He used the same Psalm, along with Zech 2:8, "Whoever touches you touches the apple of his eye," with Rom 9:4 and Rom 11:11–15.

78. Circular letter dated November 20, 1938, in Bonhoeffer, *Theological Education Underground*, 84.

79. Letter dated May 15, 1943, in Bonhoeffer, *Letters and Papers*, 81.

80. Bonhoeffer, *Life Together*, 160.

81. Ibid.

82. "A Temple Not Made with Hands," in MacLeod, *Whole Earth Shall Cry Glory*, 44–45. The psalms continue to play a central role in the worship in Iona Abbey, with a six-week cycle of some thirty-six psalms arranged around themes of justice and peace, healing, commitment, communion, leaving, and creation and welcome.

physical realities of God's creation: God is compared to a rock, a shield, a shepherd, etc., things with which the ordinary person, pray-er or otherwise, would be familiar. The metaphors of psalmody unite the melodies of heaven and the music of the human condition so that what is known in this world evokes fragments of the world to come. The created world was "the theatre of God's glory"[83] and "the dominant diction in this theater is metaphor. . . . The visible and the invisible put asunder by sin, are joined by metaphor . . . [m]etaphor is the characteristic language of prayer."[84] Such this-worldly language militates against the Neoplatonic/Gnostic tendencies. It is manifest in the prayers of George MacLeod; prayers where God's eternity, "seeps through the physical," redemption is akin to being "bought back from the pawnshop of death," the separation of death is "a veil thin as gossamer," and the difficulty of Christian discipleship feels like the "steepness of the brae."[85] Such language urges those who pray to ground their communion in the images of earthly experience.

Such earthly metaphors also enable the community of faith to affirm that all creation is "charged with the grandeur of God."[86] They unite the everyday world with God and, by including the common world in the life of prayer, this sanctifies every realm so that all creation has the potential to be a fragment of God's epiphany. In this way, "the whole earth cries God's glory."[87]

> With earthly eyes we see beneath us stones and dust
> and dross, fit subjects for the analyst's table.
> But with the eye of faith, we know You uphold.
> In You all things consist and hang together:
> The very atom is light energy,
> The grass is vibrant,
> The rocks pulsate.
> All is in flux; turn but a stone and an angel moves.[88]

When the Christian community uses such earthly metaphors in communion with God, they use the same language in their prayer that non-Christians use with clarity and meaning in their common speech. This then takes the prayer and the pray-er into lively solidarity with the language of

83. Calvin, *Institutes of the Christian Religion*, 72, 171, 341.

84. Peterson, *Answering God*, 73. For how the metaphors of the psalter link together, see Brown, *Seeing the Psalms*.

85. See MacLeod's prayers in, *Whole Earth Shall Cry Glory*, 11, 29, 60, 58.

86. Hopkins, "God's Grandeur," in *Complete Poems*, 18.

87. See MacLeod, *Whole Earth Shall Cry Glory*, 8.

88. "Man is Made to Rise," in MacLeod, *Whole Earth Shall Cry Glory*, 16.

the world.[89] It deprives both prayer and pray-er of any refuge within a pious ghetto. It is, as Bonhoeffer knew, easy for ecclesiastical language to be unconnected to the world and so be largely evacuated of any meaning for the un-churched person; words lose their force and are no longer capable of taking "the word of reconciliation and redemption to humankind and to the world."[90] In such a case, the community must search for a new language, one that would be

> quite nonreligious . . . but liberating and redeeming like Jesus's language; so that people will be alarmed and yet overcome by its power—the language of a new righteousness and truth.[91]

Such a new language will bring the pray-er and the prayer into solidarity with Christ and, through him, with all humanity.[92] This language is overtured within the psalms in melodies clearly grounded in the *cantus firmus* of Christ. Through the psalms, Christ plays to humanity in ten thousand places, the many melodies of human experience and emotion. He is found amidst the songs of sadness, doubt, and confusion as much as those of happiness, trust, and well-being. The psalms offer inimitable instruction in such polyphonic prayer because uniquely in the Scriptures they mirror life with all its highs and lows.[93] They provoke the Christian community to place their emotions with those which the Psalmist invites them to imagine may be owned by others. That is the purpose of polyphonic prayer. It is not the means by which Christians may express what they want to say to God but rather it leads the community of faith to where God is and where God is found in others. Such prayer becomes the steps by which the Christian community finds their place in the melodies of God's unfolding purposes.

And so, if the Christ worshipped by the community is acknowledged as Lord of both the church and world then their prayers will move beyond

---

89. MacLeod once prayed, "Prayer is the same word as pray-er, Lord. You can't begin to answer us till we are the words we pray." See "The Galilean Language," in Mac Leod, *Whole Earth Shall Cry Glory*, 62.

90. "Thoughts on the Day of Baptism of Dietrich Wilhelm Rüdiger Bethge," May 1944, in Bonhoeffer, *Letters and Papers*, 389.

91. Ibid., 390.

92. Bonhoeffer's quest for a language of life lived in vicarious responsibility for humanity is similar to that envisaged by MacLeod when he prayed that the church might speak for the world on its search for reconciling peace and justice with honesty and authority. See "The Galilean Language," in MacLeod, *Whole Earth Shall Cry Glory*, 62–63.

93. It was because the psalms offered the full reach of human emotion that Bonhoeffer would not allow for them to be edited in any way, especially editing out their darker and more problematic phrases. See Editor's Introduction, in Bonhoeffer, *Life Together*, 147.

a parochialism of ecclesiastical care. The community will pray not just for those known to them personally, but in polyphonic prayer will connect to the church beyond itself, to the world who do not know the Christ and, in these times of ecological degradation, to the planet itself. It will speak to God, in solidarity with places and people of suffering and brokenness or joy and celebration. Such polyphonic prayer will bring the diverse concerns of many into one.

In the daily liturgy of the abbey worship, a monthly cycle of prayer addresses the needs of the world and the life of the church, concerns of the Iona Community, its members and their families.[94] This discipline is shared by individual members dispersed around the world. This is a further evocation of the polyphony of prayer: the one prayer is shared by different people in multiple places on the same day. Add to this polyphony the daily prayers in the abbey for justice and peace and a weekly cycle that includes prayers for healing and a quiet service, and a rich polyphony is revealed.[95]

But these reflections only concern the idea of spoken prayer. We have already suggested that polyphonic prayer is more than this. The cataphatic melodies of prayer tend to be "left brain" activities that neglect the more intuitive sides of the human condition. For some personalities this is welcome and comfortable but for others it can leave the spoken prayers of worship, and therefore their experience of prayer in general, as a largely unengaging practice. There needs also to be an apophatic space that takes people into the mystery of an encounter with God. The meditative use of the rosary as well as the use of prayers such as "The Jesus Prayer" can have this effect. So too can the practice of "praying in tongues."[96]

Praying with icons has been an approved discipline of prayer in the Orthodox church since the ninth century.[97] The icon depicts a scene or per-

94. On any one day a member of the Iona Community might pray for ten other members along with thirty associates. Added to this prayer for issues such as equal opportunities, or the environment, fair trade or base Christian communities throughout the world. Their intercession may move from Eritrea to Honduras or the United Nations.

95. Some of these abbey services only continue during the periods when guests are living at the island centers, from Easter to late October each year.

96. Other practices of prayer might include the exercises of Ignatian spirituality or involve the uses of the senses. For instance, the traditional use of incense is a sensory metaphor by which worshippers can appreciate their prayers rising up as a fragrant offering to God, but other examples might include tasting honey as a reflection on Ps 81:16 or praying as in silence we shape clay in response to Jer 18. See Pritchard, *Intercessions Handbook*; and Wallace, *Multi-Sensory Church*.

97. From 726 until the middle of the ninth century, the Byzantine world disputed whether using Icons constituted idolatry.

son from history or the Bible. In using them in prayer, they become more than pieces of art or an aid to prayer, but actual channels of grace.[98] The icon is not the object of worship, but rather, spiritually connects the worshipper through Christ to the person or scene portrayed. Thus, icons become open doors through which the music of another time and place can be heard. They give to the worshipper not so much a melody of heaven, but of a different earth. Importantly, the Seventh Ecumenical Council argued that it was not only legitimate but essential to make icons of Christ because they "guarantee that the incarnation of God the Word is true and not illusory."[99] In effect, icons remind the worshipper of the bisociative and polyphonic character of Christ. When this is linked to the doctrine of creation, icons can be understood as ensuring the potential for all material creation to carry a fragmented epiphany of God. Rowan Williams notes that with the icon we see, "the boundary between God and creation is not a line between two bits of territory but the difference between the composer and the symphony, between the cloud and the rain."[100]

Another ancient practice that has reemerged as a popular form of prayer in recent years is the labyrinth. The labyrinth is similar to a maze with the one crucial difference that there are no wrong turns or dead ends. The journey undertaken is a twisting, but consistent route, looping closer to and further from the center but steadily moving there. There is then a similarly meandering return journey toward the exit. It is a pre-Christian act of meditation, which was later adopted by the church as a reflective metaphor for the journey of faith. Often the journey inwards is one of prayer and personal reflection, while the outward path considers this-worldly acts of discipleship. At the center, the *cantus firmus* of the design, is the encounter with Christ, often symbolized by Eucharist. Recent interest was sparked by the discovery of a large labyrinth on the floor of the Chartres Cathedral in France, but the idea of using the labyrinth has been adapted by many in the alternative worship movement and can be found in Christian retreat centers, at festivals, and even on the internet.[101] Usually the labyrinth is physically

---

98. For an introduction to prayer with icons see Ouspensky and Lossky, *Meaning of Icons*; Forrest, *Praying with Icons*; Jones, *Windows into Heaven*; and Williams, *Dwelling of the Light*.

99. Cited by Kallistos Ware, "The Spirituality of the Icon," in Jones, Wainwright, and Yarnold, *Study of Spirituality*, 196.

100. Williams, *Ponder These Things*, 36.

101. For instance, the Christian Conference Centre in Swanick, Derbyshire, has constructed a labyrinth on its grounds. There has been a labyrinth with "stations" along the journey for a number of years at the Greenbelt Arts Festival in the UK and there is an online labyrinth with interactive "stations" at http://www.labyrinth.org.uk /onlinelabyrinthpage1.html. See also Sewell, Sellers, and Williams, *Working with the*

walked by the worshipper but it is possible to gather a small group around a labyrinth and metaphorically make the journey in the imagination.[102] Brian and Kevin Draper, themselves pioneers in recreating the labyrinth for contemporary worship, note that

> the Labyrinth is truly multifaceted, offering many layers of meaning and numerous metaphorical connections with the Christian pilgrim in their life-journey. . . . [It is] a wonderful example (and physical demonstration) of how prayer can be both corporate and individual at the same time—people walk individually, yet everyone is involved. . . . It can incorporate less obvious "Christians" and allow for safe, inspiring and authentic spiritual exploration. And it can transform lives—by helping pilgrims to enact their walk with God visually, and physically and spiritually move closer to the divine.[103]

Finally there will be a diversity of sound and music within such worship. We have noted how polyphonic worship is open to "otherness" in ritual and people, and such openness will also characterize the "soundscape" of worship:[104] particularly the readings, the preaching, and the music and singing of the people.

The homogenizing tendencies within church worship means that Scripture readings usually are taken from one translation of the Bible, read by one person and in one language. Polyphonic readings of Scripture may wish to vary the translations used as deemed appropriate for the worship context and may involve two or more people of different gender, ethnicity, age, social backgrounds, or physical abilities, such as those who are visually impaired. It might also include reading the passages in a variety of languages, including signing for those with difficulty hearing. If so, then polyphonic worship will seek to express that diversity in the different people used to proclaim the Scripture.

This may lead to an exploration of polyphonic preaching: what does it mean to expound the Scriptures polyphonically? Literally, it means that there should be more than one voice present in the revelation of the meaning and application of the Bible. This does not deny the place of a singular proclamation undertaken by an individual, but it offers the possibility for periods of dialogue with the community on the text before the preacher prepares the sermon, or it might invite such interaction within the sermon.

Labyrinth.

102. The author has used this method to good effect on guided retreats.

103. Draper, *Refreshing Worship*, 72–73.

104. The phrase "soundscape" is borrowed from Hawn, *Gather Into One*, 274.

This enables the preacher to listen to what God says through the people. The full potential of polyphonic preaching cannot be examined here but there is much that might be explored.[105]

Likewise, in hymnody, English-speaking congregations think nothing of singing the words "amen" and "alleluia," and many will regularly sing a *Kyrie Eleison*. All these are of a language other than English but have been made familiar by repeated use. Simple chants such as *Mungu ni mwema*[106] from the Democratic Republic of Congo or *Tatanaca, mamanaca, Sarantanani*[107] from Bolivia, can be taught easily to English-speaking congregations. To sing such songs in English-speaking churches serves two aspects of polyphonic worship. First, it acknowledges that Christ is the Savior and *cantus firmus* of Christian people all around the world. By singing their words in their language, the polyphony of Christ's incarnation into other cultures is affirmed. Second, by singing the songs of other communities of faith, solidarity is expressed with their context. Thus, to sing the words of a South African lament written during the Apartheid regime, *Senzeni Na / Sono sethu* (What have we done? / What is our sin?)[108] is to join in the cries of suffering people there and all over the world.[109] The point is well made in the rhetorical comment of hymn writer Eric Routley, "How will Christians of the future sing? As members of the universal Church, or not at all."[110] The worship of the Iona Community has long attempted to celebrate this diversity of song from the global church. John Bell comments, "When we sing, however falteringly, in another tongue, we represent and experience both the universality of the Church and the grandeur of God who is not limited by anyone's mother tongue."[111] If Christ is the *cantus firmus* of such "other" people then all melodies of hymnody are bound together through him.

Thus, in each aspect of the church's worship its polyphonic character should be revealed. It will be evidenced in the bringing together of the

105. A good beginning is to be found in Murray and Murray Williams, *Multi-voiced Church*, 63–82.

106. "Know that God is Good." This song is found in the collection, Bell, *One is the Body*, 96. Used with kind permission.

107. "Men and Women Let Us Walk Together." This song is found in the collection, Bell, *Sent By the Lord*, 32. Used with kind permission of Wild Goose Publications.

108. See Bell, *Sent By the Lord*, 66–67.

109. When the same words are sung within an un-persecuted church in the West, the question becomes an inquiry as to what Christians there have done to relieve or add to the burden of others.

110. Comment by a committee member, quoted by Eric Routley, in his introduction to "Cantate Domino: An Ecumenical Hymnbook," as cited by Dawn, *Gather Into One*, inside cover.

111. Bell, "Editor's Introduction," in *Common Ground*, 7.

historical traditions of the past with the creativity of the novel. It will be seen in a wide understanding of place and it will unite through the person of Christ a wide diversity of people in terms of their gender, race, age, socio-economic status, etc. In its practices of prayer and hymnody it will bring together a people who have learned to listen and value the melodies of God in the prayers and hymnody of others. And nowhere is such polyphony more evident (or noticeably absent) than in the ecumenism practiced by a Christian community.

SECOND MOVEMENT: THE POLYPHONY OF ECUMENISM

The church is like a table
set in an open house;
no protocol or seating,
a symbol of inviting,
of sharing, drinking, eating;
an end to "them and us."

—FRED KAAN[112]

Only Christ can save us now, body and soul: politically and ecclesiastically. . . . May Iona become an ecumenical centre for the new holiness—personal as well as corporate!

—GEORGE MACLEOD[113]

I ask not only on behalf of these, but also on behalf of those who will believe in me through their word, that they may all be one . . . that they may become completely one, so that the world may know that you have sent me and have loved them even as you have loved me.

—JOHN 17:20–23

---

112. Kaan, "The Church is like a Table," 513. Used with kind permission of Oxford University Press.

113. George MacLeod, uncited reference in Ferguson, *Chasing the Wild Goose*, 94.

The prayer of Jesus for future believers was that "they may be one," so that their unity would speak to the world about the love of God. A polyphonic understanding of Christ, and therefore of the church, is of vital importance if this prayer is to be realized. Its concept is crucially instructive for the church, which wishes to speak to the world of the love of God and whose gospel claims to speak to the world concerning personal and cosmic reconciliation,[114] but whose own history and current practice remains deeply divided within itself. One contemporary prayer sums up this reality in the church: "We are one in spirit, but not in fact. History and hurt still dismember us."[115] The world can plainly see a variety of dismembering divisions (and on occasions open hostilities) that exist between the Orthodox, Roman Catholic, Anglican, Reformed, and Pentecostal traditions of the church.[116] Until such division is overcome, the world may well be justified in doubting the authenticity of the gospel. As George MacLeod once commented, "The world is dying for the lack of the reconciling Word. . . . We [the churches] may have the word 'on paper' but until we are the word, men [*sic*] will not listen, nor should they."[117]

Almost without exception these differences within the church, particularly the doctrinal disputes that have caused division through the centuries, have been premised upon the "zero-sum" logic[118] in which the acceptance of one understanding of God's revelation must negate any and all other possible interpretations. Thus, at critical times of difference the church has divided over issues that include the nature of the Trinity, Apostolic authority, the practice of the Eucharist, the methodology of Baptism, and the role of the Holy Spirit. But any utopian homogeneity of the first-century church must be acknowledged as owing more to wishful thinking than to the facts of history. James Dunn's study of the early church argues that while it is possible to identify a "unified core" for the "post-Easter kerygma," the

114. See 2 Cor 5:19 and Col 1:15–23. Colossians Chapter 3 further posits a cosmic Christ in whom there is a boundaryless unity that transcends religious, cultural, national, and economic differences.

115. Wild Goose Resource Group, *Wee Worship Book*, 99.

116. The hostilities in Ireland over the last fifty years are regularly cited as one example of conflict between Roman Catholic and Protestant Christians. There are many other instances of violent inter-Christian conflicts around the world, including many within the same tradition. This chapter considers only those melodies performed within the church and does not address interfaith conflict and dialogue, although some parallel applications will be clear. Many members of the Iona Community are engaged in aspects of such dialogue. For a brief review of Bonhoeffer's interfaith encounters, see Plant, "Dietrich Bonhoeffer's Interfaith Encounters," 19–23.

117. See Ferguson, *Chasing the Wild Goose*, 93.

118. See Cunningham, *These Three Are One*, 128–29.

emerging communities of faith actually displayed considerable "difference and disagreement" over the proportional importance assigned to varying aspects of belief and practice.[119] Critically he states that "in different circumstances" these communities of faith "can agree to differ and respect these differences as acceptable and valid."[120] He concludes that "diversity is much more obviously a feature of the beginnings of Christianity than the unity."[121] Even when apparent unity was achieved, such as that contained in the great creedal formations of the fourth and fifth centuries,[122] the unanimity contained therein often owes more to the political expedience of empire than the discerned theological accord of the church. Initially, the creeds were localized and narrative affirmations of faith rather than what they became, namely formulaic tests of universal orthodoxy by which "zero-sum logic" could identify and control conformity or heresy. Frances Young has argued that the enforced unity that results from the concept of orthodoxy could not but "breed an intolerance"[123] which would inevitably and paradoxically exacerbate division. Thus, in time, the global community of Christian faith fractured over the years into what now includes hundreds of separate denominations, some of whom consciously exclude others from their midst. Yet each denomination would wish to claim a "unity in believing"[124] through their relationship to the *cantus firmus* of Christ.

Likewise, Dunn's conclusions in respect of the early church indicate that amidst their wide diversity there remained a central unity that was located in an encounter with the person of Christ. Christ was the *cantus firmus* for the energetic fugue of Christian community. We have already shown that adopting the musical metaphor of polyphony allows for a radical reinterpretation of difference; enabling counter melodies and even dissonance to remain within relationship to the *cantus firmus*. The Trinitarian God, revealed to the church and world through Christ, is both polyphonic and boundaryless. Christ is the earthy revelation of that God. The church, as Christ existing as community, is then offered an opportunity to participate in God, to be a living alternative to monolithic homogeneity. The community

119. Dunn, *Unity and Diversity*, 30.

120. Ibid.

121. Ibid., 230. Indeed, the fact that the contemporary factions of the church all claim scriptural authority for their given positions indicates just how diverse the early church was in matters of belief and praxis.

122. The Nicene Creed was formulated in 381, although not formally adopted as an official statement of faith until the Council of Chalcedon in 451.

123. Young, *Making of the Creeds*, 15ff.

124. "Unity in Believing" is the title of an informative essay by Jean Mayland to which this section is indebted. See Mayland, "Unity in Believing," 51–74.

of faith is called to practice a polyphonic diversity wherein difference does not become the ground on which to justify exclusion or destruction but a celebration of God's diverse revelation. The denominational differences are then, as Frank Burch Brown once stated, "Different performing ensembles" of the same "Christian classic."[125] If each "performance" is understood within the context of a musical metaphor then particular denominational differences are not "heresies" to be denounced and overcome but fragments of the mystery of a polyphonic God revealed in human flesh. If each tradition has earnestly sought to respond with countermelody to Christ's *cantus firmus* in their midst, then their differing traditions are not bound to a conflict of mutual exclusivity, but are fragments of melody remaining from Christ's great song of prayer: that the church may be brought into complete unity with one another as he is one with the Father.[126]

Bonhoeffer took seriously Jesus's prayer for the church to live in unity. In time, he hinted at a theology of ecumenism, that while not being conceived within musical metaphors still owed much to their underlying polyphonic principles. He appreciated that Christ did not plead for Christian unity to benefit the community of faith but on behalf of those not within the church, so that they might know the love of God. The church existed for others and it was called to be for others, in what we have called the colony of heaven, the place of boundarylessness wherein human differences such as race, language, and nationality were transcended in a unity established through their belief in Christ.

It was during his Easter trip to Rome in 1924 that Bonhoeffer encountered an epiphanal fragment of the boundaryless "concept of the church."[127] It came to him amidst the multinational gathering of seminarians, monks, and priests of every color that attended High Mass in St. Peter's. He was not unaware that almost every person present was Roman Catholic, and few would have had no Christian allegiance, but the event nevertheless impressed itself upon him so that in his diary he simply noted "universality of the church."[128] National socialism and the *Deutsche Christen* threatened such transcending universality in the 1930s. Their philosophy directly op-

125. Brown, *Religious Aesthetics*, 179.

126. See John 17:20–23.

127. See Bethge, *Dietrich Bonhoeffer: A Biography*, 59ff. Although significant German ecumenists taught in the same faculty wherein Bonhoeffer completed his doctoral studies, he does not seem to have been particularly influenced by them. See Raiser, "Bonhoeffer and the Ecumenical Movement," 321.

128. Bethge, *Dietrich Bonhoeffer: A Biography*, 59. Bonhoeffer was not uncritical of Roman Catholicism and his encounters in Rome made him reflect more deeply on his own experience of church. See Bethge, *Dietrich Bonhoeffer: A Biography*, 60–61.

posed the international and interracial unity that Bonhoeffer argued made the church truly unique. The transcendence of boundaries and the polyphonic embrace of difference Bonhoeffer sought in the church were disappearing beneath a monophonic Nazi hatred that was marching inexorably toward conflict. Bonhoeffer was convinced that only the church could stand as an international colony of peace in such a world of conflict. But that would place the church in direct opposition to the state; an unnatural position for a Lutheran such as Bonhoeffer. The dichotomy was reinforced by the "dialectic theology" of Karl Barth who emphasized God's otherness from the world.[129] But all that changed for Bonhoeffer during his first trip to America. There, Bonhoeffer came to the critical realization that if the universal church was Christ existing as community then that church was called to be present and united in and for the world so that the love of God could be made known through it.[130] God's otherness needed to be confessed in a this-worldly discipleship and it was the church, fragmented as it was, that needed to embrace this challenge together: ecumenically and internationally.[131]

It was important that such a this-worldly witness emerged out of the ecumenical movement that understood itself to be the church militant for others. Bonhoeffer argued that it was only as a church that Christians could confess Christ as Lord and speak to the world with the authority of Christ. It was all about the search for an integral Christian truth.[132] But the ecumenical movement did not conceive of itself in those terms. It claimed to be an

---

129. Barth reacted against the liberal theologies that had flourished since Schleiermacher. WWI had left many disillusioned with the optimistic humanism that underpinned such theologies. Eventually, Bonhoeffer asserted that Barth's God became so transcendent as to become invisible and intangible to a world that needed him.

130. Bonhoeffer's first visit to America was an ecumenical experience in itself. Here he met a diverse group of friends who found a unity in their Christian discipleship. Of his four best friends in New York one was a French pacifist, one was a Swiss student of Barth, one was an African-American Baptist, and one was an Evangelical. See further, Zerner, "Dietrich Bonhoeffer's American Experiences," 261–82.

131. This is the thrust of his paper "On the Theological Foundation of the Work of the World Alliance," delivered in July 1932 in Czechoslovakia. Here, in a comparison with international socialism, Bonhoeffer stated that "Christians too will first learn to think transnationally when they have a great, common proclamation. More than anything else at the present time, we need a great unifying proclamation in the ecumenical movement." Bonhoeffer, *Ecumenical, Academic, and Pastoral Work*, 368.

132. For Bonhoeffer the ecumenical struggle was "not a matter of 'dialogue' in the talkative, compliant sense, nor of an easy concession of doctoral conflicts for a cheap unity; it was the source for integral Christian truth." See Kuhns, *In Pursuit of Dietrich Bonhoeffer*, 69.

association *of* churches from around the world, not the world church.[133] Bonhoeffer feared that much good ecumenical work could collapse the moment its ecclesial authority was challenged and he was critical of the ecumenical philosophy of mutual tolerance, calling it a "romantic-aesthetic-liberal understanding" that did not "take the question of truth seriously."[134] He claimed that Christians concerned with truth should first themselves be questioned about this truth.[135] The liberal tolerance of 1930s ecumenism was, for Bonhoeffer, a denial of the Christ's truth precisely because it was failing to concretely confess the falsehood of the *Deutsche Kirche*'s Nazi philosophy.[136] The ecumenical unity of Christ's church could not be achieved "in abstracto" through some vague compromise on doctrinal assertions that were less than relevant for the world. It could only be made known through a concrete living for others as Christ had done.[137] That could only be done as the global church, as Christ existing as an international and interracial community engaged in costly this-worldly conduct. What was needed was a theology of ecumenism that would support such a concrete international confession.

But neither ecumenism nor internationalism was popular in the Teutonic fervor of Germany to which Bonhoeffer returned in 1931. Despite this opposition, he readily accepted the invitation to the Cambridge conference hosted by the World Alliance of Promoting International Friendship Through the Churches. From then on he devoted large amounts of time and energy to the ecumenical movement: devotion that continued during his time in London[138] and Finkenwalde.[139] But for all his involvement, he

133. Bonhoeffer was not suggesting a move toward one global super-church, but was calling for the collected churches to act as one church with the authority of the historical Ecumenical Councils. See Raiser, "Bonhoeffer and the Ecumenical Movement," 319–39.

134. Bonhoeffer, *Theological Education at Finkenwalde*, 405.

135. Ibid., 408.

136. There was disagreement between Bonhoeffer and the organizers of the Fanö Conference as to whether any member of the Confessing Church would attend unless at least one was invited as an official representative. His point was to call the ecumenical movement to stand by or reject the Barmen Declaration. See Bethge, *Dietrich Bonhoeffer: A Biography*, 377ff. For a very helpful account of Bonhoeffer's struggles at this time see Moses, "Dietrich Bonhoeffer's Struggle."

137. See Duchrow, "Confessing Church and the Ecumenical Movement," 212–31.

138. It was during his time as a pastor in London (October 1933 to April 1935) that he developed a long and deep friendship with fellow ecumenist Bishop George Bell.

139. Bonhoeffer took up directorship of the seminary at Zingst in April 1935 and then Finkenwalde in June 1935 and last participated in ecumenical events in London in February 1937.

remained critical of the ecumenical movement and was to continue to argue that it must reach beyond itself as a group of like-minded Christians engaged in conversation toward agreed courses of social action and begin by developing a theology sufficient for the tasks of the time.[140] In 1932, in Czechoslovakia, he famously delivered an appeal for a coherent theology of ecumenism. He wrote:

> Whenever the church of Christ in its history has come to a new
> understanding of its nature, it has brought forth a new theology
> commensurate with this self understanding.[141]

But Bonhoeffer could find no such theology within ecumenical self-understanding. What was needed was a "theological anchorage," a center that would hold while the "waves from left and right would batter in vain."[142]

As we have hinted at already, for Bonhoeffer, this central theological anchorage was located in Christ and the doctrine of the church that he had already articulated in the dictum of *Sanctorum Communio*: "The church was Christ existing as community." As Keith Clements notes, what Bonhoeffer now did was transpose "this communal emphasis into a transnational key."[143] If Christ was Lord of every people group then the community who bears his name must include every race and nation. Only within a fully international and ecumenical community could the church make its concrete confession with authority, a confession that in this context demanded action in favor of peace.

Clements's musical reference for the theological evolution is most apposite, because even though Bonhoeffer had not yet adopted the musical imagery of *cantus firmus*, melody and countermelody, what he proposed by way of an ecumenical witness for peace at Fanö clearly fits that polyphonic model. He then wrote:

> There shall be peace because of the Church of Christ, for the
> sake of which the world exists. And this Church of Christ lives at
> one and the same time in all peoples, yet beyond all boundaries,
> whether national, political, social, or racial. And the brothers
> [*sic*] who make up this Church are bound together, through
> the commandment of the one Lord Christ, whose Word they
> hear, more inseparably than men [*sic*] are bound by all the ties

---

140. While Bonhoeffer was critical of those who looked with disregard on the work of theology but celebrated the advances in practical ecumenical projects, he was not unmindful of the need for action.

141. Bonhoeffer, *Ecumenical, Academic, and Pastoral Work*, 356.

142. Ibid., 357.

143. Clements, "Ecumenical Witness for Peace," 160.

of common history, of blood, of class and of language. All these ties, which are part of our world, are valid ties, not indifferent; but in the presence of Christ they are not ultimate bonds. For the members of the ecumenical Church, in so far as they hold to Christ, His word, His commandment of peace is more holy, more inviolable than the most revered words and works of the natural world.[144]

Thus, we can see in Bonhoeffer's theology of ecumenism an embryonic hint of his polyphonic thinking: each melody of human belonging, national, political, social, and racial is transcended into the boundaryless colony of heaven, and held in place with the others through its "ultimate bond" to the *cantus firmus* of Christ. The unity that is discovered in this polyphonic church is not for the benefit of the Christian community but for the witness of reconciliation and peace, and a witness to the world of God's love. For Bonhoeffer, only this concrete confession of a church for others would suffice.

> Only the one great Ecumenical Council of the Holy Church of Christ over all the world can speak out so that the world, though it gnash its teeth, will have to hear, so that the peoples will rejoice because the Church of Christ in the name of Christ has taken the weapons from the hands of their sons, forbidden war, proclaimed the peace of Christ against the raging world.[145]

It would be a further ten years before Bonhoeffer wrote to Bethge of the little invention of polyphony. By then he was in prison. His hopes for the church confessing a concrete example of peace to the world had collapsed into a war now five years old. In the few remaining months before his execution, ecumenism seems to have remained at the forefront of his mind. Indeed, his last known words were directed to his friend and fellow ecumenist Bishop George Bell. "Tell him . . . that with him I believe in the principle of our Universal Christian brotherhood [*sic*] which rises above all national hatreds, and that our victory is certain."[146]

Bonhoeffer died without ever articulating a comprehensive theology of ecumenism by which the church could concretely declare the love of God in the world. It has largely eluded the global church ever since, but the

144. "The Church and the Peoples of the World," in Bonhoeffer, *London*, 308.

145. Ibid., 309.

146. The message was delivered to Bishop George Bell by Bonhoeffer's fellow prisoner Captain Payne Best. See Bell, "The Church and the Resistance Movement," in Zimmermann and Gregor Smith, *I knew Dietrich Bonhoeffer*, 209–10. See also Bonhoeffer, *Conspiracy and Imprisonment*, 468–69.

struggle has been enjoined. Visser't Hooft was convinced that Bonhoeffer's arguments have had a considerable influence in this regard, particularly in moving ecumenism from a forum of conversation and cooperation, to a people grappling with the task of confessing faith in Christ amidst the this-worldly realities of life.[147] But despite far-reaching post-war developments in ecumenism, particularly the foundation of the World Council of Churches (WCC),[148] no one has yet completed Bonhoeffer's unfinished task.[149] The WCC has as its purpose the "visible unity in one faith and in one eucharistic fellowship expressed in worship and in common life in Christ."[150] This unity is not an end in itself, but is sought to give a credible Christian witness so that the world may believe, and to serve the healing of the human community and the wholeness of God's entire creation. But as with the ecumenical movement of Bonhoeffer's time the WCC has never conceived of itself as church, Christ existing as community. The WCC is a "fellowship of churches" and is self-consciously beholden to the vision of the participating churches.[151] According to one commentator this understanding leaves the WCC destined to be "a consultative forum, not an instrument to make decisions and implement them."[152] As such, the WCC retains no ecclesial character of its own; it remains an instrument of autonomous and territorial denominations working toward agreed ends. Laudable as those ends may be, the WCC has no pretension to being an Ecumenical Council of the Church or any intention to articulate a theology of ecumenism.

The ecumenical melodies to be found in the Iona Community have no such pretension either. Iona's membership is drawn from a wide range of Christian denominations and is intentionally ecumenical, but the community itself has no self-conscious theology of ecumenism nor has it any

147. Visser't Hooft, "Dietrich Bonhoeffer and the Self Understanding of the Ecumenical Movement," 198–203.

148. The World Council of Churches began in Amsterdam in August 1948. It includes over 345 denominations and fellowships from over 100 countries and represents 500 million Christians. See www.wcc-coe.org/wcc/who/index-e.html.

149. The point is well made by Ulrich Duchrow, "The Confessing Church and the Ecumenical Movement," 216ff.

150. The Constitution of the WCC. See www.wcc-coe.org/wcc/who/con-e.html.

151. Institutionally, and at their request, the Roman Catholic Church remains outside the full fellowship of the WCC although it retains a working relationship with it and is a full member of many national ecumenical organizations. While many Orthodox Churches have been part of the WCC since its beginning there have been recent tensions over mechanisms of decision making and conduct of worship. This has resulted in the 2002 "Report of the Special Commission on Orthodox Participation in the WCC." See www.wcc-coe.org/wcc/who/special-01-e.html.

152. See Lange, *And Yet it Moves*, 10.

declared desire to act with ecclesial authority. Indeed, like the WCC it rejects notions of itself as church. But unlike the WCC, the Iona Community is not beholden to varying denominational concerns.[153] Its membership is premised upon an immediacy of regularly accountable relationships gathered around the person of Christ and the Rule of the Community. As such, the Iona Community offers fragments of melodies and a polyphonic ecumenism that may yet prove helpful for the tasks of our time.

The ecumenical roots of the community can be traced to 1899 when the Duke of Argyll gifted the ruins of Iona Abbey to Church of Scotland trustees, but with the caveat that the restored abbey church should be open for worship by all sections of the Christian church. Some thirty-six years later with that work completed, George MacLeod began discussing a vision of what would in time become the Iona Community. In some ways MacLeod's initial vision was firmly ecumenical in character. He wanted to reclaim the "catholic heritage" and "collective witness" of the church.[154] He argued that the world was "in need of that sense of Universal Church which was so profound a belief in our own Roman days."[155] But he intended to achieve this not by way of an avowedly ecumenical community, but by way of a brotherhood located firmly within the Church of Scotland.[156] Apart from the artisans necessary to lead the construction work, the group that arrived on Iona in 1938 were either Church of Scotland ministers or divinity students for that denomination. It is ironic that this stoutly Presbyterian affair was soon accused of being closet Roman Catholics playing at being monks.[157]

However, the community soon became more truly ecumenical. The outbreak of war in 1939 changed its denominational bias forever. Thinking it unlikely that young ministers would apply to work on Iona while war raged in Europe, MacLeod changed the summer program into twelve weeks of retreat for clergy, divinity students, and laity. From that point on Iona became "a place of study, community learning and training in discipleship

153. Although since 1951 the Iona Community has had a formal relationship with the Church of Scotland's General Assembly, it is an autonomous charity and limited company.

154. See Ferguson, *Chasing the Wild Goose*, 51.

155. Ibid., 53.

156. Indeed, MacLeod's argument to the Iona Cathedral Trustees played on their bias toward the Reformed/Presbyterian witness in Scotland and hints at anti-Roman Catholic sentiment. In characteristic style he invoked the memory of Columba's mission and declared that his experiment would be the modern counterpart. Ibid., 52.

157. See George MacLeod's defense against such accusations in Iona Community, *Coracle*, no. 2, 18.

for the wider Church"[158] and the community's work and worship soon attracted people from a wide range of Christian traditions.[159] This ecumenical character continues today with membership being drawn from all the main denominations in Britain and some from overseas. It is also committed collectively and through the work of individual members to participating in many local and global ecumenical initiatives.[160] Its worship draws on liturgy and hymnody from numerous traditions around the world and although there remain tensions, particularly around the ecumenical celebration of Eucharist,[161] Norman Shanks argues that Iona's "kind of belonging together transcends denominations."[162] Importantly, key moments in the life of the community have been marked by great ecumenical services.[163] Ian Fraser has noted that such times of worship were not just times of celebration for the community but "provided a sign and promise of the great United Church still to come."[164]

Fraser's reference to "signs and promises" may contain the key to a functioning polyphony of ecumenism. What Bonhoeffer hoped for in 1933–34 was an anchoring theology sufficient for the new context in which the church found itself. The modern pre-war world in which Bonhoeffer called for such a new theology still believed in the compelling power of the overarching metanarratives of modernity. And at that time Bonhoeffer still believed in the authority of a comparable systematic and ecumenical theology that could equip the whole church for its confessional task. In the context of Germany in the 1930s, Bonhoeffer concretized that theme ecumenically, particularly at Fanö. He believed that only the church could confess Christ and voice the necessary international approval of the Barmen Declaration. For that to happen, the ecumenical movement had to move beyond its role of association and develop a voice as the church. But a few

---

158. Ferguson, *Chasing the Wild Goose*, 58.

159. By 1947 in addition to its members there were 5,700 signed up Friends of the Community from varying traditions, all supporting the work financially.

160. The Iona Community is a "Body in Association" with the Council of Churches for Britain and Ireland and individual members have served as consultants at WCC events.

161. This is perhaps inevitable in a community encompassing the spectrum from Quakers to Roman Catholics. No study of Eucharist is attempted here, although clearly the subject offers rich and complementary imagery to the metaphors of fragmentation and wholeness.

162. Shanks, *Iona—God's Energy*, 194.

163. The Iona Community video, *Sermon in Stone*, includes brief footage from a number of these occasions including the Queen's visit in 1958 and the 1400th anniversary of Columba's arrival on Iona in 1963.

164. Fraser, *Living a Countersign*, 12.

years later he admits that there is now "little ground" left under his feet;[165] grand schemes for theological anchorage seem less compelling. Life is now "fragmentary"; the day of the "intellectual 'life's work'" is over,[166] and what is important is that we should be able to see "in this fragment of life that we have, what the whole was intended and designed to be, and of what material it is made."[167]

Bonhoeffer was rightly never keen on idealism as a philosophy.[168] It tends to flee this-worldly reality. He wrote about the "great disillusionment" that must break through idealism in communities: "Every human idealized image that is brought into the Christian community is a hindrance to genuine community and must be broken up so that genuine community can survive."[169] But when earthly communities are visited by concrete epiphanies of Christ's ecumenical ideal ("I pray that they might all be one") then some fragments of the *cantus firmus* may indeed prove sufficient to compose the concrete melodies of a this-worldly confession. These fragments may be sufficient to inform the church as to how the ecumenical whole is planned and arranged. And if ecumenical communities such as that of Iona are understood to contain such fragments then the communities themselves become the sign and promise of the united Christian community that is to come. They represent epiphanal fragments of the boundaryless colony of heaven in which all Christians truly belong. They reveal something of its greater song on the earth by seeking to confess Christ across the boundaries of denominationalism in the concrete realities of this-worldly living. Those who belong in such communities may know these melodies now only as the first stirrings of a beckoning theme, "the beyond in our midst,"[170] but they are as fragments of the great symphony of the church and of the kingdom.

165. "After Ten Years," in Bonhoeffer, *Letters and Papers*, 38. George MacLeod used similar imagery in 1938: "Is the truth not that the old cultus has splendidly served its day and generation; it is our modern environment that has rendered it outmoded. It is not the old Reformation timbers that are in criticism, it is that they survive from a day of wooden houses. It is not the building of the old channels that has rendered them faulty, but the shifting of the subsoil of this evolving world." Cited in Ferguson, *Chasing the Wild Goose*, 52.

166. Letter dated February 23, 1944, in Bonhoeffer, *Letters and Papers*, 305.

167. Ibid, 306.

168. In *Sanctorum Communio* Bonhoeffer argued that idealism was individualistic and thus unable to comprehend the concrete other person. In denying the reality of the true "you," the true "I" was lost because the real "I" did not exist in an unmediated entity but only in responsibility vis à vis an "other." Bonhoeffer, *Sanctorum Communio*, 50.

169. Bonhoeffer, *Life Together*, 36.

170. The phrase is Bonhoeffer's. Letter dated April 30, 1944, in Bonhoeffer, *Letters and Papers*, 367.

In such an understanding, Iona functions as a community which, gathered and scattered, lives by a Rule whose purpose is to encourage a personal and communal concrete confession of Christ. If that is the task then perhaps the time has not yet come for an Ecumenical Council to proclaim a new anchorage of ecumenical theology. Perhaps that is altogether too ambitious a project for the church today. For as the world surveys the church in the early twenty-first century it cannot fail to note the persisting truth of Bonhoeffer's earlier analysis. "[The church] has become incapable of bringing the word of reconciliation and redemption to humankind and to the world. So the words we used before must lose their power, be silenced."[171] If so, then according to Bonhoeffer, being Christian, including being ecumenical, should be limited to two things, "prayer and in doing justice."[172] And until then, all Christian "thinking, talking, and organizing must be born anew,"[173] until then perhaps the Christian cause should be a "quiet and hidden" affair.[174]

If this is so, then the ecumenical task of communities of faith for the moment may be no more than to gather the fragments in prayer and release them into action for justice. The new theology for the fragmented world of today may not require an all-embracing system of ecumenical thought and sufficient anchorage may be provided by a Discipline of Counterpoint or a Rule of Life the like of which is followed by the Iona Community. Tellingly, in Iona, the members' Rule mentions no grand ecumenical imperative,[175] although the community prayer does echo Bonhoeffer's concerned vision when it speaks of "hidden things being revealed" and new ways being found "to touch the lives of all."[176] The focus of the Rule is not on ecumenism but on repeatedly calling its members to confess Christ amidst the realities of this-worldly living. It then offers a space and a relationship through which such confession can be made accountable. Each member knows that neither they nor the community have "arrived" in this regard and acknowledges that each prayer or action undertaken is but a point of departure, but a point that remains "a pious hope and a false witness" unless they seek "separately

---

171. "Thoughts on the Day of Baptism of Dietrich Wilhelm Rüdiger Bethge," in ibid., 389.

172. Ibid.

173. Ibid.

174. Ibid., 390. Eleanor S. Neel has written a provocative but unpublished paper that adopts Bonhoeffer's *Arcane Discipline* to comment on the hidden nature of the church. See Neel, "'Incognito' as a Key."

175. It does contain a specific commitment to pray for and contribute to the wider work of the church at all levels, including bodies concerned with promoting justice and peace.

176. See Appendix A, "The Rule of the Iona Community."

and together to put it into practice."[177] In this way the community knows that it is never the totality of the church but nevertheless accepts its responsibility to be the confessing fragment of the ecumenical polyphony that is to come. It is anchored in the *cantus firmus*. It sings to the world the melodies revealed among it and invites all who are willing to participate in the music. One such melody is the song of healing.

THIRD MOVEMENT: THE MELODY OF HEALING

Bring a broken heart that's bleeding,
Bring a body racked with pain,
Bring a mind and spirit needing
Power to live and love again.
Come to Jesus, come to Jesus, come to Jesus and be healed.

—I. GILLESPIE[178]

The whole earth is our hospital.

—T. S. ELIOT[179]

If the church is "Christ existing as community" and its task is to participate in the unfolding melodies of God on earth, then actions undertaken by the community of faith ought to sound in harmony with the earthly ministry of Jesus. One of the notable characteristics of Jesus's ministry was that he healed the sick; with over forty incidents of healing mental and physical illness recorded in the gospels it was a key identifying characteristic of his Messianic purpose.[180] When the disciples of John the Baptist ask if Jesus is the one their teacher anticipates, Jesus responds, "Go and tell John what you have seen and heard: the blind receive their sight, the lame walk, the lepers

---

177. Ibid.

178. "Come to Jesus" is a song written for a service of healing by Rev. Irene Gillespie and is cited in Cowie, *Prayers and Ideas for Healing Services*, 153.

179. T. S. Eliot, "East Coker IV," in *Collected Poems*, 202.

180. For a complete list of healing work described in the Gospels see Kelsey, *Healing and Christianity*, 55–56. At the commencement of his ministry Jesus declared the healing dimension to his ministry by citing the prophecy of Isa 61. See Luke 4:18. For an understanding of the different words for healing in Scripture, see Lambourne, *Community, Church and Healing*, 93ff; and Cowie, *Jesus' Healing Works and Ours*, 11.

are cleansed, the deaf hear, the dead are raised, the poor have good news brought to them."[181] But these accounts of healing differ in detail; there is no single methodology of healing adopted by Jesus. On some occasions Jesus used touch, but in others he did not; in some, healing seems dependent on the faith of the afflicted, on others it does not; in some cases he healed in public, while with others it was done in private.[182] Furthermore, while Jesus healed many of those whom he encountered, he did not heal all those around him who were also clearly in need. The gospels offer no explanation or apology as to why one was chosen and others were not.

There is then no simple methodology or guaranteed mechanism in the healing works of Jesus. The only thing they have in common is Jesus himself. His approach to the melodies of healing is decidedly polyphonic: he finds for each occasion a countermelody of healing that is relationally particular to the individual. And what was true and necessary in the time of the historical Jesus is perhaps all the more apposite today. As Stephen Pattison has rightly noted, "We live in a complicated and sophisticated society; simple or mono-dimensional responses to complex and multidimensional phenomena such as healing and illness may betoken a lack of faith in a God who somehow continues to create and to reveal himself in the chaos of contemporary existence."[183] The church response to such multidimensional phenomena is to incarnate a polyphonic Christ as a community through an engaged ministry of healing. That ministry must engage in a polyphony of practice that focuses not upon method but upon the fluid relationships that may exist between God, the healer, the healed, and society.[184] This will necessitate the community of faith engaging with the difficult discipline of listening to and participating in his *cantus firmus* within the world. In each encounter, fresh discernment will be necessary to hear the epiphanal melody appropriate for the occasion.

The church has not always risen to such a task.[185] While healing was a regular feature of the ministry of Jesus, its melodies have not always

181. See Luke 7:21–22.

182. See Wilson, *Church is Healing*, 9–10; and Kelsey, *Healing and Christianity*, 52–68.

183. Pattison, *Alive and Kicking*, 2. Pattison goes on to suggest that an adequate healing response must be not "monocular or myopic," an image that has much in common with bisociation in Christ, but in his "kaleidoscope" of perspectives on illness stops short of the full-bodied polyphony suggested herein. See ibid., 21ff.

184. The modern model of medicine eschews the communal aspect of healing in favor of an individualistic and mechanistic approach. Ibid., 22–24.

185. There was a recovery of interest in healing in the latter half of the twentieth century. The fact that Cameron Peddie in the 1960s called his book on healing "The Forgotten Talent" is perhaps illuminative. See Peddie, *The Forgotten Talent*.

been a customary refrain in the church that bears his name. This is not to say that healing has been entirely absent from the Christian community: undoubtedly, wherever faith has been expressed, melodies of healing have continued to be heard.[186] Historically, the hospitality of healing was especially nurtured by Christian monastics.[187] But locating such melodies within communities that remained self-consciously separated from the world did little to encourage the ordinary Christian or church community to regularly participate in the melodies of Christ's healing. When healing did occur, within or beyond the boundaries of the monastery, it was often regarded as a supernatural anomaly, an invasion of the world accomplished through a particularly saintly individual, holy relic, or occasioned at an especially holy site. Healing was neither regarded as a normative experience or the common responsibility of the local community of faith.[188] Matters declined further from the thirteenth century onwards. As medical and scientific knowledge increased during the Enlightenment, medicine evolved into a science that saw itself as being increasingly independent of the church and matters spiritual. Such an approach believed that healing owed more to Hippocrates and Galen than to Jesus.[189] It separated the mental from the somatic in the classic mind/body dualism that ignored the possibility of a third and spiritual dimension. All this precipitated an extended era in which it became progressively difficult for intellectually sophisticated people to believe in the possibility of direct intervention by God in this world, including the world of illness and healing.[190] While such people would perhaps admit to gaps of knowledge existing in areas such as medicine, both church and

186. Kate McIlhagga argues that healing has always been present "where the Church has offered sanctuary, forgiveness and, above all, Eucharist in any community." However, she also adds that the situations of our time call for a particular focus on the church to engage with a ministry of wholeness amidst the particular problems of suffering and pain in the world. See McIlhagga, "Church's Healing Ministry," 14.

187. From the beginnings of Western Monasticism, St. Benedict encouraged the practice of medicine among monks in a hospice at Montecassino and it became a widespread ministry of most monasteries. But by 1130, the Church Council of Clermont and the Council of the Lateran in 1139 forbade monks from practicing medicine.

188. Ian Cowie has argued that the healing works of Jesus are not supernatural interventions in the laws of nature but rather signs toward what should be truly natural for the children of God. See Cowie, *Jesus' Healing Works and Ours*, 10–11.

189. See J. W. Provonsha, "The Healing Christ," cited in Kelsey, *Healing and Christianity*, 52. A similar point is made by Lambourne, *Community, Church and Healing*, 91. Pattison notes how this is signified in the distinctive dress of the doctor being the lab coat. Pattison, *Alive and Kicking*, 23.

190. This reached its zenith in the progressive optimism of nineteenth-century Europe and the liberal theology that emerged alongside it, but began to retreat in the twentieth century. See Kelsey, *Healing and Christianity*, 346.

world considered the opportunities for God's continuance in these gaps to be increasingly rare.[191]

But in the later twentieth century, notwithstanding many great advances, trust in scientific rationalism began to erode and medicine faced new challenges as quickly as former enemies were overcome.[192] At the beginning of the twenty-first century there are a plethora of alternative medicines and healing practices running in parallel with conventional western medicine. At the same time in differing ways there has been a new anticipation of a ministry of healing taking place within the church.[193] If that healing ministry of the church is to incarnate the diverse approach adopted by Jesus, then it must be rooted in the polyphonic nature of the healing *cantus firmus*: in Christ the spiritual and the material are interwoven to the sound of polyphonic harmony. Indeed, all creation vibrates at a subatomic level and therefore may be understood as "sounding" within the universe. Following what Christian theology names as "the Fall," creation, and particularly humanity, has become cacophonic. This is true of both individuals who are physically, mentally, or spiritually unwell, and in societies that are oppressive and unjust. The salvation accomplished for the world through Christ's death and resurrection is redemption into health or wholeness.[194] If healing occurs, at either a personal or societal level it may be understood as redeeming that which has fallen and restoring it to a true relationship with the *cantus firmus* of Christ and the polyphony of God.

It is through Christ that such healing occurs and in Christ we have seen how those things that appear to be in apparent opposition may be combined in a positive and creative tension. The first consequence of this must be that in the healing of Christ, both modern medical techniques and the prayers and comfort of the community of faith are of value. It is a communal

191. Bonhoeffer was critical of the Christian Church for trying to reserve some space for a God of the gaps in the face of advancing secularism of a "world-come-of-age." He claimed that liberal theology had "allowed the world the right to assign to Christ his place within it; that it accepted, in the dispute between church and world, the—relatively mild—peace terms dictated by the world." Letter dated June 8, 1944, in Bonhoeffer, *Letters and Papers*, 428.

192. Thus, while diseases such as small pox may effectively be consigned to history, others notably HIV/AIDS have taken their place.

193. Methodologies of healing within the contemporary church are diverse. These may range in caricature from the emotionally charged environment with a charismatic individual to the quiet side chapel where every week the same few dedicated folk gather to pray for one another and those made known to them. See Cowie, *Prayers and Ideas for Healing Services*, 23–25.

194. The Greek word *sozo*, from which the English term "salvation" is derived, means to heal or to be made whole. It had both spiritual and medical associations in the time of Jesus.

process. As Lambourne suggests, healing can be understood as "a satisfactory response to a crisis, made by a group of people, both individually and corporately."[195] And as Michael Wilson notes in response, "This definition . . . emphasizes how those who surround the patient—family, friends, doctor, nurse, minister, probation officer, and others—are all involved in the situation with him."[196] Seen in this way the Christian ministry of healing is not set in opposition to the practice of modern medicine: if the polyphonic Christ is Lord of all then both medicine and prayer ought both to be part of the corporate response. There may well be times when the limits of modern medicine are exhausted and the only hope may lie in prayer but Christ ordains and remains Lord of both. Both prayer and medicine and other forms of healing can therefore be affirmed as channels of God's healing purpose. And if Christian healing is rooted not simply in prayer and spirituality but in the practical world of doctors, nurses, waiting lists, and limited resources, then polyphonic healing must be similarly concerned with the this-worldly life of public health, politics, and economics.[197]

Thus, a second consequence of the church seeking to incarnate the polyphony of Christ's healing ministry is this: time after time in Christ's healings what can be discerned is not simply the cure of presenting personal ailment, but a challenge toward a public/political healing. It is not simply that the illness is removed, but it also precipitates a collapse of the social-religious boundaries that have limited the recovery of the ill person or separated them from the "healthy" community. Along with the varying physical cures offered by Jesus, there is almost always a restoring of the individual into the socio-religious community from which they have previously been excluded. The healings point beyond their physical evidences toward the coming Kingdom of God. This fact is important if we are to truly understand a polyphony of healing. In polyphonic healing the concern is not simply focused on curing the presenting affliction, but it is about the wholeness of the person, bringing healing to their society, and bringing the earthly society closer to the kingdom of heaven. So when Jesus heals, one melody is concerned with physical cure, but a distinctive counter-harmony heralds a coming kingdom that is equally concerned with justice for those who have been marginalized by society's association of sickness with sin. Clearly, Jesus intends the former boundaries to be removed and new melodies of a boundaryless community to grow up around his *cantus firmus.*

195. Lambourne, cited in Wilson, *Church is Healing*, 17–18.

196. Ibid, 18.

197. For comment on such issues see Gordon, "The National Health Service and the Health of the Nation," in Burgess and Galloway, *Praying for the Dawn*, 31ff.

Thus, when a Gentile Roman centurion intercedes with Jesus for the health of his servant, the healing not only cures the servant, but hints at a new concept of belonging that crosses racial and political boundaries.[198] And when Jesus heals the crippled woman in the synagogue[199] no doubt he could have done so privately later or then from a distance, but he deliberately calls her into the male only assembly and addresses her as a daughter of Abraham; he intends to establish a new societal norm, a community without boundaries of gender prejudice. Likewise, curing the hemorrhaging woman is not simply about stopping her bleeding, but about publicly restoring her place in society.[200] Indeed, the fact that Mark places her story "inside" the narrative of healing Jairus's daughter further emphasizes the point: healing from Jesus goes beyond curing the external illnesses of both and moves them into a boundaryless community in which the melody of the rich, socially empowered Jairus and this melody of a poor and marginalized woman are polyphonically bound together in a new community rooted in Christ's *cantus firmus*.

Something of such a boundaryless new community is cited with approval by Bonhoeffer in one of his rare comments on the healing ministry. In *Spiritual Care* he argues that health and illness are both part of normal human life and cites with approval the practice of the Healing Center established at Bethel bei Bielefeld, where "the sick and the healthy live with one another, sharing as a matter of course daily life and worship: a continual reminder to the sick of wholeness."[201] However, despite (or perhaps because of) his father's medical pedigree, Bonhoeffer offers us little else of substance in regard to a Christian theology of healing.[202] The only practical advice offered to novice pastors in *Spiritual Care* simply instructs that while "healing of the sick in the form of laying-on of hands . . . should be made available," the pastor ought to guard against glorying in it and invoking "dangerous and exotic concepts."[203]

---

198. Matt 8:5–13. A poignant "healing" of sociopolitical division occurs with the Syro-Phoenician woman who kept asking Jesus to cast out a demon from her daughter. See Mark 7:24–30. The point is repeated in the healing of the ten lepers. See Luke 17:11–19.

199. Luke 13:10–17.

200. Mark 5:21–43.

201. Bonhoeffer, *Spiritual Care*, 56.

202. In *Spiritual Care*, Bonhoeffer offers practical advice to seminarians regarding visiting parishioners who are sick or on their death-bed but he constructs no theology of healing.

203. Ibid., 59.

Clearly, a polyphonic healing ministry of the church community addresses both the presenting patient and the social issues that precipitate or attend upon them. While Bonhoeffer is somewhat illusive on the first he provides ample reflection elsewhere on the need for the community of Christ to minister healing through socio-political inclusion. In his first pastorate in Barcelona he had spoken of the "infinite worth of that which is seemingly worthless and the infinite worthlessness of that which is seemingly so valued" in society.[204] In 1943, shortly before his arrest, Bonhoeffer again appealed passionately for the church to learn to "see the great events of world history from below, from the perspective of the outcasts, the suspects, the maltreated, the powerless, the oppressed, and reviled, in short, from the perspective of the suffering."[205]

George MacLeod had experienced something of that perspective during his years of parish ministry in Edinburgh and Glasgow. He brought it into the theology and praxis of the Iona Community. Since its beginning, the Iona Community adopted a polyphonic approach to healing that combined in harmony the praying for the cure of the person together with working at the social issues surrounding them. MacLeod began this work with no clear idea of what theology or praxis might be required for such a service, but on the simple basis that Christ had authorized his followers to "preach the gospel and heal the sick."[206] Instinctively, and almost from the inception of the community, MacLeod sought assistance and instigated specific prayers for the sick but worked tirelessly to improve the conditions that rendered people unwell. He urged others to do likewise.[207] His polyphonic approach to healing is summed up well in the oft-recited maxim that to pray for Mary suffering from tuberculosis (TB) while she is living in a dilapidated tenement in Govan and yet not be politically active in doing something about the appalling housing that causes the TB was being inconsistent.[208]

204. Bonhoeffer, *Barcelona, Berlin, New York*, 354–55. See also Kelly, "Sharing the Pain of God," 139–47.

205. "After Ten Years," in Bonhoeffer, *Letters and Papers*, 52.

206. Cowie, *Prayers and Ideas for Healing Services*, 11.

207. Requests for prayer for healing came from far and near, but as Ralph Morton recollects, while there was a latent memory of Iona as a place of healing, it was not the place but the new life found there that inspired the requests. See Morton, "Divine Healing," 21. For further reflections on prayers for healing in the early years of the Iona Community see Muir, *Outside the Safe Place*, 220–22.

208. Cited in Cowie, *Prayers and Ideas for Healing Services*, 12. The precarious tensions within such a polyphony of healing are noted by Cowie who responds to MacLeod's famous maxim about Mary with TB. "It is just as inconsistent to be convinced that you know the answers to the political problems of nations on the other side of the world and yet have nothing positive to offer Mary."

The prayers for healing conducted every Tuesday evening in Iona Abbey reflect this. In each service there is time spent in intercession for named individuals who may be suffering from a variety of illnesses but there is also space to pray for the varied social conditions that leave people far from whole. Likewise, the prayers for healing may also extend into a polyphony of concerns including various global inequities that may hinder individuals, communities, nations, and indeed the planet from fulfilling their potential. This polyphonic approach to healing is also reflected in the opening liturgical responses used in the abbey service of prayers for healing.

> Leader: We gather here in your presence, God,
>
> ALL: IN OUR NEED, AND BRINGING WITH US THE
> NEEDS OF THE WORLD.
>
> Leader: We come to you, for you come to us in Jesus,
>
> All: AND YOU KNOW BY EXPERIENCE WHAT HUMAN
> LIFE IS LIKE.
>
> Leader: We come with our faith and with our doubts;
>
> ALL: WE COME WITH OUR HOPES AND WITH OUR
> FEARS.
>
> Leader: We come as we are, because it is God who invites us to
> come;
>
> ALL: AND YOU HAVE PROMISED NEVER TO TURN US
> AWAY.[209]

Iona Community member Graham Monteith comments that these opening responses reflect some key features in the community's theology of healing, namely:

> Healing and wholeness concern not only the individual but the world. God through Jesus Christ is with us, and the world, in all our experiences of life. Healing is sought through our own volition but granted by the will of God. An unquestioning faith is not a precondition of healing. God is always in solidarity with us.[210]

Similarly, fellow member Ian MacKenzie recalls Ralph Morton saying,

> "We do not do this because we think it will work. We do this because we were told to." What he was saying was, "We're not holding a pistol to God to say, 'You've got to make this work!' . . .

209. Iona Community, *Iona Abbey Worship Book*, 90.
210. Monteith, "Service of Prayers for Healing," 19.

We're saying, 'We do this, because that's part of the ministry, and part of the witness.'"[211]

Such theologies of healing do not claim to be all encompassing, but do state a clear intention for healing to be an integral ministry of the community and for such healing to be polyphonic in nature.

This is also seen in the community's approach to the ministry of laying-on of hands. The initial prayers for healing are usually led by an individual but when the service offers the ministry of laying-on of hands close attention is paid to the dangers of exotic practice and self-glorification. On Iona, the practice of laying-on of hands seeks to avoid such dangers by ensuring that the ministry is participated in by everyone present. Members of the congregation may come forward to receive or share in the ministry as they choose, but whether they remain where they are or come forward to share in the laying-on of hands, everyone is invited to share in same prayer:

> Spirit of the living God, present with us now,
> Enter you, body, mind and spirit,
> And heal you of all that harms you,
> In Jesus' name. Amen.[212]

In turn, those who have laid hands on others are then prayed for in the same way. None of this is done to deny a place to individuals who may be especially gifted in healing. Indeed, George MacLeod and others exercised such a ministry on occasions but deliberately kept matters private.[213] But it is rather to affirm the brokenness of each human life and to establish that the gift of healing is an inclusive process entrusted to the whole community of faith.

There are other ways in which a polyphonic understanding of healing may be helpful but can only be hinted at here. When prayer is offered for healing, heaven may respond with a variety of melodies, none of which would be dissonant from Christ's *cantus firmus*, but not all of which may have been on the hearts and minds of those who prayed.[214] The obvious response is that heaven grants that which was pleaded for in prayer: that the person or situation is healed within a very short space of time. But while healing does undoubtedly occur in this way, such a response from heaven

211. In Muir, *Outside the Safe Place*, 221–22.

212. Iona Community, *Iona Abbey Worship Book*, 91.

213. Ferguson recounts one of many such incidents with staff member Ann Smith who was healed from sight problems. See Ferguson, *George MacLeod*, 385.

214. Ian Cowie relates how a woman went forward to pray for a friend but felt a strong heat on her own neck and was cured of whiplash. Cowie, *Prayers and Ideas for Healing Services*, 13.

is never guaranteed. No pistol is ever held to God. For instance, Bonhoeffer was never released from prison and was eventually executed despite the faithful prayers of friends and family. What is the individual or faith community to do when an illness or injustice continues unabated? A polyphonic understanding of healing offers a perspective that can creatively incorporate such scenarios because it accepts that heaven's healing may visit earth through a variety of fragmented epiphanies.

Sometimes when healing seems to tarry it may be that the melodies of heaven have a greater music in mind. In music there may be long pauses of silence in which nothing seems to happen as far as a particular individual is concerned. But much may be going on around them. This may be true also in regard to healing. A period of protracted illness, a time when with the Psalmist a person may repeatedly cry out, "How long O' Lord," may eventually prove to have been for the greater good of the person or community. This is not to say that God visits illness upon people in order to teach them some lesson of life, but it is to say that if circumstance brings a need for healing there is no human experience that sits beyond the reach of the healing of Christ. The Christian hope is that in the midst of such times Christ is present with them; not to necessarily remove the pain but to stand in solidarity with them. To claim that Christ was fully human means that he too experienced pain and rejection and longed for healing on occasion. To hope that life could be lived without such times would be to long for the paucity of a monophonic existence.

A polyphonic approach to healing also acknowledges that for a while the music may seem absent, but it knows too that silence is often part of the music and as such some silence may be necessary to enable a deeper healing to be worked before the presenting difficulty may be addressed. For instance, in the unity of body, mind, and spirit it may be necessary for some healing of the mind to occur before a presenting physical ailment can be addressed. It may also be that the desired healing is deliberately delayed so as to provoke the afflicted person to action. Heaven's response to prayer may not be to remove the pain or injustice but, instead, God may incite an individual to offer up a new and responsible reaction to that over which they prayed. In this way the delay is heaven's immediate response and it may make an individual or community more receptive to the unfolding melodies of God around them.

Another possible melody of healing in heaven's polyphony may be that one person's suffering becomes the way in which healing comes to others. For a number of years, an Iona Community member, Brian Gallon, was the prayer circle secretary in the abbey. He was responsible for coordinating the numerous requests for prayer received from around the world and leading the service of prayers of healing. During that time he suffered and died from cancer. Many people prayed for the healing of Brian Gallon, but he did not recover from his illness. He used to answer this apparent cruel irony by telling people that if others were healed through his weakness then he stood in the tradition of the cross where, through the wounds of Christ, the vulnerability of the world was healed. Within the polyphonic understanding of healing it may be possible to detect one such person's suffering as an essential counterpoint to the healing of others. It may also be that, for the Christian, death is the final act of healing. For them, the final act of healing comes as they move from the colony of saints militant into the homeland community of saints triumphant.

Making Melodies in the World

Three Movements

Christian piety at its best has made a significant contribution
to the social transformation of the world.

—JOHN W. DE GRUCHY[1]

New techniques entirely of the nature of the devotional life will
need to be forged. Such can only be forged by those who continue at
any cost to be involved in the world as it is.

—GEORGE MACLEOD[2]

I am a shepherd who, with his people, has begun to learn the beautiful and difficult truth: our Christian faith requires that we submerge
ourselves in this world.

—OSCAR ROMERO[3]

1. de Gruchy, *Cry Justice!*, 23.
2. MacLeod, in Iona Community, *Coracle*, no. 47, 13.
3. Romero, cited in Millar, *An Iona Prayer Book*, 21.

What is the difference between a cathedral and a physics lab?
Are not they both saying: "Hello?"

—ANNIE DILLARD[4]

PRELUDE

The church has not always viewed the world positively as a potential site for hearing the melodies of God. As we have seen, Gnostic and Neoplatonic philosophies generated a world-renouncing spirituality that has regularly dominated the self-understanding of the Christian community. In such an understanding, this world and its materiality are set at enmity with what are erroneously perceived as the more "spiritual" or "other-worldly" ambitions of God and the church.[5] But the epiphanal melodies of God are as likely to be encountered through active engagement with the material world as they are to be found within the prayers and worship of the gathered Christian community.[6] We have seen that there is a rich polyphony of such melodies to be found within the gathered church community but there also exists a vibrant mix of divine music that is revealed within the wider world.

While the previous chapter focused solely on how melodies may be made within the internal life of the church, this chapter is concerned with how Christians may encounter and recognize the fragments of God's music within the world around them. An examination of this second locus for the melodies of God is of vital importance for a deeper understanding of the new monasticism of the Christian colony. For while the church might claim to find its ultimate identity in the God of heaven, it cannot remove itself from its penultimate solidarity with the created world: the penultimate world in which God through Christ chose to act in flesh and blood.[7] The

---

4. Dillard, *Teaching a Stone to Talk*, 89.

5. Indeed, this enmity between the "sacred" and the "secular" was an understanding of world favored by Bonhoeffer while at Finkenwalde, but later rejected during *Ethics* and the prison writings. See Feil, *Theology of Dietrich Bonhoeffer*, 99ff, and particularly 125–35.

6. This positive attitude toward the world developed especially after Bonhoeffer's work with non-Christians prepared to risk their lives working in the German Resistance movement while the church did little to oppose Nazism. Ibid., 138–59.

7. See Bonhoeffer's argument concerning the "ultimate and penultimate," in *Ethics*, 146ff.

church must be, as Bonhoeffer claimed, about both prayer and righteous action.

Righteous action is then the bearer of heaven's overture;[8] it is both the proleptic epiphany of God's this-worldly music and the forerunner of the eschatological apotheosis.[9] And because in Christ the church and world are held in bisociation, the divine polyphony can be heard within such righteous action whether it is performed by Christians or by people of other or no religious faith. Christians acting in this way will do so, being conscious of their allegiance to the polyphonic Christ. But others, who claim no allegiance to Christ, may still share a parallel commitment to work for justice. However sweet the name of Jesus may sound in a believer's ear, nonbelievers may still participate in the music without ever fully recognizing its *cantus firmus*. In Luke's gospel the disciples encounter a man driving out demons. Even though he is doing so in the name of Christ, the disciples try to stop him because, they claim, he is not a follower like them. Jesus replied that they should not have prevented his action because "whoever is not against you is for you."[10] The issue at stake for the disciples is not whether the man properly recognized Christ as the Son of God, but that they were jealous of someone from outside their defined boundary participating in the purposes of God. Jesus clearly instructs them that what is important is that the work of the kingdom is accomplished, whether it is by them or by others. It is precisely because they recognize the Christ that they can identify that such this-worldly melodies are in true relationship with his *cantus firmus*: singing God's melody after him.[11]

As for those who are not avowedly Christian, until such times as they may recognize the *cantus firmus* as being Christ, the question is whether their thoughts and deeds sound in harmony with the divine music. Thus, they may presently participate in the unfolding melodies of God, but do so unconscious of the *cantus firmus* that lies beneath their own melodies of action.[12] In the

8. In an opera or oratorio the overture is played before the complete performance but contains within it hints and themes of the final music that is to come.

9. The apotheosis in music such as Liszt's "Faust" symphony or Mahler's "Resurrection" Symphony No. 2, is the final movement where all that has gone before is taken up into a "divine resolution."

10. See Luke 9:50. Cf. Luke 11:23: "Whoever is not for me is against me." These verses are not necessarily incompatible for if someone is participating in the unfolding music of God, consciously or otherwise, then they are for Christ.

11. It is akin to someone listening to Mozart's Requiem Mass and appreciating the music as music but being unaware of the biographical detail of a composer convinced that he had been commissioned to write the music for his own funeral. Once the biography is recognized the music takes on a deeper significance.

12. Bonhoeffer argued in favor of a "natural" piety of the secularists with whom

past, descriptions of such people as "unconscious" or "anonymous" Christians have been open to criticism,[13] particularly if Christians claimed to have "recognized their Christ" in the practices of other religions or secularists. In such cases it was rightly argued that Christians were unfairly claiming for themselves that which was truly "other" to them. This was clearly unacceptable to the self-aware secularist or member of another faith who did not want to be considered a Christian, whether unconscious, anonymous, or in any other way. And if the Christology asserted herein is to be maintained (namely, that Christ is a unique and particular bisociation of heaven and earth in whose *cantus firmus* the whole polyphony of life is rooted), then it is difficult to avoid some degree of such offence or criticism. But some important common ground may yet be found between Christians and non-Christians, and music may help us find a place of universal belonging.

If it is admitted by the Christian community that while fragments of God's epiphany do reside within the colony of heaven, they have not yet heard the full repertoire of God on earth, then such a self-conscious openness to continually fresh melodies of revelation will remind the community that they may still encounter God in new locations of otherness. These melodies are revealed in actions that are undertaken for the good of and on behalf of those other than themselves. In this commitment to work for the betterment of others, Christians will share with their non-Christian colleagues a commitment to making the melody of justice known in the world. Both Christians and non-Christians are then melody-makers of justice, whether or not they believe themselves to be making harmony with Christ's *cantus firmus*. All participants in such melody-making would acknowledge that a willingness to act vicariously for others has the potential to generate new challenges and understandings of justice. As such, the totality of their

---

he worked in the resistance. He referred to such people as "unconscious Christians" participating in the contrapuntal melodies of God without being conscious of Christ as their *cantus firmus*. See Letter dated July 27, 1944, in Bonhoeffer, *Letters and Papers*, 489.

13. Bonhoeffer's term may be rightfully critiqued if it is understood to mean that he unilaterally asserts an honorary Christian identity to people who themselves have expressed no desire to be included in its community of faith. Furthermore, inherent in the term "unconscious" is the suggestion that if such people were "awakened" to the claim that Christ undergirded their action for justice they could subsequently do no other than accept a Christian position on life. This is understandably offensive to avowed secularists and devout members of other faiths who are engaged in work for justice and may be seen by others in the church as reducing the particularity of the gospel. Similar critiques have been made of Karl Rahner's similar term "anonymous Christianity." See Kelly, "'Unconscious Christianity,'" 117–49. See also Knitter, "Toward a Liberation Theology," 178–200, particularly 82ff. For a wider consideration of anonymous Christianity and religious pluralism see D'Costa, "Trinitarian Différance," 28–46.

melody-making cannot be predefined by any group, including the church. This leaves open the possibility of a hitherto hidden melody of Christ being yet revealed within the world and lays before the melody-makers a common ground of mystery.

For the Christian, this means that the proleptic music located in the economy of the polyphonic God and revealed to the world in Christ does not exhaust the melodies of God's immanent polyphony. Gavin D'Costa has argued that in the "Trinitarian surplus" genuine otherness can become "a question mark" to the self-understanding of the Christian and their community.[14] And if so, then,

> in terms of the phrase "anonymous Christian," the anonymous does not relate to the self-consciousness of the Other . . . but to the manner in which the Christian does not possess God or know God without remainder, so that there is a sense in which the anonymous relates neither to the self-consciousness of the Other or the Christian, but rather to the mystery of God, who is known in Christ, yet still hidden.[15]

It is this common ground of mystery that enables the problematic terminology of "unconscious" or "anonymous Christian" to be abandoned in favor of one in which people can affirm their common commitment to participate in making the melodies of justice known in the world. Adopting this terminology does not circumvent all the criticisms of Christological particularity, but admitting to a common goal of justice-making without necessitating an identification with Christ is helpful. It provides an inclusive melody that can be made by Christians, as well as those of other or no faith commitment.

The Christian will recognize in this melody-making the boundaryless boundary that is rooted in the polyphonic Christ. The colony of heaven is known by its commitment to the polyphonic Christ as its *cantus firmus*, but must also affirm that this "mystery" to which it is dedicated and which it endeavors to share responsibly in the world has yet to reveal his entirety to that world. And, as all that exists within that world holds together in that mystery, there can be no boundaries to the potential loci of its revelation: it has a boundaryless boundary. The church that seeks to incarnate that mystery as a community of people must then also display such a boundaryless-ness in its character and will expect to encounter new epiphanal melodies of God that as yet remain hidden within the mystery of the world. If further revelation does occur then the Christian community may, in response, need

14. D'Costa, "Trinitarian Différance," 38–39.

15. Ibid., 39.

to question anew its own identifying characteristics and evolve a new self-understanding. Such a position has long been identified within the Iona Community: MacLeod argued that they were a "laboratory of cooperative living . . . working under the sign of all good laboratories—which is a Question Mark."[16] The daily prayer of the Iona Community affirms the belief that many melodies of God may still be secret in the world. "O God . . . further in all things the purpose of our community, that hidden things may be revealed to us and new ways found to touch the hearts of all."[17]

MacLeod recognized in the new monasticism of the Christian colony the penultimate world of the physical was "the only arena for the display of holiness:"[18] the legitimate identifier of true faith. He argued in favor of a witness that included "political concern, economic obligation, social betterment and scientific search," and contended that this polyphony of action ought not to be considered as "a derivative of faith," but rather, it was the stuff of which Christian faith was "molded," and through which alone faith "could be apprehended."[19] This is not to suggest that there is no room for the molding of faith within the internal life of Christian community, but rather it is to argue that the mettle of Christian holiness is tested only amidst this-worldly realities. Its testing must in turn inform the nature of the community's worship. In this way, the ultimate and penultimate realms of heaven and world are elevated above the traditional zero-sum game of mutually exclusive opposition: the traditional "two realms" between which the Christian historically had been forced to choose.[20] That choice, which places church and world in enmity, is a false one; an authentic following of Christ who is the embodied bisociation of heaven and earth involves not a choice between the two realms but the deliberate choice to hold both "melodies" together. For in Christ, "the reality of God encounters the reality of the world"[21] and Christian life is participation in that encounter, "living fully in the midst of life's tasks, questions, successes and failures, experiences and perplexities . . . [throwing oneself] completely into the arms of God."[22]

But how is the Christian to throw him or herself into the world as a Christian? While all that is created in the world may find its *cantus firmus* in

16. Iona Community, *Coracle*, no. 1, 3.

17. Iona Community, *Iona Abbey Worship Book*, 19–20.

18. MacLeod, *We Shall Rebuild*, 13.

19. Ibid., 13–14.

20. See Bonhoeffer, *Ethics*, 57ff.

21. Ibid., 159.

22. Letter dated July 21, 1944, in Bonhoeffer, *Letters and Papers*, 486.

the Christ, Christianity is not identical with the world.[23] What in the Christian will remain distinctly Christian and how, if at all, do the fragmented melodies of God encountered in the world connect with those whose revelation in the church we have hitherto considered?

In order to discover how the fragmented epiphanies of church and world unite in Christ's *cantus firmus* we turn again to the Discipline of Counterpoint. As we have defined it, this discipline requires the responsible performance by the Christian community of the mystery that is the polyphonic Christ. This mystery of the polyphonic Christ is the *cantus firmus* that underpins all Christian discipleship. It is this that is held in common by Christians both as they gather for communal worship and as they are individually scattered among the world. In healthy discipleship, Christians will perpetually move within these two loci: the colony of heaven and the surrounding world. As they do so, fragmented epiphanies of God may be encountered in either place and then are to be gathered together in the Christian colony. Each gathered fragment will inform the other and all may "polysociate" in a wider music through their relationship to the *cantus firmus*. None is ever fully separate from the other because every melody, whether it is encountered primarily within the church or world, has its foundation in Christ. There may not always be harmonious music when the melodies are gathered: there may be dissonance within the colony of new monasticism or between it and the world, but there is always in Christ the hope of a final eschatological resolution. In acknowledging the polyphonic nature of Christ who is encountered both within the world and church, the Discipline of Counterpoint enables the Christian community to bring together their encounters of Christ in prayer and worship with those in the world and vice versa. It is this discipline that unites the "two realms" of life under Christ and prevents the Christian community lapsing into world-denying piety or becoming a center of radical action with little or no sustaining spirituality. In so doing, the individual Christian and their community of faith are compelled to seek out concrete encounters with Christ beyond the church. In them, as in their Savior, work and worship and prayer and politics, sacred and secular will come together,[24] not simply as a pious hope, but as a confession of praxis.[25]

23. See Bonhoeffer, *Ethics*, 59.

24. The Iona Community affirm the joining of "work and worship, prayer and politics, sacred and secular," but this is not a statement about joining two separate spheres; rather, it acknowledges that all such apparent dichotomies are taken up into Christ.

25. Norman Shanks has noted that the community's concern for justice and peace is a confessional matter, reflecting an "inescapable biblical imperative." Shanks, *Iona—God's Energy*, 156.

But while such action must be considered a confessional matter for the individual Christian and their community, the righteous acts of justice they engage with in the world should be, according to Bonhoeffer, "a quiet and hidden" affair.[26] By "quiet," Bonhoeffer was not advocating a complete muteness concerning a Christian's confession of faith but rather he was arguing in favor of an asceticism of melody making:[27] an acknowledgment that Christians must not dare to speak to the world until their righteous actions had revealed overtures of the divine. To so speak could leave the important hopes of Christian faith (forgiveness, reconciliation, and the like) devoid of a meaningful context by which the world might understand them. For instance, to speak to the world of a gospel of forgiveness and reconciliation within the context of Nazi Germany or between white and colored South Africans during the era of Apartheid, or between Roman Catholics and Protestants amidst the "Troubles" of Northern Ireland, leaves the proclaimed music of good news ringing hollow in the air. There must be a responsible sharing of the melodies of God and that responsibility necessitates an overture of righteous action, a proleptic prelude of concrete accomplishment through which the world can experience the fragment and anticipate the whole. This is not to say that the melodies of heaven cannot be sung on earth, the Lord's Prayer constrains the Christian to participate in the divine performance precisely so that the music may be sung on earth as it is eternally performed in heaven.[28] But the primary performance of such music in the world must be a melody of righteous action that sings for itself. It will be a melody that captures the imagination of the world and provokes it into contrapuntal participation. Bonhoeffer called this "the deed that interprets itself," and argued that "when the deed [becomes] power, then the world will also demand the verbal confession."[29] He rightly distinguished this responsible sharing from occasions when the church had done nothing other than have its confession "screamed loudly in a propagandistic manner" and he argued that such a responsible word must be preserved "as the most sacred possession of the church-community."[30] To do so is an exercise of the Discipline of Counterpoint; it is to responsibly share the melodies of Christ in the

---

26. "Thoughts on the Day of Baptism of D.W.R.," May 1944, in Bonhoeffer, *Letters and Papers*, 390.

27. Frits de Lange writes of an "asceticism of speaking." See de Lange, *Waiting for the Word*, 134ff.

28. This eternal performance acknowledges the opportunity for silence and rest. Cf. Rev 8:1.

29. "The Nature of the Church," in Bonhoeffer, *Ecumenical, Academic, and Pastoral Work*, 314, fn. 329.

30. Ibid., 315.

world. A conscientious performance of these melodies will not seek as their goal the preservation or advancement of the institutional church but will hope simply for a more just world and a "better worldliness."[31] Undoubtedly, if the Discipline of Counterpoint is being properly exercised such actions would in turn affect the worshipping life of the Christian community; nevertheless, the righteous action should stand on its own in the world: "interpreting itself" to its people. Those so engaged would normatively be silent about Christ as the *cantus firmus* of their melody in the world until such times as their deeds offered a legitimate context within which they may then talk with integrity of the gospel of reconciliation and redemption.[32] It was in such "kairos" moments of opportunity that Bonhoeffer suggested the Christian community might then dare to speak to the world of Christ but they would do so, as already noted, with a

> new language, perhaps quite nonreligious, but liberating and redeeming like Jesus's language, so that people will be alarmed and yet overcome by its power—the language of a new righteousness and truth, a language proclaiming that God makes peace with humankind and that God's kingdom is drawing near.[33]

By arguing that acts of righteousness ought to be "hidden," Bonhoeffer seems to have had in mind Christ's warning to the disciples to beware of practicing righteousness before others to be seen by them (Matt 6:1).[34] He may also have had in mind the ways in which Christ often sought to keep secret his own miracles and acts of healing.[35] Of course, these acts of gracious melody are still heard in the world and there is a creative tension between letting the light shine before people and not letting the left hand become an end in itself (Matt 6:1–4).[36] But righteous actions are melodies that sing themselves before the world and are not perpetrated *in order* that the world might hear their song or as an exercise in public relations by the Christian community. Indeed, the reverse is the case: making these melodies of justice arises not out of a desire to sing one's own song, but as a result of having listened to the music of heaven and the songs of others. At its core

---

31. See Bonhoeffer, *Ethics*, 60.

32. "Thoughts on the Day of Baptism of D.W.R.," May 1944, in Bonhoeffer, *Letters and Papers*, 389.

33. Ibid., 390.

34. Bonhoeffer reflected on the hidden nature of righteousness while at Finkenwalde: See Bonhoeffer, *Discipleship*, 146ff.

35. See Matt 6:1–4. Eleanor S. Neel has helpfully traced examples of God's hiddenness throughout Christian Scripture. See Neel, "'Incognito' as a Key."

36. See Bonhoeffer, *Discipleship*, 146ff.

is an understanding of Christ as deputy:[37] the one who hears the earth's distress and the lament of the other's pain and chooses to stand in vicarious responsibility for them. For if sin is understood as "the heart turned in upon itself,"[38] then acts of righteousness are those deeds that are orientated toward the betterment of others. It is by this orientation toward others that we detect the origin of such deeds to lie within the *cantus firmus*. Righteous action begins with hearing the lament of others and joining in solidarity with their melody of distress. This is no doubt why Nazi motorbikes ran their engines outside the gas chambers of the concentration camps, to quite literally drown out the cries of the other. It illuminates why Lenin famously claimed that he could not listen to music too often because it

> affects your nerves, makes you want to say stupid nice things, and stroke the heads of people who could create such beauty while living in this vile hell. And now you mustn't stroke anyone's head—you might get your hand bitten off. You have to hit them on the head, without any mercy, although our ideal is not to use force against anyone.[39]

So if, as Bonhoeffer argues, Christ is the paradigmatic "being for others,"[40] then the Christian community ought to live in vicarious responsibility for others. As such, it is sufficient for the church to share the melody of making justice with those of other or no faith; to make "common cause with the non-Christian and the nonreligious, all without ecclesiastical and theological pretence and qualification."[41] Melody-making for justice by the Christian in, with, and for the world is then music sung not in the name of God *per se*, but in the name of the common humanity to which God in Christ binds himself in vicarious solidarity. And those who are not against this melody are deemed by Christ to be for it.[42] It is what Bonhoeffer would have understood as *mitleiden*: justice as participation in the sufferings of God within the secular life.[43] Fragments of such this-worldly melody can

---

37. See Bonhoeffer, *Ethics*, 12.

38. The definition, belongs to Martin Luther's *Lectures on Romans* which influenced Bonhoeffer's thought: see *Act and Being*, where he refers to the human spirit curving in upon itself and thus moving away from community with God and other human beings. Bonhoeffer, *Act and Being*, 46, 58, 80, 89, 137.

39. Cited in Nelson, *Music for the Revolution*, 1.

40. "Outline for a Book", in Bonhoeffer, *Letters and Papers*, 501.

41. Rasmussen, "Worship in a World Come of Age," 279.

42. Luke 9:49.

43. *Mitleiden* means compassion. See Rasmussen, "Worship in a World Come of Age," 279.

be heard in non-faith allied organizations such as the Red Cross, Amnesty International, Alcoholics Anonymous, Oxfam, World Development Movement, Greenpeace, and Friends of the Earth. Hidden in such people is the melody-making for justice typified by the unaware righteousness of Matt 25: giving food to the hungry, drink to the thirsty, clothes to the naked, a home to the stranger, and visiting the ill or those in prison. Within the Iona Community, many members are involved in making such melodies: not as Christians *per se* but as people committed to justice, peace, and the integrity of creation.[44]

As they work these silent and hidden acts of righteousness, members are discovering appropriate ways to interpret their faith in the new contexts of the world. And where it is impossible to relate these concepts to the world they, after Bonhoeffer, have discovered that "a tactful silence is better than mere repetition of words whose cultural conditioning may have rendered them meaningless."[45] But in this public silence is located their urgent struggle to reinterpret the words of the Bible and the actions of faith in ways that once again speak to the world of God's offer of reconciliation and redemption. This task is succinctly petitioned in the Iona Community prayer for "new ways to touch the hearts of all."[46] One of the melodies of God that has the potential to touch the lives of all is the practice of making peace and reconciliation.

FIRST MOVEMENT: MAKING THE MELODY OF PEACE IN THE WORLD

World peace through non-violent means is neither absurd nor unattainable. All other methods have failed. Thus we must begin anew. Non-violence is a good starting point. Those of us who believe in this method can be voices of reason, sanity and understanding amid the voices of violence, hatred and emotion.

—MARTIN LUTHER KING, JR.[47]

44. The Rule of the Iona Community specifically relates to such action. See Appendix A.

45. Kelly, "Freedom and Discipline," 314.

46. Iona Community, *Iona Abbey Worship Book*, 20.

47. King, "Dreams of Brighter Tomorrows," 34.

The whole earth is sacramental: every thing is truly every blessed thing, and it is indeed blasphemy to use the very atom to kill.

—RON FERGUSON[48]

Non-violence is about revolution. It is about finding creative, imaginative ways to overthrow all forms of tyranny and oppression, without becoming the oppressor in the process. It widens the options and holds out a possibility of a way out of the cycle of violence where dignity can be maintained.

—HELEN STEVEN[49]

It is not always easy to participate in the newly revealed melodies of God in the world. New harmonies and meaningful songs of peace and protest can be difficult music to learn. For instance, the Croat theologian Miroslav Volf was once asked by Jürgen Moltmann if he could embrace a *četnik*, those armed Serbs who had recently destroyed much of Volf's homeland. His deeply honest reply underlines the cost of being a disciple of the Prince of Peace: "No, I cannot—but as a follower of Christ I think I should be able to."[50] For the individual Christian, participating in God's melody of peacemaking will always carry a personal cost.

It was a personal cost with which Christ was familiar. While he proclaimed that the peacemakers of the world would be blessed by God, he knew also that those who sought to participate in making melodies of peace would need encouragement to "love their enemies" and to "pray for those who persecuted them."[51] He knew, too, that their enemies and persecutors, and the potential for violence, would remain ever present. But Christ repeatedly avoided violence with those who opposed him. He refused to accept for himself the warrior-king associations of Messiah-ship that might incite violent confrontations with the Romans, and he resisted provocations to precipitate such conflict. When Peter used a sword to attack those who had come to arrest him, Jesus rebuked the disciple, warning him that those who

---

48. Ferguson, *Chasing the Wild Goose*, 156.
49. Steven, "Justice and Peace Join Hands," 15.
50. Volf, *Exclusion and Embrace*, 9.
51. See Matt 5:9 and 5:43–48.

live by violence would also die by it.[52] Similarly, when he entered Jerusalem the week before his execution,[53] he did so not on a battle steed, but riding on a donkey as predicted by the prophet Zechariah. Indeed, Zechariah had foretold that the Messiah would end repeating cycles of violence: taking away "the chariots from Ephraim and the war horses from Jerusalem" and "breaking the battle bow." He would proclaim peace to the nations and his rule would extend "from sea to sea" and "to the ends of the earth."[54] At his death, Christ rejected the possible use of the legions of angels who could have delivered him from the personal cost of the crucifixion.

But Jesus did not practice nonviolence as a pragmatic tactic against a Roman Empire who held a monopoly on strength and might; rather, he saw nonviolence as a melody of heaven finding its voice on earth. It was, claims Walter Wink, "a direct corollary of the nature of God and of the new reality emerging in the world from God."[55] Echoes of this new reality had been heard in a series of fragmented melodies proclaimed by the Hebrew prophets. Isaiah described his foretaste of it as a time when "swords would be beaten into ploughshares and spears into pruning hooks," (Isa 2:4) and when "the wolf would lie down with the lamb" (Isa 11:6); when all who were thirsty could come to the waters, and when "those without money could buy and eat, [buying] wine and milk without money or price" (Isa 55:1). It was a time to bring "good news for the oppressed, bind up the broken hearted, to proclaim liberty to the captives and release to the prisoners; to proclaim the year of the Lord's favor" (Isa 61:1–2). The promise of this melody was fulfilled in Christ (Luke 4:21) and it was much more than an absence of conflict. He was the Hebrew concept of "shalom": that proleptic network of harmonious social relationships between people and with God.[56]

Not only did Christ teach and practice shalom, but the peace of Christ is in fact predicated on the polyphonic life of the Trinity: one God in perfect community. For God is not only the provider of such peace, but God's very identity is characterized by the immanent quality of shalom. Cunningham suggests that the otherness located within the immanent lives of the Father, Son, and Holy Spirit creates a genuine potential for their wills to differ, but because this conflict is never actualized, there is also within God a

---

52. See Matt 26:50–54 and John 18:1–11.

53. See Matt 21:1–11.

54. Zech 9:9–10.

55. Wink, *Engaging the Powers*, 209.

56. Shalom, the Hebrew concept of peace is to be contrasted with the Greek concept of peace (Eirene) that envisioned a harmonious balance of tranquility while the *Roman Pax* was stability maintained by the peacekeeping military might. See Kraus, *Community of the Spirit*, 133ff; and Williams and Collier, *Beginning Now*, 13–24.

genuine shalom.[57] Without this potential for difference there would be no real meaningful concept of peace but with the diversity of three agreeing to act in unity, shalom becomes personified within the polyphonic God. Christ as the second person of the divine music eternally negotiates this potential for conflict within God's own internal differentiation and together with the Father and the Holy Spirit inhabits a mutual shalom. And as the visible image of the invisible God (Col 1:15), Jesus becomes the epiphanal melody of the divine shalom in this world, inviting humanity to participate in the melody of a humanity unaffected by mimetic violence. It is this divine shalom (peace but not as the world gives it) that is left ("peace I leave with you") with the disciples and bequeathed to the church.[58]

The responsibility for participating in the this-worldly performance of shalom rested in the new realities of the post-resurrection disciples and in generations of the colony of heaven. The early Christian community inhabited a new and unique place of boundaryless social inclusion and nonviolent living for others that owed everything to the polyphonic shalom encountered in Christ. Their responsibility for participating in the melody of shalom was readily adopted by the pre-Constantine church as is evidenced in the specific Christian rejection of the Imperial State Military.[59] The writings of Justin Martyr, Origen, and Tertullian all testify to the refusal of Christians to engage in military action, claiming that "Christ in disarming Peter, unbelted every soldier."[60] But after the Constantinian Settlement, with the increasing homogenization of the gospel, the army became an integral part of ensuring the unthreatened propagation of a uniform religion. This laid the foundation for an alliance between the church and force of arms that has with notable exceptions continued ever since.

There has, of course, been controversy over whether the prior Christian denouncement of war and military participation was due to their objections to killing *per se* or owed more to their aversion to the idolatrous paganism of the army.[61] But Walter Wink asserts that this debate is largely irrelevant.[62] He concludes that both possibilities (together with his explication of the Myth

57. See Cunningham, *These Three Are One*, 238–43.

58. John 14:27.

59. Pacifism was not unknown in the ancient world, but most examples owe more to the individual pursuit of tranquility and detachment from the world than any hope to remain responsibly involved with the world in a nonviolent fashion. See the work of Brock, *Roots of War Resistance*, cited in Wink, *Engaging the Powers*, 209.

60. Tertullian, *On Idolatry*, 19.3, is among many illustrative statements cited by Wink, *Engaging the Powers*, 210.

61. For a review of varying opinions, see Hunter, "Decade of Research," 87–93.

62. Wink, *Engaging the Powers*, 211.

of Redemptive Violence)[63] are symptoms of "the domination system."[64] This
is the system of those global, national, local, and personal "powers and principalities" that have fallen from their God ordained purpose. Their march
toward monophonic homogenization (no voice but their own) stands in
direct contradiction to the polyphony of Christ and the Christian colony.
They perpetuate unjust economics, oppressive politics, domineering gender relations, racial prejudices, and hierarchical power relations that are
predicated on a hatred of difference and maintained by a violence against
diversity.[65] For the early Christians their opposition to killing and to military idolatry were one and the same, namely, an allegiance to the purposes
of shalom and as such, an opposition to the domination system personified in Rome and the empire. Here is uncovered a deeper melody of truth;
while there had been fragments of heaven's alternative revealed through the
prophets of Israel, the domination system had been largely camouflaged as
a system. It simply was the way things were. But with the epiphany of personal shalom in Christ, the system is unmasked. This reveals the "hidden
things" that Christ tells the disciples have been concealed "since the foundation of the world" (Matt 13:35).[66] These things stand in direct opposition to
melodies of vicarious action on behalf of suffering others that characterize
Christ as *cantus firmus*. The self-seeking purpose of the domination system
is to overwhelm and silence the melodies of making justice. So they stand
in opposition to the boundaryless inclusion, unifying difference, and nonviolent harmony of Christ's shalom. In the ongoing revelation of their true
character, Christ does not simply expose their falsehood, but offers creative
alternatives to their violence and overcomes their self-perpetuation through
his death and resurrection. This heralds the end to mimetic acts of violence
and the cessation of scapegoat mechanisms (including those ingrained in
Christian theology) that are designed to retrain society's longing for ven-
geance. The unmasking of these powers once hidden is the prelude to their
being engaged and redeemed.[67]

63. The Myth of Redemptive Violence is the idea that violence can be used to
satisfactorily resolve conflicts and ensure peace. Ricoeur's commentary on this myth
in *Symbolism of Evil* is the foundation of much of Walter Wink's analysis. See Wink,
Engaging the Powers, Chapter 1.

64. Ibid., 211ff.

65. Ibid., Chapters 1–5.

66. Indeed, René Girard has specifically identified such recurring cycles of violence
and domination as the "hidden things" that Christ reveals through the parables. See
Girard, *Things Hidden*.

67. The prayer for the Iona Community pre-dates the work of Girard, but synthesiz-
ing his reflections with Wink's analysis gives a deeper and fresh perspective on the community prayer. "Further in all things the purpose of our community, that hidden things

At the same time Christ offers the possibility of participating in the alternative and ordained melodies of God. The melody of peacemaking revealed to the world through Christ challenges the community of faith to resist the system without succumbing to a mimetic methodology. The gospels reveal how Jesus offered creative and disarming alternatives for nonviolent resistance, classically turning the other (right) cheek, which denies the dominator any continued power to humiliate the victim and challenges the boundaries of differing social status.[68] The cross and resurrection of Jesus attests to the ultimate powerlessness of the domination system before the melody of shalom. Pentecost bears witness to the power of the Holy Spirit, in which the domination system can be resisted in this world. The eschaton promises hope to those who live in the now and not yet that the powers can and shall be redeemed. The unmasking, engaging, and redeeming of the system is at the heart of the melody of peacemaking. Participation in such a melody ought to be a defining characteristic of the colony of heaven, a confessional matter, a commitment of belonging as determined as the traditional baptismal/confirmation vows. Within the new monasticism of the Iona Community, a commitment to making the melody of shalom is a confessional matter. Although not every member is a convinced pacifist, each person commits herself/himself to work for peace and justice in some way appropriate to their context. But while this position is by no means unique to the Iona Community, it stands in contrast the common practice of the post-Constantine church. From its sanctioning of Crusades to its blessing of battleships, the church has too often colluded with the systems of domination, complicit with its violence with little self-examination or search for alternatives.[69]

A classic example of the domination system and the church's collusion therein was the rise of Nazism in Germany during the 1930s. Nazism offers a profound example of the domination system, not simply in its desire for a totalitarian eradication of difference but also in its ability to induce in its opposition a mimetic violence of resistance.[70] And Bonhoeffer offers an honest

---

may be revealed to us and new ways found to touch the hearts of all." Iona Community, *Iona Abbey Worship Book*, 20.

68. See Wink, *Engaging the Powers*, 175ff.

69. There are, of course, sections of the church such as Quakers and Mennonites for whom peacemaking is a central concern, but peacemaking as a confessional position has been rare. The church as a whole has tended toward varying theories of the "Just War," although the strict definition of such a war is rarely appreciated by those who appeal to it. See Wink, *Engaging the Powers*, 212ff.

70. A good example is the terror bombing of civilian targets in WWII. This began with Hitler bombing Warsaw and Rotterdam, but the allies reciprocated in a systematic attempt to destroy German morale by bombing all forty-three major German cities.

refrain of the tensions and complexities of participating in the melodies of peacemaking amidst the domination system. His early theology claimed that when a people consciously submit to God's will and go to war, then "war is no longer murder."[71] In Barcelona, Bonhoeffer admitted that killing was undoubtedly a sin and wicked, but argued that pacifism was a mistaken and legalistic position that failed to be concrete, and "as a consequence it does not take in the depths of Christian decision."[72] However, by 1934 his theology had altered.[73] By then he had met Jean Lasserre and was enthralled by the Sermon on the Mount. In Germany, with the minority exception of the Confessing Church, Christians were colluding with Nazism. Soon Bonhoeffer was making passionate pleas for peace through an international and ecumenical witness at Fanö. There he confessed to colleagues that in the event of war he would pray that God would give him the strength not to take up arms.[74] He had also been influenced by the nonviolent opposition to the British in India[75] and in the next few years, secured introductions that would have enabled him to study in Gandhi's Ashram. For a variety of reasons, the trip was never possible, but despite that Bonhoeffer's commitment to peace deepened. In 1935 he wrote to his brother that "things do exist that are worth standing up for without compromise. To me it seems that peace and social justice are such things, as is Christ himself."[76] The following year he confessed to then seeing as "utterly self evident" the Christian

---

For further comment on WWII mimetic rivalry see Wink, *Engaging the Powers*, 196ff.

71. Bonhoeffer, *Sanctorum Communio*, 119.

72. See Rasmussen, *Dietrich Bonhoeffer*, 96–97.

73. Indeed, by 1932 he spoke at a Youth Peace Conference at Ciernohorské Kúpele in favor of pacifism (albeit in a contextualized form) and with Franz Hildebrant helped draft a new catechism in which he wrote, "The Church knows nothing of the sanctity of war. For in war, the struggle for existence [*Dasein*] is fought with dehumanized means. The Church that prays the Lord's Prayer calls to God only for the cause of peace." Bonhoeffer, *Ecumenical, Academic and Pastoral Work*, 262. See also James, "Growth of the Convictions," 5–12; Jehle, "Dietrich Bonhoeffer on War and Peace," 362–66; Clements, *What Freedom?*, 53–66; and Chapman, "What Would Bonhoeffer Say," 167–75.

74. As cited in Bethge, *Dietrich Bonhoeffer: A Biography*, 389.

75. Gandhi's way of life had inspired Bonhoeffer's sermon at Fanö; namely, "must we be put to shame by non-Christian peoples in the East?" Bonhoeffer, *London*, 309. For a good account on the relationship between Gandhi and Bonhoeffer see Davis, "Gandhi and Bonhoeffer," 44–49; Peck, "Significance of Bonhoeffer's Interest in India," 431–50; Wiersma, "Bonhoeffer and Gandhi," 208–11; and Poulose, "Understanding of Bonhoeffer in India," 212–15.

76. "Letter to Karl Friedrich Bonhoeffer," in Bonhoeffer, *London*, 285. See also Bethge, *Dietrich Bonhoeffer: A Biography*, 206.

pacifism that up until then he had "passionately disputed."[77] In Finkenwalde
he taught his students,

> Jesus' followers are called to peace. When Jesus called them, they
> found their peace. Jesus is their peace. Now they are not only to
> have peace, but they are to make peace. To do this they *renounce*
> *violence and strife.* Those things never help the cause of Christ.
> Christ's kingdom is a realm of peace, and those in Christ's com-
> munity greet each other with a greeting of peace. Jesus' disciples
> maintain peace by choosing to suffer instead of causing others
> to suffer. They preserve community when others destroy it. They
> renounce self-assertion and are silent in the face of hatred and
> injustice. That is how they overcome evil with good. That is how
> they are makers of divine peace in a world of hatred and war.[78]

Most of Bonhoeffer's work in the resistance reflected this commitment: to stand in solidarity with the suffering and renounce violence.[79] But
famously he then participated with other members of the resistance in a plot
to assassinate Hitler.[80] That the plot failed does not change the fact that Bonhoeffer was now willing to entertain complicity in murder. Did he forsake
the call to peace? Did he change his theology?[81] Did he too in the end suc-
cumb to mimetic violence? Both pacifism and conspiracy must somehow
flow together if Bonhoeffer meant what he said in April 1944:

> I am wholly under the impression that my life—strange as it
> may sound—has gone in a straight line, uninterrupted, at least
> with regard to how I've led it.[82]

The integrity of this unbroken course is particularly pertinent because
on the day after the failed attempt to assassinate Hitler, Bonhoeffer, in a
letter to Bethge, specifically reaffirmed that he stood by what he had written
in *Discipleship*.[83]

---

77. "Letter to Elizabeth Zinn," in Bonhoeffer, *Theological Education at Finkenwalde*,
134.

78. Bonhoeffer, *Discipleship*, 108.

79. Bonhoeffer worked on the U7 project to help Jews escape from Germany.

80. See Green, "Pacifism and Tyrannicide," 31–47.

81. Bonhoeffer would never have become a plotter on political pragmatism alone.
Rather, theology played a decisive role in his particular understanding of political re-
sistance. See Pangritz, "Sharing the Destiny of His People"; and Nation, Siegrist, and
Umbel, *Bonhoeffer the Assassin*.

82 Letter dated April 11, 1944, in Bonhoeffer, *Letters and Papers*, 352. See further
Nation, "'Pacifist and Enemy of the State," 61–77.

83. Letter dated July 21, 1944, in Bonhoeffer, *Letters and Papers*, 486. Bethge holds

It is Bonhoeffer's polyphonic approach to life and peacemaking that enables him with unbroken integrity to hold his apparently contradictory actions in tension. Christ, the *cantus firmus*, remained the epiphany of divine shalom. Peace was the "great venture" still to be dared.[84] But being conformed to the likeness of the polyphonic Christ and responsibly participating in the divine melody of peacemaking meant seriously addressing the question, "Who is Christ for us today?" Christ was to be found among those suffering under Hitler and his Nazi system of domination. Wrestling with how to make peace in such an extreme context eventually led Bonhoeffer to reject the possibility of "innocently" observing and compelled him to conspire to act violently (and sinfully) for the sake of suffering others, and in the last resort that meant tyrannicide.[85] Simple adherence to an absolute position of pacifism that retained his purity while others (and therefore Christ) suffered was insufficient.[86] For just as the melody of the divine shalom is never passive, so too Bonhoeffer could not be a pacifist: doing nothing in the face of others' struggle and pain. His life was characterized by "not always doing and daring what's random, but seeking the right thing . . . boldly [to] reach for the real."[87] And, but for the *in extremis* responsibilities that he believed arose in response to Hitler, Bonhoeffer remained as deeply committed to the music of nonviolence. He never sought to justify his participation in the planned tyrannicide as being "in tune" with the *cantus firmus*.[88] In *Ethics* he had written that

that Bonhoeffer remained consistent in this. See Chapman, "What Would Bonhoeffer Say to Christian Peacemakers Today?" 168.

84. Bonhoeffer used such phrases in his address to the Fanö Conference in August 1934. Bonhoeffer, *London*, 309.

85. Davis has argued that Bonhoeffer was still very much influenced by Gandhi at this point, particularly the spiritual discipline of "satyagraha," in which to remain "neutral" is an option which aligns one with the violence already present in the situation. See Davis, "Gandhi and Bonhoeffer," 46.

86. Indeed, he regarded the ideological purity of pacifism through public conscientious objection as a private and indulgent flight from the increased responsibility needed in the situation. He disapproved of the pacifism adopted by Hermann Stöhr, who refused to fight and, as conscientious objection was not recognized by the Nazi Regime, was shot. See Bethge, *Bonhoeffer: Exile and Martyr*, 112. In a 1985 radio interview Bethge argued that "Christians . . . have to acknowledge what is happening to victimized people and they have to accept their responsibility to try and save them, and not run away into purity and leave them. Purity is even worse then." Clements, *What Freedom*, 34.

87. "Stations on the Way to Freedom," in Bonhoeffer, *Letters and Papers*, 513.

88. Bonhoeffer asked for warning so that he might formally sever his links with the Confessing Church before any assassination occurred. He knew that his actions might mean the end of any future career as a pastor and never denied that his act was a sin.

those who, in acting responsibly, seek to avoid becoming guilty divorce themselves from the ultimate reality of human existence; but in doing so they also divorce themselves from the redeeming mystery of the sinless bearing of guilt by Jesus Christ, and have no part in the divine justification that attends this event. They place their personal innocence [*unschuld*] above their responsibility for other human beings and are blind to the fact that precisely in so doing they become even more egregiously guilty.[89]

It was in this vein that Bonhoeffer confessed his guilt before the God of shalom, but simultaneously placed his trust in that same God. So, living unreservedly in life's problems and perplexities, Bonhoeffer threw himself "completely into the arms of God."[90]

Living for God amidst life's duties and problems places an obligation upon the Christian to "seek peace and pursue it."[91] Thus, while George MacLeod became a convinced and on occasion incorrigible pacifist, a polyphony of positions on working for peace has always been found within the membership of the Iona Community. The community itself has never been pacifist in that sense of adhering to an absolute rule. However, since 1966 the community has retained as a quasi-confessional position a specific commitment within its Rule of Life for members to work for peace. This was subsequently amended into its current form, which includes a commitment to justice. It includes within it the following polyphony of commitments:[92]

We believe:

1. That the Gospel commands us to seek peace founded on justice and that costly reconciliation is at the heart of the gospel;

2. That work for justice, peace and an equitable society is a matter of extreme urgency;

[. . .]

Walter Wink notes that generations of Christians have held back from full commitment to nonviolence, citing Bonhoeffer's example and then ponders: "Had he known, both that his attempt would fail, and that it would have the effect of justifying redemptive violence in the eyes of so many Christians, I wonder if he would have done it?" Wink, *Engaging the Powers*, 225.

89. Bonhoeffer, *Ethics*, 276.

90. Letter dated July 21, 1944, in Bonhoeffer, *Letters and Papers*, 486.

91. Ps 34:14.

92. For a complete copy of the Rule, see Appendix A.

6. That social and political action leading to justice for all people and encouraged by prayer and discussion, is a vital work of the Church at all levels;

7. That the use or threatened use of nuclear weapons or other weapons of mass destruction is theologically and morally indefensible and that opposition to their existence is an imperative of the Christian Faith.[93]

And within the accountability structures of the family group members of the community, seek to participate in the melody making of peace by committing to

engage in forms of political witness and action, prayerfully and thoughtfully to promote just and peaceful social, political and economic structures.[94]

This polyphonic commitment to the melody of shalom needs to be understood as a radical alternative to the domination systems that are uncovered in Christ's presence in the world. George MacLeod instinctively grasped the truth that this involved the Christian colony in struggles against more than flesh and blood and that crucial to such resistance was for individual and community to know well the melodies of its peacemaking purpose. In a passage particularly pertinent to this book he wrote,

The fact is we live in a demonic world. At least I hope we live in a demonic world. I hope it is not as reasonable creatures that we spend these astronomical sums on preparing for a war no one can win. . . . We have always believed in principalities and powers and the rulers of wickedness in high places. The very essence of our Faith is that we have the answer through our Redeemer.

Michael must come back into our consciousness (not just our intellects). Angels must become our consciousness again . . . not floppy damsels in their nighties, but dynamic forces in the serried ranks . . . "the whole company of heaven."

It is because we have left "all that" out that the Faith has become "background music" and demonic secularism rules our souls.

By all means let us say that the secular is the realm of God's activity and that He is in and through all things, but realize He

93. For a reflection on this part of the Iona Community Rule see Galloway, *Living by the Rule*, 65–80.

94. See Appendix A.

has let loose Satan there, for our disciplining, and that Christ is also there for our salvation.[95]

For the Christian colony, the melodies of peacemaking, the polyphony of shalom can never be allowed to become "background music." This echo of angel song breaks into this world's present reality and longs for humanity to join in the performance. Such melodies are regularly rehearsed within the Christian community: as family groups gather together and, in Iona Abbey, there is a weekly evening service and short daily services of prayer for justice and peace. But such services would be but a pious hope and a false witness if members did not participate in the melodies of peace within the world. Members of the community will vary in the ways by which this music remains in the foreground of their discipleship of righteous action. Some may be said to be engaged in peace-work professionally. Many others are actively involved in organizations such as CND, the Campaign Against the Arms Trade and Trident Ploughshares. Others may express their participation in the melody of peacemaking through their lifestyle choices, or their support for others. The work is conducted within church-related and secular organizations. Some have been involved in the World Court Project regarding the international declaration of the illegality of nuclear weapons. For other members their commitment to the Rule and God's overture of peacemaking has led to direct nonviolent demonstration such as that which occurs regularly outside the Faslane Submarine Base, near Glasgow. Others have understood their participation in the melodies of peacemaking to necessitate nonviolent direct action that has ironically led to their arrest for "breach of the peace."[96] Indeed, a defense run in such cases is that given the illegality of the weapons retained on the military bases, the defendants are in fact acting "to keep the peace."[97] Rather than pay the fines with which they have been sentenced, many members have spent time in prison for their convictions. But many others who do not feel they can take this step may be found supporting the witness of such individuals, through regular "affinity groups" and practical care on the day of demonstrations and during their period of incarceration.

95. MacLeod, "Background Music," 15–16, as cited in Ferguson, *Daily Readings*, 84.

96. Accounts of the surrounding events and trials can be found regularly in various issues of *Coracle* and online at www.tridentploughshares.org.

97. On October 21, 1999, at Greenock Sheriff Court, Sheriff Margaret Gimblett upheld the defense argument of the "Trident Three" that they were keeping the law and the peace by their actions. However, on March 30, 2001, the Scottish High Court ruled that their defense was mistaken. In December 2001 the Trident Three were awarded the Right Livelihood Award (known as the alternative Nobel Prize) for their Trident Ploughshares disarmament work.

That such action is seen as an unmasking of the powers of the domination system can be seen in the reflections of Roger Gray who in 1986 at the age of seventy moved from lawful campaigner to an action of civil disobedience. After participating in a Pentecost act of worship outside the RNAD Coulport (where the Polaris missiles were housed) some campaigners then chained themselves together and knelt in prayer across the gateway of the base. Spontaneously, Roger joined. Reflecting on his subsequent arrest he wrote in the *Coracle,*

> For the first seventy years of my life I have kept the laws of the land, believing it was right to do so, but on that day of Pentecost, I believed, with the others, I was called to make that particular witness to oppose the cosmic powers of evil which, if not overcome, will lead to the destruction of life on this planet.[98]

Significantly, this act of peacemaking in the world happened after participation in an act of peacemaking worship. The day had begun with worship that had moved from penitence for complicity in the arms race to a celebration of the power of the Spirit. For these people their act of prayer was no optional extra to bolt onto their righteous action. Rather, the worship energized and sustained Roger Gray and eighteen other protestors as they participated in the penultimate melodies of God's shalom before a world of domination. Here is an example of the Discipline of Counterpoint at work; the melodies of God revealed in the church and world uniting and bisociating around the *cantus firmus* of Christ in polyphonic witness.

SECOND MOVEMENT: MAKING THE MELODY OF JUSTICE IN THE WORLD

The Bible is about revolution as well as revelation. . . . The theme of social justice echoes through the pages of Scripture like an insistent drum-beat.

—NORMAN SHANKS[99]

Certainly, we are not Christ, nor are we called to redeem the world through our own deed and our own suffering; . . . but if we want to be Christians it means that we are to take part in Christ's greatness

98. The details of these events are recorded in Steven, *Roger,* 79.

99. Shanks, *Iona—God's Energy,* 156.

of heart, in the responsible action that in freedom lays hold of the hour and faces the danger, and in the true sympathy that springs forth not from fear, but from the Christ's freeing and redeeming love for all who suffer.

—DIETRICH BONHOEFFER[100]

The melodies of peace and those of justice perpetually sound in close harmony to one another, for as Bonhoeffer once declared, "A community of peace can only exist when it does not rest on a *lie* or on *injustice*."[101] And it is precisely as the heavenly colony makes known the melodies of God on earth that the world witnesses within the boundaryless boundary how "justice and peace join hands."[102] This affirmation of the close harmony that exists between justice and peace is taken from the morning liturgy of the Iona Community, but as the Rule of the Community attests, such words become no more than "a pious hope and a false witness unless people seek separately and together to put it into practice."[103] How the melodies of justice are practiced within a community of faith will depend greatly on how they imagine God. A people who imagine God to be an omnipotent autocrat will conceive and dispense an understanding of justice in a similarly capricious and monophonic form. But that is to ill-conceive God who is polyphonic in character: God's melody of justice, as with that of God's peace, must therefore be polyphonic in form. The divine shalom (a concept as much to do with justice as it is with peace) is premised upon such a polyphonic character. And justice, like peace, requires more than the suppression of difference by the oppressive monophony of a dominating system or persons. Polyphonic justice allows the melodies of every person to find their voice through their response to the *cantus firmus*. At the core of this justice is both the ability and the willingness to listen to the voice of others, particularly those less advantaged than ourselves, to empathize and stand in solidarity with them and to welcome them into the melodies of God's community.

This is certainly the witness of the Christian Scriptures. Beginning in the Jewish Torah, God's people were exhorted not to deny justice to the poor

100. "After Ten Years," in Bonhoeffer, *Letters and Papers*, 49.

101. Bonhoeffer, *Ecumenical, Academic and Pastoral Work*, 365.

102. "Iona Community Morning Liturgy," in Iona Community, *Iona Abbey Worship Book*, 15.

103 See Appendix A, and Galloway, *Living by the Rule*, 65–80.

in legal disputations and to uphold the rights of foreigners,[104] precisely because it was so easy to ignore the voice of those who could not afford to pay to have their case heard. Biblical justice generated a social obligation for the people of God to listen to the melodies of others. It was a justice premised upon their experience of God. The prophet Micah pronounces that the Lord requires no more of humanity than to do justice, and to love kindness, and to walk humbly with your God.[105]

Jesus not only spoke about justice, but also revealed its heavenly character throughout his earthly ministry. Beginning in his incarnation, he who was of heaven did not consider equality with God as something to be grasped but took the nature of a servant and human form.[106] In so doing, he knew what it was to live in humility before others, to enter into their song, to empathize with their struggles and sufferings. In the open polyphony of his life, he revealed an inclusive appreciation of the music that others had chosen to exclude and ignore: the laments of lepers, slaves, and tax collectors, women, children, and Gentiles. He listened them into the fullness of life, not only giving them a rightful place within society but teaching them to sing a polyphonic anthem of unity in diversity through which the early church proclaimed there were no Jews nor Greeks, slaves nor free folk, male and female. For in their polyphony they were united in Christ's *cantus firmus*.[107] As these melodies of God were made known in the world there was revealed to its people a polyphonic justice that was inclusive of everyone.

Both Bonhoeffer and MacLeod shared an uncommon ear for the melodies of this righteous anthem. They did this despite coming from backgrounds of privilege. They were both male, white, and born into stable upper-middle-class families; they were physically strong and healthy, intellectually gifted and university educated, well-travelled, and financially well-resourced. Such privilege is not the usual incubus for champions of radical social action: in such environments the cacophony generated by an introspective elite often leaves little space to listen for the melodies of otherness.[108] Yet for those who had ears to hear, the music of others was

---

104. See Exod 23:6, 9; Ps 89:14; Isa 1:17; and Amos 5:15, 24.

105. Mic 6:8.

106. See Eph 2:1–11.

107. See Gal 3:28.

108. However, charges of elitism, sexism, and religious intolerance could also be leveled at both men. They shared an aristocratic elitism that did not make them particularly open to the suggestions of others. On occasion, they reveal a tendency toward what would now be regarded as sexism. Bonhoeffer's theology contains hints of anti-Semitism and for all his ecumenism, MacLeod could unashamedly engage in anti-Roman Catholic rhetoric.

there to be heard. George MacLeod heard it first in the Great War, in the trenches with the common man, and in the meetings of Toc H. But he carried the music with him to the back-street children hanging round St. Giles' in Edinburgh, the poverty of Govan tenements during the 1930s depression, and the post-war housing programs. In time, that music blossomed into the polyphonic concerns of the Iona Community and nurtured numerous personal sacrifices and communal campaigns for justice at home and around the world. Bonhoeffer heard similar countermelodies; whether it was the Barcelona drop-ins, the racially victimized African-Americans of Harlem, the slum teenagers of Grunewald, Berlin, or indeed the persecuted Jews of Europe, he continually championed the voice of the voiceless. Indeed, Bonhoeffer's "song from below" has now become a "classic" of that champion of the marginalized: liberation theology.

> It remains an experience of incomparable value that we have for once learned to see the great events of world history from below, from the perspective of the outcasts, the suspects, the maltreated, the powerless, the oppressed and reviled, in short, from the perspective of the suffering. If only during this time bitterness and envy have not corroded the heart; that we come to see matters great and small, happiness and misfortune, strength and weakness with new eyes; that our sense for greatness, humanness, justice, and mercy has grown clearer, freer, more incorruptible; that we learn indeed, that personal suffering is a more useful key, a more fruitful principle than personal happiness for exploring the meaning of the world in contemplation and action. But this perspective from below must not lead us to become advocates for those who are perpetually dissatisfied. Rather, out of a higher satisfaction, which in its essence is grounded beyond what is below and above, we do justice to life in all its dimensions and in this way affirm it.[109]

There are numerous "songs from below" that are gradually adding their voices to God's melodies of justice as revealed within the world. As they are listened into existence their songs invite the Christian colony to discover the "higher satisfaction" of the divine polyphony that will do justice to "life in all its dimensions": to the rich and poor, old and young, male and female, with the Christian and those of other or no religious faith. This music from below might include the melodies of God as they are perceived by a variety of historically marginalized or silenced groups such as women,[110] lesbians,

109. "After Ten Years," in Bonhoeffer, *Letters and Papers*, 52.
110. The feminist struggle for justice has now left few, if any, areas of life untouched

gay, bisexual, and transgendered people,[111] or those with physical or mental disabilities.[112] Regrettably, it is not possible in this study to adequately examine all such melodies from below; but by way of illustration we shall listen to two harmonies: those that address poverty and racism.

Poverty

For a long time I have known that to sit with the poor brings extraordinary blessing and insight . . . for in their freedom comes my own, and that's the place in which I wish to be found.

—MARTYN JOSEPH[113]

Poverty is an offence to God precisely because it breaks and crushes human beings made in his image; and in our society today, poverty is breaking and crushing us all, not only the poor, for it is our humanity, as well as that of the poor, that is lessened and distorted as we allow poverty to exist in our midst.

—JOHN HARVEY[114]

---

by its critique of the dominant monophony of patriarchal systems. It is itself polyphonic in nature (although Carter Heyward once called it "a cacophony of diversity"). It celebrates the multiplicity of women's experience as uniquely located in Asian, African, or Latin American women, together with the womanist theology of the developed world, women of color, the mujerista theology of Hispanic women, and various thinking contextual to the indigenous groups in which it continues to be birthed.

111. Much writing from within the Christian gay and lesbian community or those sympathetic to it, has been focused on the hermeneutics employed to interpret certain key biblical texts and the construction of an alternative Christian sexual ethic. See, for instance, Countryman, *Dirt, Greed and Sex*; and Wright Knust, *Unprotected Texts*. But many LGBTQ Christians articulate their marginalization within the church and society in general, in terms of a struggle for justice and equality. See Cleaver, *Know My Name*; and Gill, *Lesbian and Gay Christian Movement*.

112. Helpful introductions to this can be found in Eisland, *Disabled God*; McCloughry and Morris, *Making a World of Difference*; and Tataryn and Truchan-Tataryn, *Discovering Trinity in Disability*.

113. Martyn Joseph, CD, notes in *Till the End: For the MST* (Christian Aid/Pipe Records, 2002). Used with kind permission.

114. Harvey, "Bridging the Gap," cited in Paynter, *This Is the Day*, month 4, day 25.

May it not be long, Lord . . . before there are no more beggars at the door, waiting for the crumbs from the tables of the rich. . . . May it not be long before Christians in this land examine their economic priorities in the light of the Gospel, rather than its shadow.

—JOHN L. BELL[115]

Someone may be understood as economically poor[116] when they have "nowhere to externalize the cost"[117] of providing for their basic human needs. In other words, when they cannot personally bear the financial burdens of daily life and the wider community, local, national, or global, are not willing or able to accept the responsibility for those suffering from economic deprivation in their midst. When this happens, their songs of protest are silenced and excised from the harmonies of the people of the world. They may be conveniently ignored into pretended nonexistence, an experience to which every street beggar in any country will testify. Or they may be violently silenced by guns and bulldozers.[118] Either way, they are the *unmenschen*,[119] non-persons, excluded from experiencing the fullness of the relational symphony in which God has ordained they have a part to play. It is the task of the Christian community to provide a way for their songs of identity and belonging to be heard in the world; for "on Earth, God seeks to be honored by us in the other, and nowhere else."[120] As we listen to the songs of others, the music of the community we share between us is honored.

115. Excerpts from a prayer by Bell, *Jubilee Liturgy*, 17–18.

116. Gustavo Gutiérrez has distinguished real poverty (the lack of those goods required to satisfy the most basic of human needs) from spiritual poverty (an attitude of openness toward the will of God) and poverty as a commitment to be assumed by all Christians in solidarity with the poor and in protest against poverty. See Gutiérrez, "Task and Content of Liberation Theology," 25–26.

117. The phrase is borrowed from a conversation with Kathy Galloway, a former leader of the Iona Community.

118. Sadly, this experience is legion and common to the poor across the boundaries of time or geography. In times past peasants in Ireland and Scotland were "cleared" from the land on which they worked when keeping livestock became more profitable for its owners. Similarly, when the World Bank met in Manila in 1976 legal tenants in an area deemed to be an eye-sore were forcibly evicted and their homes demolished. See Fraser, *Strange Fire*, 112. A present-day instance involves the work in Brazil of *Movimento Sem Terra* (MST) in which peasant farmers campaign for land reform. In April 1996, eleven peaceful campaigners were shot dead by military police.

119. This was the Nazi term coined for non-Aryan people, literally non-persons.

120. "Thy Kingdom Come," in Bonhoeffer, *Berlin*, 295.

So liberation theologian Gustavo Gutiérrez notes that the question for our time is then not so much how to announce God in a nonreligious "world-come-of-age," but how to proclaim God as Father in an inhuman world. "How do we tell the 'non-persons' that they are the sons and daughters of God?"[121] By this he does not mean that the questions of Christian belief in a modern and postmodern world are no longer relevant, but simply that there is a greater urgency to make absolute poverty a matter of history.[122] God's justice demands that the human ability to respond to Christ and participate in the polyphonic melodies of heaven on earth cannot be denied to those whom local, national, or global society arrogantly regards as worthless non-persons. There is, claims Bonhoeffer, "the infinite worth of that which is seemingly worthless and the infinite worthlessness of that which is seemingly so valued."[123] So it is that Christ is often to be found in the midst of such people, joining with them in their otherwise unheard laments and songs of protest. As Bonhoeffer informed his Barcelona congregation, "Jesus is at the door, knocking, in reality, asking you for help in the figure of the beggar, in the figure of the degenerate soul in shabby clothes, encountering you in every person that you meet."[124] Later, he asserted that whoever attacks "the least of the people attacks Christ, who took on human form and who in himself has restored the image of God for all who bear a human countenance."[125] If the world has now truly come of age then it is a matter of justice that no individual in whom resides the image of God is denied their "response-ability" before God's *cantus firmus* in the world. Until release from poverty is achieved for all, then the melodies of God on earth remain in some part muted and all people, rich and poor, the powerful and the oppressed, those below and above, are simultaneously diminished by the place that is denied their song. "The opposite of poverty, in the Bible, is not riches, but righteousness, justice."[126]

But is the hope of polyphonic justice for the poor a credible ambition? The Hebrew Scriptures seem to assert a harsh reality that there will always be poor people in the land[127] and Jesus appears to confirm this

121. Gutiérrez, "Task and Content of Liberation Theology," 28. The concept of *mündigkeit*, a world-come-of-age, was for Bonhoeffer one in which every person was able and responsible to speak for him or herself.

122. Ibid., 28ff.

123. "The Essence of Christianity," in Bonhoeffer, *Barcelona, Berlin, New York*, 354.

124. Sermon on Rev 3:20, in ibid., 545.

125. Bonhoeffer, *Discipleship*, 285.

126. John Harvey, "Poverty—A Violence of Human Rights," cited in Paynter, *This Is the Day*, month 2, day 1.

127. See for instance Deut 15:11.

realpolitik when he tells the disciples "you will always have the poor with you."[128] However, in these Jewish Scriptures, the stated actuality of interminable poverty was not only paralleled by an exhortation for the people to be open-handed toward the needy, but included a specific social provision made for their relief through the regular communal cycle of debt cancellation.[129] These melodies of mercy and justice were specifically designed to prevent a perpetuating cycle of deepening poverty and to remind the people that everything fundamentally belonged to God. While there is no evidence that Israel ever practiced this regular rhythm of righteous economy, that need not diminish its potency: Michael Taylor claims that, at best, "jubilee, like love, is an impossible possibility. It is always there to question our self-satisfied achievements and call us on to new heights."[130] Economic jubilee is then an epiphanal fragment of heaven's polyphonic song entrusted to the colony to be shared within the world. Similarly, when Jesus claimed that the poor would always be present on earth he was intent on drawing attention to his own impending exodus and not to an inexorable social condition. From the inception of his ministry, Christ was about bringing good news to the poor and freedom to those oppressed. In acknowledging the continuing presence of the poor, Christ's intention was not to harden the hearts of the disciples so that they might walk by on the other side of another's destitution secure in cosseted religiosity. Rather, the coming of the Kingdom of God brought melodies of good news to the poor and the disciples were charged with sharing the rhythms of resurrection living and the songs of messianic freedom to "Jerusalem, Judea, Samaria and to the ends of the earth."[131] And as is evidenced in the Book of Acts, the embryonic Christian community soon responded to this challenge with melodies of "compassion and action" beginning a radical and sacrificial provision for the poor among them.[132]

In a contemporary setting these same melodies of Christ's liberation to the poor challenge the blasphemous monophony asserted by global free-trade economics that they be acclaimed the sole and comprehensive symbol of human self-determination. As Peter Selby notes,

128. See John 12:8.

129. Lev 25 provided for a Sabbath year every seven years and a year of Jubilee every fiftieth year when all slaves were freed, debts were cancelled, and the ownership of land was affirmed as belonging solely to God. See also Deut 15.

130. Taylor, *Not Angels but Agencies*, 169.

131. See Acts 1:8.

132. For instance, the quarrel between Greek-speaking Jews and Hebrew-speaking Jews in Acts 6 over the distribution of resources to widows reveals something of the seemingly normative but radical practices of the early church.

The claim of the market to be a symbol of human freedom and
responsibility comes under the judgment of those who are restricted and bound, *entmündigt*, by its operation: how else can
we describe the nations of the Two-Thirds World, whose indebtedness and whose structural adjustments programmes [are]
forced upon them. . . . How else are we to regard the individuals
and whole communities within the world's more prosperous
societies for whom the market is neither the symbol of nor the
key to their freedom, but the means by which they are reduced,
as all debtors in history have been reduced, to incapacity and
ultimately to effective slavery? Most serious of all is the fact that
since what happened to them is made to appear to come about
through the operation of the "free market" there is added to the
injury of their overwhelming poverty the insult of the conviction that they themselves are to blame.[133]

The traditional monastic vow of poverty was taken to undermine the
enslaving power that wealth may exercise over individuals and communities. It was a counter-cultural melody that refuted the claim of wealth to
determine the worth of a person. It shared something of the poetic insight
offered by Alice Walker, that "wherever there is gold there is a chain."[134]

However, as we have seen, vows of poverty were open to the misinter-
pretation that Christian discipleship required an antipathy toward and an
abandonment of the world. A more this-worldly melody is again located
in the life of the Iona Community. For while neither he nor the Iona Community has ever taken such a vow, George MacLeod understood the insight
that the "powers" behind free trade economics were not concerned with
universal equity or the freedom of all, but with promoting personal interest
and the exploitation of others. He knew, too, that the this-worldly melodies
of God heralded both liberation and justice to those oppressed in the realms
of economic practice and that these melodies of justice arose from the person and work of Christ. MacLeod argued that

the Cross be raised again at the centre of the market-place as
well as on the steeple of the Church. I am recovering the claim
that Jesus was not crucified in a cathedral between two candles,
but on a cross between two thieves; on the town garbage heap;
at a crossroad so cosmopolitan that they had to write his title in
Hebrew and in Latin and in Greek (or shall we say in English,
in Bantu and in Afrikaans?) at the kind of place where cynics

133. Selby, *Grace and Mortgage*, 26.

134. Walker, "We Alone," in *Horses Make a Landscape*, 12. Walker adds, "This could
be our revolution: to love what is plentiful as much as what's scarce."

talk smut, and thieves curse, and soldiers gamble. Because that
is where He died. And that is what He died about.[135]

Christ's *cantus firmus* compelled people into this-worldly melodies of
righteous action. One of the most demanding arenas for such engagement
was that of economics and poverty. In the Church of St. Nicholas, Liverpool, MacLeod saw a parable that powerfully illustrated his point. Above
the river Mersey stood the marketplace, the center of human activity, and
the distribution point of wealth. Before the war the parish Church of St.
Nicholas was orientated in antipathy and abandonment with its back to the
river and the marketplace. To enter the church was to turn away from the
hub of life. However, after it was bombed, a prefabricated hut was annexed
to the ruins to house the congregation's worship. Vitally, it was built to face
the other way; the surviving porch became the sanctuary, the massive doors
became windows with no stained glass that looked out on marketplace and
river. "Reality shines in—and out. For the Holy Table is now enlightened by
the River and the Marketplace, as they in turn are challenged by the Holy
Table. *One Bread is here.*"[136]

For MacLeod, such a parable was not cheap polemic: how the world
"shared its bread" was symptomatic of how well Christ's justice was shared
around the globe. Parables such as this inspired him and the community he
founded to take seriously the discipline of economics.[137] The Community
Rule on economic discipline went some way; it helped members put their
disposal of personal income under review. However, the community has
never understood this discipline to be "the solution for the economic chaos
of our times," but they do continue to affirm its importance as a point of
departure; "a response, in economic terms, and in a disciplined way, to the
biblical revelation that Christ is the Lord of all."[138] Indeed, community members have always affirmed that God's justice demanded more than personal
acts of discipline and charity. So at different levels and in a number of ways,
members have responded to the challenge of poverty through their practical involvement in local community projects, or through their churches, or
other Christian organizations such as Church Action on Poverty. At other
times, members will work with "secular" groups with whom they share

135. MacLeod, *Only One Way Left*, 38.

136. MacLeod, *We Shall Rebuild*, 13.

137. In 1984, then aged eighty-nine, George MacLeod was still encouraging others
to engage in individual, corporate, and national economic discipline. He enthusiasti-
cally endorsed Deryck Artingstall's pamphlet, "A Sane Person's A.B.C. of Economics,"
and made it required reading for the Iona Community in the May plenary of that year.

138. Harvey, "Way in the World," cited in Paynter, *This Is the Day*, month 3, day 2.

common aims and objectives. Such direct action is often a vital state of confession for Christian communities, for as Bonhoeffer claimed, there are times when the Christian community needs to go beyond bandaging the wounds of victims caught under the wheel of unjust action and proceed "to seize the wheel itself."[139] Such action would be direct political action, and if employed while seeking justice for the poor it requires poverty to be tackled at its societal core: this necessitates engagement with grant authorities and local councillors, national politicians and international financiers, all of whom shape the conditions in which poverty arose. For the Christian colony knows that while poverty makes it difficult to hear the song of one person or group it diminishes the melodies of all.

Thus, Iona Community member and longtime campaigner Erik Cramb reflects on a significant period when child poverty rose in the UK[140] and argues that

> it cannot be right . . . to deny our interdependence . . . to learn from experience that market forces favour the rich and dispossess the poor and yet do nothing about it. . . . Do we really believe that the God who called the rulers of Israel to task; who brought the rich women of Jerusalem to heel; who witnessed the worth and dignity of the poor widow, wants us to be silent on these issues and thus free to promote private religiosity?[141]

And, of course, for the Christian colony, as a global community, the struggle with poverty cannot be limited to the domestic parish but needs to be enjoined internationally. The interconnectedness of global economics can reduce whole people groups to poverty, and the Iona Community has a long record not only of charity, but of putting a spoke in the wheels of economic policy that keep such injustice turning. In one of his most quoted passages, MacLeod argued,

> It is urgent that the whole issue of international monetary finance be independently reviewed. . . . Have you ever queried the bankers? I have. Try the lower echelon of bankers and most of them will say, 'These things are too high for us, we cannot

139. This has often been translated as to "put a spoke in the wheel," but to "seize the wheel" is a better translation. See "Church and the Jewish Question," in Bonhoeffer, *Berlin*, 365, especially footnote 12.

140. Erik Cramb is specifically commenting on the years 1979–1991. See Cramb, *Fallen to Mediocrity*. Margaret Legum notes that between 1979–1997, child poverty in the UK grew from 5 million to 14.3 million. While these children were rarely starving they did display significantly increased mortality rates and revealed greater rates of addiction, crime, and illiteracy. See Legum, *It Doesn't Have to Be Like This*, 24.

141. Cramb, *Fallen to Mediocrity*, 16–17.

attain unto them', but a small minority will whisper, 'You've got something there, boy; isn't it extraordinarily cold weather for so late in the month of May?'

Try the upper echelon of bankers. I have. I wrote to the top man of a London bank, a charming man, asking his comments on a similar document to the Haslemere Declaration. He replied that the figures were inaccurate. I immediately asked which figures, but have had no reply.

They are in training for the job of international bankers. They know what is good for us. Don't consult us, the paltry crowd. But do they know what is good for us? Or are they sowing the seeds of the next war?[142]

Campaigns such as the Drop the Debt movement and the 2013 "If" Campaign have compelled international leaders to take seriously the relief of global poverty. But of course it is not simply enough to "spoke the wheel" in this manner, it is also necessary to discern new ways forward in national and global economics. Movements such as Make Poverty History and the Campaign for Trade Justice, which have included within their strategy viable economic alternatives, typified by the success of "fair trade" produce, are beginning to make a difference, economically and spiritually. As Adrian Rennie wrote,

There can be little point praying for justice and peace if we do nothing about where it really counts: through our purchasing power. If we continue to buy goods which have been made by companies whose hidden byword is exploitation, then we are really praying pretty hollow prayers.

Through the policy of Fair Trading we can be sure that the gifts and goods we buy are helping those whose needs are often ignored: the people in the poorest parts of the world who make the commodities we take for granted.[143]

Articulating a comprehensive response to poverty is clearly beyond the scope of this book, but there is an urgent need for a polyphonic economics that specifically seeks to relieve poverty by creating new policies crafted through listening not only to the masters of international finance but to those currently impoverished. One such compelling proposal came from Margaret Legum, an Iona Community member and South African national

142. Address given to the Church of Scotland General Assembly in 1968. Cited in Ferguson, *George MacLeod*, 363.

143. Rennie, "Put your money where your mouth is," cited in Paynter, *This Is the Day*, month 2, day 19.

who wrote with critical conviction against economists who perpetually assert that there is no alternative to the way things are. She has cited fellow African economists Heather Couzyn and Ronnie Lessem, who draw parallels with the world of biology to argue that "not competition but cooperation between molecules, genes, cells and organisms is what makes life possible. . . . Life did not take over the globe by combat but by networking."[144]

The full flourishing of human life is denied by continuing instances of impoverishment: the silencing of song that is occasioned by poverty diminishes the melodies of earthly justice. But such flourishing of human life remains at the core of heaven's purposes on earth. God is impatient for the full polyphony of such melodies to be sung on earth and heaven shall not wait

> for the poor to lose their patience,
> The scorned to smile, the despised to find a friend:
> Jesus is Lord;
> He has championed the unwanted;
> In him injustice confronts its timely end.
>
> Heaven shall not wait
> For the rich to share their fortunes,
> The proud to fall, the elite to tend the least:
> Jesus is Lord;
> He has shown the master's privilege—
> To kneel and wash servants' feet before they feast.
>
> Heaven shall not wait
> For the dawn of great ideas,
> Thoughts of compassion divorced from cries of pain:
> Jesus is Lord;
> He has married word and action;
> His cross and company make his purpose plain.[145]

Racism

But for Christians racism denies the unity and solidarity of all
humanity which is at the heart of the gospel.

—STANLEY HOPE[146]

---

144. Legum, *It Doesn't Have to Be Like This*, 18.

145. Bell and Maule, "Heaven Shall Not Wait," in *Heaven Shall Not Wait*, 104–5. Reproduced with kind permission of Wild Goose Publications.

146. Hope, "Light a Candle," cited in Paynter, *This Is the Day*, month 3, day 14.

God's image is not epidermal.

—JOSIAH ULYSSES YOUNG III[147]

Only he who cries out for the Jews can sing the Gregorian chant.

—DIETRICH BONHOEFFER[148]

We are not destined to be monoculture, to be uniform. The differences that exist among nations and cultures, that make other people hard to understand or attractive, are there by divine design. So, if you should happen to end up on the Costa Brava and no waiter can fulfill your need for a fish supper or hot-pea special, then thank God. . . . And if you go into the West End of Glasgow and see second and third generation Pakistani or Indian restaurateurs offering a range of curries which no cholesterol-saturated white Glaswegian could ever make, then thank God for this glorious diversity. . . . God does not want everyone to be the same. . . . The Kingdom of God is not a monoculture.

—JOHN L. BELL[149]

There is an English language proverb that suggests that "opposites attract," but human sociality often displays a marked proclivity to organize itself homogeneously: like attracting like. Having so been organized these respective factions then place around themselves clear boundaries that define both who is welcomed and accepted by the group and by extension, those who are "other" and suspect. Those who claim belonging within each boundary often perceive themselves to be in a zero-sum relationship with otherness: an "I-Thou/'us and them'" scenario that extends from the youthful cruelties of primary school playgrounds, through the intolerance of religious fundamentalism to the xenophobia that may spark and fuel international conflict. Sometimes these factional groupings are premised upon shared religious beliefs, frequently they are understood through a common language or a

147. Young, *No Difference in the Fare*, 58.
148. Bethge, *Dietrich Bonhoeffer: A Biography*, 441.
149. Bell, "Against the Monoculture," in *States of Bliss and Yearning*, 66–69.

shared culture, and often they are based upon their belonging to particular anthropological racial groups. Indeed, what is often termed "racism" is commonly a display of one group's tribal prejudice against another's nationality (the historical antipathy between the racially similar French and English) or cultural belonging (the violence during 1994 in Rwanda between Hutus and Tutsis) as much as it is specific opposition to their genetic identity as members of racial/ethnic groups such as Caucasoid (European/"White"), the Mongoloid (Southeast Asian, Chinese, Inuit, and Native Americans), the Negroid ("Black"/Colored Africans), and the Australoid (Maori/Australian Aborigines). While ethno-racial prejudice is most commonly manifest in an intolerance between anthropological categories, it is not the only way in which such partiality can be evidenced. However such intolerances are defined, ethno-racial prejudice is clearly monophonic and self-boundaried in disposition. Its elevation of sameness and its antipathy toward the limits arising out of Otherness clearly reject the possibility of Christ's incarnation pertaining to all groups within the diversity of humanity. In contradistinction, the Christian colony understands that the image of God is not epidermal, but social.[150] Christ became human precisely so that all humanity, in its richest polyphony of socio-racial difference, may be reconciled both to one another and to God. Different racial/ethnic groups may, for instance, imagine Christ to be incarnated as "one of them" and many have chosen in their art to portray Christ as Asian or Black,[151] one within their own ethnic groupings.[152] But while each artistic expression of the incarnation is valid for that ethnic group (Christ is indeed one of them), none may be thought of as exclusive. Christ, who is one of them, is also one of "otherness" and in this bisociation can be found the whole human race. True human community would not be present without such otherness.[153] Thus, the Incarnation is not boundaried by an ethnic particularity but rather it is the incarnated Christ as *cantus firmus* in whom the rich polyphony of human racial difference is held in unity.

150. The allusion comes from Young, *No Difference in the Fare*, 58. See also his "Theology and the Problem of Racism," in Jenkins and McBride, *Bonhoeffer and King*, 69–77.

151. See for instance the art of African-Americans such as Aaron Douglas's "The Crucifixion," and William H. Johnson's "Descent from the Cross," and his presentation of an all-Black cast as the family of Jesus in "Jesus and the Three Marys." For an appraisal of such work see Pinder, "Our Father, God," 223–33.

152. This is no new phenomenon; the Celtic artwork in the *Book of Kells* portrays Christ having red hair, i.e., as being one of them.

153. This is the thrust of Bonhoeffer's argument in *Sanctorum Communio* when he argues that "the union of like beings never leads *to the concept of community, but only to the concepts of sameness, of unity.*" Bonhoeffer, *Sanctorum Communio*, 43.

However, as a rule (albeit one with notable exceptions) the incarnated Christ interacted primarily within one racial boundary, his own, the Jews. Although he frequently breaks socio-religious taboos regarding Jewish purity,[154] his mission was not characterized by a deliberate overturning of racial boundaries. There is the notable exchange with the Syro-Phonecian woman,[155] the conversation with the Samaritan Woman at the Well,[156] the parable of the Good Samaritan,[157] and the proclamation that foreigners would come to feast with Abraham, Isaac, and Jacob,[158] as well as the inclusion of "outsiders" in his genealogy,[159] but as Wink notes, "Jesus nowhere flings the doors open to Gentiles."[160] While there is an unmistakable trajectory of inclusivity and boundary crossing within his ministry, Christ's disciples remain exclusively Jewish and his contact with Gentiles is self-limited.

The Jews had a long history through which they understood themselves to be the exclusive chosen people of God, a people clearly distinct and separate from others: Jewish identity was a matter of belonging to the nation as much as believing in their God. Of course, there were proleptic echoes of God's boundaryless purposes in exhortations to welcome and care for strangers,[161] and through prophets such as Isaiah,[162] but the Jewish people remained racially and religiously distinct. The two could not be separated; converts entered within the carefully constructed boundaries of both, and once inside, considered all others, the Gentiles, as those with whom contact was to be avoided. For such Gentiles to be included into the new "Christian" community of God required much imagination; from Jews and Gentiles alike. The critical moment for the embryonic church came in Acts 10 when

154. See, for instance, the occasions when he was accused of breaking the Sabbath; Luke 6:1–11; Luke 13:10–17; Luke 14:1–6; John 9:1–41, or times when he touched the unclean and ritually impure, such as lepers; Luke 5:12–16; Luke 17:11–19, or the bleeding woman; Mark 5:21–43, or foreigners/Gentiles; Mark 7:24–30; Luke 17:11–19; John 4:1–42, and associated with sinners; Luke 5:27–31; Luke 7:36–50; and Luke 19:1–10.

155. See Mark 7:24–30. This woman, clearly a Greek, is beyond the Jewish boundaries of community. Jesus appears to reject her at first and then, admiring her faith and character, makes it clear that the love of God is not just for them or those like them. In Matthew's account she is referred to as a Canaanite, traditional enemies of the Jewish people. See Matt 15:21–28.

156. See John 4:1–42.

157. See Luke 10:29–37.

158. Luke 13:28–29.

159. Neither Rahab nor Ruth, expressly mentioned in Matthew's genealogy, was a Jew. See Matt 1:5.

160. Wink, *Engaging the Powers*, 117.

161. See Exod 22:21; Lev 19:34; Deut 24:17.

162. Isa 2:2–4; 11:10–12; 25:5–6; 60:3–5.

the disciple, Peter, receives a vision from God in which he is instructed to kill and eat a selection of non-kosher food. When he protests that eating such food crosses his threshold of boundaried belonging, God declares that the former boundaries have been transcended: what heaven has now declared to be clean Peter must no longer regard as impure.[163] Within a few verses Peter encounters a devout Gentile named Cornelius and is challenged to reinterpret his recent vision as God inviting Gentiles to participate in the community of God's people. The new paradigm is confirmed when God blesses Jew and Gentile alike with the gifts of the Holy Spirit.[164]

So it was that the early church began to learn that God showed no racial favoritism and accepted people from every "nation" into the new community that was becoming the church.[165] It was this new community who would affirm that in Christ there was no "Jew nor Greek," and proclaim that Gentiles were no longer "strangers and aliens," but "citizens with the saints" and "members of the household of God . . . with Christ Jesus himself as the cornerstone."[166] This is not to say that the racial differences were forgotten or removed, but that they were overwhelmed by the unity found in Christ. The colony of heaven knew no boundaries of race; its only boundary was marked through being that space wherein the people of all races could find a polyphonic common ground through their humanity and Christ. To deny anyone their place in participating in the melodies of church, community, nation, or planet on the basis of their race or ethnicity is clearly a denial of Christ's *cantus firmus* and a silencing of the melodies of God. Participating in the fragmented epiphanies of heaven's melodies on earth will require the Christian community to perform a song of justice in which all ethnicities are equal and affirmed.

In some respects, Bonhoeffer is an unlikely source from which to learn this song and the Iona Community might on first appearances seem an improbable place in which to hear it sung. For while the Iona Community has a clear commitment to "celebrate human diversity and actively combat discrimination" on a variety of grounds, including "colour, race, ethnic and cultural background,"[167] it remains largely comprised of white Caucasians. That it has consistently addressed challenges of ethnic justice through a "Racism Matters Working Group" and that many community members are engaged in work for racial justice in the UK and around the world cannot

---

163. See Acts 10:15.

164. See further Riddell, *Threshold of the Future*, 17–18.

165. See Acts 10:35.

166. See Eph 2:11–22.

167. See Appendix A.

lessen this observation. But it would be premature to dismiss its value as an epiphanal community of heaven's racial justice on such a superficial impression. Similarly, Bonhoeffer might not be first choice of those seeking a paragon of social equality, and not simply with regard to racial equity. It cannot be avoided that Bonhoeffer's writings do reveal an aristocratic exclusivism[168] with a tendency toward sexism,[169] Euro-centricism, and even hints of anti-Semitism.[170] There is also in his life and work a problematic lacuna with regard to Africa.[171] Yet, for all that, Bonhoeffer's writings and biography has been an inspiration to those who led victims of racial oppression in South Africa during the Apartheid years.[172] Indeed, it was not just theologians and church leaders who were inspired by Bonhoeffer but all those who struggled for racial justice and discovered "fragments of his theology which have helped them to remain faithful and hopeful."[173] And it is a Black American theologian, J. U. Young III, who articulated just how inimical Bonhoeffer's life and work are to the evil of racism.[174]

From an early age Bonhoeffer's theology was equipping him to deal with the evils of *blut und boden* racism[175] that he would encounter in adult life. Long before he famously opposed the Nazi treatment of Jews or wrote about the "view from below" he articulated an understanding of the relationships between God, self, and others that denied the objectifying of otherness (which is necessary for racism to exist) and assured the legitimacy

168. See, for instance, Bertram, "Bonhoeffer's Exclusivism," 56–73.

169. For a balanced account of this see Bethge, "Bonhoeffer and the Role of Women," 169–84. For a critical assessment from a feminist perspective see Chung, "Dear Dietrich Bonhoeffer," 9–19. For a parallel feminist critique of Bonhoeffer and Martin Luther King see Muers, "Bonhoeffer, King, and Feminism," 33–42.

170. While Bonhoeffer was one of the first to oppose the Nazi treatment of Jews he did so not so much from the perspective of common human rights but in opposition to the effect of the Ayran Clause on ecclesiology. However, there is ample evidence that the early traces of anti-Semitism were excised and retracted from Bonhoeffer's theology and action. For a complete discussion on Bonhoeffer and the Jews see Bethge, "Dietrich Bonhoeffer and the Jews," 43–93; Zerner, "Church, State," 190–205; Kelly, "Bonhoeffer and the Jews," 133–66.

171. See Young, *No Difference in the Fare*, 1ff.

172. See de Gruchy, *Bonhoeffer and South Africa*; and Botman, "Is Bonhoeffer Still of Any Use?" 366–72.

173. de Gruchy, "Bonhoeffer, Apartheid and Beyond," 354. In this article de Gruchy notes that while the influence of Bonhoeffer among the common struggle cannot be underestimated, the reception of Bonhoeffer was largely restricted to a white academic elite who were themselves liberated into seeing things from below. See 359ff.

174. See Young, *No Difference in the Fare*.

175. *Blut und Boden*, literally "blood and soil" was a cry for "purity" of race and land taken up by the Nazis.

and freedom of "the other" in the "I-You" relationship.[176] For Christians, the "I-You" relationship is perpetually mediated through Christ: the You of human otherness is an image of the Divine You and hence each person's relationship to other people is orientated to their relation to God.[177] Here, says Bonhoeffer, the concept of the church comes into play. "The Christian person achieves his or her essential nature only when God does not encounter the person as *You, but 'enters into' the person as I*."[178] Tellingly, Young likens Bonhoeffer's articulation of the I-You relationship to a musical ensemble: "An asocial jazz musician, in actual performance, is an oxymoron, for, in objectifying his fellow artists all too subjectively, he fails to yield to them—fails to be with them ... fails to see that the Other ... [is a] particular living person."[179] So, "the fact that the 'alien Thou' is willed by God and is to be loved as such destroys the basis of racism, whose law is 'Thou shalt love only the Same.'"[180] And so as Young reads Bonhoeffer, the church "was to become a Christian community, in which the law of racism, Thou shalt love only the Same, would be overcome through reveling in the difference of white and black—'I and Thou.' Such difference was to be no longer a strain, but a gift, a revelation of God's love."[181] It is a fragment of heaven's apotheosis in which the monophonic tyranny of "the Same" is taken up into the polyphonic freedom of divine otherness and diversity. It is an epiphanal fragment of justice that is to be gathered into the Christian colony: a melody that is to be performed by its people.

But while the gift of this theological melody was in place, Bonhoeffer had not sung it in a crucible of genuine otherness before his sojourn in New York in 1930. As a child he had read and reread *Uncle Tom's Cabin*[182] and so was no doubt aware of the prejudice that may be encountered through racial otherness, but it invaded no more than his imagination. And while he had worked in Spain it was primarily with Germans and almost exclusively with Europeans. He had not viewed his visit to North Africa favorably.[183] So

---

176. See Bonhoeffer, *Sanctorum Communio*, Chapter 2, "The Christian Concept of Person," 34–57.

177. Ibid., 55.

178. Ibid., 56.

179. Young, *No Difference in the Fare*, 56.

180. Ibid., x.

181. Ibid., 11.

182. Bosanquet, *Life and Death of Dietrich Bonhoeffer*, 31.

183. He went to Libya with his brother Klaus in 1924 and seems to have engaged in some cultural misunderstandings. He wrote after that trip that "one should not spend a longer time in Africa without preparation, the shock is too great and increases from day to day, so that one is glad to return to Europe." Cited in Bethge, *Dietrich Bonhoeffer:*

it was in New York that Bonhoeffer first saw and was horrified at the racial prejudice perpetrated upon African-Americans such as his friend Frank Fisher and the congregation of the Abyssinian Baptist Church in Harlem where he worshipped.[184] It was here that he, "the other," was welcomed as the stranger, here that he listened to the "melodies from below" found in Negro spirituals, songs whose emotion and lyrics were rooted in the experience of slavery and still spoke loudly to the oppressed community in a racially segregated society.[185] The first person singular "I" in these spirituals spoke of the whole community.

> Nobody knows the trouble I've seen
> Nobody knows my sorrow. . .
> or
> If I had-a my way.
> I'd tear this building down
> Great God, then, if I had-a my way . . .[186]

These were more than an expression of individual suffering, as each person sung them the "I" was, says Cone, "a particular black self affirming both his or her being and being-in-community, for the two are inseparable . . . the struggle to be both a person and a member of a community was the major focus of black religion."[187] They knew that the liberation found in Christ was a bisociation of spiritual and this-worldly freedom, a freedom from which racial oppression could not exclude them.

> O freedom! O freedom!
> O freedom over me!
> An' befo' I'd be a slave,

A Biography, 59.

184. When it was obvious in an America restaurant that the black Frank Fisher was not going to be afforded the same service as Bonhoeffer they made a point of leaving. See Bethge, *Dietrich Bonhoeffer: A Biography*, 154–55.

185. Bonhoeffer was greatly impressed by the "spirituals" and was later to play recordings of them to his students in Finkenwalde. See Zimmermann, *I Knew Dietrich Bonhoeffer*, 64–65. Heinz Neumann remembers Bonhoeffer sharing the song:
Nobody knows the trouble I see
Nobody knows but Jesus
Nobody knows the trouble I see
Glory Hallelujah.
Young notes that this reflects Bonhoeffer's belief that if a person is centered in Christ then even if their life takes them to the margins of the world, that boundary edge becomes the middle, the center. See Young, *No Difference in the Fare*, 113.

186. Cited in Cone, *Spirituals and the Blues*, 58, 60.

187. Ibid., 61.

I'll be buried in my grave,
An' go home to my Lord an' be free.

My Lord delivered Daniel
Why can't he deliver me?

When Israel was in Egypt's land,
Let my people go;
Oppressed so hard they could not stand,
Let my people go;
Go down, Moses, 'way down in Egypt's land;
Tell ole Pharaoh
Let my people go.[188]

It was perhaps in the words of songs such as these that Bonhoeffer learned to identify with the voice of the racially oppressed. And perhaps herein also lies the genesis of Bonhoeffer's thinking on the Discipline of the Secret; for the lyrics of such songs conveyed, to those who knew how to listen, truths and mysteries that required them to be shared responsibly in the world. Few white persons would have understood that "Swing Low, Sweet Chariot" referred to the means by which slaves might escape the oppression of the American South, or that to "look over Jordan" meant to have reached the Ohio River, and that "a band of angels coming for to carry me home," was Harriet Tubman or some other friend coming to take them to the free states or Canada.[189]

While Bonhoeffer never explicitly stated that his ideas were formed by his experience of Black Christianity in America, it seems likely that his friendship with Frank Fisher and the Abyssinian Baptist Church informed his own secular work against the Nazi Regime. While still in America, Bonhoeffer was distressed at the deep cleft in the church in which "the 'black Christ' had to be led into the field against the 'white Christ.'" He was astounded at separatist policies that kept two ethnicities of Christians apart for word and sacrament and mystified at the silence of the "White Church" during lynchings perpetrated by the Ku Klux Klan.[190] In his first sermon in America he proclaimed that because they worshiped one God in Christ, the "marvelous mystery of the people of God . . . [rose] above all differences

188. Ibid., 40–41. Cone notes that not every Black could reconcile divine revelation with their human servitude and, alongside the "spirituals," grew up with songs known as the "seculars"; now known as "the blues," in which they sang, "I don't want to ride no golden chariot; I don't want no golden crown; I want to stay down here and be, just as I am without one plea." See Cone, *Spirituals and the Blues*, 62–63.

189. Ibid., 80–81.

190. Kelly and Nelson, *Cost of Moral Leadership*, 88.

of race, nationality and custom."[191] He promised Fisher that on his return to Germany he would make known the sufferings of Black Americans,[192] but at the time Bonhoeffer could not imagine that Germany contained anything like the racial hatred he had encountered in America. He wrote to his brother, "Our Jewish question is a joke by comparison; there won't be many people who claim they are oppressed here. At any rate, not in Frankfurt."[193]

That opinion changed rapidly in April 1933. When the Nazi persecution of the Jews began, Bonhoeffer was one of the first to offer a melody of resistance. His initial objections owed more to his theology than a concept of humanitarian liberalism; raising his objections to the Aryan legislation that sought to evict from the church all Christians who could trace a Jewish heritage. He claimed that "racial purity" had replaced baptism and the church had thus fallen into heresy. But in an essay entitled "The Church and the Jewish Question,"[194] he developed his argument further, advocating that Christians should go beyond merely questioning how the anti-Jewish law impacted the church. The melody of justice that affirmed God's revelation in the face of others necessitated Christians taking action in solidarity with Jews and in their defense, action that would "seize the wheel"[195] of the Nazis. H. E. Tödt notes that at this time, "Bonhoeffer was . . . the only one who considered solidarity with Jews, especially non-Christian Jews, to be a matter of such importance as to obligate the Christian Churches to risk a massive conflict with the state."[196] In August 1933, Bonhoeffer wrote, "It is the task of the Christian proclamation to say: here, where Jew and German stand together under God's word, is the Church, here it is proven whether or not the Church is still the Church."[197] It was with the ambition to help the Confessing Church prove their worth as the church that he agreed to lead their seminary at Finkenwalde. Before doing so he had considered spending time with Gandhi in India to learn more about the nonviolent patterns of resistance (*satyagraha*) and no doubt his opposition to racism would have been strengthened by such a time, but the urgency of events in Germany drew him back. Within a few years the Gestapo closed the seminary and Bonhoeffer became increasingly disillusioned with the equivocal position

191. "Sermon for Armistice Day Sunday," November 9, 1930, in Bonhoeffer, *Barcelona, Berlin, New York*, 581.

192. Zimmermann, *I Knew Dietrich Bonhoeffer*, 64–65.

193. Letter to Karl-Friedrich, January 21, 1931, cited in Bethge, *Dietrich Bonhoeffer: A Biography*, 151.

194. Bonhoeffer, *Berlin*, 362–73.

195. Ibid., 365.

196. H. E. Tödt, in Bethge, "Dietrich Bonhoeffer and the Jews," 63.

197. Bethge, *Dietrich Bonhoeffer: Man of Vision*, 207.

taken by the Confessing Church in respect of the Jews and the Nazi regime. The low point came in 1938 when many pastors capitulated to the *Konsistorium* and accepted the Oath of Loyalty to Hitler[198] and then failed to offer any resistance to the shameful events of *Kristallnacht*.[199]

By then Bonhoeffer was deprived of students and banned from writing. There was, it seemed, only one forum left where he could raise the song of heaven's protest to racial injustice. He sought more immediate and secular ways by which he could not only denounce the racism of the state, but also take action that put a "seized the wheel" of Nazi *rassenhygiene*.[200] So, during his double life as a member of *Abwehr*, he performed many of the melodies of God's racial justice in secret, taking great personal risk to act for the most defenseless of others. He enabled the escape of Jews from Germany and travelled abroad to communicate plans of the anti-Nazi conspiracy to the allies. In the end, he accepted the guilt of his part in the plot to assassinate Hitler because he believed his church to be already guilty of remaining silent while the blood of the innocent cried to heaven. And in the end it was such action that led to his death. It was from prison that he wrote of "the view from below," but he had been seeing it and singing the laments of its people for many years before. It was his unending hope that justice would be done to life in all its dimensions from a higher satisfaction, whose foundation would be beyond any talk of from below or from above. The challenge to the Christian community is to offer a place for all the melodies of race to belong and find their voices in response to Christ.

Bonhoeffer was a significant influence on many of the early members of the Iona Community and they too have consistently sought to oppose the presence of racism wherever it is encountered. In the late 1950s and early 1960s many new members went to work overseas: to Pakistan, South Africa, Kenya, Northern Rhodesia, Nigeria, Nyasaland, and India.[201] They did not do so with the specific intention to combat racism (although some inevitably did so) but their encounters with otherness when shared with

198. The *Konsistorium*, led by Dr. Friedrich Werner, was the official body of the Reich Church, which could grant politically legitimate ordination. Werner used legal, financial, and administrative pressures to force many Confessing Church pastors to assent to an oath of faithful obedience to the Führer, the German Reich, and its people.

199. On November 9, 1938, 7,500 Jewish shops and 171 synagogues were destroyed. It was called "Crystal Night" because of the extensive remnants of broken glass. The Confessing Church was silent in the face of such blatant racial violence.

200. Literally "racial hygiene"; *rassenhygiene* was the Nazi policy that weak elements must not be allowed to prosper or reproduce and was the premise upon which the handicapped were culled, and for the Jewish holocaust. See Young, *No Difference in the Fare*, 29ff.

201. See Ferguson, *Chasing the Wild Goose*, 83.

the community "at home" inevitably generated difficult questions of global justice and equity between peoples.[202] Within the worship of the community, the singing of songs from around the world in the language of their origin, such as those collected in Malawi by Tom Colvin, reminded the Christian colony that God is fully present in the Other and enabled expressions of solidarity.[203] This practice has increased in recent years through the work of the Wild Goose Resource Group. But vital as such disciplines may be to the responsible sharing of the polyphonic Christ within the spiritual life of the church, this-worldly action for racial justice is also needed. Often this has been accomplished by questioning, even as Bonhoeffer did, the legitimacy of the actions of the state or some other racial oppressor. On other occasions it has required aid being brought to the victims of racism and sometimes it has required members to "seize the wheel" of injustice. MacLeod's maiden speech in the House of Lords questioned the legitimacy of the Commonwealth Immigrants Bill, legislation that was being pushed through in a week and was designed to stop the influx of Kenyan Asians into Britain. Many Asians had gone from India to Kenya to support the British colony in the previous century. On Kenyan independence they could choose between Kenyan citizenship and the right to live and work in the former colony or retain their British citizenship that they believed would allow them to live and work in Britain. The proposed legislation restricted access to Britain on racial conditions.[204] MacLeod denounced the bill as racist.[205] Indeed, in 1992, Stanley Hope, an Iona Community member and longtime campaigner for racial justice, argued in a brief but searing pamphlet that since the Second World War the intention behind every governmental development in UK immigration law has been intentionally racist, seeking to "restrict entry to the UK on the basis of colour."[206] Overseas, many community members were involved in challenging the legitimacy of racist legislation and institutions: a prime example was the opposition of Iona

202 For more detailed accounts of the work for justice and peace in Africa, see Muir, *Outside the Safe Place*, 242ff.

203. Alison Swinfen, a community member has argued that the imperialism associated with certain languages including English is a matter of social justice. See Swinfen, "Living Words, Living Worlds," 9–11.

204. The bill, which was subsequently enacted, required an applicant to show a "substantial UK connection" to be permitted residency in Britain. This was deemed to necessitate a connection "by birth or ancestry." Thus, Asians leaving Kenya, despite holding UK passports, were denied access to the only country where they had a connection but white settlers from Kenya were welcomed. See Hope, *Liberty to the Captives*, 8–9.

205. See Ferguson, *George MacLeod*, 363.

206. Hope, *Liberty to the Captives*, 9.

members to the Central African Federation, an exploitative regime formed on Britain's initiative, which denied Africans land rights and revenues from industry, particularly mining. It collapsed in 1963. More recently, the work of community member Yousouf Gooljary Wright in equipping black people in England with "survival skills" to overcome the "persistent ideology in English society of discriminatory practice in employment and education"[207] is just one example of bandaging the wounds of the victims of racism. There have been occasions to seize the wheel also. In the 1960s, members Andrew Ross and Albert McAdam were forced to leave Malawi after speaking out against oppression there and Graeme Brown, a onetime leader of the community, was refused permission to return to his position as principal of a theological college in South Africa after the protest he and others made against Apartheid.

Poverty and racism are just two of the melodies generated by participating in the performance of heaven's justice in the world. We have already noted that prejudice over gender equality, sexual orientation, and disability also demand consideration and in a "post 9/11" world, bringing the metaphor of polyphony to bear on matters of interfaith dialogue may prove to be of great import. Each is connected to Christ the *cantus firmus* and each will bear upon the other. Clearly these and other melodies of justice sound in close harmony with matters of peace and conflict resolution. Sharing these melodies responsibly in the world is the task of the Christian community. But to the melodies of peace and justice must be added one further counterpoint, one that may prove to be the defining melody of our time: the song of all creation, the lament of the earth and her distress.

THIRD MOVEMENT: SINGING THE INTEGRITY OF CREATION

O God, enlarge within us the sense of fellowship with all living things, our brothers, the animals, to whom thou gavest the earth as their home in common with us.

We remember with shame that in the past we have exercised the high dominion of man with ruthless cruelty, so that the voice of earth, which should have gone up to thee in song, has been a groan of travail.

207. See "Leaven in the Lump," an interview with Yousouf Gooljary-Wright by Karen Attwood, in Iona Community, *Coracle*, no. 4/3 (February 2003) 15.

May we realise that they live not for us alone but for themselves
and for thee and that they love the sweetness of life.

—BASIL THE GREAT[208]

The earth remains our mother, just as God remains our Father, and
our mother will only lay in the Father's arms those who remain true
to her. Earth and its distress—that is the Christian's Song of Songs.

—DIETRICH BONHOEFFER[209]

In You all things consist and hang together:
The very atom is light energy,
The grass is vibrant,
The rocks pulsate.
All is in flux; turn but a stone and an angel moves.
Underneath are the everlasting arms.
Unknowable we know You, Christ beneath us.

—GEORGE MACLEOD[210]

This prayer of George MacLeod's, "Man is Made to Rise," is a celebration of
creation in which he detects beneath the polyphony of vibrant grass, pulsat-
ing rocks, and the perpetual flux of all that is created, a *cantus firmus* of
divine cradling; the everlasting ground bass of God. Many of MacLeod's
prayers call upon the imagery of nature[211] as if it is an epiphanal countermelody to the divine song in which all things hang together.[212] For him,

208. This prayer, often attributed to Basil the Great (c. 330–379), is cited in Mc-
Donagh, *Greening of the Church*, 167. He offers no original reference and it may be that
Basil is not the author, but that need not diminish the sentiment of the prayer.

209. "Basic Questions of a Christian Ethic," in Bonhoeffer, *Barcelona, Berlin, New
York*, 378. Translation altered to follow that of Rasmussen, *Earth Community, Earth
Ethics*, 297.

210. MacLeod, "Man is Made to Rise," in *Whole Earth Shall Cry Glory*, 16.

211. See prayers such as "Eternal Seeping Through the Physical," "The Glory in the
Grey," and "A Veil Thin as Gossamer," in MacLeod, *Whole Earth Shall Cry Glory*, 11,
13, 60.

212. He was not unique in this. Down through the centuries many examples can be
found in the writings of Celtic Christians such as St. Columba, as well as in Hildegard of

"matter mattered":[213] the earth and sea and sky were "a harmony of colour" in which the "air of the eternal seep[ed] through the physical."[214] The physical creation was valued in heaven because it reverberated with the song of God. Jürgen Moltmann argues that there "sleeps a song in everything,"[215] and thus when Genesis speaks of God's Spirit hovering over the waters of creation we should envisage not a brooding dove but the vibrating "song of creation," in which "the word names, differentiates and appraises. But the breath is the same in all the words, and binds the words together." He adds:

> We should think of the fundamental resonances of music out of which sounds and rhythms emerge. . . . In the quickening breath and through the form-giving word, the Creator sings out his creatures in the sounds and rhythms in which he has his joy and his good pleasure.[216]

In such a scenario, matter would matter to God; it would be God's delight. But this understanding is in contradistinction to the strong anti-materiality that we have seen persistently pervading much of historical Christianity. This has propounded a theology concomitant with its suspicions of materiality, a theology that objectified creation and asserted humanity's dominance over the natural. The dangers of such an unhelpful paradigm were amplified when married to the individualism and scientific experimentation that characterized the Enlightenment. In this, individuals were isolated "from other people except through contracts and from nature except as a resource base from which to amass wealth."[217] Nothing in this social paradigm encouraged the church to be a community that embraced mutually sustainable relationships with the realm of nature. So it was in 1967, that Lynn White famously laid the burden of blame for contemporary ecological degradation at the door of historical Christianity. Particularly, he

---

Bingen (1098–1178) and St. Francis of Assisi (1182–1226). More recent examples can be found in the theologies of Teilhard de Chardin and Matthew Fox.

213. The phrase "matter matters" was a favorite of MacLeod's: in a sermon in 1948 he wrote, "What really is the gospel? . . . Is it that the physical, the earthly, is of passing account . . . and that matter does not matter, while spirit matters everything? . . . Christ is the key to every living thing." MacLeod, "The Church in the Modern World," cited in Ferguson, *Daily Readings*, 60. See also Collins, *God's Earth*; and Lowes, "Up Close and Personal: In the End Matter Matters," in Edwards, *Earth Revealing Earth*, 125–43.

214. MacLeod, *Whole Earth Shall Cry Glory*, 11.

215. The line from J. von Eichendorff is quoted in Moltmann, *Jesus Christ for Today's World*, 96.

216. Ibid.

217. McFague, *Life Abundant*, 102.

understood the Genesis accounts of creation as condoning the exploitation of creation as a solely human resource.[218] He wrote,

> We shall continue to have a worsening ecological crisis until we reject the Christian axiom that nature has no reason for existence but to serve man. . . . Both our present science and our present technology are so tinctured with orthodox Christian arrogance towards nature that no solution for our ecological crisis can be expected from them alone.[219]

In the article, White revealed some ignorance of theological history[220] but he did succeed in provoking many and varied Christian responses both in reply to his criticisms and addressing the ecological crisis facing the planet.[221] Most of these agree that the fault lies not in the Christian heritage or texts *per se*, but in the church's infidelity to their roots, i.e., their unwillingness to accept the communal and ecological responsibilities entrusted to them in Eden, their reluctance to acknowledge their recapitulation in Christ's incarnation, and their ongoing refusal to listen to the current laments of earth's distress. Never before has the very existence of the planet and its varied species (including the human race) been under threat by the irresponsible actions of humanity whose systemic anthropocentrism threatens all creation by its unchecked and self-serving monophony. Never before has there been such a necessity to develop a theology that addresses the global community and articulates the interdependence of all multi-voiced creation (with humanity being but one constituent part) upon its *cantus firmus*. And if the Christian colony is to share the mystery of the polyphonic Christ responsibly then their participation in the melodies of a sustainable ecological lifestyle will be perhaps *the* defining righteous action in the twenty-first century.

218. White, "Historical Roots of our Ecological Crisis," 1203–7.

219. Ibid., 1203.

220. See McFague, *Life Abundant*, 161. McFague rightly notes that while post-Enlightenment Christianity may be guilty of White's critique, it has not been true for all of Christian history. She notes that the recapitulation of creation through Christ's resurrection was a major theme in the work of Irenaeus and comments that similar reflection can also be found within the works of Augustine and Aquinas. McDonagh notes that while Christian theology has predominately focused on the divine/human relations, there have been persistent strains of a more cosmic context. See McDonagh, *Greening of the Church*, 165ff. See also Deane-Drummond, *Eco-Theology*, 82–85.

221. For excellent introductions see Deane-Drummond, *Eco-Theology*; McDonagh, *Greening of the Church*; McFague, *Life Abundant*; and Rasmussen, *Earth Community*. See also Ruether, *Gaia and God*; Page, *God and the Web of Creation*; and Grey, *Sacred Longings*.

We turn first to the responsibilities given to humanity in the Garden of Eden. In the King James translation of Genesis 1 we read,

> So God created man in his image, in the image of God created he him; male and female created he them. And God blessed them, and God said unto them, "Be fruitful, and multiply, and replenish the earth, and subdue it: and have dominion over the fish of the sea, and over the fowl of the air, and over every living thing that moveth upon the earth.[222]

Lynn White saw in this commandment to subdue and have dominion over creation something akin to the "domination system," i.e., a violent trajectory toward monophonic exploitation of the nonhuman creation, an aggressive silencing of the many melodies of created shalom. If this was what was commanded by God, then White's criticisms of the Christian position would be valid. And insofar as the church has adopted such a reading of the biblical text, his critiques remain legitimate.[223] But such an understanding misinterprets the biblical command through an unjustified anthropocentric hermeneutic that has eschewed the true responsibility entrusted to humanity in the Garden of Eden. Before human beings were ever given "dominion over the earth" we learn that they were made in the image of God. And if God is understood polyphonically, then we see that it is in the very character of the divine to exist in mutually affirming and sustaining relationship with the melodies of Otherness. As we have seen, the Father is distinctly differentiated from the Son and Holy Spirit, the Son from the Spirit and the Father, and the Spirit from the Son and Father. Yet there is a unity in this diversity: three parts to the great music of the divine; "each so *for* and *in* the others that they cannot but comprise one *being*."[224] And if humanity is made in the image of such a polyphonic deity, and it is from such a God that dominion over nature is granted to them, then the character of the dominion they receive must similarly be identified by a mutually affirming sustainability: they will mirror God's polyphonic way in their ways of dominion.[225] In accepting this charge of polyphonic dominion,

222. Gen 1:26–28, KJV.

223. Sallie McFague acknowledges that particularly in western history, since the Enlightenment, White's criticisms have more validity. See McFague, *Life Abundant*, 161. Similarly, Jürgen Moltmann argues that "the Christian belief in creation as it has been maintained in the European and American Christianity of the Western churches is therefore not guiltless of the crisis on the world today." Moltmann, *God in Creation*, 21.

224. See Lowes, "Up Close and Personal," 131–32.

225. See Rasmussen, *Earth Community*, 280. This view of dominion is now widely accepted, but as recently as 1995 Roman Catholic teaching asserted to the contrary: "everything in creation is ordered to man and everything is made subject to him." See

they will recognize their integrated part as but one created voice amidst a diverse materiality so interconnected that it cannot but comprise one being of created order. For as the poets tell us, "no matter how many times removed," humanity remains a "cousin to volcanoes and leaf-buds."[226] The dominion exercised by humanity thus requires them to listen "to the entire orchestration of creation, and not to allow the apparently minor melodies to be silenced."[227] The task of dominion with which humanity is charged in Eden is to teach the world (and indeed all nonhuman creation beyond it) to sing in perfect harmony comprised of mutually sustaining relationships. In essence, it requires nothing other than that they perform their unique part in this creaturely counterpoint,[228] affirming that they are but one (albeit privileged) interwoven melody among the polyphony of the cosmic shalom.

Each part must therefore sing of both their common likeness and their difference. The fact that Adam is fashioned out of this nonhuman creation (dust of the ground)[229] and will return to it[230] merely emphasizes the point that it is not incumbent upon him or his descendants to objectify creation, placing it at a distance from himself. Humanity, as with other melodies of creation, is not valued primarily because of its own existence but because of its relationship with Christ's *cantus firmus* and the polyphonic life of God and all creation. It is in recognition of this that, for instance, the Hebrew book of Proverbs acknowledges that "four things on earth are small and yet exceedingly wise: . . . ants . . . badgers . . . locusts . . . and lizards."[231] Every created being is "fathered or mothered into being," rescued from "nonbeing" by the first person of the Trinity, is shaped in its particularity by the

---

Pope John II, *Gospel of Life*, 60–61, as cited in Rasmussen, *Earth Community*, 229. Roman Catholic thinking has progressed considerably under Pope Francis as was seen in the 2015 Papal encyclical, "Laudato Si."

226. The lines are taken from Norman MacCaig, "No End, No Beginning," as cited by Page, *God and the Web of Creation*, xii. Page adopts the metaphor of the spider's web not only because it is a pattern of interconnection, but because when one part shakes, it all shakes. But there are weaknesses in the metaphor: it is an image whose purpose is entrapment and death rather than liberation and life, and as such raises potentially uncomfortable parallels between the role of spider and God. However, Page's central thesis is correct, namely that Christian doctrines of creation need to be reformed from their anthropocentrism and reconstructed in ways that enable all creation, human and nonhuman, to declare their very being as a valued response to God's gift of life.

227. Cunningham, *These Three Are One*, 262.

228. Indeed, as humanity reaches into the cosmos, this responsibility should be extended to all that exists beyond the earth.

229. Gen 2:7.

230. Gen 3:19.

231. Prov 30:24–28.

Word and then located within the larger communion of all being, divine and created, by the Spirit.[232] Each being within the universe, human and nonhuman, should therefore "be viewed more or less as *subject*—at least insofar as it partakes of the subjectivity of the divine personal subjects who give themselves to and through it—as well as *object*."[233]

All life as subject should therefore be revered as God's sacrament, "the material is shot through with the spiritual" because, as Ron Ferguson suggests, there is a "withinness of God in all life."[234] Each created being within it, nonpersonal as well as personal, is the subject of its own being.[235] It is the responsibility of each subject to live in contrapuntal relationship to Christ's *cantus firmus*.[236] As such, theologies that seek to include an ecological dimension but interpret human dominion as no more than a benign stewardship[237] remain insufficient guides for singing the integrity of creation because they perpetuate the objectifying distance between human and nonhuman creation.[238] They deny the mutuality of nurturing relationship that resides at the core of every creature's responsibility and simultaneously encourage humanity in their arrogant assumptions that having so damaged creation, the earth is now theirs to heal. However inspiring it may be to regard the human vocation as something akin to Hebrew idea of "*tikkun olam*"[239] (gathering and refashioning the fragments of our broken earth), ecological shalom will only be accomplished if, in part, the earth is allowed to heal herself; to sing her own song. Stewardship, no matter how benign, fails to appreciate the degree of mutuality located between cooperative musicians or the deep way in which a composer and their composition may shape one another.

232. Lowes, "Up Close and Personal," 134.

233. Ibid.

234. Ferguson, *Chasing the Wild Goose*, 156. This view of creation as sacrament not only has a long pedigree within the Celtic tradition but within Orthodox Christianity too. See Evdokinov, "Nature," 1–22; and Koyama, "Eucharist," 80–90.

235. Lowes, "Up Close and Personal," 134.

236. For a study of the interdependence of ecosystems see Prance, *Earth Under Threat*.

237. For instance, see Hall, *Imaging God*.

238. This same point is addressed by Scott, "Christ, Nature, Sociality," 413.

239. The ancient idea of "*tikkun olam*," literally "repair of the world," comes from the seventeenth-century Jewish mystic, Isaac Luria. He argued that God drew in the divine breath in order to make room for creation and in the space placed vessels into which was poured the brilliance of divine light. This was too brilliant for the vessels that shattered all over the universe. Since then the work of human beings has been to mend and transform these vessels in the repair of the world. See Grey, *Outrageous Pursuit of Hope*, 40.

However, the vocation of teaching the world to sing in response to its *cantus firmus* may on occasion require humanity to demonstrate and initiate the song. Humanity may be required to cantor the music to the world or to even sing vicariously for the realm of nature. In initiating harmonies of worship to God, humanity as the world's "high priest" and "secretarie" of God's praise[240] may loosen what Moltmann calls "the dumb tongue of nature."[241] This is not to suggest that the melodies of creation do not sound in the ears of heaven apart from and even without humanity[242] (if humanity is the high priest of creation then it is surely a priesthood of all believers). But it is to agree with Rasmussen that "human beings are the singers of the cosmic song and tellers of its tale in a special way; we can represent creation and give voice to it in cosmic liturgy of praise and transfiguration."[243] In performing this responsibility, humanity does not dominate to the exclusion of the melodies of nature, but rather empowers their polyphony. What is being sustained by their music is neither the earth nor human existence upon it, but the contrapuntal relationship each has with the *cantus firmus*.

All this is reaffirmed in the incarnation. Here, the Son of God, the one in whom all things were made,[244] takes material form. Here, God is confirmed as more than an absentee composer who might objectify the music he created and from which he then may distance himself.[245] Through Christ, God decides to locate God's self within the music of temporal and material life; he is the "all in all."[246] As we have seen, this places a unique responsibility upon humanity who are made in God's image. But while nonhuman creation does not share in this unique responsibility, it is nonetheless clear that if such a being has been sung into its existence by God and is held

240. The allusions are taken from George Herbert's poem "Providence," in Patrides, *English Poems of George Herbert*, 129.

241. Moltmann, *God in Creation*, 71.

242. Rasmussen notes that in Haydn's oratorio *The Creation*, when all creation is completed except for humanity, the angel Raphael sings in praise of all that has been accomplished, but then notes that one thing is yet missing. He does not yet know what it will be and indeed the aria ends without the creation of humanity, but in his song Raphael described their responsibility in the created order. "There wanted yet that wond'rous being . . . that grateful should God's pow'r admire . . . and with heart and voice [God's] goodness praise." See Rasmussen, *Earth Community*, 238.

243. Ibid.

244. John 1:3.

245. Diarmuid O'Murchu makes this same point, paralleling humanity's stewardship to God as an absent landlord. See O'Murchu, *Poverty, Celibacy, and Obedience*, 66ff.

246. See Col 3:11 and 1 Cor 15:28.

together in Christ's *cantus firmus*, then each constituent part, from waterfall to antelope, has a particular harmony to perform. As the Psalmist says,

> Praise the LORD from the heavens . . .
>
> Praise him, sun and moon;
> Praise him, all you shining stars! . . .
> Praise the LORD from the earth,
> you sea monsters and all deeps,
> fire and hail, snow and frost,
> stormy wind fulfilling his command!
> Mountains and all hills,
> Fruit trees and all cedars!
> Wild animals and all cattle,
> Creeping things and flying birds!
>
> Kings of the earth and all peoples,
> princes and all rulers of the earth!
> Young men and women alike,
> Old and young together.[247]

With regard to the animal kingdom, Rasmussen notes that in the second biblical account of creation the animals were first considered as potential companions to Adam and while none prove to be wholly sufficient the important reflection remains "the aboriginal companion character of all creatures."[248] The Celtic tradition that so inspired MacLeod and the Iona Community abounds in legends of Columba and other saints being befriended by animals, even ferocious ones.[249] Indeed, that same tradition goes further and asserts,

> There is no plant in the ground
> But is full of His virtue,
> There is no form on the strand
> But is full of His blessing . . .
>
> There is no life in the sea,
> There is no creature in the river,
> There is naught in the firmament, . . .
>
> There is no bird on the wing,

247. Ps 148:1–3, 7–12.

248. Rasmussen, *Earth Community*, 275. Ian Bradley notes that when Jesus is driven into the desert (Mark 1:13) he is said to be with the wild animals and emerged untouched by them, perhaps even having had them as companions. Bradley, *God is Green*, 76.

249. See Bradley, *Celtic Way*, 55ff. For a detailed account of the Celtic traditions relationship to creation, see Low, *Celtic Christianity and Nature*.

There is no star in the sky,
There is nothing beneath the sun,
But proclaims His goodness.[250]

Likewise, theologians have contended that the whole divine majesty can be found substantially present "in a single grain"[251] and that "all things made by the Word live in the Word and are life."[252] Poets correspondingly assure us that creation is "charged with the grandeur of God"[253] and compel our spirits to "make sensuous the glories of God."[254] Ancient saints exhort that if we would know the Creator, we must understand created things[255] and modern seers declare that "the whole earth shall cry glory."[256] Being made in the image of God places upon the Christian community a unique counterpoint of ecological responsibility and its performance must remain its primary concern. However, such a performance, while obliged to respond to its *cantus firmus*, must also attune itself to the polyphony found within the realm of nature's song and encourage its rendition too.[257]

It is important to realize that locating Christ's *cantus firmus* within the material world of human and nonhuman creation is not to reduce God and creation to a vaguely symbiotic pantheism.[258] While it may be true that all creation finds a commonality in its relationship to the *cantus firmus*, God remains God, and so cannot be simply reduced to "being everything."[259] The finite simply cannot hold the infinite.[260] While the boundaries between

250. "Jesu Who Ought to Be Praised," in Carmichael, *Carmina Gadelica*, 45.

251. Martin Luther, *Weimarer Ausgabe*, 32.134.34–136.36, as cited in Rasmussen, *Earth Community*, 273.

252. Eriugena, "Eriugena's Homily," 87.

253. Hopkins, "God's Grandeur," in *Complete Poems*, 18.

254. D. Gwenallt Jones, "Cnawd as Ysbryd" (Flesh and Spirit), cited in Allchin, *Resurrection's Children*, 61.

255. St. Columbanus, cited in de Waal, *World Made Whole*, 82.

256. MacLeod, *Whole Earth Shall Cry Glory*, 8.

257. This analysis follows that of Sallie McFague in *Life Abundant*, 166ff.

258. Such symbiotic pantheism is propounded in some aspects of Gaia philosophy. See Lovelock, *Gaia*. His ideas have been taken up by eco-feminist theologians such as Ruether, *Gaia and God*.

259. Jacques Pohier takes the phrase "God is God, so God is not everything" as the title for the final chapter in his book, *God In Fragments*, 261ff.

260. Reformed theology has traditionally asserted "*finitum non capx infiniti*," the finite created order cannot hold the infinite of God. In contrast, Lutheran theology has argued "*finitum capax infiniti*," the created order is the place where God is to be found. This led Luther to famously propose a bold panentheism whereby the Divine majesty could be found entirely within one grain. Bonhoeffer offers an alternative, namely "*Finitum capax infiniti non per se sed per infinitum*"—the finite can hold the infinite, not by

humanity and nonhuman creation may be beneficially transcended to facilitate the practical and theological necessities of mutual creaturely sustainability, "creation," as George MacLeod once prayed, "is not enough." Though
the "sap of life in our bones and being" is God's, "in the garden that is each
of us" there is "always the thorn . . . always in the beauty, [there is] the tang
of sin, in our consciences."[261] And this remains the fundamental separation
between God and creation and the tension that is uniquely bisociated in
Christ. Creation's music, the melodies of materiality, however beautiful, are
always foreshadowed by its bondage to decay. Even in the Christ who was
without the "tang of sin," his materiality was yet bound to go the way of all
flesh. The polyphonic music of the Trinitarian God exists both before and
beyond the melodies of creation; it is free from such decay. God neither
needs creation nor to be in relationship with it for that self-sustaining music
to exist. God and creation, including humanity, are thus definitively distinct. This was the clear understanding of Bonhoeffer's theology.

> That which lives and is creative is not something divine; instead
> it is and remains a work that is creaturely, that has been created,
> that is separate from the Creator and under the Creator's free
> command.[262]

God and God's creation do not serve each other's needs in symbiotic
codependency but rather it is precisely this difference between God and creation that marks the freedom of the Creator's love for the world, especially
humanity.[263] It is in the human response to that love that their responsibility
is located. However, clearly God has freely chosen to bring the world into
existence and through Christ to remain as its *cantus firmus*. In so doing the
infinite is to be found within the finite: *finitum capax infiniti*. God is then
both simultaneously beyond creation and bound to it as the "beyond in its
midst"; the Creator chooses to bisociate with creation. This is not pantheism
but a more subtle melody of panentheism[264] in which the eternally transcendent Christ participates in the immanent particularity of every created
thing.[265] As Bonhoeffer argued, "The finite cannot take on the infinite by

---

itself, but it can by the aid of the infinite! See "Lectures on Christology," in Bonhoeffer,
Berlin, 346.

261. MacLeod, *Whole Earth Shall Cry Glory*, 8–10.

262 Bonhoeffer, *Creation and Fall*, 58.

263. The point is made by Williams, "Bonhoeffer, the Sixties and After," 5–6.

264. By "panentheism" is meant an understanding of the world as existing in God
without seeking to negate or diminish the transcendence of God. It does not imply a
mutuality between creation and creator.

265. Luther's panentheism argued that while the divine majesty could be found

itself, but only through the infinite": creation bears the melodies of Christ because his *cantus firmus* makes it possible.[266]

In the incarnation, Christ, the Emmanuel, is revealed as both the good and the God of material existence.[267] As we have seen, human and nonhuman creation share in the responsibility of offering up reciprocating countermelodies in response to their common Christological *cantus firmus*. The elements respond in obedient harmony, "Who then is this, that even the wind and sea obey him."[268] But for humanity, and particularly those within the Christian community, the task entrusted to them is to participate in the melody of earthly dominion as exercised by Christ in inaugurating the Kingdom of God. So if the contemporary Christian colony is to be the body of Christ existing as a this-worldly community, then they must revisit the ministry of Jesus to discover who Christ is for today's ecological age and how he may inform the unique responsibilities entrusted to humanity. It is to the historical and earthbound Jesus that the Christian community must look if they are to hear the clearest fragments of God's compelling melody of mutual sustainability.

The gospel narratives offer some limited witness as to an ecological sensitivity in Christ: he shows an intimacy with the processes of creation and a contemplative appreciation of its elemental presence and does this

---

within a single grain, still that same majesty was so large that neither this world not a thousand worlds could encompass it. In his commentary on the Eucharist he wrote, "God in his essence is present everywhere in and through the whole creation in all its parts and in all places, and so the world is full of God and God fills it all, yet God is not limited to or circumscribed by it, but is at the same time beyond and above the whole creation." Luther, *Luther's Works*, 37:59, as cited in Rasmussen, *Earth Community*, 278–79. A similar argument, although one drawing more on the work of the Holy Spirit, is found in Moltmann's theology of creation, where he argues that "if we understand the Creator, his creation, and the goal of that creation in a trinitarian sense, the Creator through his Spirit *dwells* in his creation as a whole, and in every individual created being, by virtue of his Spirit holding them together and keeping them in life." See Moltmann, *God in Creation*, xii. Page has proposed her own term, "pansyntheism," with which she hopes to distance herself from the pantheism in which Creator and Creation are so often conflated, but which identifies her with a theology that affirms the role of God to be *with* (as opposed to "above" or "in") creation. See Page, *God and the Web of Creation*, 40.

266. "Lectures on Christology," in Bonhoeffer, *Berlin*, 346. For a lucid appreciation of how Bonhoeffer's Christology can prove foundational to a theology of ecology, see Burkholder, "Christological Foundations for an Ecological Ethic," 338–56.

267. This celebration of materiality is never far from the life of the Iona Community. In the abbey cloisters sits the Jacob Lipchitz sculpture "The Descent of the Spirit." It depicts the Holy Spirit visiting the Virgin Mary and bringing God to earth. It is a permanent reminder of what MacLeod referred to as the "earthed life."

268. Mark 4:41.

while within a predominately urban existence.[269] But it is anachronistic and, as McFague argues, "futile to rummage about with fig trees and hens, trying to make Jesus into a nature lover."[270] But she is nevertheless right to assert that the way Christ exercises dominion in the unfolding Kingdom of God can be extended to the created environment. She writes,

> His parables, which overturn conventional human hierarchies, should include the hierarchy of humans over nature; his heal-ing stories can be extended to the deteriorating ecosystems of our planet; his practice of eating with outcasts is pertinent to the extension of species and loss of habitats due to human over-development and consumption.[271]

This is dominion as understood and practiced by earth's *cantus firmus*: it is an invitation extended to humanity into new ways of hearing the music of the world, and to join with it in mutually fulfilling relationships with God, themselves and the whole created order. It is epitomized in the Parable of the Wedding Banquet in Luke 14:15–24, wherein the expected boundaries of society are overcome and those who would have been otherwise excluded are invited to participate in the celebration of life. What this parable reveals and what is heard throughout the ministry of Jesus, is a polyphony of lament issuing from the oppressed. And today that must include the songs of protest rising up from victimized nonhuman species and the suffering earth itself. It is, as we have seen earlier, what Bonhoeffer described as the importance of "the view from below."

If Christ is Christ for today's ecological crises then the Christian colony must again see the whole of creation with the view from below. They must learn to listen to the songs from the boundaries and include them in their own: not only to the hymns of human suffering, but to the laments of nonhuman species, the cry of the earth and her distress. As early as 1929 Bonhoeffer was drawing on ancient mythology to make exactly this point.

> It is only through the depths of the earth, only through the storms of a human conscience, that the window to eternity opens itself up to us.
>
> An ancient and profound legend tells us the giant Antaeus, who was stronger than all the men [sic] of the world. No one could defeat him until during one battle his adversary lifted him up off the ground, whereupon the giant lost the power that had

---

269. See McDonagh, *Greening of the Church*, 158ff.

270. McFague, *Life Abundant*, 167.

271. Ibid.

flowed into him only from his contact with the earth. Those who would abandon the earth, who would flee the crisis of the present, will lose all the power still sustaining them by means of eternal, mysterious powers. The earth remains our mother just as God remains our Father and only those remain true to the mother are placed by her into the Father's arms. Earth and her distress—that is the Christian's Song of Songs.[272]

And while this is far from being a systematic theology of sustainable ecology, Bonhoeffer's concern for a responsible deputyship, both for the present day and the future tomorrow,[273] together with this passion for "the earth and her distress," contains compelling insights for the contemporary Christian colony. For instance, Keith Clements argues that Bonhoeffer's personal hopes for the future were theologically paralleled with a sense of vicarious responsibility for those generations that were yet to come. It was not, as in the songs of the Hitler Youth, that the future belonged to them, but rather, that in faith, they belonged to the future reign of God and were called to manifest their "belonging to that community, however modestly, in the here and now."[274] Furthermore, in imagining the bond between God and creation as being akin to the reciprocal relationship that is to be found in marriage (Father God and Mother Earth), Bonhoeffer implies that fidelity to God can only be properly lived as a fidelity to the earth.[275] As late as 1944 Bonhoeffer is still pressing home the point, telling Bethge that the Christian has no "ultimate escape route out of their earthly tasks and difficulties into eternity. Like Christ . . . they have to drink the cup of earthly life to the

272. "Basic Questions of a Christian Ethic," in Bonhoeffer, *Barcelona, Berlin, New York*, 377–78.

273. In *Ethics*, Bonhoeffer's concern for the world of the penultimate was always integrated with the future world of final justification in the eschatological Christ. In this, the church is bound to the historical future but in such a way that its vision of the ultimate must not hinder the fulfillment of her historical responsibility. See Bonhoeffer, *Ethics*, 149ff. Likewise, two years before his own engagement he had written to his friend Sutz arguing that marriage was "an affirmative gesture to the world and the world's future," a symbol of man's desire to build, to which God says 'Yes.'" See Bosanquet, *Life and Death of Dietrich Bonhoeffer*, 239. Likewise, in prison, while considering the "Present and Future" he wrote that we must be ready "to think and to act with an eye on the coming generation and to be ready to move on without fear or worry." Bonhoeffer, *Letters and Papers*, 50. Wolfgang Huber notes that Bonhoeffer's notion of responsibility is not just concerned with "care for" (Fürsorge) but includes prospective care (Vorsorge), specifically the prospective care for a shared realm of living together. See Huber, "Bonhoeffer and Modernity," 15.

274. See Clements, "Community in the Ethics of Dietrich Bonhoeffer," 25.

275. This point is made by Larry Rasmussen in "Bonhoeffer's Song of Songs and Christianities as Earth Faiths."

last drop. . . . This-worldliness must not be abolished ahead of its time."[276] The theme even appears in his love letters to Maria von Wedemeyer: "Our marriage must be a 'yes' to God's earth. It must strengthen our resolve to do and accomplish something on earth. I fear that Christians who venture to stand on earth on only one leg will stand in heaven on only one leg too."[277] Bonhoeffer is therefore repeatedly specific in his rejection of the religious inclination to be other-worldly. He claims that the church has tended toward this ever since they "hit upon the devious trick of being religious, yes even 'Christian' at the expense of the earth" so that "[w]henever life begins to become oppressive and troublesome we just leap in the air with a bold kick and soar relieved and unencumbered into the so-called eternal fields. We leap over the present. We disdain the earth; we are better than it."[278] But if the church is to be Christ existing as a community, then faithfulness to the *cantus firmus* will be made manifest in the melodies that bind them "with oaths of fealty to the Earth, to misery, to hunger, to death."[279]

But in making such oaths of fealty to the earth it is not just the life and ministry of Jesus that must be revisited by the Christian colony. If "creation is not enough" then neither are the parables, miracles, and daily acts of righteousness performed by Jesus. It is to the suffering song of crucifixion and the victory cry of resurrection that the colony must ultimately listen, because it is there that God completes that liberating work which humanity and creation could not accomplish for themselves.[280] In his death and resurrection the *cantus firmus* overcomes all that would deny the polyphony of life or would enslave it to monophonic oppression. On Good Friday, as his followers scattered in terror or watched in horror, creation hid in darkness, trembled in earthquake, and feared that the song of life had failed and lay silenced for all time. As Julian of Norwich put it,

> Even heaven and earth languished for grief in their own peculiar
> way when Christ died. It is their nature to know him to be their

276. Letter dated June 27, 1944, in Bonhoeffer, *Letters and Papers*, 447–48. Bonhoeffer retained an affirmation of loyalty to the earth without deifying the finite creation as had occurred within the Nazi *cri de cœur* of "*Blut und Boden*," (Blood and Soil). For a detailed discussion see Rasmussen, *Earth Community, Earth Ethics*, 298–302.

277. Bonhoeffer and Von Wedemeyer, *Love Letters from Cell 92*, 64.

278. See "Thy Kingdom Come," in Bonhoeffer, *Berlin*, 285–86. Translation taken from Kelly and Nelson, *Testament to Freedom*, 89.

279. "Thy Kingdom Come," in Bonhoeffer, *Berlin*, 289.

280. It is argued here that salvation is more than merely "illustrative," revealing to the world new insight to an existing situation, but rather is "constitutive," i.e., it establishes a new situation between God and creation. For a detailed discussion see Gunton, *Actuality of Atonement*.

God, from whom they draw all their powers. When he failed, then needs must that they too most properly should fail to the limit of their ability, grieving for his pains.[281]

But on Easter Sunday failure is swallowed up in victory, death is overcome, all fear is cast out by the perfect love of Jesus's song of liberation. His *cantus firmus* is heard anew and harmonies of joy resonate throughout the cosmos. From sin, all forms of life-denying action and monophonic dominion have no claim to be the final note. There is a future music that calls to all creation from beyond itself, a music in which the melodies of past events announce eternal consequences that are to be heard both in the now and the not yet. Along with all creation, the individual Christian and their colony of heaven inhabit this world of the now and are conscious of that which is not yet. The eternal redemption of humanity is accomplished but there remains an ongoing work of sanctification that echoes to each person from the eschaton. Likewise, the effects extend beyond humanity. The essential goodness of creation is liberated. St. Paul writes,

> Creation waits with eager longing for the revealing of the children of God . . . in hope that the creation itself will be set free from its bondage to decay and will obtain the freedom of the glory of children of God. We know that the whole creation has been groaning in labor pains until now; and not only the creation, but we ourselves, who have the first fruits of the Spirit, groan inwardly while we wait for our adoption, the redemption of our bodies.[282]

Through the reality of the resurrection all visible creation is touched, given a new significance, called by the echoes of the future melody wherein everything is reconciled to God[283] through the *cantus firmus* and all creation learns to sing in perfect harmony. This is, as Moltmann suggests, "a cosmic event," the "first act in the new creation of the world"[284] and in it "we find the road to harmony again in Him."[285] Sing to the Lord a new song: this is the new reality, the colony of heavenly relationship that Isaiah envisages keeps breaking into the now.

The wolf shall live with the lamb,

---

281. Julian of Norwich, *Revelations of Divine Love*, 91.

282. Rom 8:19, 21–23.

283. See 2 Cor 5:19.

284. Moltmann, *Jesus Christ for Today's World*, 83.

285. "Eternal Seeping Through the Physical," in MacLeod, *Whole Earth Shall Cry Glory*, 11.

the leopard shall lie down with the kid,
the calf and the lion and the fatling together.[286]

The wilderness and the dry land shall be glad
The desert shall rejoice and blossom.[287]

For you shall go out in joy,
and be led back in peace;
the mountains and hills before you
shall burst into song,
and all the trees of the field shall clap their hands.[288]

Declaring, as Bonhoeffer suggested, "oaths of fealty to the earth," committing themselves to live as if "our mother will only lay in the Father's arms those who remain true to her" is an important part of the Rule of the Iona Community. Within the Rule that commits members to act for justice and peace in society it is stated:

We believe:

that God has given us partnership as stewards of creation and that we have a responsibility to live in a right relationship with the whole of God's creation;

and:

that, handled with integrity, creation can provide for the needs of all, but not for the greed which leads to injustice and inequality and endangers life on earth.[289]

While the description of humanity as "stewards" falls short of the theology outlined above, this aspect of the Rule is a clear statement of community members' intentions to remain true to the earth, their mother, and to listen and respond to her distress, making melody with the songs of creation. In recent years, members of the community have added an annual audit of their eco-footprint to their regular accountability on peace and justice issues. This commitment seeks to attain a regular 5 percent reduction of their eco-impact year on year.

However, long before this section of the Rule was composed and almost in prophetic anticipation of the current ecological crises, George MacLeod had both envisioned and incarnated a concern for the integrity

286. Isa 11:6.

287. Isa 35:1.

288. Isa 55:12.

289. See Appendix A, "Rule of the Iona Community." For a reflection on this part of the Iona Community Rule see Galloway, *Living by the Rule*, 72–78.

of creation. In the late 1930s he was readily appreciative of a theology that saw something of Christ in all things, but there were few others thinking similarly or constructing praxis rooted in such a theology. In the early 1940s these ecological concerns attracted him to the Russian Orthodox philosopher Nicolas Berdyaev and the anthroposophy of Rudolf Steiner. Steiner's work particularly was not easily accommodated into traditional Christian doctrine[290] and MacLeod was no systematic theologian. But his was a concern with praxis, at a time when Barth's theology of transcendence dominated European thought and there were few others addressing the concerns that he intuitively knew would be critical in the years to come. By the 1950s he had electricity generated by wind power in the abbey and his car had been refitted with a diesel engine specifically for ecological reasons.[291] He was unsuccessful in persuading the community to establish a market garden on Iona or to assist in crofting on Mull.[292] But in the 1970s, after ceding the leadership of the Iona Community and approaching his eightieth birthday, he initiated a new experiment to be undertaken at the old manse at Fuinary. His dream was for a new interdenominational and self-sufficient agricultural community that would live simply "as a preface to an understanding with the underprivileged Third world"[293] and offer hospitality to groups wishing to explore alternative lifestyles. MacLeod managed to persuade Alec and Anne Walker to join him, but despite the best efforts of all the vision proved impracticable and illusory.[294]

In this, as on many other occasions, George MacLeod heard the first strains of a new melody before the tune was widely known or loved. In the 1970s he proposed that a windmill be installed on Iona[295] and argued that Camas should become "an ecological community exhibiting an alternative lifestyle, with a full-time horticulturalist on the staff."[296]

290. Macleod's fascination with Berdyaev owed much to the Russian's mysticism and resonating social analysis. Rudolf Steiner's anthroposophy was more problematic; it offered no place for God, whether transcendent or immanent, and sought simply to develop the spirit of man.

291. Ferguson, *George MacLeod*, 305, 307.

292. Ian Fraser recalls that one summer MacLeod made little effort to tend the lettuce in a small garden he had already created by the youth huts and suggests that MacLeod hadn't thought the whole prospect of the market garden through in sufficient detail. Private conversation with Ian Fraser, August 2005.

293. Paper prepared by George MacLeod announcing the "Fuinary Intention," cited in Ferguson, *George MacLeod*, 386.

294. Ibid., 387.

295. The proposal was rejected on technical grounds by the then Secretary of State for the Environment Rt Hon. Tony Benn.

296. Ferguson, *George MacLeod*, 388.

In his proposals for Camas, MacLeod's vision has proved more possible. Camas is a group of former fishing cottages situated on the Ross of Mull in a secluded bay, over a mile away from the nearest road. The cottages were originally purchased pursuant to MacLeod's vision for them becoming a center for deprived urban young people. This vision persists and it is now an accredited activity center offering a wide range of outdoor pursuits to youth groups, schools, social work groups, and church groups. But it is also a community with a distinct fealty to the earth. Until 2010, when health and safety legislation for hosting outdoor pursuit groups required some structural changes to the buildings, there was no electricity at all; light came from the sun and the stars or candles. Still, heat comes to the common rooms with a fireplace from a managed supply of peat dug and dried on site. The (cold) water was collected rain-water. There is now provision for limited hot water providing there has been enough sun or wind energy to create it. Until the recent past the waste collected from the dry toilets was used to fertilize the garden from which many of the daily vegetables are harvested. The addition of flush toilets has not weakened the resolve of the community to live as simple and ecologically sustainable life as possible. The center is also used occasionally for themed adult weeks often focusing on ecological matters. Since the rebuilding of the abbey, Camas has traditionally been the site where new members have come for weeks of practical work, a series of physically demanding and necessary common tasks that help to "build" community and which emphasize the community's bisociation of work and worship.[297]

Not all such projects have met with equal success. The restored abbey is a difficult building to light and heat, and in the past a well-intentioned if ultimately ill-conceived idea to do so using the considerable energy of tidal ebb and flow unfortunately floundered. But the MacLeod Centre now heats much of its water from solar panels, and in purchasing food for the island centers, preference is given to local suppliers and community-based projects. All of this, successes and failures alike, reflect the community's attempts to sing the integrity of creation, joining their voices with those of all creation in response to Christ's *cantus firmus.*

As with other aspects of the Rule it is not simply a community commitment: each member has the personal responsibility to discern what this commitment means within the context of their daily living and then to remain accountable for their action within the network of family groups and the wider community gatherings. For some, this commitment has led them

297. For an excellent reflection on the place of Camas within the witness of the Iona Community see Galloway, *Living by the Rule,* 102–14.

to full-time work for sustainable development and environmental justice. For instance, one community member recently gave up his job to purchase a small cottage and three-quarters of an acre of land at Beaudesert Park, England, to work on a Christian eco-project. There they have developed a wider range of activities that connect creation and faith, including a series of five "reflective gardens," inspired by the Ignatian exercises, "Seeing God in all things."[298]

For others, it has meant taking ecological considerations to the heart of their chosen professions or domestic arrangements. For many more it has meant a conscious rethinking of daily life choices: for instance, choosing power supplies that utilize renewable sources, or deliberately seeking not to purchase food and other goods that have been transported over long distances and thus necessitated the burning of polluting fuels. Many have chosen to grow as much of their own produce as possible, either amidst their rural context or in suburban gardens and city allotments. For many, it has occasioned rigorous programs of recycling resources and composting waste and for some the deliberate choice to forsake the personal use of cars. And in keeping with their commitment that the Rule does not become a "pious hope and false witness," many community members have enabled their local churches to consider these issues and have been part of initiatives at local and national government to place the practical implementation of sustainable patterns of living at the heart of policy.

These commitments and many others like them are far from being unique but by placing them at the center of their understanding of the gospel, the Iona Community declares them to be a vital part of making the melodies of God in the world.

298. See www.reflectiongardens.org.uk.

CHAPTER 10

Cadenzas and Conclusions

Never fear.
The kingdom of heaven's
for all
for all
who just sing and play
playing their heart out
orchestrally
communally
in harmony
the sound of heaven's
chief occupation
Spirit-inspired preoccupation
to follow the maestro
singing and playing
playing and singing
beyond expectation.

We didn't know
we had it in us
to play and sing
to sing and play
so radiantly

so accurately

so precisely together

in harmony

each performing

our own vocation

each rapt up

in a symphony

beyond ourselves

in the kingdom of heaven

playing our heart out.

—FRANCES YOUNG[1]

The conclusion of a solo musical performance is often marked by a cadenza. It is a virtuosic passage performed in response to all that has gone before it. This practice began as an ornamental flourish but it soon evolved into the opportunity for a concerto musician to display their technical and creative prowess through melodic improvisation. Symbolically, it extemporized on the "penultimate note of the bass."[2] The cadenza is then the final occasion for the performer to bring some concluding and personal comment to all that has gone before and offers an apposite metaphor for this final chapter. The improvisation of a cadenza arises organically out of the preceding melodies as written by the composer and performed by the orchestral community. Yet it is a unique and personal moment of recital by the individual. As Young notes,

> In order to improvise effectively, the performer not only has to have technical competence, but also needs to understand musical theory, the rules of harmony and counterpoint, the accepted conventions of development, the stylistic character of the work within which the cadenza is to figure. She has to have sensitivity to the actual score of that work, its form, its themes, and subjects, and their "generative" potential.[3]

In other words, to perform a "cadenza of Christian discipleship," the individual must have nurtured an *askesis* of personal rehearsal which shows

1. "A Mozart Concerto," in Young, *Art of Performance*, 183–84.

2. See Albert Cohen, "Performance Theory," in Christensen, *Cambridge History of Western Music Theory*, 548.

3. Young, *Art of Performance*, 160.

that they have listened and responded to the *cantus firmus*. They must have been true to the melodies of community called into being by God and established through Scripture, sacrament and historical tradition, and yet be true to the personality of the individual as well as the context of auditorium and audience. In many respects, this book has sought to be one such cadenza. Its stated intention was to articulate a theology of community through the metaphors of music, particularly that of polyphony. Adopting this as its central image, the book has sought to perform something unique in the theology of Christian community while yet remaining true to the Scriptures, doctrines, and traditions of the church and its theologians. The metaphor of polyphony has provided a fresh Christology which takes seriously the Christian claim that heaven and earth are bisociated in and through the incarnate God. That incarnate God has been described as the *cantus firmus*, the one in whom difference and particularity are affirmed and yet through whom all boundaries are transcended. This understanding of Christ has facilitated a unique understanding of praxis for the community which seeks to perform the earthbound countermelodies that God calls into existence. It has done so by establishing a unique paradigm in which multiple images of the Christian community may inform and strengthen one's imagination and by showing how diverse theologies may coexist in a fecund Christ-centered relationship. Vitally, the metaphors of polyphony and *cantus firmus* have demonstrated how Christ is Lord of the world and church, concerned with work as well as worship, politics as well as prayer, and the secular along with the spiritual. However, hopefully this book has done more than articulate a theology that demands that the activities of Christians within the life of the church and what is commissioned through their presence in the world should inform and shape each other. It has also posited a Discipline of Counterpoint, through which such a polyphonic praxis may be attempted.

Like any musical cadenza, performing this book has depended upon the mind of the great Composer and the orchestral community of the faithful, and it hopes to make some small effect upon the lives of all those gathered in the auditorium of creation. But it has been a performance with acknowledged limits.

It has drawn deeply on Bonhoeffer and particularly the evocative imagery of his *Letters and Papers*. But in these he offers only tantalizing fragments of the potential he glimpsed in the synergy of theology and music, the metaphor of polyphony and the performance of what we have termed the "Discipline of Counterpoint." The book has never sought to be a statement of the theology of Bonhoeffer and has less attempted to be a projection of what he might have said or done had he lived longer. But it has sought to be true to the man whose overwhelming concern in life and work was the character of the Christian community and its place in the world.

It has also engaged at length with George MacLeod and the contemporary Iona Community. It has not sought to present Iona or its founder as the perfected embodiment of polyphonic community. The community would readily acknowledge that it has not perfected anything, least of all how to be the body of Christ, and that it is just one of many colonies of heaven seeking to practice something like a worldly monasticism. By its own admission it has no pretensions to the importance of its existence. In its early days its members affirmed that the community would continue just as long as God required its existence.[4] Today, it confesses to be "a disposable tool, not an everlasting institution; it is only a tiny part of the Church's witness"[5] Yet, as Ferguson has noted, "The numbers of Members and Associates joining, the continued appeal of the developing Iona program and the response to its mainland work would seem to indicate that if the Iona Community were to disband today it would need to be reinvented tomorrow."[6] So while acknowledging the shortcomings of the Iona Community, it has been suggested that within the fragmented melodies of its history and current membership there can be detected persistent intimations of a polyphonic Christ and the countermelodies he calls into being.

The book has left unexamined many areas that others may have felt vital. So, for instance, there has been no detailed inquiry into the varying manifestations of the character of the Eucharist when understood through the metaphor of polyphony. Similarly, there has been no extension of the discussion on ecumenism to consider how a polyphonic community might develop a theology and praxis of Eucharist. Neither has there been any examination of how the metaphor of polyphony will assist the more difficult but no less urgent arena of interreligious dialogue. Little attention has been given to the phenomenon of time, how it is comprehended in music and theology, and how these understandings might be bisociated. Furthermore, a myriad of ethical considerations have, of necessity, fallen beyond the remit of the book. However, it is hoped that the prevailing metaphors of polyphony, *cantus firmus*, and the Discipline of Counterpoint might offer fruitful contributions to matters such as sexual ethics where polarizing positions and zero-sum mentalities do little to reflect the bisociation of unity and diversity revealed in the polyphonic Christ. There is much potential research in these and parallel areas of interest.

4. Ferguson, *Chasing the Wild Goose*, 160.

5. Ibid., 161.

6. Ibid.

Another area in which there remains much work to be done is the interaction of theology and the arts, particularly as to how practices other than music might inform Christian doctrine, praxis, and spirituality. It is anticipated that the metaphor of polyphony will provide a helpful paradigm for further interdisciplinary research and discussions.

And finally there has been little explicit consideration of the missional character of polyphonic communities of new monastic praxis. It is hoped that the proposed bisociation of work and worship, prayer and politics, secular and sacred, offer an incarnational approach to the mission of God that brings together the former poles of Word and action, evangelism and social justice. It is acknowledged that there do remain unanswered here significant questions about evangelism and wider mission in a post-Christendom world.[7]

The book has sought to be no more than one improvisation upon Christ's *cantus firmus*, offering one performance of participation in the polyphony of God. And as Young notes, "there is bound to be improvisation if we are to sing love-songs that are at once our own, and yet inspired by and integrally related in theme and style to the classics provided by the repertoire we have inherited."[8]

As such, the preceding pages are neither a blueprint for the reform of the church nor are they a manifesto for any alternative form of Christian community. With one final mix of metaphor, we might say all this is far less a comprehensive road map and more akin to snapshots of the journey so far, in which can be glimpsed the new and distant horizons of tomorrow. What has been written is not the thing itself, it has perhaps not even well described the thing itself, it has been, at best, a new song sung to the Lord and "an echo of a tune" that has not yet been fully heard.[9]

In this concluding chapter, the score may have reached its final page, the baton may be stilled, the orchestra silenced, and the audience departing, but the music has not ended. It is hoped that one day, in the fullness of time and grace, it may find a place in the melodies of heaven's community. But until then,

> O sing to the LORD a new song;
> sing to the LORD, all the earth.

---

7. There is an ever increasing bibliography attached to this subject, but see Kreider and Kreider, *Worship and Mission After Christendom*; Murray, *Post-Christendom*; Kalu, Vethanayagamony, and Chia, *Mission After Christendom*; Stone, *Evangelism after Christendom*; and Frost, *Exiles*.

8. Young, *Art of Performance*, 167.

9. See Lewis, *Weight of Glory*, 31.

Sing to the LORD, bless his name;
tell of his salvation from day to day.
Declare his glory among the nations,
his marvelous works among all the peoples.[10]

10. Ps 96.

The Rule of the Iona Community
As It Was until 2014

Our five-fold Rule calls us to:

1. Daily Prayer and Bible-reading
2. Sharing and accounting for the use of our money
3. Planning and accounting for the use of our time
4. Action for Justice and Peace in society
5. Meeting with and accounting to each other

1. Daily Prayer and Bible Reading

We are asked to pray for each other, for our common concerns, and for the wider work of the church, on a daily basis. We are also asked to read the Bible on a regular and frequent basis. Together with prayer requests and topics in the Members booklet, the use is commended of *Pray Now* (published by St. Andrew Press) or *With All God's People* (published by the WCC, Geneva), or such other resources as mentioned in the Community's "Spirituality Tool-kit."

2. Sharing and Accounting for the Use of Our Money

a. We are asked, first, to account to each other for the use of our income.

b. We are then asked, in Family Groups, to agree our individual baseline commitments and special circumstances and expenses: thus arriving at a personal disposable income figure from which the amount to be given (a tithe—10% in most cases) can be deducted.

c. The amount to be given should be divided up as follows:

  i   to the wider work of the Church, and to bodies concerned with promoting justice and peace, world development, etc.—60%

  ii to the work of the Iona Community—20%

  iii purposes decided by the Family Group—10%

  iv to purposes decided by the Common Fund Trustees on behalf of the Community—5%

  v   to the Travel Pool—5%

The accounting year for each of these amounts is from 1st January to 31st December.

3. Planning and Accounting for the Use of Our Time

This discipline seems to have its origins in the early days of the Community, when craftsmen doubted the ability of ministers to work an eight-hour "shift!" Through it, we are all asked to plan our time, in such a way that proper "weighting" is given, not simply to work, but equally to leisure, to time for family, to developing skills or acquiring new ones, to worship and devotion, to voluntary work—and to sleep!

4. Action for Justice, Peace and Integrity of Creation

Our act of commitment on justice and peace is, as was also said of the earlier Act of Commitment on Peace, "a point of departure." It will remain no more than a pious hope (and a false witness) unless we seek, separately and together, to put it into practice.

Justice and Peace Commitment

We believe:

  1. that the Gospel commands us to seek peace founded on justice and that costly reconciliation is at the heart of the Gospel;

  2. that work for justice, peace and an equitable society is a matter of extreme urgency;

3. that God has given us partnership as stewards of creation and that we have a responsibility to live in a right relationship with the whole of God's creation;

4. that, handled with integrity, creation can provide for the needs of all, but not for the greed which leads to injustice and inequality, and endangers life on earth;

5. that everyone should have the quality and dignity of a full life that requires adequate physical, social and political opportunity, without the oppression of poverty, injustice and fear;

6. that social and political action leading to justice for all people and encouraged by prayer and discussion, is a vital work of the Church at all levels;

7. that the use or threatened use of nuclear and other weapons of mass destruction is theologically and morally indefensible and that opposition to their existence is an imperative of the Christian faith.

As Members and Family Groups we will:

8. engage in forms of political witness and action, prayerfully and thoughtfully, to promote just and peaceful social, political and economic structures;

9. work for a British policy of renunciation of all weapons of mass destruction and for the encouragement of other nations, individually or collectively, to do the same;

10. celebrate human diversity and actively work to combat discrimination on grounds of age, colour, disability, mental wellbeing, differing ability, gender, race, ethnic and cultural background, sexual orientation or religion;

11. work for the establishment of the United Nations Organisation as the principal organ of international reconciliation and security, in place of military alliances;

12. support and promote research and education into non-violent ways of achieving justice, peace and a sustainable global society;

13. work for reconciliation within and among nations by international sharing and exchange of experience and people, with particular concern for politically and economically oppressed nations;

14. act in solidarity with the victims of environmental injustice throughout the world, and support political and structural change in our own countries to reduce our over consumption of resources.

5. Meeting with and Accounting to Each Other

We are asked to do this

  a) In Family Groups

  b) In Plenaries

We are also asked to give a written undertaking at the beginning of January each year (through the "With-us" card) that we are "with the Community" in commitment to the Rule.

Along with the "With-us" card, we are asked to send a short personal assessment to the Leader of how we are keeping the Rule.

The Rule of the Iona Community
As It Is from 2015

As Members of the Iona Community we commit ourselves to:

1. Daily prayer, worship with others and regular engagement with the Bible and other material which nourishes us;

2. Working for justice and peace, wholeness and reconciliation in our localities, society and the whole creation;

3. Supporting one another in prayer and by meeting, communicating, and accounting with one another for the use of our gifts, money and time, our use of the earth's resources and our keeping of all aspects of the Rule;

4. Sharing in the corporate life and organisation of the Community.

ASSOCIATE MEMBERS are invited to keep the Rule whereas Full Members are held accountable for their keeping of the Rule.

Justice, Peace and Integrity of Creation

Commitment

We believe:

1. that the Gospel commands us to seek peace founded on justice and that costly reconciliation is at the heart of the Gospel;

2. that work for justice, peace and an equitable society is a matter of extreme urgency;

3. that God has given us partnership as stewards of creation and that we have a responsibility to live in a right relationship with the whole of God's creation;

4. that, handled with integrity, creation can provide for the needs of all, but not for the greed which leads to injustice and inequality, and endangers life on earth;

5. that everyone should have the quality and dignity of a full life that requires adequate physical, social and political opportunity, without the oppression of poverty, injustice and fear;

6. that social and political action leading to justice for all people and encouraged by prayer and discussion is a vital work of the Church at all levels;

7. that the use or threatened use of nuclear and other weapons of mass destruction is theologically and morally indefensible and that opposition to their existence is an imperative of the Christian faith.

As Members and Family Groups we will:

8. engage in forms of political witness and action, prayerfully and thoughtfully, to promote just and peaceful social, political and economic structures;

9. work for a policy of renunciation by our own nations of all weapons of mass destruction and for the encouragement of other nations, individually or collectively, to do the same;

10. celebrate human diversity and actively work to combat discrimination on grounds of age, colour, disability, mental wellbeing, differing ability, gender, race, ethnic and cultural background, sexual orientation or religion;

11. work for the establishment of the United Nations Organisation as the principal organ of international reconciliation and security, in place of military alliances;

12. support and promote research and education into nonviolent ways of achieving justice, peace and a sustainable global society;

13. work for reconciliation within and among nations by international sharing and exchange of experience and people, with particular concern for politically and economically oppressed nations;

14. act in solidarity with the victims of environmental injustice throughout the world, and support political and structural change in our own countries to reduce our over-consumption of resources.

Our working principles

Our passion

We are motivated by our shared commitment to Jesus Christ and his proclamation of a just and generous new order; by our own experience of the common life, and by a creative spiritual practice of prayer, song, silence and sacrament.

Our movement

We seek to offer practical support, mutual encouragement, challenge and inspiration to our members, staff and friends in our common task. We are committed to ongoing dialogue and learning and to prayer and action for health.

Our centres

Our centres on Iona and Mull strive to be places of hospitality, sanctuary and challenge, which offer the experience of the common life and exposure to the concerns of the Iona Community to those who live in them and those who visit.

Our publications

We seek in all our publications to inform, to reflect, to inspire and to bring about personal and political transformation. We have a bias to material that is based on practice, and which furthers the task of the Community.

Our environmental values

We strive in our practice for the highest environmental goals. We travel by public transport wherever possible. We are committed to reducing our energy consumption and environmental impact. We actively seek suppliers who share these goals.

Our social values

We deplore social injustice. We respect all our members, staff, guests and partners, irrespective of age, race, gender, religion, sexuality, disability, or health status. We actively campaign for social justice at all levels and have a particular commitment to inclusion of people living in poverty.

Our economic values

We deplore economic injustice. We are committed to the common good, to trade justice and to a critique of economic policies that increase poverty and inequality. We support our work through our own giving and our trading operations. We operate a balanced budget, try to bank and invest ethically and purchase fairly-traded goods. Our residential staff are paid the same, regardless of job. We seek to minimise salary differentials for non-residential staff.

Participation

Ours is a common task. Everyone has the opportunity to share in leadership, in policy-making and spiritual practice. Our structures are democratic, and we strive for consensus. We give our leaders a mandate to act fast and effectively, but expect them to listen and respect the views of all. In particular, we are committed to extending the full participation of young people, within and beyond our movement.

Accountability

Our Rule binds us to mutual accountability. We aim to be fully transparent and accountable for our use of money and time, and to operate with ethical codes of conduct.

Citizenship and partnership

We seek social transformation, and encourage our members to be engaged in civic and political structures at all levels. We actively seek collaboration with all people of goodwill who share our commitment to just and non-violent action, irrespective of nationality, religion or political creed. Working both outside and within military organisations, members are committed to standing against militarism and the arms trade and for mediation and reconciliation founded on justice.

Bibliography

Adamnan of Iona, Saint. *Life of St. Columba*. Translated by Richard Sharpe. London: Penguin, 1995.

Adams, Ian. *Cave, Refectory, Road: Monastic Rhythms for Contemporary Living*. Norwich, UK: Canterbury, 2010.

Allchin, A. M. *Resurrection's Children: Exploring the Way towards God*. Norwich, UK: Canterbury, 1998.

Allchin, Donald, and D. Densil Morgan. *Sensuous Glory: The Poetic Vision of D. Gwenallt Jones*. Norwich, UK: Canterbury, 2000.

Allen, Loyd. "A Brief History of Christian Devotion." *Faith and Mission* 7 (Spring 1990) 3–18.

Anderson, Ray S. *Historical Transcendence and the Reality of God: A Christological Critique*. Grand Rapids: Eerdmans, 1975.

Anderson, Walter Truett, ed. *The Fontana Postmodernism Reader*. London: Fontana, 1996.

Anson, Peter F. *The Call of the Cloister: Religious Communities and Kindred Bodies in the Anglican Communion*. Edited by A. W. Campbell. London: SPCK, 1964.

Arbuckle, Gerald A. *From Chaos to Mission: Refounding Religious Life Formation*. London: Chapman, 1996.

Astley, Jeff, Timothy Hone, and Mark Savage, eds. *Creative Chords: Studies in Music, Theology and Christian Formation*. Leominster, UK: Gracewing, 2000.

Attali, Jacques. *Noise: The Political Economy of Music*. Minneapolis: University of Minnesota Press, 2002.

Augé, Marc. *Non-places: Introduction to an Anthropology of Supermodernity*. Translated by John Howe. London: Verso, 1997.

Augustine, Saint, Bishop of Hippo. *On Christian Teaching*. Translated by R. P. H. Green. Oxford: Oxford University Press, 1997.

Ayers, Lewis, and Gareth Jones, eds. *Christian Origins: Theology, Rhetoric and Community*. London: Routledge, 1998.

Baab, Lynn M. *Personality Type in Congregations: How to Work with Others More Effectively*. Bethesda, MD: Alban Institute, 1998.

Bainton, Roland. *Here I Stand: A Life of Martin Luther*. Tring, England: Lion, 1987.

Ballard, Paul H. "Worship in a Secular World: Bonhoeffer's Secret Discipline." *The Princeton Seminary Bulletin* 68 (1975) 27–36.

Ballard, Paul H., and Pamela D. Couture, eds. *Creativity, Imagination and Criticism: The Expressive Dimension in Practical Theology*. Cardiff: Cardiff Academic Press, 2001.

Balthasar, Hans Urs von. *Truth is Symphonic: Aspects of Christian Pluralism.* San Francisco: Ignatius, 1987.

Bamford, Christopher. *The Voice of the Eagle: The Heart of Celtic Christianity.* Great Barrington, MA: Lindisfarne, 2000.

Banks, Robert. *Paul's Idea of Community: The Early House Churches in their Cultural Setting.* Rev. ed. Peabody, MA: Hendrickson, 1998.

Barclay, William. *The Letters to Philippians, Colossians, Thessalonians.* The Daily Study Bible. Edinburgh: Saint Andrew, 1961.

Barnes, A. "Discipline of the Secret." In vol. 5 of *The Catholic Encyclopedia.* New York: Robert Appleton, 1909. http://www.newadvent.org/cathen/05032a.htm.

Barrett, C. K. *A Critical and Exegetical Commentary on the Acts of the Apostles.* Vol. 1, *Preliminary Introduction and Commentary on Acts 1–14.* Edinburgh: T. & T. Clark, 1994.

Barry, Patrick. *Saint Benedict and Christianity in England.* Ampleforth Abbey, UK: Ampleforth Abbey Press, 1995.

Barth, Karl. *Church Dogmatics.* Edited by G. W. Bromiley and T. F. Torrance. 4 volumes in 13 parts. Edinburgh: T. & T. Clark, 1936.

———. *The Epistle to the Philippians.* Translated by J. W. Lietch. London: SCM, 1962.

———. *Wolfgang Amadeus Mozart.* Translated by Clarence K. Pott. Reprint, Eugene, OR: Wipf and Stock, 2003.

Barton, Stephen C. "New Testament Interpretation as Performance." *Scottish Journal of Theology* 52 (1999) 179–208.

———. *The Spirituality of the Gospels.* London: SPCK, 1992.

Begbie, Jeremy, ed. *Beholding the Glory: Incarnation through the Arts.* London: Darton, Longman and Todd, 2000.

———. "Play it (Again): Music, Theology and Divine Communication." In *Creative Chords: Studies in Music, Theology and Christian Formation,* edited by Jeff Astley, Timothy Hone, and Mark Savage, 56–64. Leominster, UK: Gracewing, 2000.

———. *Resounding Truth: Christian Wisdom in the World of Music.* London: SPCK, 2008.

———, ed. *Sounding the Depths: Theology Through the Arts.* London: SCM, 2002.

———. *Theology, Music, and Time.* Cambridge Studies in Christian Doctrine 4. Cambridge: Cambridge University Press, 2000.

———. *Voicing Creation's Praise: Towards a Theology of the Arts.* Edinburgh: T. & T. Clark, 1991.

Bell, G. K. A. "The Church and the Resistance Movement." In *I Knew Dietrich Bonhoeffer: Reminiscences By His Friends,* edited by Wolf-Dieter Zimmermann and Ronald Gregor Smith, 209–10. London: Collins, 1966.

Bell, John L. "Battering the Babies Heads." Unpublished paper delivered at Swansea University, 2000. Copy obtained from the author.

———. "Editor's Introduction." In *Common Ground: A Song Book for All the Churches,* 6–7. Edinburgh: Saint Andrew, 1998.

———. *A Jubilee Liturgy: An Order of Service for the Millennium.* Glasgow: Wild Goose, 1999.

———. *One is the Body: Songs of Unity and Diversity.* Glasgow: Wild Goose, 2002.

———. "Reforming Worship." *Ministry Today* 11 (October 1997) 6–18.

———, ed. *Sent By the Lord: Songs of the World Church.* Vol. 2. Glasgow: Wild Goose, 1991.

———. *The Singing Thing: A Case for Congregational Song.* Glasgow: Wild Goose, 2000.

———. *States of Bliss and Yearning: The Marks and Means of Authentic Christian Spirituality.* Glasgow: Wild Goose, 1998.

Bell, John L., and Graham Maule. *Enemy of Apathy.* Vol. 2, *Wild Goose Songs.* Glasgow: Iona Community, 1988.

———. *Heaven Shall Not Wait.* Vol. 1, *Wild Goose Songs.* Glasgow: Iona Community, 1987.

———. *Love from Below.* Vol. 3, *Wild Goose Songs.* Glasgow: Iona Community, 1989.

———. *Poverty, Chastity, Obedience—A Vocation for Today.* Glasgow: Iona Community, 1985.

Bell, John L., et al. *Composing Music for Worship.* Edited by Stephen Darlington and Alan Kreider. Norwich, UK: Canterbury Press, 2003.

Bell, Richard H., ed. *The Grammar of the Heart: New Essays in Moral Philosophy and Theology.* San Francisco: Harper and Row, 1988.

Benson, Bruce Ellis. *Liturgy As a Way of Life: Embodying the Arts in Christian Worship.* Grand Rapids: Baker Academic, 2013.

Berger, Peter L. *The Precarious Vision: A Sociologist Looks at Social Fictions and Christian Faith.* New York: Doubleday, 1968.

Bertram, Robert. "Bonhoeffer's Exclusivism." In *Reflections on Bonhoeffer: Essays in Honor of F. Burton Nelson,* edited by Geffrey B. Kelly and C. J. Weborg 169–84. Chicago: Covenant, 1999.

Best, Thomas F., and Dagmar Heller, eds. *Worship Today: Understanding, Practice, Ecumenical Implications.* Faith and Order Paper 194. Geneva: WCC, 2004.

Bethge, Eberhard. *Bonhoeffer: An Illustrated Introduction in Documents and Photographs.* Translated by Rosaleen Ockenden. London: Collins, 1979.

———. *Bonhoeffer: Exile and Martyr.* London: Collins, 1975.

———. *Dietrich Bonhoeffer: A Biography—Theologian, Christian, Man for His Times.* Rev. ed. Minneapolis: Fortress, 2000.

———. "Dietrich Bonhoeffer and the Jews." In *Ethical Responsibility: Bonhoeffer's Legacy to the Churches,* edited by John D. Godsey and Geffrey B. Kelly, 43–93. Toronto Studies in Theology 6. New York: Edwin Mellen, 1981.

———. *Dietrich Bonhoeffer: Man of Vision, Man of Courage.* New York: Harper and Row, 1985.

———. *Friendship and Resistance: Essays on Dietrich Bonhoeffer.* Grand Rapids: Eerdmans, 1995.

———. *Prayer and Righteous Action in the Life of Dietrich Bonhoeffer.* Belfast: Christian Journals, 1979.

Bethge, Renate. "Bonhoeffer and the Role of Women." In *Reflections on Bonhoeffer: Essays in Honor of F. Burton Nelson,* edited by Geffrey B. Kelly, and C. John Weborg, 169–84. Chicago: Covenant, 1999.

de Bhaldraithe, Eoin. "Early Christian Features Preserved in Western Monasticism." In *The Origins of Christendom in the West,* edited by Alan Kreider, 153–78. Edinburgh: T. & T. Clark, 2001.

Biot, François. *The Rise of Protestant Monasticism.* Baltimore: Helicon, 1963.

Black, Max. *Models and Metaphors: Studies in Language and Philosophy.* Ithaca, NY: Cornell University Press, 1962.

Blout, Brian K., and L. Tubbs Tisdale, eds. *Making Room at the Table: An Invitation to Multicultural Worship.* Louisville: Westminster John Knox, 2001.

Blume, Friedrich. *Protestant Church Music: A History*. London: Victor Gollancz, 1975.

Bonhoeffer, Dietrich. *Act and Being: Transcendental Philosophy and Ontology in Systematic Theology*. Edited by Wayne Whitson Floyd, Jr. Translated by H. Martin Rumscheidt. Dietrich Bonhoeffer Works 2. Minneapolis: Fortress, 1996.

———. *Barcelona, Berlin, New York: 1928–1931*. Edited by Clifford J. Green. Translated by Douglas W. Scott. Dietrich Bonhoeffer Works 10. Minneapolis: Fortress, 2008.

———. *Berlin: 1932–1933*. Edited by Larry L. Rasmussen. Translated by Isabel Best and David Higgins. Dietrich Bonhoeffer Works 12. Minneapolis: Fortress, 2009.

———. *Christ the Center*. Translated by Edwin Robertson. San Francisco: Harper and Row, 1978.

———. *Conspiracy and Imprisonment: 1940–1945*. Dietrich Bonhoeffer Works 16. Minneapolis: Fortress, 2004.

———. *Creation and Fall: A Theological Exposition of Genesis 1–3*. Edited by John W. de Gruchy. Translated by Douglas Stephen Bax. Dietrich Bonhoeffer Works 3. Minneapolis: Fortress, 1997.

———. *Discipleship*. Dietrich Bonhoeffer Works 4. Minneapolis: Fortress, 2001.

———. *Ecumenical, Academic, and Pastoral Work: 1931–1932*. Edited by Victoria J. Barnett et al. Translated by Anne Schmidt-Lange et al. Dietrich Bonhoeffer Works 11. Minneapolis: Fortress, 2012.

———. *Ethics*. Edited by Clifford J. Green. Translated by Reinhard Krauss et al. Dietrich Bonhoeffer Works 6. Minneapolis: Fortress, 2005.

———. *Fiction from Tegel Prison*. Edited by Clifford J. Green. Translated by Nancy Lukens. Dietrich Bonhoeffer Works 7. Minneapolis: Fortress, 2000.

———. *Letters and Papers From Prison*. Edited by John W. de Gruchy. Translated by Isabel Best et al. Dietrich Bonhoeffer Works 8. Minneapolis: Fortress, 2010.

———. *Life Together/Prayerbook of the Bible*. Edited by Geffrey B. Kelly. Translated by Daniel W. Bloesch and James H. Burtness. Dietrich Bonhoeffer Works 5. Minneapolis: Fortress, 1996.

———. *London: 1933–1935*. Edited by Keith Clements. Translated by Isabel Best. Dietrich Bonhoeffer Works 13. Minneapolis: Fortress, 2007.

———. *Meditating on the Word*. Translated and edited by David McI. Gracie. Cambridge, MA: Cowley, 1986.

———. *Sanctorum Communio: A Dogmatic Enquiry into the Sociology of the Church*. Edited by Clifford J. Green. Translated by Reinhard Krauss and Nancy Lukens. Dietrich Bonhoeffer Works 1. Minneapolis: Fortress, 2000.

———. *Spiritual Care*. Translated by Jay C. Rochelle. Philadelphia: Fortress, 1985.

———. *Theological Education at Finkenwalde: 1935–1937*. Edited by H. Gaylon Barker. Dietrich Bonhoeffer Works 14. Minneapolis: Fortress, 2013.

———. *Theological Education Underground: 1937–1940*. Edited and translated by Victoria J. Barnett. Dietrich Bonhoeffer Works 15. Minneapolis: Fortress, 2012.

———. *The Young Bonhoeffer: 1918–1927*. Edited by Paul Duane Matheny et al. Translated by Mary C. Nebelsick. Dietrich Bonhoeffer Works 9. Minneapolis: Fortress, 2003.

Bonhoeffer, Dietrich, and Maria von Wedemeyer. *Love Letters from Cell 92: The Correspondence Between Dietrich Bonhoeffer and Maria von Wedemeyer, 1943–1945*. Edited by Ruth Alice von Bismark and Ulrich Kabitz. Translated by John Brownjohn. Nashville: Abingdon, 1995.

Bosanquet, Mary. *The Life and Death of Dietrich Bonhoeffer.* New York: Harper and Row, 1968.

Bosch, David J. *Transforming Mission: Paradigm Shifts in Theology.* Maryknoll, NY: Orbis, 1991.

Botman, H. Russel. "Is Bonhoeffer Still of Any Use in South Africa?" In *Bonhoeffer for a New Day: Theology in a Time of Transition,* edited by John W. de Gruchy, 366–72. Grand Rapids: Eerdmans, 1997.

Boyce Tillman, June. "Even the Stones Cry Out: Music, Theology and the Earth." In *Through Us, With Us, In Us: Relational Theologies in the Twenty-First Century,* edited by Lisa Isherwood and Elaine Bellchambers, 153–78. London: SCM, 2010.

Bradley, Ian C. *Abide With Me: The World of Victorian Hymns.* London: SCM, 1997.

———. *Celtic Christianity: Making Myths and Chasing Dreams.* Edinburgh: Edinburgh University Press, 1999.

———. *The Celtic Way.* London: Darton, Longman and Todd, 1993.

———. *Colonies of Heaven: Celtic Models for Today's Church.* London: Darton, Longman and Todd, 2000.

———. *Columba: Pilgrim and Penitent.* Glasgow: Wild Goose, 1996.

———. *God is Green.* London: Darton, Longman and Todd, 1990.

Brown, Dale. "Bonhoeffer and Pacifism." *Manchester College Bulletin of Peace Studies Institute* 11 (June 1981) 32–43.

Brown, Frank Burch. *Religious Aesthetics: A Theological Study of Making and Meaning.* London: Macmillan, 1990.

Brown, William P. *Seeing the Psalms: A Theology of Metaphor.* Louisville: Westminster John Knox, 2002.

Bruce, James. *Prophecy, Miracles, Angels and Heavenly Light? The Eschatology, Pneumatology, and Missiology of Adomnan's Life of Columba.* Reprint, Eugene, OR: Wipf and Stock, 2007.

Brueggemann, Walter. *The Land: Place as Gift, Promise and Challenge in Biblical Faith.* Overtures to Biblical Theology 1. London: SPCK, 1978.

———. *The Message of the Psalms: A Theological Commentary.* Minneapolis: Augsburg, 1984.

———. *Texts Under Negotiation: The Bible and Postmodern Imagination.* London: SCM, 1993.

Burgess, Ruth, and Kathy Galloway, eds. *Praying for the Dawn: A Resource Book for the Ministry of Healing.* Glasgow: Wild Goose, 2000.

Burgess, Yvonne. *The Myth of Progress.* Glasgow: Wild Goose, 1996.

Burkholder, Benjamin J. "Christological Foundations for an Ecological Ethic: Learning from Bonhoeffer." *Scottish Journal of Theology* 66 (2013) 338–56.

Burnham, F. B., ed. *Postmodern Theology: Christian Faith in Pluralist World.* New York: HarperCollins, 1989.

Burton-Christie, Douglas. *The Word in the Desert: Scripture and the Quest for Holiness in Early Christian Monasticism.* New York: Oxford University Press, 1993.

Busing, Paul F. W. "Reminiscences of Finkenwalde." *The Christian Century* 78 (September 20, 1961) 1108–11.

Calvin, John. *Institutes of the Christian Religion.* Edited by John T. McNeill. Library of Christian Classics. Philadelphia: Westminster, 1960.

Carlile, J. C. *A Colony of Heaven.* London: Hodder and Stoughton, n.d.

Carmichael, Alexander. *Carmina Gadelica: Hymns and Incantations, Collected in the Highlands and Islands of Scotland in the Last Century.* Edinburgh: Floris, 1992.

Carter, Guy C., and R. Van Edyen, eds. *Bonhoeffer's Ethics: Old Europe and New Frontiers.* Kampen, Netherlands: Kok Pharos, 1991.

Chadwick, Owen, ed. *Western Asceticism.* Library of Christian Classics 12. London: SCM, 1958.

Chandler, Andrew, ed. *The Terrible Alternative: Christian Martyrdom in the Twentieth Century.* London: Cassell, 1998.

Chapman, G. Clarke. "What Would Bonhoeffer Say to Christian Peacemakers Today?" In *Theology, Politics, and Peace,* edited by Theodore Runyon, 167–75. Maryknoll, NY: Orbis, 1989.

Chitty, Derwas J. *The Desert a City: An Introduction to the Study of Egyptian and Palestinian Monasticism under the Christian Empire.* Oxford: Blackwell, 1966.

Christensen, Thomas, ed. *The Cambridge History of Western Music.* Cambridge: Cambridge University Press, 2002.

Chung, Hyun Kyung. "Dear Dietrich Bonhoeffer." In *Bonhoeffer for a New Day: Theology in a Time of Transition,* edited by John W. de Gruchy, 9–19. Grand Rapids: Eerdmans, 1997.

Clapp, Rodney. *A Peculiar People: The Church as Culture in a Post-Christian Society.* Downers Grove, IL: InterVarsity, 1996.

Cleaver, Richard. *Know My Name: Gay Liberation Theology.* Louisville: Westminster John Knox, 1995.

Clements, Keith W. "Community in the Ethics of Dietrich Bonhoeffer." In *Studies in Christian Ethics* 10 (1997) 16–31.

———. "Ecumenical Witness for Peace." In *The Cambridge Companion to Dietrich Bonhoeffer,* edited by John W. de Gruchy, 154–72. Cambridge: Cambridge University Press, 1999.

———. *Learning to Speak: The Church's Voice in Public Affairs.* Edinburgh: T. & T. Clark, 1995.

———. *A Patriotism for Today: Dialogue with Dietrich Bonhoeffer.* Bristol: Bristol Baptist College, 1984.

———. *What Freedom? The Persistent Challenge of Dietrich Bonhoeffer.* Bristol: Bristol Baptist College, 1990.

Cobb, Peter G. "The Architectural Setting of the Liturgy." In *The Study of Liturgy,* edited by Cheslyn Jones et al., 528–41. London: SPCK, 1992.

Cohen, Albert. "Performance Theory." In *The Cambridge History of Western Music,* edited by Thomas Christensen, 534–53. Cambridge: Cambridge University Press, 2002.

Cole, Basil. *Music and Morals: A Theological Appraisal of the Moral and Psychological Effects of Music.* New York: Alba, 1993.

Collins, Paul. *God's Earth: Religion as if Matter Really Mattered.* Sydney: Dove, 1995.

Cone, James H. *The Spirituals and the Blues.* Maryknoll, NY: Orbis, 2001.

Countryman, L. William. *Dirt, Greed and Sex: Sexual Ethics in the New Testament and Their Implications for Today.* London: SCM, 1996.

Cowie, Ian. *Jesus' Healing Works and Ours.* Glasgow: Wild Goose, 2000.

———. *Prayers and Ideas for Healing Services.* Glasgow: Wild Goose, 1995.

Craig, Maxwell, ed. *For God's Sake . . . Unity: An Ecumenical Voyage with the Iona Community.* Glasgow: Wild Goose, 1998.

Cramb, Erik. *Fallen to Mediocrity, Called to Excellence: An Affirmation of the Spirit of Community in Britain.* Glasgow: Wild Goose, 1991.

Crawford, Nathan. *Theology as Improvisation: A Study in the Musical Nature of Theological Thinking.* Studies in Systematic Theology 13. Leiden: Brill, 2013.

Cray, Graham, Ian Mosbsy, and Aaron Kennedy, eds. *New Monasticism as Fresh Expression of Church.* London: Canterbury, 2010.

Crichton, J. D. "A Theology of Worship." In *The Study of Liturgy*, edited by Cheslyn Jones et al., 3–31. London: SPCK, 1992.

Cross, Simon. *Totally Devoted: The Challenge of New Monasticism.* Milton Keynes, UK: Authentic Media, 2010.

Cummings, Charles. *Eco-Spirituality: Towards a Reverent Life.* Mahwah, NJ: Paulist, 1991.

———. *Monastic Practices.* Kalamazoo, MI: Cistercian, 1986.

Cunningham, David. S. *These Three Are One: The Practice of Trinitarian Theology.* Oxford: Blackwell, 1998.

Dahill, Lise E. "Probing the Will of God: Bonhoeffer and Discernment." *A Journal of Theoloy* 41 (2002) 42–8.

Davies, John Gordon. *A New Dictionary of Liturgy and Worship.* London: SCM, 1986.

Davis, Dena. "Gandhi and Bonhoeffer." In *Manchester College Bulletin of the Peace Studies Institute.* 11 (June 1981) 44–49.

Dawn, Marva, and Eugene H. Peterson. *The Unnecessary Pastor: Rediscovering the Call.* Grand Rapids: Eerdmans, 2000.

Day, Thomas I. *Dietrich Bonhoeffer on Christian Community and Common Sense.* Toronto Studies in Theology 11. New York: Edwin Mellen, 1982.

D'Costa, Gavin. "Trinitarian Différance and World Religions: Postmodernity and the 'Other.'" In *Faith and Praxis in a Postmodern Age*, edited by Ursula King, 28–46. London: Cassell, 1998.

Dean-Drummond, Celia. *Eco-Theology.* London: Darton, Longman and Todd, 2008.

De Certeau, Michel. *The Practice of Everyday Life.* Translated by Steven Rendall. Berkeley: University of California Press, 1988.

De Gruchy, John W., ed. "Bonhoeffer, Apartheid and Beyond: The Reception of Bonhoeffer in South Africa." In *Bonhoeffer for a New Day: Theology in a Time of Transition*, edited by John W. de Gruchy, 353–65. Grand Rapids: Eerdmans, 1997.

———, ed. *Bonhoeffer for a New Day: Theology in a Time of Transition.* Grand Rapids: Eerdmans, 1997.

———. *Bonhoeffer and South Africa: Theology in Dialogue.* Grand Rapids: Eerdmans, 1984.

———, ed. *The Cambridge Companion to Dietrich Bonhoeffer.* Cambridge: Cambridge University Press, 1999.

———. *Cry Justice!* London: Collins, 1986.

———. *Dietrich Bonhoeffer: Witness to Jesus Christ.* London: Collins, 1988.

De Gruchy, John W., Stephen Plant, and Christiane Tietz, eds. *Dietrich Bonhoeffer's Theology Today: A Way Between Fundamentalism and Secularism?* Munich: Gutersloher Verlagshuas, 2009.

De Kerckhove, Derrick. *The Skin of Culture: Investigating the New Electronic Reality.* Toronto: Somerville, 1995.

De Lange, Frits. *Waiting for the Word: Dietrich Bonhoeffer on Speaking about God.* Grand Rapids: Eerdmans, 2000.

De Waal, Esther. *Seeking God: The Way of St. Benedict.* London: Fount, 1996.

————. *A World Made Whole: Rediscovering the Celtic Tradition.* London: Fount, 1991.

Dickinson, Emily. *The Complete Poems of Emily Dickinson.* Edited by Thomas H. Johnson. London: Faber and Faber, 1970.

Dillard, Annie. *Pilgrim at Tinker Creek.* New York: HarperPerennial, 1999.

————. *Teaching a Stone to Talk: Expeditions and Encounters.* New York: HarperPerennial, 1992.

Draper, Brian, and Kevin Draper. *Refreshing Worship.* Oxford: Bible Reading Fellowship, 2000.

Dryden, John. "A Song for St. Cecilia's Day." In *The Time of the Spirit: Readings Through the Christian Year,* edited by George Every, Richard Harries, and Kallistos Ware, 58. Crestwood, NY: St. Vladimir's Seminary Press, 1984.

Duchrow, Ulrich. "The Confessing Church and the Ecumenical Movement." In *The Ecumenical Review* 33 (1981) 212–31.

Dulles, Avery Robert. *Models of the Church: A Critical Assessment of the Church in All its Aspects.* 2nd ed. Dublin: Gill and Macmillan, 1988.

Dumas, André. *Dietrich Bonhoeffer: Theologian of Reality.* Translated by Robert McAfee Brown. New York: Macmillan, 1967.

Duncan, Denis. *Health and Healing: A Ministry to Wholeness.* Edinburgh: Saint Andrew, 1988.

Dunn, James D. G. *Unity and Diversity in the New Testament: An Inquiry into the Character of Earliest Christianity.* 2nd ed. London: SCM, 1990.

Dunn, Marilyn. *The Emergence of Monasticism from the Desert Fathers to the Early Middle Ages.* New York: Blackwell, 2000.

Dupré, Louis, and Don E. Saliers, eds. *Christian Spirituality: Post Reformation and Modern.* New York: Crossroad, 1989.

Dyson, R. W., ed. *Augustine: The City of God Against the Pagans.* Cambridge: Cambridge University Press, 1998.

Echlin, Edward P. *Earth Spirituality: Jesus at the Centre.* New Alresford, UK: Arthur James John Hunt, 1999.

Edwards, Denis, ed. *Earth Revealing, Earth Healing: Ecology and Christian Theology.* Collegeville, MN: Liturgical, 2001.

Ehrlich, Rudolf T. "Some Observations on the 'New Theology' and on Dietrich Bonhoeffer and his Ecclesiology." *Scottish Journal of Theology* 22 (1969) 30–59.

Eisland, Nancy L. *The Disabled God: Toward a Liberatory Theology of Disability.* Nashville: Abingdon, 1994.

Eliot, T. S. *Collected Poems: 1909–1962.* London: Faber and Faber, 2002.

Eriugena, John Scotus. "Eriugena's Homily on the Prologue to the Gospel of St. John." In *The Voice of the Eagle,* translated by Christopher Banford, 67–114. Great Barrington, MA: Lindisfarne, 2000.

Evdokimov, Paul. "Nature." *Scottish Journal of Theology* 18 (1965) 1–22.

Every, George, Richard Harries, and Kallistos Ware, eds. *The Time of the Spirit: Readings Through the Christian Year.* Crestwood, NY: St. Vladimir's Seminary Press, 1984.

Feil, Ernst. *The Theology of Dietrich Bonhoeffer.* Translated by Martin Rumscheidt. Philadelphia: Fortress, 1985.

Ferguson, Everet. "Catechesis and Initiation." In *The Origins of Christendom in the West,* edited by Alan Kreider, 229–68. Edinburgh: T. & T. Clark, 2001.

Ferguson, Ron, ed. *Daily Readings with George MacLeod.* Glasgow: Wild Goose, 2001.

Ferguson, Ronald. *Chasing the Wild Goose: The Story of the Iona Community.* Glasgow: Wild Goose, 1998.

———. *George MacLeod: Founder of the Iona Community.* Glasgow: Wild Goose, 2001.

Fiddes, Paul S. *The Creative Suffering of God.* Oxford: Clarendon, 1988.

———. *Participating in God: A Pastoral Doctrine of the Trinity.* London: Darton, Longman and Todd, 2000.

———. *Past Event and Present Salvation: The Christian Idea of Atonement.* London: Darton, Longman and Todd, 1989.

Finlay, Ian. *Columba.* London: Gollancz, 1979.

Finney, John. *Fading Splendour: A New Model of Renewal.* London: Darton, Longman and Todd, 2000.

Floyd, Wayne Whitson, Jr. "Other, Stranger—Enemy: Bonhoeffer and the Myth of Redemptive Violence." Unpublished paper, Bonhoeffer Archive, Union Theological Seminary, New York.

Floyd, Wayne Whitson, Jr., and Charles Marsh, eds. *Theology and the Practice of Responsibility: Essays on Dietrich Bonhoeffer.* Valley Forge, PA: Trinity, 1994.

Ford, David F. "Holiness Past and Present: Bonhoeffer, Holiness and Ethics." Paper presented at Durham University, May 18, 2000.

———. "Prayer and Righteous Action: Exploring Bonhoeffer's Suggestion." *New Blackfriars* 66 (July 1985) 336–47.

———. *Self and Salvation: Being Transformed.* Cambridge: Cambridge University Press, 1999.

Ford, David F., and Dennis L. Stamps, eds. *Essentials of Christian Community: Essays for Daniel W. Hardy.* Edinburgh: T. & T. Clark, 1996.

Forrest, Jim. *Praying with Icons.* Maryknoll, NY: Orbis, 1997.

Forrester, Duncan B. *Christian Justice and Public Policy.* Cambridge: Cambridge University Press, 1997.

Foster, Richard J. *Money, Sex and Power.* London: Hodder and Stoughton, 2000.

Fowl, Stephen E., ed. *The Theological Interpretation of Scripture: Classic and Contemporary Readings.* Oxford: Blackwell, 1996.

Fowl, Stephen E., and L. Gregory Jones. *Reading in Communion: Scripture and Ethics in Christian Life.* Reprint, Eugene, OR: Wipf and Stock, 1998.

Fraser, Bruce. "The Interpretation of Novel Metaphors." In *Metaphor and Thought*, edited by Andrew Ortony, 329–41. 2nd ed. Cambridge: Cambridge University Press, 1993.

Fraser, Ian M. *Living a Countersign: From Iona to Basic Christian Communities.* Glasgow: Wild Goose Publications, 1990.

———. *Strange Fire: Life Stories and Prayers.* Glasgow: Wild Goose, 1994.

Fritz, William. "Symphonie Bonhoeffer: Dietrich Bonhoeffer and Music." In *Journal of Church Music* 25 (Summer 1983) 4–7.

Frost, Michael. *Exiles: Living Missionally in a Post Christian Culture.* Peabody, MA: Hendrickson, 2006.

Galloway, Kathy. *Living By the Rule: The Rule of the Iona Community.* Glasgow: Wild Goose, 2010.

———, ed. *The Pattern of Our Days: Liturgies and Resources for Worship.* Glasgow: Wild Goose, 1996.

————. "Put Your Hand in My Side: Communities of Hope and Unity in Worship." In *For God's Sake . . . Unity: An Ecumenical Voyage with the Iona Community*, edited by Maxwell Craig, 13–30. Glasgow: Wild Goose, 1998.

————. *Starting Where We Are: Liberation Theology in Practice, the Story of a Neighbourhood Centre*. Glasgow: Wild Goose, 1998.

————. *A Story to Live By*. London: SPCK, 1999.

————. *Talking to the Bones: Poems, Prayers and Meditations*. London: SPCK, 1996.

————. *Walking in Darkness and Light: Sermons and Reflections*. Edinburgh: Saint Andrew, 2001.

————. "The Worship of the Iona Community." In *Worship today: Understanding, Practice, Ecumenical Implications,* edited by Thomas F. Best and Dagmar Heller, 222–30. Geneva: WCC, 2004.

Gardiner, Craig. "The Fragments and the Whole: An Examination of the Life and Works of Dietrich Bonhoeffer with Particular Attention to Stellvertretung as a Unifying Theme in His Biography and Theology." Unpublished MTh thesis, Cardiff University, 2000.

————. "Worship in the Middle of the Village: The Reality that Shines In and Out." In *Dietrich Bonhoeffer's Theology Today: A Way Between Fundamentalism and Secularism?*, edited by John W. de Gruchy, Stephen Plant, and Christiane Tietz, 262–73. Munich: Gutersloher Verlagshuas, 2009.

Garrett, James Leo, Jr., ed. *The Concept of a Believers' Church: Addresses from the 1967 Conference*. Scottdale, PA: Herald, 1969.

Geddes and Grosset. *Celtic Mythology*. New Lanark, Scotland: Geddess and Grosset, 1999.

Gestrich, Christof. "God Takes Our Place: A Religious-Philosophical Approach to the Concept of Stellvertretung." *Modern Theology* 17 (July 2001) 313–34.

Giles, Gordon. "Performing Theology Authentically." In *Creative Chords: Studies in Music, Theology and Christian Formation*, edited by Jeff Astley, Timothy Hone, and Mark Savage, 76–88. Leominster, UK: Gracewing, 2000.

Giles, Richard. *Re-pitching the Tent: Reordering Your Church Building for Worship and Mission*. Collegeville, MN: Liturgical, 1999.

Gill, Sean, ed. *The Lesbian and Gay Christian Movement: Campaigning for Justice, Truth and Love*. London: Cassell, 1998.

Girard, René. *Things Hidden Since the Foundation of the World*. Translated by Stephen Bann and Michael Metteer. Stanford: Stanford University Press, 1987.

Godsey, John D. "Dietrich Bonhoeffer and Christian Spirituality." In *Reflections on Bonhoeffer: Essays in Honor of F. Burton Nelson,* edited by Geffrey B. Kelly and C. John Weborg, 77–86. Chicago: Covenant, 1999.

————. *The Theology of Dietrich Bonhoeffer*. Philadelphia: Westminster, 1960.

Godsey, John D., and Geffrey B. Kelly, eds. *Ethical Responsibility: Bonhoeffer's Legacy to the Churches*. Toronto Studies in Theology 6. New York: Edwin Mellen, 1981.

Goldsmith, Malcolm. *Knowing Me, Knowing You: Exploring Personality Type and Temperament*. London: SPCK, 1994.

Gordon, Allan. "The National Health Service and the Health of the Nation." In *Praying for the Dawn: A Resource Book for the Ministry of Healing*, edited by Ruth Burgess and Kathy Galloway, 31–36. Glasgow: Wild Goose, 2000.

Gorringe, Timothy. *Discerning Spirit: A Theology of Revelation*. London: SCM, 1990.

Graham, John. *A Century of Welsh Music*. London: Kegan Paul, Trench, Trubner, 1923.

Grainger, Roger. *The Message of the Rite: The Significance of Christian Rites of Passage.* Cambridge: Lutterworth, 1988.

Green, Clifford. *Bonhoeffer: A Theology of Sociality.* Rev. ed. Grand Rapids: Eerdmans, 1999.

———. "Bonhoeffer's 'Non-Religious Christianity' as Public Theology." In *Dialog* 26 (Fall 1987) 275–80.

———. "Human Sociality and Christian Community." In *The Cambridge Companion to Dietrich Bonhoeffer* edited by John W. de Gruchy, 113–33. Cambridge: Cambridge University Press, 1999.

———. "Pacifism and Tyrannicide: Bonhoeffer's Christian Peace Ethic." In *Studies in Christian Ethics* 18 (2005) 31–47.

———. "Sociality and Church in Bonhoeffer's 1933 Christology." *Scottish Journal of Theology* 21 (1968) 416–34.

Green, Ian. "Build My Church—Some Theological Considerations on the Theme of Church Design." *Ministry Today* 11 (October 1997) 27–36.

Greer, Rowan A. *Broken Lights and Mended Lives: Theology and Common Life in the Early Church.* Pennsylvania: Pennsylvania State University Press, 1986.

Greggs, Tom. *Theology Against Religion: Constructive Dialogues with Bonhoeffer and Barth.* London: T. & T. Clark, 2011.

Grenz, Stanley J., and John R. Franke. *Beyond Foundationalism: Shaping Theology in a Postmodern Context.* Louisville: Westminster John Knox, 2001.

Grenz, Stanley J., and Robert E. Olson. *20th Century Theology: God and the World in a Transitional Age.* Exeter, UK: Paternoster, 1992.

Grey, Mary C. *Beyond the Dark Night: A Way Forward for the Church?* London: Cassell, 1997.

———. *The Outrageous Pursuit of Hope: Prophetic Dreams for the Twenty–First Century.* London: Darton, Longman and Todd, 2000.

———. *Prophecy and Mysticism: The Heart of the Postmodern Church.* Edinburgh: T. & T. Clark, 1997.

———. *Sacred Longings: Ecofeminist Theology and Globalisation.* London: SCM, 2003.

———. "The Shaking of the Foundations—Again! Is There a Future for the Christian Theology?" Von Hügel Lecture, 1994. Cambridge: Von Hügel Institute, 1995.

———. "A Vanished Integrity? Epiphanies of Grace in a Fragmented World." Anne Spencer Memorial Sermon, University of Bristol, Anglican Chaplaincy Church, February 1995. Copy obtained from the author.

Grimley, Anthony, and Jonathan M. Wooding. *Living the Hours: Monastic Spirituality in Everyday Life.* Norwich, UK: Canterbury, 2010.

Gunton, Colin E. *The Actuality of Atonement: A Study of Metaphor, Rationality and the Christian Tradition.* Edinburgh: T. & T. Clark, 1988.

———. *Promise of Trinitarian Theology.* Edinburgh: T. & T. Clark, 1991.

Gutiérrez, G. "The Task and Content of Liberation Theology." In *The Cambridge Companion to Liberation Theology,* edited by Christopher Rowland, 19–38. Cambridge: Cambridge University Press, 1999.

Gwynn Williams, W. S. *Welsh National Music and Dance.* London: Curwen, 1932.

Hall, Douglas John. *Imaging God: Dominion as Stewardship.* Grand Rapids: Eerdmans, 1986.

Hall, Stuart G. *Doctrine and Practice in the Early Church.* London: SPCK, 1991.

Hammond, Peter. *Towards a Church Architecture.* London: Architectural, 1962.

Harmless, William. *Augustine and the Catechumenate*. Collegeville, MN: Liturgical, 1995.

Harrison, Carol. *Augustine: Christian Truth and Fractured Humanity*. Oxford: Oxford University Press, 2000.

Harvey, Barry. "The Body Politic of Christ: Theology, Social Analysis, and Bonhoeffer's Arcane Discipline." *Modern Theology* 13 (July 1997) 319–46.

Hauerwas, Stanley. *After Christendom: How the Church is to Behave if Freedom, Justice, and a Christian Nation Are Bad Ideas*. Nashville: Abingdon, 1991.

———. *Christian Existence Today: Essays on Church, World and Living In Between*. Grand Rapids: Baker, 1995.

———. *Performing the Faith: Bonhoeffer and the Practice of Nonviolence*. London: SPCK, 2004.

———. *Vision and Virtue: Essays in Christian Ethical Reflection*. Notre Dame: University of Notre Dame Press, 1981.

Hauerwas, Stanley, and William H. Willimon. *Resident Aliens: Life in the Christian Colony*. Nashville: Abingdon, 1989.

———. *Where Resident Aliens Live: Exercises for Christian Practice*. Nashville: Abingdon, 1996.

Hawn, C. Michael. *Gather Into One: Praying and Singing Globally*. Grand Rapids: Eerdmans, 2003.

Hawthorne, Gerald F. *Philippians*. Word Biblical Commentary 43. Waco, TX: Word Books, 1983.

Hick, John, and Paul Knitter, eds. *The Myth of Christian Uniqueness: Towards a Pluralistic Theology of Religions*. Maryknoll, NY: Orbis, 1988.

Hinson, Glenn E. "Spiritual Preparation for Apocalypse: Learning from Bonhoeffer." In *Cistercian Studies* 23 (1988) 156–68.

Holloway, Richard. *Dancing on the Edge: Faith in a Post Christian Age*. London: Fount, 1997.

———. *Godless Morality: Keeping Religion Out of Ethics*. Edinburgh: Canongate, 1999

Holness, Lyn, and Ralf K. Wustenberg, eds. *Theology in Dialogue: The Impact of the Arts, Humanities, and Science on Contemporary Religious Thought, Essays in Honor of John W. de Gruchy*. Grand Rapids: Eerdmans, 2002.

Holst, Imogen. *Gustav Holst: A Biography*. Oxford: Oxford University Press, 1988.

Holt, Bradley P. *A Brief History of Christian Spirituality*. Oxford: Lion, 1993.

Hooft, William A. Visser't. "Dietrich Bonhoeffer and the Self-Understanding of the Ecumenical Movement." *The Ecumenical Review* 28 (1976) 198–203.

Hope, Stanley. *Liberty to the Captives: Christianity, Racism and the Law in the UK*. Glasgow: Iona Community Working Group on Interfaith and Racism, 1992.

Hopkins, Gerard Manley. *The Complete Poems With Selected Prose*. London: Fount Classics, 1996.

Hopper, David H. *A Dissent on Bonhoeffer*. Philadelphia: Westminster, 1975.

House, Paul R. *Bonhoeffer's Seminary Vision: A Case for Costly Discipleship and Life Together*. Wheaton, IL: Crossway, 2015.

Huber, Wolfgang. "Bonhoeffer and Modernity." In *Theology and the Practice of Responsibility, Theology and the Practice of Responsibility: Essays on Dietrich Bonhoeffer*, edited by Wayne Whitson Floyd, Jr., and Charles Marsh, 5–20. Valley Forge, PA: Trinity, 1994.

Hugo, Victor. *Les Misérables.* Translated by Charles E. Wilbour. London: Everyman's Library Classics, 1998.

Hume, Basil. *Searching for God.* London: Hodder and Stoughton, 1977.

Huntemann, Georg. *The Other Bonhoeffer: An Evangelical Reassessment of Dietrich Bonhoeffer.* Translated by Todd Huizinga. Grand Rapids: Baker, 1993.

Hunter, David G. "A Decade of Research on Early Christians and Military Service." *Religious Studies Review* 18 (1992) 87–94.

Iona Community. *The Coracle, Rebuilding the Common Life: Foundation Documents of the Iona Community.* Glasgow: Wild Goose, 1988.

———. *Iona Abbey Worship Book.* Glasgow: Wild Goose, 2001.

———. *Iona Community Members' Prayer Book.* Glasgow: Internal Community Publication, 2017.

Isherwood, Lisa, and Elaine Bellchambers, eds. *Through Us, With Us, In Us: Relational Theologies in the Twenty-First Century.* London: SCM, 2010.

Jackson, W. F. *St. Augustine's De Musica: A Synopsis.* Westport, CT: Hyperion, 1949.

James, Eric. "The Growth of the Convictions of Dietrich Bonhoeffer Concerning War and Peace." *Christian Action Journal* 75 (Winter 1974) 5–12.

Jamison, Christopher. *Finding Sanctuary: Monastic Steps for Everyday Life.* London: Weidenfeld and Nicolson, 2006.

Jehle, Herbert. "Dietrich Bonhoeffer on War and Peace." In *A Bonhoeffer Legacy: Essays in Understanding,* edited by A. J. Klassen, 362–66. Grand Rapids: Eerdmans, 1981.

Jenkins, Willis, and Jennifer M. McBride, eds. *Bonhoeffer and King: Their Legacies and Import for Christian Social Thought.* Minneapolis: Fortress, 2010.

Jenson, Michael P. *Martyrdom and Identity: The Self on Trial.* London: T. & T. Clark, 2010.

Jenson, Robert W. *The Triune God.* Vol. 1, *Systematic Theology.* Oxford: Oxford University Press, 1997.

———. *The Works of God.* Vol. 2, *Systematic Theology.* Oxford: Oxford University Press, 1999.

Jones, Carolyn M. "Dietrich Bonhoeffer's Letters and Papers from Prison: Rethinking the Relationship of Theology and Arts, Literature and Religion." *Literature and Theology* 9 (September 1995) 243–59.

Jones, Cheslyn, Geoffrey Wainwright, and Edward Yarnold, eds. *The Study of Spirituality.* London SPCK, 1992.

Jones, Cheslyn, et al., eds. *The Study of Liturgy.* London: SPCK, 1992.

Jones, James. *Jesus and the Earth.* London: SPCK, 2003.

Jones, L. Gregory. *Embodying Forgiveness: A Theological Analysis.* Grand Rapids: Eerdmans, 1995.

Jones, Simon. *Windows into Heaven.* Oxford: Lion, 1998.

Jones, W. Paul. *Theological Worlds: Understanding the Alternative Rhythms of Christian Belief.* Nashville: Abingdon, 1989.

———. *Trumpet at Full Moon: An Introduction to Christian Spirituality as Diverse Practice.* Louisville: Westminster John Knox, 1992.

———. *Worlds Within a Congregation: Dealing with Theological Diversity.* Nashville: Abingdon, 2000.

Jordan, William. "Augustine on Music." In *Grace, Politics and Desire,* edited by Hugo A. Meynell, 123–35. Calgary: University of Calgary Press, 1990.

Julian, of Norwich. *Revelations of Divine Love.* Translated by Clifton Wolters. London: Penguin, 1966.

Kaan, Fred. "The Church is Like a Table." In *Rejoice and Sing: United Reformed Hymnbook.* Oxford: Oxford University Press, 1991.

Kalu, Ogbu U., Peter Vethanayagamony, and Edmund Kee-Fook Chia, eds. *Mission After Christendom: Emergent Themes in Contemporary Mission.* Louisville: Westminster John Knox, 2010.

Keller, Timothy. *Counterfeit Gods: When the Empty Promises of Love, Money and Power Let You Down.* London: Hodder and Stoughton, 2009.

Kelly, Geffrey B. "Bonhoeffer and the Jews: Implications for Jewish—Christian Reconciliation." In *Reflections on Bonhoeffer, Essays in Honor of F. Burton Nelson,* edited by Geffrey B. Kelly and C. John Weborg, 133–66. Chicago: Covenant, 1999.

———. "Freedom and Discipline: Rhythms of A Christocentric Spirituality." In *Ethical Responsibility: Bonhoeffer's Legacy to the Churches,* edited by John Godsey and Geffrey B. Kelly, 307–32. Toronto Studies in Theology 6. New York: Edwin Mellen, 1980.

———. "Freedom and Obedience: Reflections on the Spiritual Legacy of Dietrich Bonhoeffer." *Weavings* 3 (May–June 1988) 14–25.

———. "An Interview With Jean Lasserre." In *Union Seminary Quarterly Review* 27 (Spring 1972) 149–60.

———. "Prayer and Righteous Action." In *The Cambridge Companion to Dietrich Bonhoeffer,* edited by John W. de Gruchy, 246–68. Cambridge University Press, 1999.

———. "Sharing in the Pain of God: Dietrich Bonhoeffer's Reflections on Christian Vulnerability." In *Communion, Community, Commonweal: Readings For Spiritual Leadership,* edited by J. S. Mogabgab, 139–47. Nashville: Upper Room, 1995.

———. "'Unconscious Christianity' and the 'Anonymous Christian' in the Theology of Dietrich Bonhoeffer and Karl Rahner." *Philosophy and Theology* 9 (1995) 117–49.

Kelly, Geffrey B., and C. J. Weborg, eds. *Reflections on Bonhoeffer: Essays in Honor of F. Burton Nelson.* Chicago: Covenant, 1999.

Kelly, Geffrey B., and F. Burton Nelson. *The Cost of Moral Leadership: The Spirituality of Bonhoeffer.* Grand Rapids: Eerdmans, 2003.

———. *A Testament to Freedom: The Essential Writings of Dietrich Bonhoeffer.* New York: HarperCollins, 1995.

Kelly, J. N. D. *Early Christian Doctrines.* 5th ed. London: Continuum, 2004.

Kelsey, Morton T. *Healing and Christianity: In Ancient Thought and Modern Times.* London: SCM, 1973.

Kemp, Walter H. "Polyphonous Christian Community of Dietrich Bonhoeffer." In *Lutheran Quarterly* 28 (February 1976) 6–20.

———. "The 'Polyphony of Life': References to Music in Bonhoeffer's Letters and Papers From Prison." In *Vita Laudanda: Essays in Memory of Ulrich S. Leupold,* edited by Erich R. W. Schultz, 137–54. Waterloo: Wilfrid Laurier University Press, 1976.

Kenneson, Philip D. "Worship Wars and Rumours of Worship Wars." In *Reviews in Religion and Theology* 2 (May 1996) 72–75.

Ketcherside, W. Carl. *Colony of Heaven.* St. Louis: Mission Messenger, n.d.

Keyes, Richard. *Chameleon or Tribe? Recovering Authentic Christian Community.* Downers Grove, IL: InterVarsity, 1999.

Kierkegaard, Søren. *Philosophical Fragments.* Translated by Niels Thulstrup. 2nd ed. Princeton: Princeton University Press, 1962.

Kilde, Jeanne Halgren. *Sacred Power, Sacred Space: An Introduction to Christian Architecture and Worship.* Oxford: Oxford University Press, 2008.

King, Martin Luther, Jr. "Dreams of Brighter Tomorrows." *Ebony* 20 (March 1965) 34–35.

King, Ursula, ed. *Faith and Praxis in a Postmodern Age.* London: Cassell, 1998.

————. *Feminist Theology from the Third World: A Reader.* London: SPCK, 1994.

Kirkpatrick, Matthew D. ed. *Engaging Bonhoeffer: The Impact and Influence of Bonhoeffer's Life and Thought.* Minneapolis: Fortress, 2016.

Klassen, A. J., ed. *A Bonhoeffer Legacy: Essays in Understanding.* Grand Rapids: Eerdmans, 1981.

Knitter, Paul F. "Toward a Liberation Theology of Religions." In *The Myth of Christian Uniqueness: Towards a Pluralistic Theology of Religions,* edited by John Hick and Paul Knitter, 178–200. Maryknoll, NY: Orbis, 1988.

Knowles, David. *Christian Monasticism.* New York: McGraw-Hill, 1969.

Koestler, Arthur. *The Act of Creation.* London: Arkana, 1989.

Kohler, R. F. "The Christocentric Ethics of Dietrich Bonhoeffer." *Scottish Journal of Theology* 23 (February 1970) 27–40.

Koyama, Kosuke. "The Eucharist: Ecumenical and Ecological." *Ecumenical Review* 44 (January 1992) 80–90.

Kraus, Norman C. *The Community of the Spirit: How the Church Is in the World.* rev. ed. Scottdale, PA: Herald, 1993.

Kreider, Alan, ed. *The Origins of Christendom in the West.* Edinburgh: T. & T. Clark, 2001.

————. *Worship and Evangelism in Pre-Christendom.* Cambridge: Grove, 1995.

Kreider, Alan, and Eleanor Kreider. *Worship and Mission After Christendom.* Milton Keynes, UK: Paternoster, 2009.

Kreider, Eleanor. *Enter His Gates: Fitting Worship Together.* London: Marshall, Morgan and Scott, 1989.

Kuhns, William. *In Pursuit of Dietrich Bonhoeffer.* London: Burns and Oates, 1967.

Küng, Hans. *Mozart: Traces of Transcendence.* London: SCM, 1992.

————. *On Being a Christian.* London: Collins, 1977.

Kvale, Steiner. *Psychology and Postmodernism.* London: SAGE, 1992.

Lakeland, Paul. *Postmodernity: Christian Identity in a Fragmented Age.* Minneapolis: Fortress, 1997.

Lambourne, R. A. *Community, Church and Healing.* London: Darton, Longman and Todd, 1963.

Lange, Ernst. *And Yet it Moves: Dream and Reality of the Ecumenical Movement.* Belfast: Christian Journals, 1978.

Lash, Nicholas. *Theology on the Way to Emmaus.* London: SCM, 1986.

Lasserre, Jean. "Remembrances of Dietrich Bonhoeffer." *International Bonhoeffer Society for Archive and Research, English Language Section* 31 (February 1986) 1–4.

Lawrence, C. H. *Medieval Monasticism: Forms of Religious Life in Western Europe in the Middle Ages.* 2nd ed. London: Longman, 1989.

Leclercq, Jean. *The Love of Learning and the Desire for God: A Study of Monastic Culture.* New York: Fordham University Press, 1974.

Lee, Philip J. *Against the Protestant Gnostics.* New York: Oxford University Press, 1987.

Legum, Margaret. *It Doesn't Have to Be Like This: Global Economics: A New Way Forward*. Glasgow: Wild Goose, 2003.

Leibholz-Bonhoeffer, Sabine. *The Bonhoeffers: A Portrait of a Family*. Chicago: Covenant, 1994.

Lewis, C. S. *The Weight of Glory: A Collection of Lewis' Most Moving Addresses*. London: William Collins, 2013.

Loades, Ann, ed. *Feminist Theology: A Reader*. London: SPCK, 1990.

Lockley, Harold. *Dietrich Bonhoeffer, His Ethics and its Value for Christian Ethics Today*. Swansea, UK: Phoenix, 1993.

Long, Thomas G. *Beyond the Worship Wars: Building Vital and Faithful Worship*. Bethesda, MD: Alban Institute, 2001.

Loughlin, Gerard. *Telling God's Story: Bible, Church and Narrative Theology*. Cambridge: Cambridge University Press, 1996.

Lovelock, J. E. *Gaia: A New Look at Life on Earth*. Oxford: Oxford University Press, 2000.

Low, Mary. *Celtic Christianity and Nature: Early Irish and Hebridean Traditions*. Edinburgh: Edinburgh University Press, 1996.

Lowes, Anthony. "Up Close and Personal: In the End Matter Matters." In *Earth Revealing, Earth Healing: Ecology and Christian Theology*, edited by Denis Edwards, 125–43. Collegeville, MN: Liturgical, 2001.

Maas, Robin, and Gabriel O'Donnell, eds. *Spiritual Traditions for the Contemporary Church*. Nashville: Abingdon, 1990.

MacArthur, E. Mairi. *Columba's Island: Iona From Past to Present*. Edinburgh: Edinburgh University Press, 1995.

Macgregor, G. H. C. *The New Testament Basis of Pacifism*. New York: Fellowship Publications, 1954.

MacIntyre, Alasdair. *After Virtue: A Study in Moral Theory*. 2nd ed. London: Duckworth, 1985.

MacLeod, George F. "Abundant Life On Earth." In *The Way to God: Broadcast Talks, Second Series*, edited by C. C. Martindale, C. E. Raven, and G. F. MacLeod, 123–36. London: SCM, 1935.

———. "As it Is in Heaven." In *The Way to God: Broadcast Talks, Second Series*, edited by C. C. Martindale, C. E. Raven, and G. F. MacLeod, 137–51. London: SCM, 1935.

———. *Govan Calling: Sermons and Addresses*. London: Methuen, 1934.

———. *Only One Way Left*. Glasgow: Iona Community, 1956.

———. *The Place of Healing in the Ministry of the Church*. Glasgow: Iona Community, n.d.

———. *Speaking the Truth in Love: The Modern Teacher's Task*. London: SCM, 1936.

———. *We Shall Rebuild: The Work of the Iona Community on Mainland and on Island*. Glasgow: Iona Community, 1962.

———. *The Whole Earth Shall Cry Glory, Iona Prayers by Rev. George F. MacLeod*. Glasgow: Wild Goose, 1985.

———. *With Singing Hands: Studies from "We Shall Rebuild."* Melbourne: Presbyterian Board of Religious Education, 1946.

MacMillan, James. "Sound of Heart." *Third Way* 22 (June 1999) 18–21.

Macmurray, John. *Persons in Relation*. New York: Humanities Press, 1991.

———. *The Self as Agent*. London: Faber and Faber, 1969.

Manley Hopkins, Gerard. *The Complete Poems with Selected Prose*. London: Fount, 1996.

Maries, Andrew, John L. Bell, and Michael Joncas. "Music in the Mission of the Church." Papers from the Sing our God Together Conference, Birmingham, Alabama, 1996. Mildenhall, UK: Decani, 1996.

Markofski, Wes. *New Monasticism and the Transformation of American Evangelicalism*. New York: Oxford University Press, 2015.

Marsh, Charles. *Reclaiming Dietrich Bonhoeffer: The Promise of His Theology*. Oxford: Oxford University Press, 1994.

———. *Strange Glory: A Life of Dietrich Bonhoeffer*, London: SPCK, 2014.

Marshall, Howard. "Climbing Ropes, Ellipses and Symphonies: The Relation between Biblical and Systematic Theology." In *A Pathway into the Holy Scripture*, edited by P. E. Satterthwaite and D. F. Wright, 199–220. Grand Rapids: Eerdmans, 1994.

Marshall, Howard I., and David Peterson, eds. *Witness to the Gospel: The Theology of Acts*. Grand Rapids: Eerdmans, 1998.

Martin, Ralph P. *New Century Bible Commentary: Philippians*. London: Oliphants, 1976.

Marty, Martin E. *The Place of Bonhoeffer: Problems and Possibilities in His Thought*. London: SCM, 1963.

Matt, Daniel C., trans. *The Essential Kabbalah: The Heart of Jewish Mysticism*. San Francisco: HarperSanFrancisco, 1997.

Matthews, John W. "Responsible Sharing of the Mystery of Christian Faith: *Disciplina Arcani* in the Life of Dietrich Bonhoeffer." In *Reflections on Bonhoeffer: Essays in Honor of F. Burton Nelson*, edited by Geffrey. B. Kelly and C. J. Weborg, 114–26. Chicago: Covenant, 1999.

Mayland, Jean. "Unity in Believing." In *For God's Sake . . . Unity: An Ecumenical Voyage with the Iona Community*, edited by Maxwell Craig, 51–74. Glasgow: Wild Goose, 1998.

Mayne, Michael. *Learning to Dance*. London: Darton, Longman, and Todd, 2001.

Mays, James Luther, ed. *Interpreting the Gospels*. Philadelphia: Fortress, 1981.

McCloughry, Roy, and Wayne Morris. *Making a World of Difference: Christian Reflections on Disability*. London: SPCK, 2002.

McDonagh, Sean. *The Greening of the Church*. Maryknoll, NY: Orbis, 1990.

———. *Passion for the Earth: The Christian Vocation to Promote Justice, Peace and the Integrity of Creation*. London: Geoffrey Chapman, 1994.

McFadyen, A. I. *Bound to Sin: Abuse, Holocaust and the Christian Doctrine of Sin*. Cambridge: Cambridge University Press, 2000.

———. "The Call to Discipleship: Reflections on Bonhoeffer's Theme 50 years on." *Scottish Journal of Theology* 43 (1990) 461–83.

———. *The Call to Personhood: A Christian Theory of the Individual in Social Relationships*. Cambridge: Cambridge University Press, 1990.

McFague, Sallie. *Life Abundant: Rethinking Theology and Economy for a Planet in Peril*. Minneapolis: Fortress, 2001.

———. *Metaphorical Theology: Models of God in Religious Language*. Minneapolis: Fortress, 1982.

———. *Models of God: Theology for an Ecological, Nuclear Age*. Minneapolis: Fortress, 1987.

————. *Speaking in Parables: A Study in Metaphor and Theology.* 2nd ed. London: SCM, 2002.

McGinn, Bernard, John Meyendorff, and Jean Leclercq, eds. *Christian Spirituality: Origins to the Twelfth Century.* London: SCM, 1989.

McIlhagga, Kate. "The Church's Healing Ministry." In *Praying for the Dawn: A Resource Book for the Ministry of Healing,* edited by Ruth Burgess and Kathy Galloway, 13–14. Glasgow: Wild Goose, 2000.

McIntosh, Mark A. *Mystical Theology: The Integrity of Spirituality and Theology.* Oxford: Blackwell, 1998.

McKinnon, James, ed. *The Early Christian Period and the Latin Middle Ages.* Vol. 2, *Source Readings in Music History,* edited by Oliver Strunk. London: Norton, 1998.

————. *Music in Early Christian Literature.* Cambridge: Cambridge University Press, 1987.

Mellers, Wilfred. *Bach and the Dance of God.* London: Faber and Faber, 1980.

Merton, Thomas. *Bread in the Wilderness.* Collegeville, MN: Liturgical, 1963.

————. *Conjectures of a Guilty Bystander.* Garden City, NY: Doubleday, 1966.

————. *The Wisdom of the Desert.* Tunbridge Wells, UK: Burns and Oates, 1997.

Metaxas, Eric. *Bonhoeffer: Pastor, Martyr, Prophet, Spy.* Nashville: Thomas Nelson, 2010.

Meynell, Hugo A., ed. *Grace, Politics and Desire: Essays on Augustine.* Calgary: University of Calgary Press, 1990.

Milbank, John. "Postmodern Critical Augustinianism: A Short Summa in Forty-Two Responses to Unasked Questions." *Modern Theology* 7 (April 1991) 225–37.

————. *Theology and Social Theory: Beyond Secular Reason.* Cambridge: Basil Blackwell, 1991.

Millar, Peter. *An Iona Prayer Book.* Norwich, UK: Canterbury, 1998.

————. *Waymarks: Signposts to Discovering God's Presence in the World.* Norwich, UK: Canterbury, 2000.

Miller, Calvin. *The Singer Trilogy: The Mythic Retelling of the Story of the New Testament.* Downers Grove, IL: InterVarsity, 1990.

Minear, Paul S. *Images of the Church in the New Testament.* Philadelphia: Westminster, 1960.

Mobsby, Ian, and Mark Berry. *A New Monastic Handbook: From Vision to Practice.* Norwich, UK: Canterbury, 2014.

Moffat, James A. R., trans. *The Bible: James Moffatt Translation.* San Francisco: HarperSanFrancisco, 1994.

Mogabgab, John S. "Active Waiting." *Weavings* 2 (January–February 1987) 2–43.

————, ed. *Communion, Community, Commonweal: Readings for Spiritual Leadership.* Nashville: Upper Room, 1995.

Moltmann, Jürgen. *The Church in the Power of the Spirit: a Contribution to Messianic Ecclesiology.* 2nd ed. London: SCM, 1992.

————. *The Crucified God: The Cross of Christ as the Foundation and Criticism of Christian Theology.* London: SCM, 1974.

————. *Experiences of God.* London: SCM, 1980.

————. *God for a Secular Society: The Public Relevance of Theology.* London: SCM, 1999.

————. *God in Creation: An Ecological Doctrine of Creation.* London: SCM, 1985.

————. *Jesus Christ for Today's World.* London: SCM, 1994.

————. *The Open Church: Invitation to a Messianic Lifestyle.* London: SCM, 1978.

————. *The Source of Life: The Holy Spirit and the Theology of Life.* London: SCM, 1997.

Moltmann, Jürgen, and Jürgen Weissbach. *Two Studies in the Theology of Dietrich Bonhoeffer.* New York: Scribner, 1967.

Monteith, Graham W. "The Service of Prayers for Healing of the Iona Community: A Historical and Theological Perspective." In *Praying for the Dawn: A Resource Book for the Ministry of Healing,* edited by Ruth Burgess and Kathy Galloway, 17–22. Glasgow: Wild Goose, 2000.

Moore, Gareth. "Singing a New Song: Music and Justice in the Bible." *Theology* 107 (2004) 159–68.

Mootry, Maria, and Gary Smith. *A Life Distilled: Gwendolyn Brooks, The Poetry and Fiction.* Urbana: University of Illinois Press, 1988.

Morris, Kenneth Earl. *Bonhoeffer's Ethic of Discipleship: A Study in Psychology, Political Thought, and Religion.* University Park: Pennsylvania State University Press, 1986.

Morton, T. Ralph. "Divine Healing." *Coracle* 22 (July 1952) 20–22.

————. *The Household of Faith: An Essay of the Changing Pattern of the Church's Life.* Glasgow: Iona Community, 1951.

————. *The Iona Community: Personal Impressions of the Early Years.* Edinburgh: Saint Andrew, 1977.

Moses, John A. "Dietrich Bonhoeffer's Struggle for the 'True Church' in Germany Under Nazi Rule." Unpublished seminar held at St. Mark's Theological Centre, Canberra, May 23, 1996. Bonhoeffer Archive, Union Theological Seminary, New York.

Muers, Rachel. "Bonhoeffer, King, and Feminism: Problems and Possibilities." In *Bonhoeffer and King: Their Legacies and Import for Christian Social Thought,* edited by Willis Jenkins and Jennifer M. McBride, 33–42. Minneapolis: Fortress, 2010.

————. *Keeping God's Silence: Towards a Theological Ethics of Communication.* Oxford: Blackwell, 2004.

Muir, Anne. *Outside the Safe Place: An Oral History of the Early Years of the Iona Community.* Glasgow: Wild Goose, 2011.

Muller, Denis G. "Bonhoeffer's Ethic of Responsibility and its Meaning for Today." *Theology* 100 (1997) 108–15.

Murray, Stuart. *Church After Christendom.* Milton Keynes, UK: Paternoster, 2004.

————. *Post-Christendom: Church and Mission in a Strange New World.* Milton Keynes, UK: Paternoster, 2004.

Murray, Stuart, and Sian Murray Williams. *Multi-voiced Church.* Milton Keynes, UK: Paternoster, 2012.

Nation, Mark Thiessen. "Discipleship in a World Full of Nazis: Dietrich Bonhoeffer's Polyphonic Pacifism as Social Ethics." In *The Wisdom of the Cross: Essays in Honor of John Howard Yoder,* edited by Stanley Hauerwas et al. 249–77. Grand Rapids: Eerdmans, 1999.

————. "The First Word Christians Have to Say About Violence is 'Church': On Bonhoeffer, Baptists, and Becoming a Peace Church." In *Faithfulness and Fortitude: Essays in Conversation With the Theological Ethics of Stanley Hauerwas,* edited by Mark Thiessen Nation and Samuel Wells, 83–116. Edinburgh: T. & T. Clark, 2000.

————. "'Pacifist and Enemy of the State': Bonhoeffer's 'Straight and Unbroken Course' from Costly Discipleship to Conspiracy." *Journal of Theology for Southern Africa* 77 (1991) 61–77.

Nation, Mark Thiessen, Anthony G. Siegrist, and Daniel P. Umbel. *Bonhoeffer the Assassin: Challenging the Myth, Recovering His Call to Peacemaking.* Grand Rapids: Baker, 2013.

Neel, Eleanor S. "A Comparison of the Spiritual Principles Operative in the *Sanctorum Communio* with Those of Contemporary Secular Organization such as Amnesty International as Evidence of the Non-Religious Interpretation of the Gospel." Unpublished paper presented at the Fourth International Bonhoeffer Conference, Hirschluch, Germany, 1984. Bonhoeffer Archive, Union Seminary, New York.

———. "'Incognito' as a Key to the Future Church's Way of Being and Working in the World." Unpublished paper, Bonhoeffer Archive, Union Seminary, New York.

Nelson, Amy. *Music for the Revolution: Musicians and Power in Early Soviet Russia.* University Park: Pennsylvania State University Press, 2004.

Nelson, F. Burton. "The Relationship of Jean Lasserre to Dietrich Bonhoeffer's Peace Concerns in the Struggle of the Church and Culture." *Union Seminary Quarterly Review* 40 (1985) 71–84.

Newell, Philip J. *Echo of the Soul: The Sacredness of the Human Body.* Norwich, UK: Canterbury, 2000.

———. *Listening for the Heart Beat of God: A Celtic Spirituality.* London: SPCK, 1997.

Newman, John Henry. *The Church of the Fathers; St. Chrysostom; Theodoret; Mission of St. Benedict; Benedictine Schools.* Vol. 2, *Historical Sketches.* London: Longmans, 1906.

Niebuhr, H. Richard. *Christ and Culture.* New York: Harper & Row, 1951.

Ní Riain, Nóirín. "The Specificity of Christian Theosony: Towards a Theology of Listening." PhD diss., University of Limerick, 2003.

O'Donohue, John. *Anam Cara: Spiritual Wisdom from the Celtic World.* London: Bantam, 1997.

O'Meara, Dominic J. *Plotinus: An Introduction to the Enneads.* Oxford: Clarendon, 1995.

O'Murchu, Diarmuid. *Poverty, Celibacy and Obedience: A Radical Option for Life.* New York: Crossroad, 1999.

Orr, James, ed. *The International Standard Bible Encyclopedia.* Vol. 4, *Naarah-Socho.* Reprint, Grand Rapids: Eerdmans, 1986.

Ortony, Andrew, ed. *Metaphor and Thought.* 2nd ed. Cambridge: Cambridge University Press, 1993.

O'Siadhail, Micheal. *Our Double Time.* Newcastle upon Tyne, UK: Bloodaxe Books, 1998.

———. *Poems 1975–1995: Hail!, Madam Jazz, A Fragile City.* Newcastle upon Tyne, UK: Bloodaxe Books, 1999.

Otto, Rudolph. *The Idea of the Holy: An Enquiry into the Non-Rational Factor in the Idea of the Divine and its Relation to the Rational.* Translated by John W. Harvey. 2nd ed. London: Oxford University Press, 1950.

Ouspensky, Leonid, and Vladimir Lossky. *The Meaning of Icons.* Crestwood, NY: St. Vladimir's Seminary Press, 1983.

Page, Ruth. *God and the Web of Creation.* London: SCM, 1996.

Pangritz, Andreas. *Karl Barth in the Theology of Dietrich Bonhoeffer.* Translated by Barbara Rumscheidt and Martin Rumscheidt. Grand Rapids: Eerdmans, 2000.

———. "Point and Counterpoint—Resistance and Submission: Dietrich Bonhoeffer on Theology and Music in Times of War and Social Crisis." In *Theology in Dialogue:*

The Impact of the Arts, Humanities, and Science on Contemporary Religious Thought, Essays in Honor of John W. de Gruchy, edited by Lyn Holness and Ralf K. Wustenberg, 28–42. Grand Rapids: Eerdmans, 2002.

———. "Sharing the Destiny of His People." In *Bonhoeffer for a New Day: Theology in a Time of Transition,* edited by John W. de Gruchy, 258–77. Grand Rapids: Eerdmans, 1997.

Panikkar, Raimundo. *Blessed Simplicity: The Monk as Universal Archetype.* New York: Seabury, 1982.

Patrides, C. A. *The English Poems of George Herbert.* London: Dent, 1974.

Pattison, Stephen. *Alive and Kicking: Towards a Practical Theology of Illness and Healing.* London: SCM, 1989.

———. "Public Theology: A Polemical Epilogue." *Political Theology* 2 (2000) 57–76.

Paynter, Neil, ed. *This Is the Day: Readings and Meditations from the Iona Community.* Glasgow: Wild Goose, 2002.

Peck, William J., ed. *New Studies on Bonhoeffer's Ethics.* Toronto Studies in Theology 30. Lewiston, NY: Edwin Mellen, 1987.

———. "The Significance of Bonhoeffer's Interest in India." *Harvard Theological Review* 61 (July 1968) 431–50.

Peddie, Cameron. *The Forgotten Talent.* London: Fontana, 1966.

Pelikan, Jaroslav. *The Melody of Theology: A Philosophical Dictionary.* London: Harvard University Press, 1988.

Peterson, Eugene H. *Answering God: The Psalms as Tools for Prayer.* New York: Harper Collins, 1991.

———. *Christ Plays in Ten Thousand Places: A Conversation in Spiritual Theology.* London: Hodder and Stoughton, 2005.

———. *Under the Unpredictable Plant: An Exploration in Vocational Holiness.* Grand Rapids: Eerdmans, 1992.

Phillips, John A. *The Form of Christ in the World: A Study of Bonhoeffer's Christology.* London: Collins, 1967.

Pickstock, Catherine. "Ascending Numbers: Augustine's *De Musica* and the Western Tradition." In *Christian Origins: Theology, Rhetoric and Community,* edited by Lewis Ayres and Gareth Jones, 185–215. London: Routledge, 1998.

Pinder, Kymberly N. "'Our Father, God; Our Brother, Christ; or Are We Bastard Kin?' Images of Christ in African American Painting." *African American Review* 31 (1997) 223–33.

Plant, Stephen. *Bonhoeffer.* London: Continuum, 2004.

———. "Dietrich Bonhoeffer's Interfaith Encounters." *Discernment* 3 (1988) 19–23.

———. *Taking Stock of Bonhoeffer: Studies in Biblical Interpretation and Ethics.* London: Routledge, 2014.

Plant, Stephen, and Ralf K. Wüstenberg, eds. *Religion, Religionlessness and Contemporary Western Culture: Explorations in Dietrich Bonhoeffer's Theology.* Oxford: Peter Lang, 2008.

Pohier, Jacques. *God In Fragments.* Translated by John Bowden. London: SCM, 1985.

Poole, Roger. "Bonhoeffer and the Arcane Discipline." In *Ethical Responsibility: Bonhoeffer's Legacy to the Churches,* edited by John D. Godsey and Geffrey B. Kelly, 271–91. Toronto Studies in Theology 6. New York: Edwin Mellen, 1981.

Porritt, Jonathon. *Seeing Green: The Politics of Ecology Explained.* Oxford: Basil Blackwell, 1984.

Postman, Neil. *Amusing Ourselves to Death: Public Discourse in the Age of Show Business.* London: William Heinemann, 1986.

Poulose, Poulose Mar. "The Understanding of Bonhoeffer in India." In *Bonhoeffer's Ethics: Old Europe and New Frontiers,* edited by Guy C. Carter, and R. Van Edyen, 212–15. Kampen, Netherlands: Kok Pharos, 1991.

Poythress, Vern S. *Symphonic Theology: The Validity of Multiple Perspectives in Theology.* Phillipsburg, NJ: P & R, 2001.

Prance, Ghillean. *The Earth Under Threat: A Christian Perspective.* Glasgow: Wild Goose, 1996.

Price, Peter B. *Undersong: Listening to the Soul.* London: Darton, Longman and Todd, 2002.

Pritchard, John. *The Intercessions Handbook: Creative Ideas for Public and Private Prayer.* London: SPCK, 1997.

Pugh, Jeffrey C. *Religionless Christianity: Dietrich Bonhoeffer in Troubled Times.* London: T. & T. Clark, 2008.

Rahner, Karl. *Karl Rahner in Dialogue: Conversations and Interviews, 1965–1982.* Edited by Paul Imhof and Hubert Biallowons. Translated by Harvey D. Egan. New York: Crossroad, 1986.

Raiser, Konrad. "Bonhoeffer and the Ecumenical Movement." In *Bonhoeffer for a New Day: Theology in a Time of Transition,* edited by John W. de Gruchy, 319–39. Grand Rapids: Eerdmans, 1997.

Rasmussen, Larry. "Bonhoeffer's Song of Songs and Christianities as Earth Faiths." Paper presented at the International Bonhoeffer Conference, Berlin, 2000. Copy obtained from the author.

———. *Dietrich Bonhoeffer: Reality and Resistance.* Nashville: Abingdon, 1972.

———. *Earth Community, Earth Ethics.* Maryknoll, NY: Orbis, 1996.

———. *Moral Fragments and Moral Community: A Proposal for Church in Society.* Minneapolis: Fortress, 1993.

———. "Worship in a World Come of Age." In *A Bonhoeffer Legacy: Essays in Understanding,* edited by A. J. Klassen, 268–80. Grand Rapids: Eerdmans, 1981.

Rasmussen, Larry L., and Renate Bethge. *Dietrich Bonhoeffer: His Significance for North Americans.* Minneapolis: Augsburg, 1989.

———. "Bonhoeffer's Family and Its Significance for His Theology." In *Dietrich Bonhoeffer: His Significance for North Americans,* 1–30. Minneapolis: Augsburg, 1989.

Rausch, Thomas P. *Radical Christian Communities.* Reprint, Eugene, OR: Wipf and Stock, 2002.

Reynolds, Terrence. *The Coherence of Life Without God Before God: The Problem of Earthly Desires in the Later Theology of Dietrich Bonhoeffer.* Lanham: University Press of America, 1989.

Rich, Adrienne. *The Dream of a Common Language: Poems, 1974–1977.* New York: Norton, 1978.

Ricoeur, Paul. *Figuring the Sacred: Religion, Narrative and Imagination.* Edited by M. I. Wallace. Translated by D. Pellauer. Minneapolis: Fortress, 1995.

Riddell, Michael. *Threshold of the Future: Reforming the Church in the Post-Christian West.* London: SPCK, 1998.

Riddell, Mike, Mark Pierson, and Cathy Kirkpatrick. *The Prodigal Project.* London: SPCK, 2000.

Rilke, Rainer Maria. *Later Poems.* Translated by J. B. Leishman. London: Hogarth, 1938.

————. *Selected Poems.* Translated by J. B. Leishman. London: Penguin Classics, 2000.

Robertson, Edwin. *The Shame and the Sacrifice: The Life and Preaching of Dietrich Bonhoeffer.* London: Hodder and Stoughton, 1987.

Robinson, John A. T. *Honest to God.* London: SCM, 1963.

Rochelle, Jay C. "Gospel in a Secular World; Mystery and Relationship." In *Reflections on Bonhoeffer: Essays in Honor of F. Burton Nelson,* edited by Geffrey. B. Kelly and C. J. Weborg, 315–33. Chicago: Covenant, 1999.

Routley, Eric. *The Man for Others.* New York: Oxford University Press, 1964.

Rowland, Christopher, ed. *The Cambridge Companion to Liberation Theology.* Cambridge: Cambridge University Press, 1999.

Ruether, Rosemary Radford. *Gaia and God: An Ecofeminist Theology of Earth Healing.* London: SCM, 1993.

Rumscheidt, Martin. "The Formation of Bonhoeffer's Theology." In *The Cambridge Companion to Dietrich Bonhoeffer,* edited by John W. de Gruchy, 50–70. Cambridge: Cambridge University Press, 1999.

Satterthwaite, P. E., and D. F. Wright, eds. *A Pathway into the Holy Scripture.* Grand Rapids: Eerdmans, 1994.

Schaff, Philip, ed. *The Work of St. John Chrysostom.* Vol. 9, *A Select Library of the Nicene and Post-Nicene Fathers of the Christian Church.* Reprint, London: T. & T. Clark, 1996.

Schlingensiepen, Ferdinand. *Dietrich Bonhoeffer, 1906–1945: Martyr, Thinker, Man of Resistance.* London: T. & T. Clark, 2010.

School(s) for Conversion: 12 Marks of a New Monasticism. Edited by the Rutba House. Eugene, OR: Cascade, 2005.

Scott, Michael. *A Celtic Odyssey.* London: Warner Books, 1985.

Scott, Peter. "Christ, Nature, Sociality: Dietrich Bonhoeffer For an Ecological Age." *Scottish Journal of Theology* 53 (2000) 413–30.

Selby, Peter. *Grace and Mortgage: The Language of Faith and the Debt of the World.* London: Darton, Longman and Todd, 1997.

Sewell, Ruth, Jan Sellers, and Di Williams. *Working with the Labyrinth: Paths for Exploration.* Glasgow: Wild Goose, 2013.

Shanks, Norman. *Iona—God's Energy: The Spirituality and Vision of the Iona Community.* London: Hodder and Stoughton, 1999.

Shapiro, Nat. *An Encyclopedia of Quotations About Music.* New York: Da Capo, 1977.

Sheldrake, Philip. *Living Between Worlds: Place and Journey in Celtic Spirituality.* London: Darton, Longman and Todd, 1995.

————. *Spaces for the Sacred: Place, Memory, and Identity.* London: SCM, 2001.

————. *Spirituality and Theology: Christian Living and the Doctrine of God.* London: Darton, Longman and Todd, 1998.

Sider, Ronald. *Evangelism and Social Action: In a Lost and Broken World.* London: Hodder and Stoughton, 1993.

Simpson, Ray. *Exploring Celtic Spirituality: Historic Roots for our Future.* London: Hodder and Stoughton, 1995.

————. *A Pilgrim Way: New Celtic Monasticism for Everyday People.* Buxhall, Suffolk: Kevin Mayhew, 2005.

Sine, Tom. *The Mustard Seed Conspiracy: You Can Make a Difference in Tomorrow's Troubled World.* London: MARC, 1981.

————. *Wild Hope: Crises Facing the Human Community on the Threshold of the 21st Century.* London: Word Books, 1991.

Smith, Ronald Gregor, ed. *World Come of Age: A Symposium on Dietrich Bonhoeffer.* London: Collins, 1967.

Soskice, Janet Martin. *Metaphor and Religious Language.* Oxford: Clarendon, 1987.

Staniforth, Maxwell. *Early Christian Wrings: The Apostolic Fathers.* Harmondsworth, UK: Penguin, 1987.

Steven, Helen. "Justice and Peace Join Hands: Further Probing with Ian M. Fraser." *Coracle* 3 (February 2000) 15.

————. *Roger: An Extraordinary Peace Campaigner.* Glasgow: Wild Goose, 1990.

Stewart, A. Monica. *T. Ralph Morton: A Biographical Pamphlet.* Glasgow: Iona Community, n.d.

Stewart, Columba. *Prayer and Community: The Benedictine Tradition.* London: Darton, Longman and Todd, 1998.

Stockton, Ian G., and Hugh Searle. *Bonhoeffer Fifty Years On.* Cambridge: International Bonhoeffer Society, British Section, 1994.

Stone, Bryan. *Evangelism After Christendom: The Theology and Practice of Christian Witness.* Grand Rapids: Brazos, 2007.

Surin, Kenneth. "*Contemptus Mundi* and the Disenchanted World: Bonhoeffer's 'Discipline of the Secret' and Adorno's 'Strategy of Hibernation.'" *Journal of the American Academy of Religion* 53 (September 1985) 383–410.

Swan, Laura. *The Forgotten Desert Mothers: Sayings, Lives and Stories of Early Christian Women.* New York: Paulist, 2001.

Swinfen, Alison. "Living Words, Living Worlds." *Coracle* 4 (February 2003) 9–11.

Tataryn, Myroslaw, and Maria Truchan-Tataryn. *Discovering Trinity in Disability: A Theology for Embracing Difference.* Maryknoll, NY: Orbis, 2013.

Taylor, John V. *The Christ-Like God.* London: SCM, 1992.

Taylor, Mark. "Polyrhythm in Worship: Caribbean Keys to an Effective Word of God." In *Making Room at the Table; An Invitation to Multicultural Worship,* edited by Brian K. Blout and Leonora Tubbs Tisdale, 108–28. Louisville: Westminster John Knox, 2001.

Taylor, Michael. *Not Angels but Agencies: The Ecumenical Response to Poverty—A Primer.* London: SCM, 1995.

Telfer, William, ed. *Cyril of Jerusalem and Nemesius of Emesa.* Library of Christina Classics 4. London: SCM, 1960.

Templeton, Elizabeth. *The Strangeness of God: Essays in Contemporary Theology.* London: Arthur James, 1994.

Thiselton, A. C. *Language, Liturgy and Meaning.* Grove Liturgical Study 2. Nottingham: Grove, 1975.

Thomas, R. S. *Collected Poems: 1945–1990.* London: Phoenix, 2000.

Thomson, Leonore. *Personality Type, An Owner's Manual: A Practical Guide to Understanding Yourself and Others Through Typology.* Boston: Shambhala, 1998.

Tillich, Paul. *The Shaking of the Foundations.* London: Pelican, 1962.

Tomlinson, Dave. *The Post-Evangelical.* London: SPCK, 1995.

Vanier, Jean. *Community and Growth.* rev. ed. London: Darton, Longman and Todd, 1989.

Viladesau, Richard. *Theology and the Arts: Encountering God through Music, Art and Rhetoric.* Mahwah, NJ: Paulist, 2000.

Volf, Miroslav. *After Our Likeness: The Church as the Image of the Trinity*. Grand Rapids: Eerdmans, 1998.

———. *Exclusion and Embrace: A Theological Exploration of Identity, Otherness, and Reconciliation*. Nashville: Abingdon, 1996.

Walker, Alice. *Horses Make a Landscape Look More Beautiful*. New York: Harcourt Brace, 1984.

Walker, Andrew. *Telling the Story: Gospel, Mission and Culture*. London: SPCK, 1998.

Wallace, Mark I. *Fragments of the Spirit: Nature, Violence and the Renewal of Creation*. Harrisburg, PA: Trinity, 2001.

Wallace, Sue. *Multi-Sensory Church*. Bletchly, UK: Scripture Union, 2002.

Walls, Andrew, and Kathy Ross. *Mission in the 21st Century: Exploring the Five Marks of Global Mission*. London: Darton, Longman and Todd, 2008.

Ward, Graham, ed. *The Postmodern God*. Oxford: Blackwell, 1997.

Washington, James Melvin, ed. *A Testament to Hope: The Essential Writings of Martin Luther King, Jr*. San Francisco: Harper and Row 1986.

Watson, Francis. "Theology and Music." *Scottish Journal of Theology* 51 (1998) 435–63.

Watson, J. R. *The English Hymn: A Critical and Historical Study*. Oxford: Oxford University Press, 1999.

Weaver, John. *Earthshaping, Earthkeeping: A Doctrine of Creation*. London: SPCK, 1999.

Webber, Robert E. *Blended Worship: Achieving Substance and Relevance in Worship*. Peabody, MA: Hendrickson, 1994.

———. *Planning Blended Worship: The Creative Mixture of Old and New*. Nashville: Abingdon, 1998.

Wells, Richard C., and Ray Van Neste. *Forgotten Songs: Reclaiming the Psalms for Christian Worship*. Nashville: B & H, 2008.

West, Charles C. "The Church in the World." *Theology Today* 18 (January 1962) 493–502.

Westermann, Claus. *The Psalms: Structure, Content, and Message*. Minneapolis: Augsburg, 1980.

White, James F. *Introduction to Christian Worship*. rev. ed. Nashville: Abingdon, 1990.

White, Lynn. "The Historical Roots of our Ecological Crisis." *Science* 155 (1967) 1203–07.

White, Susan J. *Christian Worship and Technological Change*. Nashville: Abingdon, 1994.

Wiersma, Jürgen. "Bonhoeffer and Gandhi: Measure and Movement for Political Ethic of Resistance." In *Bonhoeffer's Ethics: Old Europe and New Frontiers*, edited by Guy C. Carter and R. Van Edyen, 208–11. Kampen, Netherlands: Kok Pharos, 1991.

Wild Goose Resource Group. *A Jubilee Liturgy: An Order of Service of the Millennium*. Glasgow: Wild Goose, 1999.

———. *A Wee Worship Book: Fourth Incarnation*. Glasgow: Wild Goose, 1999.

Wilken, John. "Bonhoeffer: Church and Ecumenism." *The Heythrop Journal* 10 (January 1969) 162–79.

Wilken, Robert L. *The Christians as the Romans Saw Them*. New Haven: Yale University Press, 1984.

Williams, H. A. *Poverty, Chastity and Obedience: The True Virtues*. London: Mitchell Beazley, 1975.

Williams, Rowan. "Bonhoeffer: the Sixties and After." Bonhoeffer Society, British Section Conference, January 1991. Bonhoeffer Archive, Union Theological Seminary, New York.

———. *Christian Spirituality: A Theological History from the New Testament to Luther and St. John of the Cross.* Atlanta: John Knox, 1979.

———. "Defining Heresy." In *The Origins of Christendom in the West,* edited by A. Kreider, 313–36. Edinburgh: T. & T. Clark, 2001.

———. *The Dwelling of the Light: Praying With Icons of Christ.* Norwich, UK: Canterbury, 2003.

———. "God's Workshop." Lecture delivered at Shaping Holy Lives Conference, April 29, 2003. http://rowanwilliams.archbishopofcanterbury.org/articles.php/654 /shaping-holy-lives-a-conference-on-benedictine-spirituality.

———. *Grace and Necessity: Reflections on Art and Love.* London: Continuum, 2005.

———. *Lost Icons: Reflections on Cultural Bereavement.* Edinburgh: T. & T. Clark, 2000.

———. *On Christian Theology.* Oxford: Blackwell, 2000.

———. *Open to Judgement: Sermons and Addresses.* London: Darton, Longman and Todd, 1994.

———. *Ponder These Things: Praying With Icons of the Virgin.* Norwich, UK: Canterbury, 2002.

———. "Postmodern Theology and the Judgment of the World." In *Postmodern Theology: Christian Faith in Pluralist World,* edited by Frederic B. Burnham, 92–112. New York: HarperCollins, 1989.

———. *Silence and Honey Cakes: The Wisdom of the Desert.* Oxford: Lion, 2003.

———. "The Suspicion of Suspicion: Wittgenstein and Bonhoeffer." In *The Grammar of the Heart: New Essays in Moral Philosophy and Theology,* edited by Richard H. Bell, 36–53. San Francisco: Harper and Row, 1988.

Williams, Rowan, and Mark Collier. *Beginning Now: Peacemaking Theology.* London: Dunamis, 1984.

Willmer, Haddon. "Costly Discipleship." In *The Cambridge Companion to Dietrich Bonhoeffer,* edited by John W. de Gruchy, 173–89. Cambridge: Cambridge University Press, 1999.

Wilson, Jonathan R. *Living Faithfully in a Fragmented World: Lessons for the Church from MacIntyre's After Virtue.* Harrisburg, PA: Trinity, 1997.

Wilson, Michael. *The Church is Healing.* London: SCM, 1966.

Wilson-Dickson, Andrew. *A Brief History of Christian Music: From Biblical Times to the Present.* Oxford: Lion, 1997.

Wilson-Hartgrove, Jonathan. *New Monasticism: What It has to Say to Today's Church.* Grand Rapids: Brazos, 2008.

Wind, Renate. *Dietrich Bonhoeffer: A Spoke in the Wheel.* Grand Rapids: Eerdmans, 2000.

Wink, Walter. *Engaging the Powers: Discernment and Resistance in a World of Domination.* Minneapolis: Fortress, 1992.

———. *Naming the Powers: The Language of Power in the New Testament.* Philadelphia: Fortress, 1984.

———. *Unmasking the Powers: The Invisible Forces that Determine Human Existence.* Philadelphia: Fortress, 1986.

Wood, Diana, ed. *The Church and the Arts.* Oxford: Blackwell, 1995.

Woodhead, Linda. "Theology and the Fragmentation of the Self." *International Journal of Systematic Theology* 1 (March 1999) 53–72.

Wordsworth, William. *The Major Works*. Oxford: Oxford World Classics, 2000.

Workman, Herbert B. *The Evolution of the Monastic Ideal: From the Earliest Times Down to the Coming of the Friars*. 2nd ed. London: Epworth, 1927.

Wren, Brian. *Praying Twice: The Music and Words of Congregational Song*. London: Westminster John Knox, 2000.

———. *What Language Shall I Borrow? God-Talk in Worship, A Male Response to Feminist Theology*. London: SCM, 1989.

Wright Knust, Jennifer. *Unprotected Texts: The Bible's Surprising Contradictions about Sex and Desire*. New York: HarperOne, 2011.

Wüstenberg, Ralf K. *A Theology of Life: Dietrich Bonhoeffer's Religionless Christianity*. Grand Rapids: Eerdmans, 1998.

Yearsley, David. *Bach and the Meanings of Counterpoint*. Cambridge: Cambridge University Press, 2002.

Yeats, W. B. *Selected Poems*. Edited by John Kelly. London: Orion, 2002.

Yoder, John Howard. *Body Politics: Five Practices of the Christian Community Before the Watching World*. Scottdale, PA: Herald, 1992.

———. *The Priestly Kingdom: Social Ethics as Gospel*. Notre Dame: University of Notre Dame Press, 1984.

York, Terry W. *America's Worship Wars*. Peabody, MA: Hendrickson, 2003.

Young, Alexander. *Chronicles of the Pilgrim Fathers of the Colony of Plymouth: From 1602 to 1625*. Boston: Little and Brown, 1841.

Young, Frances. *The Art of Performance: Towards a Theology of Holy Scripture*. London: DLT, 1990.

———. *The Making of the Creeds*. London SCM, 2002.

Young, Josiah Ulysses, III. *No Difference in the Fare: Dietrich Bonhoeffer and the Problem of Racism*. Grand Rapids: Eerdmans, 1998.

Zerner, Ruth. "Church, State and the 'Jewish Question.'" In *The Cambridge Companion to Dietrich Bonhoeffer*, edited by John. W. de Gruchy, 190–205. Cambridge: Cambridge University Press, 1999.

———. "Dietrich Bonhoeffer's American Experiences: People, Letters and Papers from Union Seminary." *Union Seminary Quarterly Review* 31 (Summer 1976) 261–82.

Zimmermann, Wolf-Dieter, and Ronald Gregor Smith, eds. *I Knew Dietrich Bonhoeffer: Reminiscences By His Friends*. Translated by Käthe Gregor Smith. London: Collins, 1966.

Index of Names

Index of Subjects